THE ROAD TO YORKTOWN

The French Campaigns in the American Revolution, 1780-1783

by

Louis-François-Bertrand du Pont d'Aubevoye, comte de Lauberdière

Translated and annotated

by Norman Desmarais

Savas Beatie

California

Library of Congress Cataloging-in-Publication Data

Names: Lauberdie`re, Louis François Bertrand Dupont d'Aubevoye, comte de, 1759-1837. | Desmarais, Norman, editor, translator.
Title: The Road to Yorktown: the French campaigns in the American Revolution, 1780-1783 / edited by Norman Desmarais.
Other titles: Journal de l'Arme´e, aux ordres de Monsieur le Comte de Rochambeau, pendant les campagnes de 1780, 1781, 1782, 1783 dans l'Ame´rique septentrionale. English | French campaigns in the American Revolution, 1780-1783
Description: El Dorado Hills, CA: Savas Beatie, [2020] | Includes bibliographical references and index. | Summary: "Serving as aide-de-camp on General Rochambeau's staff, the young and well-educated Count of Lauberdière enjoyed a unique perspective of the war. He rubbed shoulders with some of the Revolution's most important personalities (including George Washington and Lafayette), and was in the epicenter of many of the war's momentous events. Lauberdière kept one of the most remarkable diaries of the entire American Revolutionary War. His journal covers a host of topics and his keen eye and sharp descriptions of the Army's daily activities and movements provide a wealth of information for inquisitive readers and historians." — Provided by publisher.
Identifiers: LCCN 2020009824 | ISBN 9781611214833 (hardcover) | ISBN 9781611214840 (ebook)
Subjects: LCSH: Lauberdière, Louis François Bertrand Dupont d'Aubevoye, comte de, 1759-1837—Diaries. | United States—History—Revolution, 1775-1783—Personal narratives, French. | United States—History—Revolution, 1775-1783—Campaigns. | United States—History—Revolution, 1775-1783—Participation, French.
Classification: LCC E265 .J6813 2020 | DDC 973.3/24—dc23
LC record available at https://lccn.loc.gov/2020009824

First edition, first printing

SB

Savas Beatie
989 Governor Drive, Suite 102
El Dorado Hills, CA 95762
Phone: 916-941-6896
www.savasbeatie.com
sales@savasbeatie.com

Our titles are available at special discounts for bulk purchases. For more details, contact us at sales@savasbeatie.com.

MIX
Paper from responsible sources
FSC www.fsc.org FSC® C011935

Proudly printed in the United States of America.

To my good friend and fellow researcher Robert Selig, who first introduced me to Count de Lauberdière's diary. Bob is the most knowledgeable person I know about the expédition particulière and the one I consult whenever I have a question about it.

Louis-François-Bertrand du Pont d'Aubevoye,
comte de Lauberdière

Table of Contents

Table of Contents (continued)

Table of Contents (continued)

Maps, photos, and illustrations have been interspersed throughout this book for the convenience of the reader.

From the pen of

Louis-François-Bertrand du Pont d' Aubevoye, comte de Lauberdière

"When the Treaty of Alliance was signed with America, the British did not fail to paint us in the darkest colors to the Americans. At the arrival of our army, fear had already alienated many inhabitants."

"Mrs. Arnold played the actress, pretended to be ill, sobbing, ignorant of the despicable action of her husband."

"The British are very brave but they only fight well when the forces are equal or when they have superiority."

"We hardly see an unhappy man in America because a young man's and a young girl's desire and inclination make them decide to get married."

"The Americans are beginning to want nothing to do with the English except the language."

"We often find beauties, lovely girls in the country. They bring their flocks to pasture. They truly fulfill the idea we have of the shepherdess and which we no longer find in Europe except in the pastorals and in the poets."

"General Washington's demonstration of joy upon seeing us join him was very moving."

"The enemy began firing. . . . We did not respond with a single musket shot. The march was rapid. The Baron had the charge beaten and penetrated the redoubt. We did not have any need for ladders. The same zeal, the same bravery animated the commander and the soldiers and we took the work sword in hand."

Introduction

In early April of 1777, a 19-year-old Frenchman named Marie Joseph Paul Yves Roch Gilbert du Motier, Marquis de Lafayette set sail for America. Upon arrival, he joined the fledgling Continental Army in its struggle against the British empire. Lafayette's name and contributions remain storied lore in the tale of the birth of the United States.

Less well known are the names of those who followed Lafayette to North America. By 1780, hundreds of other young Frenchmen were in the camps and battlefields across America. They included: 25-year-old Donatien Marie Joseph de Vimeur, Vicomte de Rochambeau, son of the general; Mathieu Dumas (27); Count Hans Axel von Fersen (26); Joseph Louis César Charles, Comte then Duc de Damas (22); Alexandre-Théodore-Victor, Comte de Lameth (20) and Louis-François-Bertrand du Pont d'Aubevoye, Comte de Lauberdière (21). All of these men served as staff officers for General Rochambeau.

Like all young men in their circumstance, they headed off to war burdened with fear and excitement. The element of fear was because many were leaving home for the first time to participate in combat in an unknown country more than 3,000 miles away. Many would never see their families and friends again, like 13-year-old drummer François Gogue, who died at a hospital in Providence, Rhode Island, on November 5, 1780.

Excitement tempered their fear, beckoned as they were to adventure in a foreign land. They would be shoulder-to-shoulder with their country's former enemies and have a chance to observe these people who spoke a different language, wore unusual clothes, and practiced unfamiliar customs, mannerisms, and styles of dress.

There was great eagerness in France for the war from the very beginning. Brigadier General Louis Duportail made that clear to the Minister of War, the Comte de St. Germain, on November 12, 1777, when he reported: "There is a hundred times more enthusiasm for this revolution in a single cafe in Paris than in all the united colonies."[1]

French Involvement

The French Enlightenment thinkers, called the philosophes, laid the ideological foundations for both the American and French revolutions. Charles-Louis de Secondat, Baron de La Brède et de Montesquieu (1689-1755) developed the idea of the separation of powers and the need to divide power among the executive, legislative, and judicial branches of government, particularly in his book *The Spirit of the Laws*, which went through eighteen printing in less than two years of its original printing in 1748.

François-Marie Arouet (1694-1778), better known by his pen name Voltaire, used sarcasm and irony to advocate intelligent political authority based on the rule of law. During his entire literary and professional life, Voltaire advocated freedom of thought in all of its forms and the ability to ensure social and political organizations do not silence voices—particularly those of dissent. Most of his political views were based on the ideas of John Locke (1632–1704) and Isaac Newton (1642-1726/27). Voltaire distrusted democracy, which he saw as propagating the idiocy of the masses and was very critical about other people's ideas. Essentially, he believed enlightened despotism to be the key to progress and change. Only an enlightened monarch or an enlightened absolutist, advised by philosophers like himself, could bring about change. It was in the king's interest to improve the power and wealth of his subjects and kingdom. He considered the French bourgeoisie to be too small and ineffective, the aristocracy parasitic and corrupt, the commoners ignorant and superstitious, and the church as a static force useful only as a counterbalance since its "religious tax," or the tithe, helped to create a strong backing for revolutionaries. Voltaire was a firm advocate of secular rule.

1 Louis Duportail to St. Germain, 12 November 1777 in Walker, Paul K. et al. *Engineers of Independence: A Documentary History of the Army Engineers in the American Revolution, 1775-1783.* Historical Division, Office of Administrative Services, Office of the Chief of Engineers, 1981 pp. 175-177.

Jean-Jacques Rousseau (1712-1778) remains the most celebrated of the French political philosophers. His works, particularly *The Social Contract* (1762), developed the principles of general will and the importance of a social contract between people and government.

The increasing absolutism of the French monarchy directly shaped French political philosophy. The role and influence of representative institutions in France were diminishing. In direct contrast, at this time the British Parliament saw a growth in political power and the importance of legislatures surged in the British North American colonies. While the Americans, and even many Britons, adopted the ideas and concepts that shaped the democratic ideals of the American Revolution, there were few practical outlets for corresponding anti-monarchical views in France. This became important as French adherents to the philosophies of Montesquieu and Rousseau, such as Lafayette (1757–1834) and Mathieu Dumas (1753–1837), traveled to the colonies to fight for democracy.

During the eighteenth century, the British and French fought for domination in Europe and around the globe. This conflict spilled over into the established colonies. The Treaty of Paris ended the Seven Years' War (known as the French and Indian War in America) in 1763 and marked the end of French territorial ambitions in North America. The conflict's end saw the emergence of a mainly European foreign policy regarding Great Britain. France lost Canada, officially called the Province of Québec, after 1763. Nearly all of Québec's population, about 85,000, were of French ancestry except for 2,000 to 3,000 British or American newcomers. France's loss of territory included all the land explored by the French in the Ohio and Mississippi River valleys. These territories were annexed to Canada, which now extended all the way south to Louisiana.

The economic system known as mercantilism, which exploited the colonies for the benefit of the mother country, shaped the trade laws of the period. France reasoned any steps loosening the bonds between the colonies and the mother country would naturally diminish overall British power. Scottish philosopher Adam Smith (1723–1790), in his famous treatise *An Inquiry into the Nature and Causes of the Wealth of Nations*, opposed mercantilism and advocated free trade.

When the war ignited between Britain and her American colonies in 1775, many colonists believed the French would welcome an opportunity to retaliate and regain their country (New France). The concentration of some 800 British troops in southeastern Canada, coupled with the fluid and undefended borders, invited raids from both sides.

While the majority of colonists viewed France as a natural ally in the struggle with Britain, others remained distrustful of French ambitions. Many recently divorced British subjects shared the mother country's hatred for the French. For generations, English and Americans had been taught to despise the government, religion, and culture of France. The fact that the French had been their bitter enemies during the French and Indian War was still fresh on the minds of many.

Moreover, the French were predominantly Catholic. Many colonists came to America in search of religious freedom and, particularly, to escape the Inquisition run by the Catholic Church. Consequently, there was a strong distrust and hatred of Catholicism in the colonies in the eighteenth century.

Despite the continuing rhetoric of hostility, the Americans conducted a clandestine illegal trade with France and the French West Indies. This relationship helped pave the way for France's allowance of American privateers in her ports and those of her colonies in the West Indies. Such areas served as vital havens for prizes captured at sea. The West Indies were also later used as main ports for receiving supplies from France before transferring them on to the American colonies.

King Louis XVI appointed Charles Gravier, the comte de Vergennes, as his foreign minister in 1774. One of Vergennes's priorities was to reduce British power, both as revenge for the humiliation of the Treaty of Paris in 1763, and as a way to make France's own position in Europe strong enough to deal with challenges from other nations. Vergennes was patient, and did not want France to act too soon for the consequences were severe. The Treaty of Paris of 1763, for example, prohibited France from aiding and abetting any of England's enemies; such actions would be considered an act of war by Britain. France could not risk, at least not yet, entering another war without some reasonable expectation of victory.

When news of the outbreak of hostilities reached France, many aristocrats, imbued with the ideas of the philosophes, wanted to to foster their careers by coming to aid the Americans in their struggle for liberty. King Louis could not openly condone such actions, but he could turn a blind eye to them. As a result, Brigadier General Louis Lebègue de Presle Duportail arrived in America in February 1777, and the Marquis de Lafayette four months later in June. They were the first of many Frenchmen who would volunteer to serve the Continental Army.[2]

2 Others included: Pierre Colomb; Charles-François, Vicomte Dubysson des Hays; Matthias Alexis Fermoy; René-Etienne-Henri de Vic Gayault de Boisbertrant; Jean-Joseph Gimat de Soubadère; Jean-Michel-Gabriel Houdin de Saint-Michel; Baptiste Gouvion; Luc de LaCorne; Alexandre-Théodore-Victor, comte de Lameth; Jean-Baptiste-Joseph Chevalier de Laumoy; Augustin-François L'Epine; the Marquis de Malmédy; Augustin Mottin de la Balme; Louis-Pierre Penot Lombart; Philippe Hubert, Chevalier de Preudhomme de Borre; Philippe François Rastel, Sieur de Rocheblave; Lieutenant Colonel François Louis Teissedre de Fleury; Ann-Louis Toussard; Philippe Charles Jean Baptiste Tronson du Coudray; Armand Charles Tuffin, Marquis de la Rouërie; Jean-Gaspard Vence and Pierre-Jean-François Vernier.

The Marquis de Saint Simon commanded a body of 200 volunteers and Major General Vicomte François de Fontanges recruited 2,979 "Europeans" and 545 "Colored: Volunteer Chasseurs, Mulattoes, and Negroes, at St. Domingue [Haiti]. The Volunteer Chasseurs, called the Fontanges Legion, included young men who would become famous in the Haitian revolution.[3]

The odds of an American victory, however, were slim. It was not until the Battle of Germantown outside Philadelphia in September 1777, coupled with the decisive American defeat of General John Burgoyne at Saratoga the following month, that France made up its mind. King Louis XVI decided it was time to side with the Americans and openly entered the Revolutionary War by signing the Treaty of Amity and Commerce and the Treaty of Alliance on February 6, 1778. The king dispatched Admiral Comte Jean-Baptiste-Charles-Henri-Hector d'Estaing to America with a fleet of 12 ships of the line, three frigates, and approximately 4,000 French soldiers. They arrived off New York in June of 1778. Sir Richard Howe's fleet of nine ships in New York harbor became Admiral d'Estaing's first target. When he arrived off Sandy Hook on July 9, however, d'Estaing discovered that the water was too shallow for his ships to get at the British fleet. The French admiral and General George Washington decided instead to attack the British at Newport, Rhode Island, the second largest British seaport at the time.

The French and British fleets were preparing for battle off Rhode Island in August when heavy winds struck just as the battle was getting underway. The high winds made it impossible to wage a fleet-level action, and the opposing ships engaged in combat individually. Both sides suffered severe damage and returned to port to refit. The first effort at French-American cooperation was unsuccessful and increased anti-French sentiment.

The events off Rhode Island, along with his government's instructions to regain territory for France, compelled Admiral d'Estaing to take his fleet south to attack the British colonies in the Caribbean. He successfully captured Grenada but was recalled to aid in the American siege of British-held Savannah, Georgia. D'Estaing's fleet captured the 50-gun *Experiment*, the frigate *Ariel*, and two store

3 Some of these men included: Pierre Astrel, Pierre Auba, Louis Jacques Beauvais, Jean-Baptiste Mars Belley, Martial Besse, Guillaume Bleck, Pierre Cangé, Jean-Baptiste Chavannes, Pierre Faubert, Laurent Férou, Jean-Louis Froumentaine, Barthélemy-Médor Icard, Gédéon Jourdan, Jean-Pierre Lambert, Jean-Baptiste Léveillé, Christophe Mornet, Pierre Obas, Luc-Vincent Olivier, Pierre Pinchinat, Jean Piverger, André Rigaud, Césaire Savary, Pierre Tessier, Jérome Thoby, Jean-Louis Villate, and Henri Christophe, future king of Haiti.

ships carrying the £30,000 payroll for the Savannah garrison along with Brigadier General George Garth, on his way to take command of the British in Georgia.

With is fleet off the seaport, D'Estaing demanded General Augustine Prevost surrender the city. Prevost declined, and the Franco-American forces hurried their ensuing attack. D'Estaing, remembering his experience at Rhode Island, chose not to risk his fleet in a position dangerously exposed to hurricanes. He abandoned plans of a systematic approach by regular parallels and prepared for a more immediate attack, which in turn failed. D'Estaing suffered a pair of wounds in the fighting that followed, and the French army boarded ships on October 20, 1779, and sailed to the West Indies. The second attempt at Franco-American cooperation ended in much the same atmosphere of bitterness and disillusion as the first.

King Louis XVI planned to send 12,000 troops to America in 1780 under the command of Lieutenant General Jean Baptiste Donatien de Vimeur Comte de Rochambeau (1725–1807). As only 32 transports could be assembled to carry them to America, only 5,800 men embarked for the long journey. By the time the transports returned to France for the remaining troops, the soldiers had been redeployed elsewhere, or had returned to their peace-time assignments.

General Rochambeau's arrival in Newport, Rhode Island on July 11 marked the beginning of a new and decisive phase of Franco-American military cooperation. A series of British strategic blunders, the decision of Admiral François Joseph Paul Comte de Grasse to move his large French fleet north from the West Indies to support the allied armies of Rochambeau and Washington, and the skillful operations of Lafayette in Virginia, contributed to the victorious Yorktown campaign and the end of British military power in America.[4]

Louis François Bertrand Dupont d'Aubevoye de Lauberdière

Rochambeau's nephew, Louis François Bertrand Dupont d'Aubevoye de Lauberdière, one of the general's aides-de-camps, lived a rather extraordinary life full of accomplishments and adventure on both sides of the ocean.

Louis François was born at the château de l'Auberdière (formerly Lauberdière) in Bocé (Maine-et-Loire) in the province of Anjou, on October 27, 1759. He was the son of Louise-Jeanne-Claire Le Gros de Princé and François-Charles-Mathieu

4 For the best overall treatment of the Yorktown Campaign, with good coverage of French participation, see Jerome A. Greene, *The Guns of Independence: The Siege of Yorktown, 1781* (Savas Beatie, 2005).

du Pont d'Aubevoye, seigneur de Lauberdière (1723-1795), a musketeer in the king's guard and Knight of Saint-Louis (chevalier de Saint-Louis).

Louis François entered military school in Paris (Collège militaire de la Flèche) on October 7, 1767 with a recommendation from Étienne-François de Choiseul-Beaupré-Stainville, Count then duc de Choiseul (1758) and duc d'Amboise (1764), head of the government of King Louis XV between 1758 and 1770. He entered the royal military academy, l'École Royale Militaire, on October 3, 1773, and left as a gentleman to join the Saintonge Regiment with the rank of sub-lieutenant on January 30, 1778.

Louis François was promoted to captain in the Royal Normandy Cavalry Regiment on April 15, 1780, and served as a staff officer and aide-de-camp of General Rochambeau during the American campaigns. Louis François and his cousin, Colonel Donatien-Marie-Joseph de Vimeur, vicomte de Rochambeau, at 21 and 26 years of age respectively, were the youngest of General Rochambeau's six aides-de-camp. On June 13, 1780, Louis François was appointed sub-assistant quartermaster general in the expeditionary corps while serving as an assistant of the army staff.

After the conclusion of the American Revolution, Lauberdière was promoted to assistant quartermaster general on December 2, 1787, and elevated to lieutenant-colonel on June 11, 1789. He was admitted to the Order of the Cincinnati in 1789 and became a Knight of St. Louis in 1790. The officer was sent to Ireland at the beginning of the French Revolution on a reconnaissance mission. While there, he met Caroline Macnamara Hussey (December 28, 1772- 1834), and the couple married on June 16, 1790, at the church of Saint-Sulpice in Paris. Later, during the French Revolution, Count de Lauberdière was posted to the Northern Army as a colonel.

Lauberdière returned to Ireland in 1791, but during this tour the British authorities arrested and held him as a prisoner of war from May 1793 to June 1800. After his exchange, his uncle, Marshal Rochambeau, recommended him to Napoléon Bonaparte, who was then First Consul. Lauberdière resumed his service as staff officer of the Army of Italy, and thereafter with the Army of Germany, and distinguished himself at the battles of Elchingen and Jena.

Lauberdière represented Maine-et-Loire in the legislature in 1804, was reelected in 1808, and was afterwards known as Dupont-Lauberdière. He left the legislature the following year to fight in Poland with the Grand Army, where he suffered a serious wound at Deppen (and for which he was awarded the medal of the Legion of Honor). Lauberdière served as chief of staff of the Lasalle division on

January 2, 1807, and was promoted to the rank of brigadier general the following month on February 12.

Through a new act of the senate, he managed another reelection. The title of Baron of the Empire became his on June 3. From 1808 to 1811, Lauberdière was appointed to Spain. On February 12, 1812, he commanded Madrid in the Spanish War, and participated in many engagements. Lauberdière also added the post of governor to his impressive list of appointments; while still employed in Westphalia, in Northern Germany in 1812, he served as governor of the provinces of Leon, Zamora and Toro.

Lauberdière was given command of the 32nd army division in 1813, headquartered at Hamburg. He ordered the bridges of Haya and Nieubourg blown up and captured Brême from the Russians. He commanded the Wessel line on August 26, 1813, and directed the retreat to Wessel at the end of October 1813 after the Battle of Leipzig.

The revolt of the Hanseatic countries of Westphalia and Holland brought General Dupont-Lauberdière to the banks of the Ijssel and Rhine rivers. King Louis XVIII promoted him to Lieutenant General of the King's Armies on August 23, 1814 and he became Commander of the Legion of Honor.

Lauberdière commanded the 15th Army division at Rouen from April 17, 1815, to July 21, 1815, and was elected representative of the Baugé district in the Chamber of One Hundred Days on May 23, 1815.

After the return of Louis XVIII, Lauberdière expressed his Royalist sentiments. He claimed that he was forced to take the command when he wanted to board a ship to go to England. On November 13, 1815, however, the Duc de Castries linked Lauberdière to the Bonapartists three years earlier. Lauberdière was the candidate of the liberal opposition in the elections of 1815 and 1820, and returned to his estate after this legislative session and retired on January 1, 1816.

Lauberdière tried unsuccessfully to get reelected to the Chamber of Deputies, followed by an unsuccessful appeal to be raised to the position of peer of France in 1822. King Charles X granted him a private audience on March 13, 1825. On January 9, 1831, he gained the post of general counsel, but chose to resign later same year.

He grieved the death of his wife in 1834 and had her buried at the l'Auberdière chapel. He died a few years later, on February 8, 1837, and was buried at the same chapel, leaving behind no children.

The Manuscript

Lauberdière kept a diary during his time in America. His "Journal de l'armée aux ordres de monsieur le comte de Rochambeau pendant les campagnes de 1780, 1781, 1782, 1783, dans l'Amérique septentrionale" remained in private hands in France until its owner, "Ms. Weelen," donated it to the Bibliothèque Nationale (the national library of France) in February 1978. An article about the journal by Michèle Sacquin appeared in the *Bulletin de la Bibliothèque Nationale* in 1979. The fact that this remarkable and invaluable journal has never been published or translated until now is remarkable.[5]

Lauberdière kept his journal in four separate booklets now bound in a single quarter-leather volume with brown marbled covers. The booklets have a sequentially printed number in the upper right corner of each folio. The upper left corner has a page number written in pencil. This number is sequential for the text of the manuscript; title pages, blank pages, maps, and inserts (newspaper issues and other documents) are not numbered in pencil, but they do have a printed page number.

The text is generally written in a fine hand with very few corrections, strikeouts, or ink blotches, suggesting that it may have been rewritten from an earlier manuscript. Many memoirs of the war were written when the soldiers were advanced in years and wanted to record their recollections for their grandchildren or to submit them for pension applications. Some diaries, originally kept during the war, were recopied for the same purpose. This one was not. Lauberdière was not eligible for a pension from Congress nor did he and his wife have children (and hence no grandchildren). He kept the journal primarily for his own purposes. Hence, he is very frank and blunt in expressing his thoughts about the people he met and the locations he visited.

Unfortunately, the booklets were bound so tightly that some words at the end or beginning of lines on the inner margins (gutter) cannot be fully read. It is often possible to deduce the word from the initial letters and the context. When this is not possible, or if a word or sequence of words cannot be read due to faded ink or bleeding through the page, the text is marked "illegible." Sometimes characters are somewhat legible, but their combination cannot be understood. Consonants like m, n, u, v, w, and vowels like a, e, o can often look alike and sometimes be difficult

5 Michèle Sacquin, *Bulletin de la Bibliothèque Nationale* (1979), pp. 51-57. All documents refer to her only as Ms. Weelen. Her brother, Jean-Edmond Weelen, owned the manuscript and instructed her to give it to the Bibliotheque Nationale upon his death in 1978.

to interpret. Such cases are indicated as "unintelligible." Words that are not clear or could have multiple meanings are indicated with a question mark if not positively clear.

Proper names of places and people are often misspelled or spelled phonetically, which is to be expected. Sometimes, places undergo name changes. In these cases, the first instance of a name will appear as written in the manuscript with a note identifying the person or place more completely. Subsequent instances will have the proper spelling or modern name. For example, "Crompond" is usually written "Crompound" in the journal. The town, now known as Yorktown Heights, New York, not to be confused with Yorktown, Virginia, is transcribed as Yorktown Heights in the second and subsequent occurrences.

As General Rochambeau's nephew and aide-de camp, Lauberdière had a unique perspective on the war and the French army in America, and his literate and informative journal reflects this. Indeed, nothing remotely comparable has appeared in the war's literature. His diary contains a detailed account of the army's camp in Newport, the march to Yorktown, combat, and the march back, and the people he met and the places he visited along the way. His observations—lively, frank, and clear—are not only fresh and original to the study of this period, but offer glimpses into the strains of the unlikely alliance that won American independence.

Lauberdière describes the reception (or lack of it) that the French encountered wherever they traveled in America. His descriptions of the anti-French prejudice he found everywhere, and how General Rochambeau dispelled those prejudices and won over the populace, are invaluable. The young French officer also discusses the total absence of culture—in his opinion—within the colonies, and how the colonials attempted to imitate European manners and styles. He marveled at Philadelphia's adoption of Parisian fashions in the brief time between his visits to the city, and recalled his fascinating visit to George Washington's home at Mount Vernon, complete with pointed comments about his wife Martha. Lauberdière also penned a lengthy detailed account of Admiral de Ternay's death and funeral, touching accounts of friendships, and a description of a Quaker wedding that he thought resembled a funeral more than a celebration. There's even an account of General Rochambeau's arrest for the destruction of property. By 1783, each nationality had accepted the other's customs, which they used to express their sadness and cordiality as the French departed Boston to return to France.

Acknowledgments

I want to thank Dr. Robert Selig for bringing this diary to my attention and for all his help in obtaining a copy of it and introducing me to contacts at the Society of the Cincinnati. He also provided encouragement and assistance in the translation process and reviewed early drafts of the manuscript.

Theodore P. Savas, Managing Director at Savas Beatie deserves credit for his perspicacity and enthusiasm in being the first to publish this diary. It is astounding that it has not been published in almost 250 years and that its first public exposure comes in this English translation.

Michael Coker helped edit and organize the text and footnotes. We had several enjoyable conversations and I am now happy to count him among my friends.

J. David Dameron and Theodore Savas created the modern maps for Jerome A. Greene's book *The Guns of Independence: The Siege of Yorktown, 1781*. They graciously granted permission to use several, which are interspersed in this volume.

Marketing Director Sarah Keeney and Media Specialist Sarah Closson at Savas Beatie also deserve credit for their innovative marketing ideas and their strong efforts to bring this volume to public awareness.

Finally, thanks to those in the production department who worked so hard to design my book. They did a fine job.

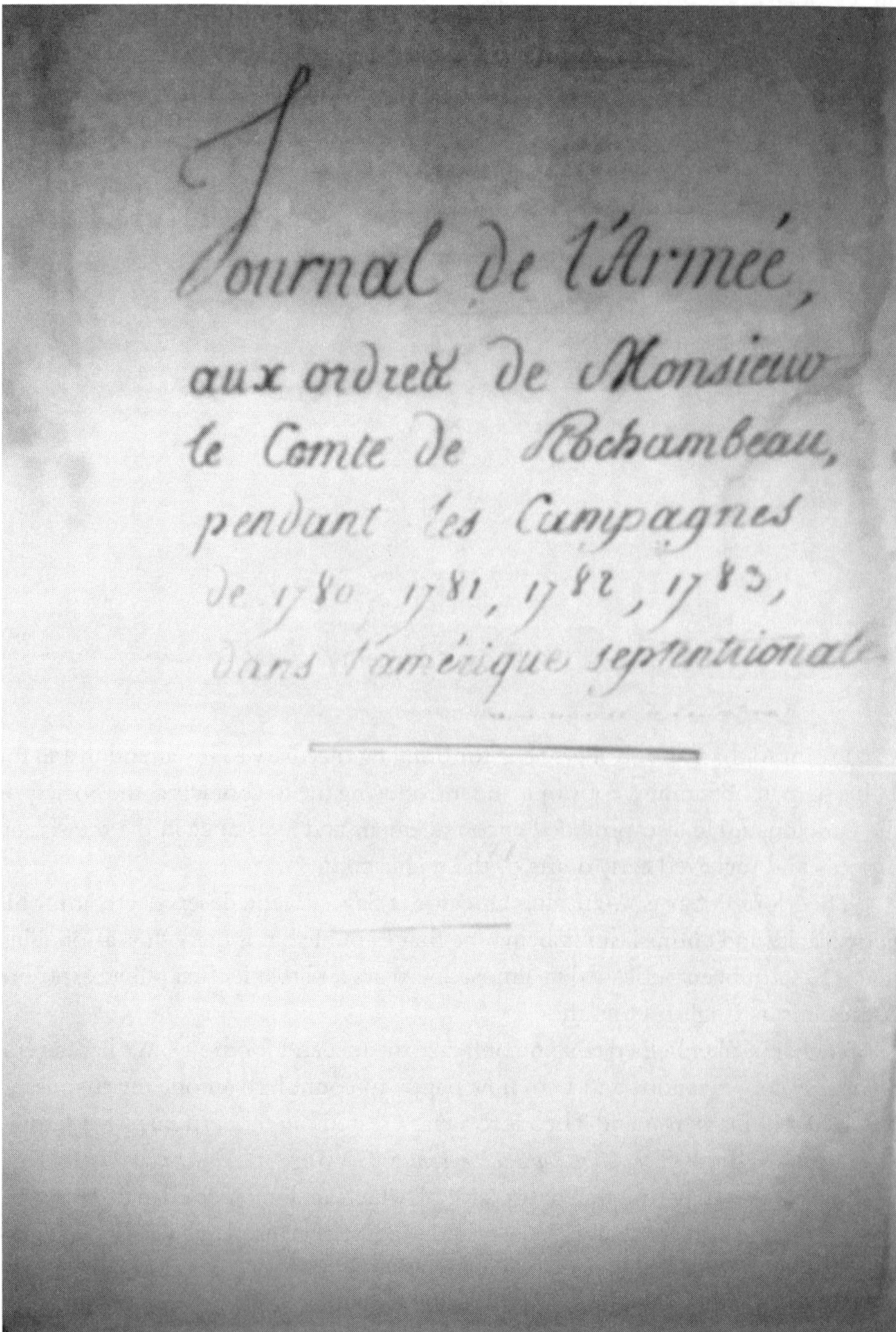

Journal de l'Armeé,
aux ordres de Monsieur
le Comte de Rochambeau,
pendant les Campagnes
de 1780, 1781, 1782, 1783,
dans l'amérique septentrionale

The title page of Louis de Lauberdière's journal.

Bibliothèque Nationale

Campaign of 1780

Introduction

Louis François Bertrand Dupont d'Aubevoye de Lauberdière began his journal summarizing the causes of the War of American Independence and the beginning of hostilities. He recounted Count d'Estaing's mission to America and the siege and attack of Savannah. American losses in the battles of Long Island, Manhattan, White Plains, Brandywine and Germantown are discussed, as is the occupation of Philadelphia and Rhode Island, to emphasize the nascent country's need for help.

Congress sent Benjamin Franklin to Paris as an envoy to seek France's help. King Louis XVI granted the request and appointed the Count de Rochambeau as general over 8000 men on March 1, 1780. This force marched to Brest, scheduled to board transports under the command of the Chevalier de Ternay. Conflicts between the army and the navy delayed boarding until April 1780. Bad weather struck shortly after departure, forcing a return to Brest.

The expedition set sail again in May. The weather soured once more in the Gulf of Gascogne. Despite another setback, the French fleet reached the Bermudas, on June 21. Five British vessels and a smaller frigate, commanded by Captain William Cornwallis, brother of the famous Lord Charles Cornwallis were on the horizon. Lauberdière blamed the Chevalier de Ternay for hesitating to attack, giving the weaker enemy time to prepare for battle.

At this engagement, the French captured a British sloop of war. From their prisoners they learned of Lord Cornwallis's capture of Charleston, SC the only major port the Americans had left in the South. This news underscored just how urgent and necessary the arrival of the French had become.

After two months at sea, the fleet headed to the Chesapeake Bay. Lookouts sighted ships, which forced them to reverse direction. Fearing these ships were part of Admiral Graves's fleet, which they had engaged at Bermuda, de Ternay convened a Council of War. The council decided to navigate to Rhode Island. Lauberdière noted the captains were all discontent with their leader, predicting the men would never forgive him for passing up two good opportunities for easy victories.

The Ile de France, *with 350 men of the Bourbonnais Regiment aboard, got lost in a thick fog. She proceeded to Boston, the rendezvous point, and the troops marched to Newport, arriving on July 28.*

The fleet entered Newport Harbor after a passage of seventy-one days. Many of the French sailors and soldiers were seasick and depressed, perhaps stung by the missed opportunities during their Atlantic passage. Morale suffered another blow when the grand reception they expected upon arrival in a friendly port failed to materialize.

Lauberdière described the organization of the army and the state of Rhode Island at the time of their arrival. Other diarists outlined the order of debarkation. However, Lauberdière is the only one who identified the location. This revelation does not come until October 17, when General Rochambeau orders his bored and sulking troops to drill and engage in war games.

After landing, the French fortified the area. With British ships appearing off Newport daily, they prepared their defenses. Lauberdière captures Rochambeau's call for strict discipline in camp. This display of military bearing thawed the American prejudices of the inhabitants and started to win their trust and respect. No doubt, their payments in cash for whatever they needed helped relations. However, all of the diarists suspected they were being taken advantage of due to difficulties in language, different customs and the ready availability of much-desired currency.

After a brief account of the Battle of Rhode Island two years earlier, Lauberdière recounted the arrival of a delegation of twenty-two Iroquois, Illinois and Four Nations Indians. These dignitaries arrived on August 29, 1778 travelling to Newport to pay their respects to General Rochambeau and King Louis. He described their customs, especially their dance. In return, the Native Americans received gifts from the king and a Capuchin was sent to honor their request for a priest.

Generals Washington and Rochambeau met in conference at Hartford to plan the campaign. Lauberdière described the initial uneasiness of both generals but the proceedings remain secret. During the absence of the French officers, the army feared an attack on Newport, which never materialized.

Lauberdière described the forts at West Point; Major General Benedict Arnold's treachery; Major John André's capture, trial and execution; General William Heath's appointment as commander at West Point to replace Arnold; the Battle of Camden; the death of Baron de Kalb and General Nathanael Greene's appointment as head of the southern army. These accounts are not in chronological order, as the author recorded the events not as a history, but as a personal memoir for his own recollection. He also expressed frustration when the second part of the army failed to materialize. He noted General Rochambeau sent his son to France with dispatches seeking an update to this situation while also supplying as much intelligence as he could for his countrymen.

General Rochambeau kept his idle troops engaged with drills and war games. They also were set to work, rebuilding the wharves and many houses destroyed by the British for firewood during their occupation. A delegation of Abenaki and Micmac Indians arrived the evening of October 20 to request charity. This delegation stayed for roughly ten days, receiving gifts from the French similar to the delegation mentioned two-years earlier.

The troops entered winter quarters on November 1. A detachment went to "the continent" to cut wood, while Rochambeau made a reconnaissance in Connecticut. After a visit to the quarters of Lauzun's hussars, Rochambeau journeyed to Boston. While Rochambeau was in this city, the Chevalier de Ternay died from natural causes. The Baron de Vioménil sent Lauberdière to notify Rochambeau of the loss. Rochambeau's early departure from Boston allowed him arrive on the evening de Ternay was buried. Lauberdière described de Ternay's funeral and reflected upon his character.

Lauberdière closed out 1780 by describing Boston and its fortifications, the siege, the battle of Bunker Hill, and British and American Christmas customs.

The Diary: Campaign of 1780

A very close relative of the general whom the King selected to command his troops in America, I was his aide-de-camp and assistant quartermaster general of his army. These two tasks allowed me to observe all the events that happened to us very closely and to report on them. I write for myself, for my own satisfaction and to remember, one day, certain periods of the most extraordinary and most glorious revolution recorded by history. I shall make a few recollections. I will speak about what struck me the most in a little-known country which is little understood in Europe and which deserves to be better known. In my journal, I will try to relate everything truthfully and with the greatest accuracy.

About the American War

In summary, the war in America was sparked by the violent means which the British ministry used to execute the act of Parliament to raise taxes, to increase those same taxes and to change the Constitution and the internal government of many of these colonies, in violation of natural and civil rights of those same colonies.

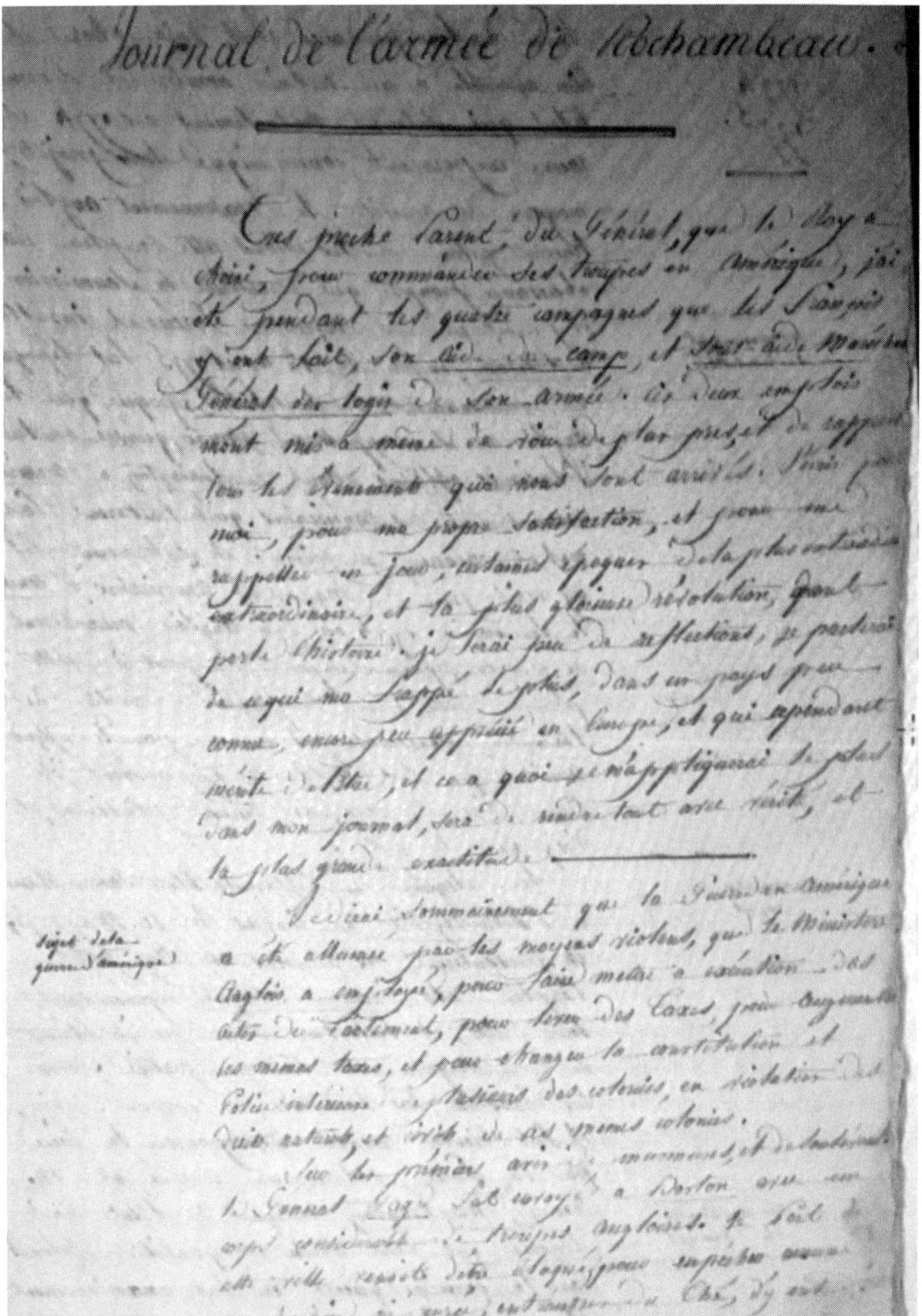
Journal de l'armée de Rochambeau.

A page from Lauberdière's journal.

Bibliothèque Nationale

General Gage was sent to Boston with a large body of British troops at the first reports of riots and rebellion. The port of this city was blockaded to prevent any merchandise, such as tea, from entering.

Beginning of Hostilities

Several leaders cherished and held dear the idea of independence and banded together already by 1774. They even discussed their plans and the means for success. The British government no longer found, among its colonists, that acceptance and prompt obedience characteristic of submission. Some sentries were pressured and assaulted at Boston. Hostilities finally broke out on April 18, 1775, a time which the British will remember only with pain. Several officers, going from Lexington to Concord, encountered some Americans whom they treated very badly and took to prison. They inquired if there were any American magazines at Concord. The following day, the 19th, 4 or 500 British marched from Boston to capture the bridge at this first town. A company of militiamen from Lexington mustered and marched to oppose them. As soon as the British sighted them, they fired on them, killing several and dispersing the rest.

Congress Assembles & Mr. Washington Appointed General

Delegates from the various states assembled in Congress at Philadelphia on May 10, 1775[1]. They presented their appeals to the King and to the people of Great Britain, advocating their rights and sincere intention to continue getting along with the mother country. But the vexations and the hostilities did not cease, so Congress soon resolved to repel force with force. It authorized an army and unanimously voted Mister George Washington as general. He was a delegate from the state of Virginia who served in the capacity of colonel during the last war. Events proved that a choice was never more celebrated and with good reason.

The fermentation of the minds, the desire to defend liberty, soon became to find new soldiers. Everyone enlisted with pleasure and marched toward Boston. More than 25,000 men soon mustered.

1 The First Continental Congress met from September 5 to October 26, 1774. The Second Continental Congress convened in Philadelphia, Pennsylvania, on May 10, 1775, with representatives from twelve of the thirteen colonies. This body essentially acted as the national government during the balance of the war, with its delegates voting to raise armies, direct strategy, and appoint diplomats, and ratified the Declaration of Independence on July 4, 1776.

Battle of the *Belle Poule*

Meanwhile, France sought revenge for the Peace of 1763. She secretly sent military supplies to the Americans. The armies observed each other in 1776 and 1777. They had a mutual hatred of England in dispatches and negotiations. France armed them in her ports. Finally, in June 1778, the French frigate *Belle Poule*, on a cruise in the English Channel, encountered the British frigate *Arethusa* which demanded to board. She was part of a fleet still out of sight. M. de la Clocheterie, captain of the *Belle Poule*, courageously and honorably defended our flag. He detested the British bravado and fought for three hours. The battle was fierce and bloody on both sides until the moment that the *Arethusa*, a little stronger than the *Belle Poule*, withdrew from combat, badly beaten and ready to sink.

Marquis de la Fayette

Several French officers had already gone to offer their services to the Americans, including the Marquis de la Fayette. He had already served two campaigns under the command of General Washington and won the esteem and recognition of the American army. He soon attained the rank of major general[2] and returned to France in 1779. He served in the capacity of assistant quartermaster general under the Count de Vaux who commanded a body of 40,000 men on the coast of Normandy and Brittany and was supposed to land in Great Britain. Great expenses were made at Le Havre and Saint-Malo where the troops were gathered for a planned landing which never occurred.

Count d'Estaing & Siege and Attack of Savannah

Count d'Estaing[3] was sent to the West Indies in February 1778 with 18 ships of the line to protect our possessions and to bring assistance to the Americans in case of a declaration

2 This note is part of the manuscript: "M. de la Fayette was now 23 years old and captain of dragoons. His rank in America and the rapidity with which he was promoted will not seem surprising when we consider a person of rare personal merit would be expected to transfer to an emerging country and be obliged to draw some general officers from the classes of society. Knox was a bookseller, Heath a butcher."

3 Admiral Comte Jean–Baptiste–Charles–Henri–Hector d'Estaing (1729-1794) held the ranks of Admiral in the French Navy and Lieutenant General in the Army. He played a prominent role in helping the Americans gain independence. In 1793, he testified on behalf of Marie Antoinette and was brought to trial himself, convicted, and executed by guillotine the following

of war. He appeared several times on their coasts but the bad weather and strong wind put an end to the plans. Finally, there was nothing lacking in this paragon of success when he came to lay siege to Savannah, the capital of Georgia, which was occupied by the British at the end of 1779. He could barely land 2 or 3000 men. The American General Lincoln, who commanded at Charleston, brought him some reinforcements. As soon as the trench was open, the attacks began immediately and without orders. The French were twice repulsed with much loss. D'Estaing received two wounds in a place where a single attack drove him. He then reboarded his ship (the *Languedoc*) and returned to France, after having engaged in several sea battles in the course of his two campaigns. He lost the island of St. Lucia and attacked her again with great loss after having taken the island of Grenada and winning the naval battle of the same name but without changing the state of affairs for the Americans.

The Americans had already conducted five victorious campaigns. They were victorious at the beginning,[4]

State of the United States

and as long as patriotism compelled them to take up arms, they suffered great losses. They lost the Battle of Long Island, the island of that name, the island of New York, the Battle of White Plains, the Battle of Brandywine, Germantown. Philadelphia was captured and evacuated, Rhode Island was in enemy hands for four years. The Americans who, in taking up arms, believed the war would only last a short time, were tired of it and faltered daily. The army was neither dressed nor paid and often on the verge of starvation, even though General Washington commanded no more than 4 or 5000 men. Only a few officers of the army still demonstrated courage and firmness. The paper money which was thought to be of use to procure silver depreciated daily. Several families who exchanged their silver for paper were ruined.

Doctor Franklin
Request for Help

Benjamin Franklin, who was sent as an envoy to Paris at the beginning of the Revolution, along with Mr. de la Fayette, who received instructions on departing America,

---

year. The former admiral had a sense of humor. Before his execution, d'Estaing wrote, "After my head falls off, send it to the British, they will pay a good deal for it!"

4 This note is part of the manuscript: "Boston was evacuated. Burgoyne surrendered his army as prisoners of war, lost the battle of Saratoga. Trenton was surprised…"

depicted the status of the thirteen United States and strongly requested help which became more and more urgent. France had only shown a mild interest up to this point. She signed a Treaty of Alliance with the United States, recognized her independence but the aid she sent only helped them to conduct the war. A good general and troops were needed.

General Jean Baptiste Donatien de Vimeur, comte de Rochambeau

National Park Service, Colonial National Historical Park, Yorktown Collection

March 1780
Count de Rochambeau Appointed General
Requests Granted

This was pretty much the state of affairs when it was decided to send French troops to America. All Paris, for two months, nominated the Count de Rochambeau as lieutenant general to command them. The King approved and put 8000 men under his command on March 1, 1780. They consisted of the Bourbonnais, Neustrie, Auvergne, Soissonnais, Rouergue, Saintonge, Royal Deux Ponts infantry regiments, 400 men of the Auxonne artillery regiment and 600 men of Lauzun's[5] Legion, half infantry, half cavalry. Rochambeau selected as camp marshals the Baron and Viscount de Vioménil[6], the Chevalier de Chastellux[7] and M. de Wittgenstein.

Chevalier de Ternay

All the troops were immediately ordered to march to Brest. They arrived about the end of the month at which time the transport vessels which were to transport troops were loaded. The fleet which was to convoy them was put under the command of the Chevalier de Ternay.[8] It was composed of the 80-gun ships *Duc de Bourgogne* and *Neptune*, the 74-gun *Conquérant*, 64-gun *L'Eveillé*, *La Provence*, *Le Jason* and *l'Ardent*; the 32-gun frigates *La Surveillante*, *l'Amazone* and *Hermione*.

5 Armand Louis de Gontaut–Biron, Duc de Lauzun (1747-1793) was a colonel of a Legion of French volunteers in Rochambeau's army. Brion was guillotined for political intrigue during the French Revolution.

6 Antoine Charles du Houx baron de Vioménil (1728-1792) and his son Charles Gabriel du Houx vicomte de Vioménil. The father was second-in-command of the expeditionary force sent to America. Charles was his father's aide-de-camp. The elder was shot in the knee while defending the king against an assault of a Parisian mob in 1792. He died of complications of this injury the following year.

7 François-Jean de Beauvoir, chevalier de Chastellux, maréchal de camp (1734-1788) served as an English translator. In 1786 he published his memoirs of the American Revolution *Voyages de M. le Marquis de Chastellux dans l'Amérique septentrionale, dans les années 1780, 1781 et 1782*.

8 Admiral Charles Louis d'Arsac Chevalier de Ternay (1723-1780) commanded the fleet that brought Rochambeau's army to America. Hemmed in by the six-month blockade of Newport, the Admiral grew ill, and died from typhus after lingering for over a week. As a member of the Knights of Malta, he swore to three monastic oaths, that forbade him marriage.

Lafayette's Departure

It was essential to keep this expedition and armament secret because the British suspected the purpose from reports they received. They put a number of vessels equal to ours under the command of Admiral Graves[9] to follow them to whatever part of the world they would sail. The Marquis de la Fayette was ordered to go give the particulars of our arrival to Congress. So as not to give any suspicion that we were associated with him, he left from Rochefort at the beginning of March aboard the *Hermione* commanded by the Count de la Touche. He brought with him Mr. Ethis de Corny,[10] Commissioner of War, to carefully prepare and to procure everything necessary for our landing, to buy horses for the artillery, the cavalry, food and finally to gather general information about the country in secrecy.

Rochambeau Arrives at Brest Finds Difficulty for Embarkation

Rochambeau arrived at Brest on March 26. He expected to find everything ready for immediate boarding. Everything that Prince de Montbarey, the Minister of War, promised him was already there. Even bombs and bullets had arrived. Everything concerning the Navy was very late. Mr. de Sartines, Minister of the Navy, assured that it would be ready very early and that we would find more vessels than necessary to transport the troops. But Mr. de Sartines was badly informed for, either the government's intention was really to send only 6000 men or, through Mr. de Sartines's fault, we truly lacked transports after making the reassignments. We could barely find enough to embark 3 to 4000 men. Mr. de Rochambeau complained to the Court forcefully and with reason. The Court responded that even though he could embark only 3,000 men, he needed to leave as the reinforcements were urgently needed. Mr. Hestace, Harbormaster of the Port of Brest, found a few more vessels which were immediately armed. We executed some drills in the Landernau River[11] and boarded more men on each vessel the following day.

9 Samuel Graves (1713-1787) was British commander-in-chief of the North American squadron in 1774-1775.

10 Louis-Dominique Éthis de Corny (1736-1790) came to America with Lafayette and served as commissary of war. Corny actively supported the French Revolution, losing his fortune in the upheaval. An acquaintance, William Short, claimed this trauma caused his death.

11 The river runs southwest from L'Elorn to Brest.

April 1780
The Troops Board

Finally, a new reassignment was made. They found place for the Bourbonnais, Soissonnais, Saintonge, Royal Deux-Ponts regiments, the Legion and chasseurs and artillery comprising a body of 6000 men. The artillery was placed at the back of the hold. The Bourbonnais Regiment boarded on April 4; the Deux-Ponts on the 5th, the Soissonnais on the 6th, the Legion on the 7th, the artillery battalion on the 8th and the Saintonge Regiment which was camped on the other side of the harbor at Crozon and Camaret on the 9th. The Neustrie, Rouergue and Auvergne regiments were ordered to remain in Brittany under the command of Mr. de Wittgenstein, designated the second division of Rochambeau's army. This general was promised that he would leave as soon as the transports were ready: a promise given to gain time but without any intention of keeping it.

Merchant Captains

We experienced difficulties on the part of the Navy. There has always been a sort of insidious antipathy, at best, between the Navy and the Army. Whether due to disagreement or to misunderstanding, these men later denied all the deceptions from the beginning. We had great difficulty boarding our baggage. The stowage was badly and hastily done on the ships of the line. The king paid for everything on his account by the ton. All the transports and, despite the strict ban, all the merchant captains boarded wines and other things detrimental to the embarkation, the troops' baggage and magazines.

April 1780

Mr. de Rochambeau's recommendation to the king for my nomination as one of his aides-de-camp (the 5th)[12] with the rank of captain.

I was, at this time, still a sublieutenant in the Saintonge Regiment. Mr. de Rochambeau, who did not want to reveal the object of his mission and wanting to make us believe that he could go to Gibraltar or elsewhere, had not yet named his staff which would have assured that he was forming a separate army corps. The king expressly forbade bringing more than six aides-de-camp, four of whom had already been appointed. The others would be named

12 The other aides-de-camp were Count Hans Axel von Fersen, Joseph Louis Cesar Charles, comte then duc de Damas, Alexandre-Théodore-Victor, comte de Lameth, Mathieu Dumas and Karl Friedrich von Closen.

once underway. There was no fear of divulging the secret. He told me that he would do what was expected of him to promote me during the course of the war, that I could prepare myself and be at peace and to embark awaiting my regiment. My company boarded the 300-ton *Père de Famille*. I made the crossing on board this vessel.

The Convoy Appears
Return to Brest
May 1780
Commission of Captain April 15

Everybody was ordered to sleep aboard on April 14. The winds blew to the West for some time. They turned on the afternoon of the 15th and the Chevalier de Ternay seized the moment to get underway. The vessels of the convoy weighed anchor first. They hoisted all their sails and went out the inlet. They were ordered to anchor in Bertheaume harbor. The fleet departed Brest. The winds turned to the West during the night and became very violent and remained so the following day which obliged the Chevalier de Ternay to give the signal for the convoy to return to Brest. (I received the rank of captain this day). Nobody, except certainly Mr. de Rochambeau, was upset by this adversity… There were a few officers who tendered their resignation. The weather being very stormy, I became very ill. I was only 20 years old and I have since noticed that young men suffered from seasickness more frequently than older men but some discomfort is good. If I suffered a bit of uneasiness, a bit of illness, I, at least, had the satisfaction that I should see, at this departure, my fate secured for the war. The Count de Rochambeau sent me to the Saintonge Regiment on a captain's commission and told me that he selected me as aide-de-camp to replace de Collot who was appointed quartermaster general. At the same time, he gave me the position of sub-aide. I was very happy. I remained on board the *Père de Famille*.

We occupied ourselves by restoring a bit of order, reloading the most necessary supplies for the troops which were forgotten or rather which were refused in bad faith. We returned to port to await a favorable wind which only occurred on May 2 when it turned to the North East.

May 1780
Departure of the
Chevalier de Ternay, of the Army

The Chevalier de Ternay gave the signal to get underway at dawn. He himself set the example. He was the first one under sail and immediately went out the inlet, followed by all the vessels of the fleet in convoy. We rounded the Pointe de Saint Mathieu at 8 a.m. We passed the Rash[13] after which we got ourselves ready to rally the laggards. The 32-gun frigate *La Bellone* escorted us as far as Cape Finisterre near the other side of the Isle of the Saints and discovered nothing. She then came to report to the Chevalier de Ternay who ordered her into service. He and all his fleet took the rear of the convoy. The frigates sometimes covered the flanks, sometimes the head or the rear of the entire fleet. We sailed to our destination in this order, realigning every day, two or three hours before nightfall, to rally the stragglers.

Bad Weather in the Gulf of Gascogne

The first days of our navigation were pleasant. Gaiety reigned on board, the wind was good and the weather mild but that didn't last long. Very bad weather soon greeted us. The wind turned to the Southwest, directly contrary to our route. We were buffeted in the Gulf of Gascogne. You can imagine, under these circumstances, how our troops appeared aboard. Three-quarters of them were seasick. I was terribly seasick. *La Provence* had her little mast broken, as did several other vessels in the convoy. This bad weather lasted five days, during which we saw Cape Ortégal[14] several times and noticed the wind shift to the northeast on the 15th, allowing us to round Cape Finisterre. This passage is always difficult.

Rallying Point

Only Mr. de Rochambeau, the Chevalier de Ternay, the Baron de Vioménil, and the Chevalier de Chastellux knew where we were headed. In the event we became separated, there was a rallying point indicated to each captain in a sealed packet which should be opened only in the presence of the staff of the vessel. That point was Boston.

June 1780

We passed to the south of the Azores and encountered other contrary winds. We were at 33 ½° latitude after which we went to the Bermudas, always with superb weather and without any boardings. Nothing noteworthy happened. Uneasiness began to be felt on board because of the heat and the large number of people on board the vessel.

13 Pointe du Raz.

14 Coruña, Spain.

Battle of the Bermudas

On June 21, on crossing the Bermudas, we signaled the vessels. At 11 a.m., *La Surveillante* reconnoitered them and signaled six. *L'Eveillé* and the *Neptune* were ordered to chase. It was a fleet of five vessels and a frigate commanded by Captain Cornwallis, brother of the general of that name which had escorted, up to a certain latitude, a convoy headed from Jamaica to England. One of the enemy vessels was much farther ahead of the others and was soon joined by our chasing vessels. The Chevalier de Ternay had them form a line and gave the slow sailers of his fleet time to join the leaders. Everyone was astonished that the *Neptune* and *L'Eveillé* did not attack the vessel which they overtook. She had only 64 guns and was more than two leagues from the rest of the squadron. But the Chevalier de Ternay thought that he was escorting a convoy which he only had to defend and to bring her to safety and that the object of his mission was not to fight but to land us as soon as possible. Several of his vessels could have been damaged and detained and his progress delayed which was already quite high. The little desire that he had to fight gave the enemy time to launch their vessel, which maneuvered very well, and to get in line to gain the wind and to close in more narrowly. Then, after different maneuvers, the battle began at long range at 6:30 p.m. We received several volleys on all sides but to little effect. The approaching nightfall allowed the combatants to break off easily. During this action, the convoy arrived to the lee of the squadron.

Despite the reasons alleged in favor of the Chevalier de Ternay, he would never redeem himself in the eyes of the Navy and the witnesses of this battle for not having vigorously attacked an enemy much weaker than he both in numbers and vessel strength. He could have taken the first in the midst of his fleet. The English fight little or very badly against superior forces. *L'Ardent* caught up with two frigates in 1779, seeing some vessels approaching, we had ten or twelve men killed and 15 wounded in this battle.

The General lit his fires that night and we continued our route without any other encounter with the enemy.

Charleston Captured by the British

We captured an English sloop of war with six officers aboard on the 22nd. They informed us that Lord Cornwallis captured Charleston. They were bringing news of the capitulation to England. This was the only port the Americans had left in the South. Our arrival became more and more urgent and necessary.

July

We already began to enter into the third month of our cruise since our departure from France. As I already said, we were all ignorant of the landing site, so, as we approached the Chesapeake Bay, we all believed that this was the destination. We sounded and found bottom at 18 fathoms. We sailed toward the Virginia capes when we discovered vessels ahead of us at sundown on July 5.

Change of Direction at Chesapeake Bay

The Chevalier de Ternay, who was to go to the Chesapeake Bay to reconnoiter and to learn if Rhode Island had been evacuated, turned around at the sight of vessels. He feared Admiral Graves's fleet had joined the vessels which we engaged at Bermuda. This thought and his great anxiety to escape caused him to make a mistake. He sent me to reconnoiter the van of the frigates. He signaled a false route for the night which was neither seen nor understood because of the advancing nightfall. The convoy passed the night in constant fear. Several officers of the vessels pretended having seen other vessels. The fact is that it was the 44-gun *Romulus* and four frigates that were exiting the bay. The night was very dark. Two enemy frigates followed us and caught up with us without being observed. A little before dawn, they found themselves a little athwart the *Duc de Bourgogne* which they recognized as a ship only by the sound of her bell. They fired a volley and gave chase. The Chevalier de Ternay wanted to assure himself if these frigates formed part of a fleet. He would discover nothing in full daylight before distancing his vessels.

For these reasons, he declined to give chase, after which he signaled to *l'Eveillé*, to the *Amazone* and to *la Surveillante* but the time lost at sea and elsewhere is difficult to regain. The frigates were hotly pursued. They threw their cannons and some carriages overboard and everything which could lighten their progress. Despite that, we observed, for half an hour, that our chasers gained on them greatly when the Chevalier de Ternay, who believed seeing otherwise, signaled for them to give up the chase. This order greatly pleased the captains of our vessels and, in general, all the spectators who prided themselves in knowing which vessels we saw the night before.

Council of War
Chevalier de Marigny Captain of the Ardent

The same day, 6, we held a council of war after dinner. The sea was calm. We put everything in order. All the captains went aboard the Chevalier de Ternay. The heat was excessive. We had a large number of sick on board and three-quarters of the vessels of the fleet and of the convoy lacked water. We were on the coast of America. We had to land somewhere, anywhere. The Chevalier de Ternay detailed, in the council, the reasons for his conduct on the day of combat and the change of direction at the Chesapeake. Despite all the reasons, good or bad, the captains were all discontent with him. He asked who was sent to reconnoiter the previous evening. The Chevalier de Marigny[15] responded "it is not today that we can know; it was yesterday," thus expressing well that we should have conducted ourselves otherwise. The Chevalier de Marigny (Bernard) was a very brave and excellent officer. It was he who, in 1779, commanding the frigate *la Junon*, captured *l'Ardent* with la *Charmante* and given command of her.

July 1780
It is Decided to go to Rhode Island

Our destination had always been Rhode Island. The result of the council of war was that having learned, from the little vessel which we captured, about what we wanted to learn in the Chesapeake, we had to sail to this first location and fight the enemy who would oppose us with whatever forces were available. We then set sail for Rhode Island.

L'Ile de France Goes Astray

We had very thick fog the 7th and the following days. Despite all the signals those days, *l'Ile de France*, with 350 men of the Bourbonnais Regiment aboard, got separated. La *Surveillante*, repeating the signals, fired a cannon shot with ball which happily only pierced our mainsail.

Martha's Vineyard

We sighted Norman's Island[16] and Martha's Vineyard on the 9th. There are still many native Indians on these two islands.

15 Charles-René-Louis, vicomte de Bernard de Marigny (1740-1815) was a French vice admiral who commanded the Brest fleet. In 1775, Marigny nearly died from poisoning after sleeping on his freshly repainted ship. A year of rest restored his health, and Marginy served in seven naval engagements during the American Revolution. Just before his death in 1815 he gained the title of Commandant of the Navy at the Port of Brest.

16 Possibly Nantucket.

Block Island

We sailed between Martha's Vineyard and Rhode Island on the 10th. We sighted Block Island and we anchored at the harbor of this island.

Land Sighted
The Count de Rochambeau Lands
The Fleet and the Convoy Enter Newport Harbor
July 1780

We weighed anchor on the morning of the 11th. We landed and reconnoitered Rhode Island. The rising fog was still very heavy and forced us to anchor. It lifted around noon. The Chevalier de Ternay got ready and only wanted the last vessel in port. He went aboard the *Amazone*. The Count de Rochambeau and Mr. de Béville[17], Quartermaster General of the Army, wanted to be the first ashore to reconnoiter and immediately select a campsite. They disembarked the *Amazone* at 3 o'clock in the afternoon and the convoy and the fleet entered Newport Harbor at 5 p.m. after a passage of 71 days.

One has to experience seasickness, the apathy and the depression where we are in order to define it and to have passed 3 ½ months on the water to understand the pleasure we have to recover, so to speak, the use of our legs, the ability to drink fresh water and to breathe fresh, pure air on arriving on land. Our long passage was one of the more pleasant ones. It is impossible to conduct a more urgent convoy than the one done by the Chevalier de Ternay, but he missed two good occasions for his own glory. His entire fleet had an opinion and would never forgive him.

Admiral Graves Arrives at New York

Admiral Graves was sent to pursue us with seven vessels. He left the port of Portsmouth the same day we left Brest but the wind we experienced in the Gulf of Gascogne forced him to return. He then chased le *Fargès* for a long time, a vessel from the Indies which lost him. We played the fable of the tortoise and the hare with him. We proceeded slowly but surely. We arrived at Newport on the 11th and he arrived in New York on the 13th.

17 Jacques de Béville was Quartermaster General of the Army.

Admiral Thomas Graves

National Park Service, Colonial National Historical Park, Yorktown Collection

Battle of the *Hermione*

We found the *Hermione* at Newport which had left in the month of March with Mr. de la Fayette. After disembarking her passengers, she went on a cruise and had fought the 32-gun English frigate *Iris*. The battle lasted an hour with an equal loss of men without gaining any advantage. The Comte de la Course was badly wounded in the arm and Mr. Daguesse, his second, was also wounded.

July 1780
Mr. Rochambeau's Reception

Nobody disembarked on the 11th. The Count de Rochambeau, as I said, went ashore with Mr. de Béville to reconnoiter a position. He found almost nobody to speak with, no American troops. A Quaker named Mr. Wanton approached him and loaned him some horses and offered him some tea at his house which Mr. de Rochambeau accepted. He asked if the Americans had a commander in town. Mr. Greene[18], Colonel of the Rhode Island Regiment, who was at Newport with a dozen men was brought to him. He was the first one to whom Mr. de Rochambeau spoke about his mission. Greene was a relative of the governor of the state. He immediately sent an express to him to inform him of our arrival. The Baron de Vioménil did not think it prudent to leave Mr. de Rochambeau alone on land. He had the grenadier company of the Bourbonnais Regiment disembark to be his guard.

Location Chosen for the Camp

We can enter Newport Harbor by three different passages. The first between the part of Rhode Island called the Neck and the island of Conanicut. The second between Conanicut and the continent; the third going around the island passing between the eastern part and the continent and going north. This passage is called the Sakonnet Passage. Newport is built at the most secure part of the island, at the entrance to the Neck. This is where Mr. de Rochambeau placed his camp along the city, the right adjacent to the harbor, the left going out to the east all the way to the edge of the sea, in such a way that a vessel could not appear without being seen. We just had the coast to guard; the whole region was ours.

Formation of the Small Army into Brigades

The Bourbonnais and Royal Deux-Ponts Regiments made up the first brigade. The Baron de Vioménil was attached to it. The Soissonnais and Saintonge regiments formed the

18 Colonel Christopher Greene (1737-1781), the cousin of General Nathanael Greene, commanded Fort Mercer in 1777, fought at the battle of Rhode Island in 1778 and took command of the lines in Westchester County, New York, in the spring of 1781.

second under the command of the Viscount de Vioménil. Lauzun's Legion, under the command of Brigadier the Duc de Lauzun, formed the advance guard, at the point of the Neck near Mr. Collins's house where we find the Conanicut passage. This deployment concluded, the grenadiers and chasseurs disembarked on the 12th.

The State Addresses Him

The same day, Governor Greene[19] complimented and addressed Mr. de Rochambeau before the state assembly. He responded that he was only the advance guard of a much larger corps which the king wanted to send to America's aid, that we would all follow General Washington's orders and that it would give him great pleasure to contribute to his success. The city was illuminated that night.

The Troops Disembark

The artillery was unloaded on the 13, 14, 15, and 16 and the troops were all in camp the night of the 16th. The artillery park was placed at the right of the camp.

Establishments for the Sick

It was essential to set up magazines and especially hospitals for the army and the navy. This was immediately taken care of. We had more than 800 sick which is not surprising due to the length of the crossing and the heat we experienced.

July 1780
The *Hermione* Sets Sail

The Chevalier de Ternay had the *Hermione* go out to cruise the coasts to search for the *Ile de France*. Of 5000 men, we only had 3600 fit for service. That was the opportune moment for the enemy. They did not delay in showing themselves.

19 William Greene (1731-1809) served as governor of the Colony of Rhode Island and Providence Plantations from 1778-1786. Greene largely stayed out of politics after his defeat in the election of 1786 but served as an elector for presidents and vice presidents in the first electoral college Rhode Island participated in.

Sir Henry Clinton

National Park Service
Colonial National Historical Park
Yorktown Collection

State of Rhode Island at Our Arrival

Before speaking about the state and the condition of the country which we now inhabit, I should say that the island of Rhode Island, once flourishing, was now desolate. We could barely see, in Newport houses, a few Negroes whose masters had fled, leaving them to guard them. The British were their masters for four years and had burned and destroyed many of the plantations on the island and houses in the city. Two parties (as in the rest of the 13 states) shared it. The Tories or royalists who were in the majority were particularly well treated during the British occupation. The Whig or American party was always horribly vexed and barely survives. They did not know us; we found few resources. When the Treaty of Alliance was signed with America, the British did not fail to paint us in the darkest colors to the Americans. At the arrival of our army, fear had already alienated many inhabitants. Mr. de Rochambeau had a proclamation published throughout the countryside assuring safety and protection for everyone. Strict discipline, the sight of money encouraged some and then the others. Little by little, they all brought us merchandise in abundance and hope.

July 1780
About the Army
Americans at the Same Time

Mr. the Count de Rochambeau immediately dispatched a courier to General Washington informing him of our arrival. This general's army barely consisted of 1500 men and there was much to fear for the freedom of America if we delayed coming to her aid. Our presence revived them. Little by little, we saw proclamations appear, edicts to have levees. The British had conducted a very fine campaign but Sir Henry Clinton surely lost hope of the great successes he promised.

The Enemy Appear off Newport

The troops had barely disembarked when Mr. de Rochambeau began to make his position respectable. This precaution achieved its purpose a short time later. Admiral Arbuthnot,[20] reinforced by Graves's squadron, appeared in sight of Newport on the 19th with a large number of transports with troops on board. Clinton was on board the 90-gun *London.* Even though we had dug in along the coast, we were still almost unready to receive the enemy and I don't know what might have happened if they immediately attempted a landing and tried to force the passage. Our vessels were not all anchored because the landing presented obstacles and everything was in turmoil. More than half of the crews aboard were not in condition to service their cannons. On our side, we must remember that we had more than 700 ill and 350 men aboard the *Ile de France* of whom we had no news. The Navy did not exert itself for a landing. When Mr. de Rochambeau wanted to place the heavy artillery, it was found at the bottom of the hold along with the ammunition.

July 1780

Necessity gave added force to the orders which were reiterated. The two battalions of grenadiers and chasseurs commanded by the Brigadier Count de Custine[21] were marched to the point of the Neck where they passed the night in bivouac.

Batteries Set Up

The morning of the 20th, this party found itself in a state of defense. They worked prodigiously through the night. The artillery was placed early. Our seven vessels anchored and, despite the advice of the inhabitants, Mr. de Rochambeau prepared for a strong defense in case he was attacked.

20 Admiral Mariot Arbuthnot (1711-1794) was commander-in-chief of the British North American squadron. In 1793, a year before his death, Arbuthnot advanced to the post of Admiral of the Blue, the third highest ranking in the British navy.

21 Adam Philippe comte de Custine (1740-1793) was a French general who joined Rochambeau's Expédition Particulière (Special Expedition) supporting the American colonists. In 1782 he dined at Mount Vernon, presenting Mrs. Washington with porcelain dishes produced at his factory in France.

The Viscount of Noailles is Sent to Conanicut Island

To cover the right of the squadron, which was only a quarter cannon range from Conanicut island, Mr. de Rochambeau sent the Viscount of Noailles[22] there with the second battalion of the Soissonnais Regiment. They took possession of the dominant hill on a very narrow part of the island where they could make a good defense, as the enemy landing at the point would have to cross there.

From the 20th to the 23rd, the enemy was always in sight, often very close to land. Sometimes, several vessels dared to remount. They received some of our preparations and our dispositions. A council of war was held aboard the *London* which saw the leaders divided. Mr. Arbuthnot always wanted to attack and attempt to land; but Mr. Clinton was of the opposite opinion. They finally left us for a chase and the enemy disappeared after having missed its only opportunity to really attack us successfully.

Effect of the Appearance of the British in the Area

The news of the appearance of the British soon spread through the countryside. A company of volunteers on horseback came to offer its services to our general. The officers of Connecticut and Massachusetts marched to join us also. The enemy was no longer in sight. Mr. de Rochambeau thanked the company for its goodwill and sent to stop the militia's march, enjoining them, all the while, to come at the first request. We had already stressed that we needed provisions. We had not been attacked at that opportune moment after all, which left us nothing to fear later. In addition, Mr. de Rochambeau did not want to alienate Connecticut where the enemy might go.

The Fleet Changes Anchorage

The fleet formed part of our forces at Rhode Island and reciprocally could not leave us for her defense. The fleet's anchorage near Conanicut occasioned a division of our forces such that, if the enemy had landed in several places and had attempted to force a passage, it was not possible to reinforce those troops who would have to defend this island. Communication was very long. Mr. de Rochambeau consulted Captain Gardner, a very good Whig and an excellent sailor, who knew the harbor perfectly. He asked him if there was another anchorage out of range of the cannons and bombs from Conanicut island. He

22 Louis-Marie, viscount de Noailles (1756-1804) served under his brother-in-law the Marquis de Lafayette in America during the American War for Independence. He was the French officer who concluded the capitulation of Yorktown in 1781.

responded that he knew one and, on Gardner's advice, the Chevalier de Ternay anchored his fleet with the right against Rose Island which was decided to be made a good port. The center was divided by Goat Island, where there were already batteries, and the left at Brenton's Point where a fort was located defended by twelve pieces of heavy cannon and four mortars. Conanicut island was abandoned, leaving only a small post for signals which were agreed upon along the entire coast, in case the enemy landed anywhere.

Conduct and Response of Mr. de Rochambeau

Mr. de Rochambeau initially used a lot of firmness. The inhabitants and the state assembly advised him to abandon his post given the inferiority of his forces compared to the numbers which the British could have. He responded that he would never abandon the Navy and that he would be buried with his last soldier. This conduct and the strict discipline which ruled the Army then restored to us part of the inhabitants which old national prejudices partially alienated from us. We needed great gentleness with a people naturally slow and whose customs differed greatly from ours. We paid in full everywhere and the difficulty of language (given our limited use of English) did not make matters easier. It soon increased at the sight of money. Our allies were very greedy for ours. Despite that, they showed very good faith on every occasion when our ignorance of their language would give them an advantage. The only people we had to complain about were the French horsemen who travelled in America for two or three years. Our awareness of them always made us suspect.

Establishment at Providence

We put the peace which the enemy gave us to good use for our defenses. The entire army greatly needed it after such a long passage and our first labors. Mr. de Corny, of whom I already spoke, established some warehouses before our arrival. He set up a hospital at Providence at a college perfectly exposed where all the necessary aid was transported. The Newport City Hall and some churches were taken for the same purpose and almost all the sailors and soldiers went there, three quarters of them with scurvy.

General Washington's Plans

Our arrival in America was soon known in all 13 states and seemed to awaken and revive everyone. As soon as we saw 5,000 good troops, we thought the English would soon disappear and that we could undertake any enterprise against them with the present assistance. This thought was not only that of the people. General Washington was then making plans. He did not yet know Mr. de Rochambeau. He did not know what kind of man he was dealing with. He feared making erroneous plans, doubted every undertaking. That's why he thought it prudent to have them approved by a general of the same country. Mr. de la Fayette wrote him several letters regarding the conduct of the war. An attack on New York seemed to be the preferred plan. Mr. Washington admitted the garrison was 15,000. He thought the Hook was weak. He said if we entered first, we had nothing to fear against much superior forces, that if the Chevalier de Ternay was blocked by Arbuthnot, we could certainly do without the Navy, that the French could march immediately to join the American Army which he hoped would increase from 10 to 12,000 men about August 15 to then embark at Morrisania Point and to land on Long Island . . .

Mr. de Rochambeau responded quite negatively to these plans which seemed poorly designed. He showed how impracticable he thought it was with our resources. The Chevalier de Ternay responded to the sentence which said that, once inside the Hook, we would be unbeatable, not stronger than us; that consequently weaker than Arbuthnot, he could not think about engaging him. Mr. de Rochambeau repeated that it the Navy could not move, he could not leave it unprotected. Mr. de la Fayette wrote him another long letter to urge him, seemed to give him some advice and told him that the point of Rhode Island seemed of little interest….. Mr. de Rochambeau responded that the court sent him to this post which he did not choose, that when he saw a good plan adopted militarily, he did not need a spur to put it into execution. He responded to a long dispatch in a rather dry letter and, at the same time, he requested General Washington the favor of communicating his orders directly to him. He said that he would find him always ready to carry them out and to use his zeal for the cause which he came to defend. Moreover, they would conduct much more business and deliberate much better in an enterprise he advocated and which he demanded absolutely and that he himself would determine the time and place.———. This letter produced its effect. Confidence and esteem took the place of management and, from that time on, good understanding, so essential, began and continued between the two generals.

The Detachment of the Bourbonnais Regiment aboard the Ile de France Arrives at Newport

We received news of the *Ile de France* on the 24th. After becoming separated from the fleet, she sailed to Boston. The Chevalier de Bressolles, Lieutenant Colonel of the Bourbonnais Regiment, commanded the 350 men of this regiment who were aboard. He had this detachment march toward Newport. They arrived at camp on the 28th, having left only a few sick men behind.[23]

August

Mr. de Guichen

At the beginning of August, we learned the details of the three battles that Mr. de Guichen[24] fought against Admiral Rodney off Martinique and we flattered ourselves that he would come pass the winter in our area and furnish us with the means to engage the enemy.

Mr. de Rochambeau Fortifies Himself

Mr. de Rochambeau profited from their distance to regroup and strengthen his position. He reopened and fortified some redoubts which had previously been occupied by the British and demolished others which were more detrimental than useful for defense. No use was made of the old lines which the British made, as they were susceptible to being captured and enfiladed in many places. In general, all their works on Rhode Island do little honor to their engineers.

His Army Passes in Review

We employed 400 men every day in our entrenchments until the 25th, St. Louis day, when Mr. de Rochambeau passed the Army in review. He had the troops perform a feu de joie. All the forts fired three cannon shots per piece and the fleet 21 per vessel. This review attracted a great number of people. All our regiments were admired. They deserved to be. Moreover, this was a very natural feeling for people who had never seen any troops other than their militias. We only had 400 men help us in our work under the command of General Heath.[25] It was especially he who showed his surprise. The former Englishmen

23 Gilbert de Bressolles, a lieutenant colonel in Rochambeau's army, was a hard-charging officer who suffered several sabre wounds at the Battle of Minden in 1759. His horse was shot out from him during a sortie in Cassel in 1762.

24 Luc Urbain du Bouëxic de Guichen (1712-1790) was a French admiral who distinguished himself in the battle off Ushant on July 27, 1779. He fought three battles with Admiral Rodney in April and May 1780, including the Battle of Martinique.

25 Major General William Heath (1737-1814) served as commander of the Eastern Department.

could hardly believe that it was the French. The general began exclaiming "I am quite in rapture." (I am in ecstasy). They were paraded. The music attracted particular but mediocre attention from the curious—a very natural effect which novelty produces among everybody. Our general was greatly complimented. All these demonstrations were necessary for a people imbued with prejudice against us and knowing us better and following us everywhere, returned daily to the French from their estrangement.

General Sullivan[26] commanded the land troops who were to attack Rhode Island in 1778 while Mr. d'Estaing was to do so for the sea. General Sullivan came to Newport on the 27th. It was he who commanded the American troops who landed on Rhode Island in 1778 to attack by land while Mr. d'Estaing was supposed to do so by sea. First of all, the plan was perfectly well executed and Mr. d'Estaing put to flight the 4000 British who defended Newport and would certainly have been captured. But excessive ambition lost it. Admiral Howe[27], with two vessels less than the French, arrived off Rhode Island but could provide no assistance as Mr. d'Estaing was already there. The latter believed that this was a good opportunity for a double victory. He left his station to chase Howe but he was barely out of the port when a terrible wind arose and dispersed his entire fleet and dismasted his vessel. He was on the verge of being captured himself by the 50-gun ship *Renown* which flanked him and cannonaded him the entire day. In the state of distress in which he found himself, he might also have had the shame of surrendering to him, such a despicable enemy, a 90-gun ship if he had not been disengaged by one of his own at the end of the day. He went to Boston to refit where he exerted astounding effort to repair his fleet and the prompt and good deployments he made.

If the enemy, who did not suffer, had attacked him, they would have regained their reputation in the eyes of the Americans who had suffered such a great loss.

Sullivan did not forgive him. He unleashed himself against him and even put some indecent things about Mr. d'Estaing and the French in the following day's orders. Instead of attacking, the Americans were forced to abandon their works and retreat. They were

26 Major General John Sullivan (1740-1795) commanded the Congressional land troops at the Battle of Rhode Island.

27 General Richard Howe (1726-1799) entered British naval service at the age of 14. By 1776 he was appointed head of the North American station. Although sympathetic to the colonists' plight, and favoring reconciliation, he fought fiercely to restore British rule. Howe defeated the French attempt to take Newport in 1780. In 1782, he was appointed to command the English Channel fleet, where he oversaw the final relief mission of Gibraltar. He later served as first lord of the Admiralty before resuming his old post as head of the Channel Fleet upon the outbreak of the French Revolution, and was in command at Ushant ("Glorious First of June") on June 1, 1794. Howe's prestige was such that he was called upon to help pacify mutineers at Spithead in 1797.

very worried and lost some men, but, despite that, they retreated in good order and re-embarked at Bristol Ferry.

Now Member of Congress

Sullivan was one of the American generals who had served best since the beginning of the war. He was educated and Mr. de Rochambeau was not embarrassed to show him the Army and our new fortifications. He asked him how and in what manner he would have conducted his attacks if Mr. d'Estaing had not departed. General Sullivan first showed him his camp which was placed on a height dominating the British works. He was to go out at nightfall, leaving the fires lit, to make two attacks. One, a feint on the left, the true one on the right of their lines where there was a low valley. There was a swamp in the middle of the valley. He would have marched along the edge and arrived at the lines without being discovered. He was very surprised to find a considerable fort at this location with cannons enfilading the valley from one end to the other which made him say that he believed we could not be attacked from that side. This general has since retired from the military and is presently a member of Congress for the state of Massachusetts Bay.

I will continue to detail the military actions of this war even though they seem strange to the French, they can only be of interest, in a journal of campaigns, to those who followed them. It is with this in mind that I recount the following anecdote.

Delegation of Natives

A delegation of 22 Iroquois, Illinois and Four Nations Indians arrived at Newport on the 29th. They heard that the French, American allies, had come to their aid. The British wanted to persuade them otherwise. They came to touch with their hands and to see with their eyes. It was about the beginning of the address that one of the principals of the band who spoke French spoke to Mr. de Rochambeau in the name of the other delegates and their nations. He complimented him on his fortuitous arrival and then expressed their satisfaction at seeing some Frenchmen again whom they greatly enjoyed as neighbors in Canada, that they would always love them and that they could not be any more devoted to them, to their father the King of France. It is thus they always referred to and always call the general. They also elaborated on their natural hatred for the British and the need they had for a minister of the Catholic religion to which they were permanently associated. Each French sentence the speaker delivered, he repeated in the Indian language. His companions responded in two or three words in sign of approval.

During the speech, the members of the delegation squatted on the ground like monkeys. They had pipes and lit them. Mr. de Rochambeau responded with kindness, telling them that he was expressly charged by the King, their father, to learn whether they were still good subjects, that he wanted to protect them and that he was convinced that as an American ally, he would never turn to the side of the English, their enemy and his.

He assigned them an empty house in the city where straw was placed for them. They were invited to dine the following day. Two grenadiers were posted at their door to prevent them from going out.

The General Gives Them Gifts from the King

The following day, the 30th, they came to headquarters. Mr. de Rochambeau gave them gifts from the King. They were holy medals; earrings; bracelets which they put on their arms and forearms, all silver; shirts; woolen blankets for which they showed great appreciation. They then dined, drank and ate abundantly. We had taken the precaution to put much water in the wine because they become very wicked when they are drunk. They were greatly astonished when the second course was served and the desert afterward. In general, for savages, they conducted themselves very decently. I had two at my side for whom I asked expressly for several dishes which they served with great dexterity.

They Saw the Army

After dinner, Mr. de Rochambeau showed them the Army under arms which they viewed attentively and with admiration. Lauzun's hussars particularly surprised them. They were paraded at the gallop which pleased them greatly.

September

They were entrusted to me and Count Fersen[28] on the 31st to bring them aboard the squadron. We showed them in detail everything that might excite their curiosity and after having also satisfied ours, they left on September 2, very content of their delegation.

28 Count Hans Axel von Fersen (1755-1810) was a Swedish nobleman who served as a French officer in America, one of Rochambeau's aides-de-camp. Fersen enjoyed a long friendship with Marie Antoinette. In 1791, he tried unsuccessfully to intervene to save the Queen's life. He fell victim to mob violence in Sweden in 1810.

Their Customs and Practices

These people could show us a slice of the ancient sites in their tastes, their customs, their mannerisms. They are lazy; they have few or no fixed lodgings; they live only by hunting. Their women do all the work inside and outside of their cabins and, if they travel, they carry the baggage. They are not as cruel as those who have never seen civilized people. However, they should not be provoked for they then follow their natural ferocity and they almost immediately scalp their enemy who insults them. Their clothing is very simple and very economical for it consists only of a little apron made to conceal their private parts and which doesn't descend any lower. In the winter, they cover themselves with a woolen blanket. They put great art in painting themselves or, better said, to smear their faces with different colors. It seemed to me the most precious for them was a dark blue. I observed their grooming at which they spend much time. They all have a little mirror and they decorate their faces in color with different designs according to their taste: ovals, squares, lines—straight, curved, angular. . . . They have no beard. They pluck it as soon as it appears at 18 or 20 years. A white shirt has no air of neatness among them, for they put all sorts of colors on those we gave them. Their color is olive. Their hair is a shiny black which they keep short. They also paint their hair and decorate their head with feathers on which they put some color. Once they've been to war, they pierce their ears. Some attach ribbons which hang down to their shoulders. One is cut in circles, the other in squares, diamonds, hearts. They attach pendants, bows, little charms, often all together. They almost all have the separation between the nostrils pierced, to which they attach rings which hang down to the upper lip. That does not prevent them from eating.

Uniqueness of their Dance

One of their great pleasures is the dance. That of the Negroes expresses sensuality, theirs expresses war. It is a double jump in place, on one leg then on the other, hitting the ground hard in between and accompanied by piercing cries, contortions and awful movements. They gather together for pleasure which always begins and ends with horrible and certainly frightening cries for which there would be no warning. They have no other instrument but a type of drum with only a hide. They only dance three, four, or five together. The dancers are always armed with an unsheathed sabre or a sword. The others take two pieces of wood which they beat in time one against the other to accompany the drum.

After the first three or four loud cries, they begin to sing in a low voice. The dancers then put themselves in movement. My description ends here because it would be too difficult to describe the bizarre and strange effect of this type of music, of the song of the spectators, the sharp and discordant cries of the dancers, their hitting of feet, all followed in the most precise manner. They don't make any figures. They turn one against the other without any order, very different from us who keep ourselves straight in dancing. They are almost doubled over. We thought our curiosity cost us dearly. There were a lot of people in the dance hall. They burst the floor while dancing. Happily, it only collapsed a little at a time and everyone had time to leave. Their natural uncleanliness, their frequent use of tobacco, the prepared colors with which they cover their skin, the sweat . . . . give them an unpleasant odor which is so strong that after purchasing a woolen belt decorated with pearls from them and washing it several times, the odor never was removed.

We Send Them a Capuchin as They Requested

Some time after their departure, we sent them a Capuchin chaplain from the *Jason* who was well received, as he never returned. He only had a limited pass.

Our Works Continue
September 1780

Mr. de Rochambeau ceaselessly continued work on the fortifications. Our works were pushed a little further from Newport than the old British lines and, unlike theirs, did not require a lot of men to defend them. Without being in force anywhere, they were constructed in the most advantageous positions. Their fire crossed and swept everything in front. If the enemy had landed anywhere, the general's plan was always to go out to fight them. If he were repulsed, he would retreat into his entrenched camp. He wanted to put only 1500 men in the forts and keep the rest in reserve in order to immediately counterattack whatever the enemy might have taken before he made camp. For this reason, almost all our redoubts were open by the gorge. There was only a mile from the right to the left of our works.

The general staff of the Army opened communications along all the landing sites. These first works completed, the colonels drilled their regiments who had not taken up arms since our departure from France.

General Washington's and
Rochambeau's Conference at Hartford

Mr. de Rochambeau did not know General Washington. For a long time, he requested an interview with him, the result of which could only produce good results for the general affairs. He left for Hartford, the capital of Connecticut and the designated site, on the 18th.

The Chevalier de Ternay accompanied him along with Mr. Desandroüins,[29] Colonel commanding the engineers, and the counts de Fersen and Charles Damas,[30] two of his aides-de-camp.

The Situation Becomes Critical During his Absence

During the absence of the major generals, we found our situation the most critical it had ever been. The naval officers particularly demonstrated an uneasiness to displace themselves and, what was even more remarkable, land troops acted only by force and to serve with the naval forces.

Mr. the Chevalier de Guichen commanded the navy in the West Indies at that time. We prided ourselves that having spent the winter in our region, he might procure for us the means of operating or at least to match the English forces. Crossing the Bermudas, he encountered a ship coming to Newport. He only sent his compliments to Mr. de Rochambeau and de Ternay and told them that he was very upset about their situation but that he was on his way to France, escorting a merchant fleet. Thus, instead of announcing the arrival of his army, we were told of the arrival of Sir George Rodney at New York with 12 ships of the line which, joined with those of Graves and Arbuthnot, made a total of 25 vessels against our seven. The enemy immediately prepared to come attack us and embarked their troops.

The Batteries of Rhode Island at the Entrance to the Harbor

The right of our fleet was perfectly anchored on Rose Island which covered it. There was only one very insignificant earthwork with a few cannons. Navy Brigadier Chevalier Destouches[31] and the Baron de Vioménil went there and deemed it necessary to immediately construct a large barrier and to fortify it well with large cannons. The Chevalier

29 Jean Nicolas Desandrouïns (1729-1792) commanded the French artillery during the American campaigns. Illness prevented him from taking part in the siege of Yorktown. However, his prior service secured him a special French pension and membership in the Society of the Cincinnati.

30 Joseph François Louis Cesar Charles de Damas, comte then duc de Damas (1758-1829) was a colonel and one of Rochambeau's aides-de-camp. In 1791, he joined with the fleeing royal family in Varennes. After his capture, he was sentenced to death but ultimately pardoned.

31 Charles René Dominique Sochet, Chevalier Destouches (1727-1794) second-in-command of the French Navy, assumed command after the death of Admiral de Ternay.

de Kerenet,[32] Lieutenant Colonel of Engineers, immediately determined the dimensions and ordered 400 men to work on it. It was already usable on the 20th and the battery had 44 pieces of cannons, 36 or 24 or 18 pounders, on the 21st. Four 8-inch mortars were also placed there. The fire of this work crossed with that of the vessels at Goat island and Brenton's Point where there were 4 12-inch mortars such that, as soon as an enemy vessel passed Rose Island, it would receive 300 cannon shots per volley, those from land with red balls.[33] The vessels could not turn around because of the rocks.

Terror and Panic of the Sailors

Also, extreme anxiety or fear sometimes manifested itself among us or magnified objects which didn't exist. One fine day, at noon, the weather was rather foggy, when the sentiments of which I want to speak suddenly took hold of our Navy. We heard cries everywhere aboard the vessels, from the main deck to below deck. There is the enemy! Great activity everywhere, general confusion, orders, counter orders etc. etc. etc. The fog lifted after an hour. Fire, men! In every direction along the horizon, there was not a single enemy armed vessel. General shame reigned on board. The matches were extinguished, the cannons housed. Next time, men, look with greater attention or take your glasses, but no more terror, especially panic!

Return of Our General

To our great regret, the enemy never appeared. Mr. de Rochambeau and the Chevalier de Ternay returned from the conference at Hartford on the 26th after having left General Washington who resumed the route of his army where his presence would become so necessary.

32 Guillaume Querenet de la Combe (1731-1788) served as Lieutenant Colonel of Engineers in the French army. As second in command of Rochambeau's engineers, he directed the French engineering work at Yorktown in place of Colonel Desandrouins who was ill. He was promoted to colonel on December 5, 1781. He died at Mézières after breaking his leg.

33 Hot shot are cannon balls heated enough to become red hot. If these balls lodged in the side of a wooden vessel, they could start a fire.

American Forts at West Point

The Americans, not being masters of the course of the North River,[34] erected various works on the shores of this river which they lost and retook at one time or another during the course of the war. After the capture of Fort Montgomery in 1777, Mr. Washington chose West Point as the most suitable location for his plan to prevent the enemy from penetrating any higher and to block the river. He made it a respectable post. The warehouses and the American army's munitions of war were located there along with the cannons captured at Saratoga. The defense of this important post could only be given to a man of proven bravery and talent. The general finally chose Benedict Arnold.

Arnold's Treason
American Major General Benedict Arnold's Treachery

This man, a native of New Haven, a small port on the Sound[35] in Connecticut, was raised from the business of horse trader to major general after having served his country for five years with the greatest distinction, having received three gunshots and enjoying great respect. He had just deserted to the persecutors and the enemies of the same country for whose liberties he risked his life. After the English evacuated Philadelphia, Mr. Washington appointed Arnold as commandant. He committed some fraud in this city and found the means to turn the public funds to his profit. He was accused and appeared before a court-martial. He could have been broken and dismissed but he was a useful man. He was given a severe reprimand with the full knowledge of General Washington. Arnold then conceived the abominable plan for revenge by treachery as soon as the occasion presented itself.

Mr. André, Adjutant General of the British Army

It was only such an infamous act which could put the British in possession of West Point. They also felt the importance of the proposals Arnold made to them when he became commandant of this post. To better execute his plans, he wanted to discuss them with someone whose talents could respond to his views and to those of Sir Henry Clinton.

34 Hudson River.

35 Long Island Sound.

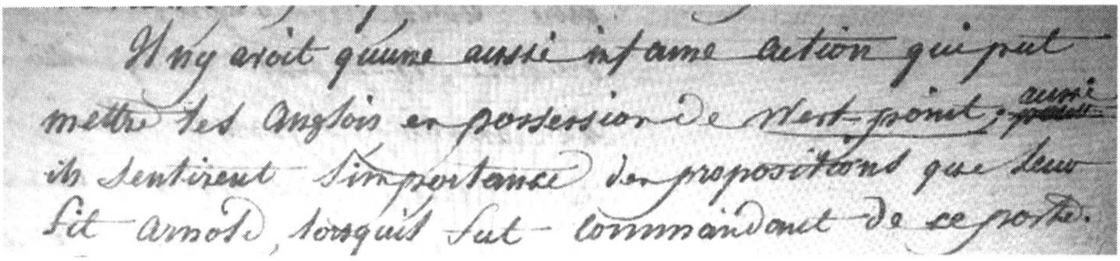
Il n'y avoit qu'une aussi infame action qui put mettre les Anglois en possession de West-point, aussi ils sentirent l'importance des propositions que leur fit Arnold, lorsqu'il fut commandant de ce poste.

The latter chose Mr. André,[36] Adjutant General (Major General) of his army, a young man full of talent in whom he had the greatest confidence. This officer boarded the frigate *Vulture*, went up the North River as far as Haverstraw Bay below the forts of Verplanck's and Stony Point and was put ashore near Mr. Smith's house. Arnold, on his part, went there, going down river. The traitor had an interview with André during which he told him that he sent many troops away from West Point under the false pretense of cutting wood ... He gave André the plans of the earthworks, the status of the last inspections, a copy of a very interesting council of war, some plans of attack—all signed in his hand.

The *Vulture* ran aground almost under the cannon of the Stony Point fort. Colonel Livingston,[37] who commanded there and who saw Arnold cross, sent a request for permission to take some big guns and to fire on this frigate. Arnold ignored the request and found some excuse, but the colonel had two four-pounders which he had fired on this frigate which he might have badly damaged if the rising tide had not refloated it and allowed it to get away. This cannonade was the cause for the cruel situation in which André found himself a short time later.

Stopped by Militiamen as a Spy

The interview finished, he wanted to return to his vessel but the cannonade kept him away. He decided instead to return to New York by land, fearing capture. After Arnold's insistent requests, he decided to remove his uniform and to change. Thus, he crossed from the right bank to the left bank of the river where he encountered three militiamen which the cannon shots attracted out of curiosity. They asked him about the noise they heard. André

36 John André (1750-178) was aide-de-camp to Sir Henry Clinton in New York and head of the British spy ring. He personally negotiated with General Benedict Arnold for the plans of the defenses of West Point. Andre's was captured, tried and executed for treason by American forces. Alexander Hamilton remarked "Never perhaps did any man suffer death with more justice, or deserve it less."

37 Colonel James Livingston (1747-1832) was responsible for raising and leading the 1st Canadian Regiment of the Continental Army during the invasion of Canada. He played a crucial role in unmasking Benedict Arnold's treachery and continued to serve in the war until 1781.

was seized, disconcerted and his countenance changed. After a few more questions, the militiamen arrested him near Tarrytown. André immediately offered them his watch, a horse which was given to him and 400 guineas to allow him to pass. Nothing could corrupt them. They judged the importance of the detainee by his offers. Arnold commanded the entire region. They sent a messenger to advise him that they stopped an Englishman they suspected was a spy. Not knowing who he might be and realizing that everything would be discovered, he ordered that his best horse be saddled.

It was the morning of the 26th and Mr. Washington was returning from Hartford with Mr. de la Fayette who was coming to breakfast with him this day. The French general sent two aides-de-camp ahead of him. Seeing him ready to leave instead of remaining for breakfast, they asked him where he wanted to go. He responded that he did not expect General Washington to arrive for several more hours, he was going to inspect the posts. He whispered a word in his wife's ear and mounted his horse. He lodged near the river. He found his canoe, boarded it and rowed out to the *Vulture*. Colonel Livingston, seeing him pass near Stony Point, suspected him and wanted to fire upon him, but having nothing to justify his suspicions, nothing then bothered the traitor in his escape.

We can easily picture Mr. Washington's astonishment who was ready for breakfast with Mrs. Arnold, when André was brought to him after being searched and it was discovered that the husband of the pretty woman at whose place he was staying was only a vile person! He in whom he had placed all his confidence! He who had the greatest role in the capture of Burgoyne and of 7000 British, the elite of their army at Saratoga!

Mrs. Arnold played the actress, pretended to be ill, sobbing, ignorant of the despicable action of her husband. A Frenchman ignores the tears shed by a beauty. Mr. de la Fayette who knew how to join love to arms, gave her, whom he loved much, his most generous assistance.

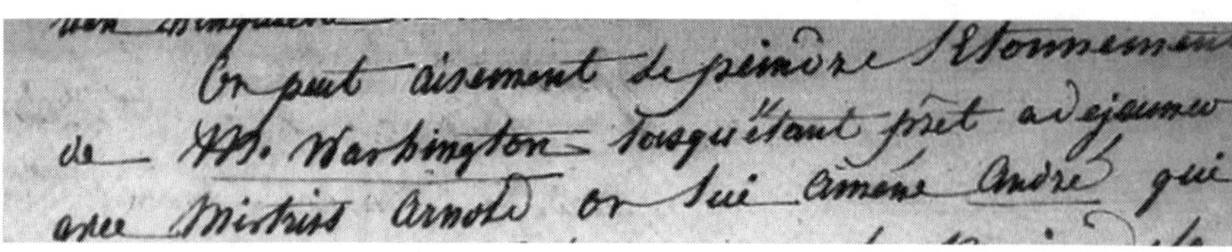
On peut aisement de peindre l'Etonnement
de Mr. Washington lorsqu'etant prêt a dejeuner
avec Mistriss Arnold on lui amene André qui

William Heath Appointed Commander at West Point in Arnold's Stead, His Qualifications

Mr. Washington's first concern was to bring back the troops which Arnold had dispatched, to oversee the security of West Point on all sides, and he appointed General Heath to command the militias. He was the most trustworthy man, the best citizen who could replace the greatest traitor. He was with us during the entire summer at Newport.

This general was never guilty of such gross actions since the beginning of the war. He was regarded as one of the good officers of the American line. He was born at Roxbury near Boston, was a butcher by trade and had become a rich farmer. He was one of the first to take up arms at Boston and soon rose to the rank of major general. The lack of fortune having prevented many of his veterans from continuing in the service and his own permitting him to remain, he became one of the first general officers. He has wit and it is because of his honesty that General Washington chose him.

If Arnold's treachery is despicable and base on the one hand, we cannot excessively admire the greatness of spirit of the militiamen into whose hands André fell. Without this nobility of sentiment, without this patriotism, West Point would have been handed over. What would then become of the American army? It was the most mortal blow, the most fatal which could be struck against the United States. Arnold would have said that he was surprised while he withdrew a strong detachment from the garrison and perhaps continued to mask his conduct for a long time afterward. [the rest of the line is crossed out].

André's arrest, which was immediately brought to a general court-martial, resulted in the exchange of many letters between General Clinton and General Washington. Every response demanded the traitor — before releasing the unfortunate [André]. Congress awarded 100 guineas to each of the three militiamen who captured him.

Arrival of the Frigate *la Gentille* at Newport and Mr. de Choisy, Brigadier

The frigate la *Gentille*, bound from Martinique, arrived at Newport on the 27th. She had Mr. de Choisy,[38] Brigadier, aboard, known for the capture and subsequent excellent defense of Cracow. The minister did not want to employ him. At 60 years old, he was returning to Versailles to request a transfer to 1500 leagues from his homeland. This is an example for all officers who tender their resignation when their regiments embark. We can say, in general, to the praise of the land troops, that, during this entire war, they conducted themselves perfectly in the colonies and on the vessels and that the young people of the court always requested very ardently to go serve in the army under Messrs. de Bouillé[39] and de Rochambeau.

38 Lieutenant General Claude Gabriel marquis de Choisy (1723-1800) commanded Lauzun's Legion at the siege of Yorktown. Founding Father Benjamin Franklin presented him with the Libertas Americana medal for his service in America.

39 François Claude Amour, marquis de Bouillé (1739-1800) was governor of the Caribbean islands of Guadeloupe, Martinique and St. Lucia. He was involved in organizing, provisioning, and leading troops in a number of actions in the West Indies. He returned to France where he

October
Execution of Mr. André at Orangeburg
Mrs. Arnold

The fate of the unfortunate André, who did not come as a spy and who was arrested disguised as one, interested all the members of the court assembled to judge him. Everybody complained, damning Arnold. He was judged according to the law and condemned to be hanged. Even the eyes of his enemies welled with tears when they saw his sentence carried out and him executed on October 2 at Orangeburg. He wrote a letter the previous evening to General Washington full of energy and submission without baseness. He requested to be granted the death of a soldier, to be shot, and not to end on a gibbet of infamy and disgrace. This letter brought regrets but produced no effect. He was 28 to 30 years old and enjoyed the advantages of a very distinguished birth, a spirit of knowledge and a figure most pleasing to women. It was perhaps the source of his misfortune. When the British were masters of Philadelphia, he aroused of Miss Shippen's[40] (later Mrs. Arnold) charms and was much liked. It was said that she had no part in the defection of her husband but the opinion of many is that it is because of her that André came to correspond with Arnold. The latter was poorly received by the English because of the death of André. They gave him the agreed-upon sum for his treason. He was always known to be very avid of the means to acquire money. He could not find a more vile one than to sell his honor in betraying a post and his fellow citizens. If his plan succeeded, the British would have become masters of all the North River and would absolutely cut off all communication by land between the northern and southern states. Thus divided, what would become of them?

---

held military commands in the country's northeast at the time of the French Revolution. A committed Royalist, he was a leading conspirator involved in the royal family's failed flight in 1791. This failure forced him into exile. He died in exile in London and is mentioned as a hated Royalist in the French national anthem, La Marseillaise.

40 Margaret (Peggy) Shippen (1760-1804) was General Benedict Arnold's wife. For her services, Shippen was given an annual sum for the care of her children from Queen Charlotte and King George presented the family with a lump sum. While visting her family in Philadelphia in 1791, protests at her presence broke out. Due to her husband's business ventures, she died heavily in debt in New Brunswick.

Battle of Camden
Battle of Camden in Carolina
Death of Baron de Kalb

General Cornwallis[41] commanded an army corps after the capture of Charleston in May. The Americans appointed General Gates[42] to oppose him, the same one who captured Burgoyne at Saratoga on October 17, 1777. This general was English and served as aide-de-camp in the war of 1756. He was then major of a regiment, but he left this position to come to Virginia, on the Carolina border, with his entire family. After several marches and changes of position on both sides, the two generals met at Camden, South Carolina. Gates's advance guard was attacked vigorously. Some dragoons fought well but were defeated because they weren't supported. They folded back to the army without orders. The militiamen then took flight. Nothing could stop them and the Americans were completely routed.

The Baron de Kalb,[43] a Brigadier in the French service who transferred to the Americans, commanded a reserve which held firm but finally was forced to retreat. He was captured and bayoneted as he retreated. Mr. du Buisson, his aide-de-camp, made every effort to save him but was captured along with the general and beaten with the butt of the musket. The Marquis de la Rouerie's American regiment of dragoons, under the name of Armand's Legion, was cut to pieces and destroyed.[44]

The rout was such that many of the soldiers fled as far as 20 or 30 miles. General Gates lost his head entirely. He gave no orders and, the day after the battle, he was 90 miles or 30 leagues from his army. Brigadier General Smallwood,[45] with a few Maryland troops and

41 General Charles Cornwallis (1738-1805) commanded British troops in the South, surrendering his forces at Yorktown.

42 Horatio Gates (1726-1806) was appointed to command Congressional forces in the South in the summer of 1780, after General Benjamin Lincoln had surrendered Charleston. His defeat at the Battle of Camden in in South Carolina in 1780, and intrigues against George Washington tarnished his promising career.

43 Major General Johann von Robais, Baron de Kalb (1721-1780) served as a major general in the Continental Army during the American Revolutionary War. He was mortally wounded while fighting the British Army during the Battle of Camden.

44 Charles-François du Buysson (1752-1786) was a distant cousin of the Marquis de Lafayette and aide-de-camp to the Baron DeKalb. He was seriously wounded attempting to help the baron at the battle of Camden and was taken prisoner.

45 William Smallwood's brigade was part of General Horatio Gates's army at the Camden disaster. His men held their ground for a time, garnering Smallwood a promotion to major general.

levies, was able to gather some of those who fled and retreated so that, happily again, not all was lost despite the loss of men on the American side which was not very considerable. The British only gained a battlefield. Cornwallis had advanced without knowing very much where he was going and, lacking supplies, soon afterward was obliged to return to Charleston.

The American General Gates Withdraws to his Property in Virginia

This battle occurred on October 3. Arnold's treachery was too recent. Eyes were cast on Horatio Gates after his defeat. He was forced to resign and retire to his property where he lived ignored. The Americans should never forget him however because he was the first one to strike a decisive and fatal blow to British tyranny, that he defeated 7000 enemy troops and acquired 60 pieces of cannon, almost the only ones they had at the time.

General Greene Replaces Him as Head of the Southern Army

General Gates was appointed to command the southern army. This choice was generally applauded.

I speak of the feats of the army of our unfortunate allies. It is true, I have nothing to say about the French! We are here awaiting our second division, without the present resources, without news from France—we conduct a great diversion. We have seven vessels in port, a handful of brave men in camp. The enemy does not dare form a detachment nor send any vessels. American commerce, more free, begins to revive. Their ships, so pursued, arrive richly loaded without being harassed. Boston Philadelphia… enrich themselves. Our presence only works to great good. Peace and confidence are reborn. The army recruits more easily. To see the big picture is something good, something real. But our silver, in circulating, devalues the paper money. It has greatly depreciated since our arrival. Many families will be ruined. Our stores, our necessary purchases exhaust our treasury. Our funds decrease. It is only our ardor, our desire, that seem to increase and which circumstances entail.

Mr. de Sartines,[46] where is your promise to find vessels for our second division? Make them leave if they haven't already. May our comrades arrive soon and draw us out of the somber tranquility in which we live. The soldiers under canvas want to see the enemy, want to hear the cannon. In the absence of the British, Mr. de Rochambeau created some and, on the eighth, he drilled the army on the point where the real enemy might land. We pretended that a fleet entered our harbor and planned a landing.

Our General Drills the Army

We put 1500 men under the command of the Viscount de Vioménil who was at Stauder's house. It was there that our enemies first began to take possession of a few houses along the shore. Mr. de Rochambeau kept the rest of the troops with him for the imminent attack to which he joined the American Rhode Island Regiment commanded by Col. Greene. These troops were divided into two columns. Mr. de Rochambeau personally led the left column. The Baron de Vioménil commanded the right. The grenadier and light infantry battalions formed a separate one.

The attack began with several discharges of cannon, well-executed to create a complete effect of the fictitious enemy leaving their boats and forming quickly. At the same time, the column of grenadiers advanced to dislodge the enemy from the houses as they began to establish themselves there. During this musket fire, the Baron de Vioménil turned their right under the protection of a hill which concealed his movement. When he was ready and the attack was fully engaged, Mr. de Rochambeau had the charge sounded. Everything advanced in good order. The enemy disappeared and reassembled on the seashore.

An Accident Happens

An accident occurred during this drill. A cannoneer cleaning a piece lost an arm by the sponge. The one who was aiming it had neglected to cover the touchhole with his thumb. An ember remaining from the preceding shot ignited and the charge caught fire.

Other accidents might have also happened, always caused by the cannon. Many of our navy officers, wanting to witness this drill, rented horses. They were usually poor horsemen

46 Antoine Raymond Jean Gualbert Gabriel de Sartine comte d'Alby (1729-1801) served as Lieutenant General of Police of Paris (1759–1774) during the reign of Louis XV and as Secretary of State for the Navy (1774–1780) under King Louis XVI.

and wanted to remove all doubt about it, as three or four were thrown on the ground with each cannon shot.

Violent Storm

We experienced a very violent wind the night of the 9th to the 10th. Almost all the tents of the camp were knocked down and torn. The vessels in the harbor were beached and a transport ship in port broke its cables and was dashed upon the shore (la *Cibèle*). This blast of wind was felt almost all over the world at the same time. Barbados, Jamaica, St. Domingue suffered greatly. The same hurricane struck Europe.

Mr. the Count de Rochambeau had the same drill at the point of Stauder's house on the 11th, just as on the eighth. It was not executed with enough precision or vivacity. It's only when we are outside the lines and near the one giving orders that we can see the mistakes and know how important it is to have well-informed officers and experienced soldiers. The former understand the orders they receive more easily with experience. In the execution, the latter are more prompt, often foresee the objectives and march with greater assurance.

A skirmish is an image of a real battle when it is well-conceived and it is also educational. The only real difference, I think, is saving the blood of a large number of brave men. Our general, then, could not make better use of the leisure time which the English gave or to which our small number reduced us, than to accustom his soldiers to the sound of the musket and the cannon, to teach them to march without fear especially on the land where they would really fight if the enemy appeared.

On the days when there were not enough soldiers occupied with different duties or the army did not drill together, the individual regiments were kept busy by their colonels. I hardly ever saw the administration of an unwarranted punishment and which sometimes fell on men who had finished their leave and did not want to reenlist and who were retained in violation of the agreement made with them when they first enlisted. On the other hand, necessity, distance required it. The regulations order blows with the flat of the sabre. So be it. Corporal punishment inflicted at the time of the offense can sometimes be felt better, have better effect than any other; but I would always greatly blame the superior officers of the Bourbonnais Regiment for having made a type of sabre or iron bar which they substituted for the sabre of the corporals to punish their unfortunate soldiers. Severity well-applied with firmness are qualities in an officer but inhumanity, unreasonable harshness, should never be known. I saw several soldiers from the Saintonge and Bourbonnais spit blood after a beating. In the aftermath, as with students under the iron rule of a teacher, as novices in the art of war, the punishment was applied on their buttocks.

All our colonels were imbued with the same zeal. Their regiments were well dressed; some were drilled very perfectly, others passably so. They loved to have their corps under orders, bowed under the tiring yoke of obedience, but they themselves could not submit. Always setting examples, not listening to orders received, adding their own interpretations to them, changing them. . . . These dangerous mistakes, damaging to the service, the vexations were unknown, not reaching Mr. the Count de Rochambeau who would have surely have reprimanded or punished them. In his eyes, we led a model and mild life but no less active than the rest of the army. We mounted a rotating 24-hour guard at his quarters. A saddled horse was kept at the picket day and night to be constantly ready to bring orders or to warn him of anything that was happening. If there were none, his four other aides-de-camp, not being in service, would always accompany him on his errands day or night.

If a vessel was signaled, we were soon at the end of the Neck to determine whether she would enter the port or pass by, whether it was coming from France, or whether it was part of our second division.

Military Drills

The 17th, Mr. de Rochambeau had the army drill at Wood Castle, the landing point five miles from camp, always pretending a fleet protecting its boats, landing men ashore. We marched in three columns. The right one was composed of Lauzun's Legion and a battalion of the Soissonnais Regiment under the command of the Duc de Lauzun. They advanced to attack and draw the enemy's attention while the center column composed of the grenadiers and light infantry, where Mr. de Rochambeau was, took a hill or rock dominating the beach where the enemy was forming. The grenadiers made a lively and sustained fire to give the Baron de Vioménil, who had the rest of the army with him, time to turn the enemy's right flank in his favor from a curtain. His movement decided, the general sent him the order to charge along with the right column where Lauzun's cavalry was. This drill was well-executed. Our only regret was that our cannon could only frighten some sea gulls and wild ducks &&.

Delegation of Abenaki and Micmac Indians

A delegation of Abenaki and Micmac Indians arrived the evening of the 20th. They began, as the first ones we saw, by addressing the general. They seem to have come to request charity rather than to cement a treaty of alliance. They insisted much on the gifts the English made to them, hoping that we would give them even more.

We gave them a few pairs of bracelets and some blankets. I was charged to show them the camp, to bring them aboard the fleet. Two days after their visit they were dismissed.

Sent to 1500 Leagues
Arrives with 2,500,000#

Upon his arrival in America, Mr. de Rochambeau told the state assembly that we were only the vanguard of a much larger body which the king was sending. The Americans were beginning to find the delay a bit long and wanted an explanation. Mr. de Rochambeau was forced to draw his sword before them. Becoming well-aware that he had erred about the politics at the court of Versailles, he sent a general 1500 leagues with a handful of people which the first warm engagement could cut in half. How, with what could he silence the mouths of our allies. Would it be with money? They arrived here with 2,500,000 livres. All our purchases, all our establishments had reduced us to nothing. No news from Europe, no hope, how to proceed?

Rochambeau's Dignitary Sent to France

To better depict the situation, Mr. de Rochambeau thought he should choose his son to send back to France with dispatches. He feared that he would be taken at sea, so he had him learn them by heart. They contained the results of the Hartford conference, the state of the country in general, of the two armies in particular, the resources they could find, the planned operations, the state of our finances....

The English sent cruisers daily to observe us but, on the 27th, the weather was very heavy and overcast. The Chevalier de Ternay profited from this moment to have the *Amazone* go out with Mr. de Rochambeau aboard. This frigate commanded by the Chevalier de la Pérouse[47] set sail with a violent northwest wind, escorted by the *Hermione* and *Surveillante* which were to accompany him up to a certain latitude and then to return to cruise between Newport and Boston. Despite the fog, the frigates were chased by three enemy vessels which fortunately only chased them to [unintelligible] where the *Amazone* had her little mast broken.

47 Jean François de Galaup, comte de La Pérouse (1741-1788) was a French naval officer and explorer whose expedition vanished in Oceania. He victoriously led the frigate L'*Astrée* in the naval battle of Louisbourg, July 21 1781, defeated the English frigate *Ariel* in the West Indies. He escorted a convoy to the West Indies in December 1781, participated in the attack on St. Kitts in February 1782 and then fought in the defeat at the Battle of the Saintes against the squadron of Admiral Rodney.

Winter Quarters
November
The Troops Go Into Quarters

Mr. de Béville and the staff of the army were busy for some time preparing winter quarters. All our posts, all our forts were finished and in good order. The weather was becoming brisk and consequently made every attempt on the part of the enemy difficult. Mr. de Rochambeau determined to have the troops enter the town on November 1. The second brigade was only quartered on the second and the infantry and the Legion were quartered at the Neck near their camp. The hussars remained camped because there was nothing for them to do.

Although these quarters were difficult to build for a very small army, and the extreme harshness of the climate of the preceding winter (previously unknown in these regions, forced the British to destroy several of the city's wharves, a large number of houses and parts of several others for lack of wood. They were rebuilt at an even better price than new barracks. When they were ready, individual owners wanted to acquire them without dislodging. We had to change the minds of our new allies but, in the end, abuse became considerable. We resorted to the use of force or authority, as needed. The artillery horses were put under cover in the ropewalks. Without having rendered any disagreeable service, three quarters of them were in a very pitiful state. They were purchased very dearly but poorly chosen. The administration of the teams was ignorant and bad in this matter. They learned their trade as a repellent but the lesson cost the king dearly for we were obliged to sell 200 horses which cost 600 livres for 6, 12 or 15 livres.

Lauzun's Hussars Take Their Camp at Lebanon, a Village in Connecticut

On the fifth, the hussars of Lauzun's Legion departed their camp on the Neck for Providence and then for Lebanon in Connecticut to make their quarters there. This is the location of the birthplace and actual residence of Governor Trumbull, an old man of 80 years. He was the governor of Connecticut for the British for 20 years. When his fellow citizens took up arms, he quit the party of his first master to embrace that of liberty. The assembly of the state then chose him unanimously for governor. He is now incapable. He never had very great talents. His strong attachment to the cause is now, with his age, the best recommendation and the finest title he can ever offer to his fellow citizens. The hussars made their own barracks. As the village was unable to contain them all, 50 remained at Newport for various duties.[48]

There is no post office in America. Mr. de Rochambeau, to counter the slowness and delays of the country's mail, established various little posts of hussars along the route from Newport to General Washington's army to perform that service. Some American dragoons were also employed in the service. Correspondence thus became more certain, much easier and more expeditious.

Lord Cornwallis Defeated by Militia Colonels

On the 12th, we learned of the defeat of part of Lord Cornwallis's advance guard in the Carolinas. As I already said after the victory of the battle of Camden, he was obliged to retreat for lack of provisions. He spent several days at Charleston and advanced in the country. At his approach, several militia captains mustered their men and before any of them assumed command, they marched to the enemy commanded by Major Ferguson. He himself was killed, 600 British were killed or taken with the baggage.

A Detachment is Sent to the Continent to Cut Wood

On the 14th, Mr. de Rochambeau sent a detachment of 400 men to go cut wood near Taunton for the army. This provisioning of prime necessity was not very easy because of the transport and the distance. The Chevalier de Ternay sent transports to be loaded. The cold and the thaw came each in their turn. Fortunately, the vessels could return to the harbor and the Taunton River, so that we were at ease in this regard.

We were not always equally comfortable regarding provisions and munitions in general. Our administrators, accustomed to easy and not arduous work in Europe, were disoriented in this country where the king's order is ignored or there are no warehouses already established. The agents did not know English and were ignorant of the resources of the country as was their leader who wanted to manage everything from his office without budging, without mounting a horse. Forage was always lacking. We decided to give the job and the duty of furnishing the other munitions to an American man of merit who was

48 Jonathan Trumbull (1710-1785) was the only man who served as governor in both an English colony and an American state, and he was the only governor at the start of the American Revolutionary War to take up the Patriot cause.

Lieutenant General Charles Cornwallis

National Park Service, Colonial National Historical Park, Yorktown Collection

charged with this duty. In the Continental Army, it was Colonel Wadsworth[49] who presented himself and one named Mr. Carter. They were given a 5% commission on everything they purchased. Our agents then were only charged with delivery.[50]

I will not talk about what the soldiers did in camp during the winter, about what the officers reported to their hosts, about the way our colonels passed their time. I shall leave the French there.

General Washington Makes his Army Forage
They Enter Winter Quarters

The Americans were still camped. The weather was very brisk but General Washington still wanted his army to make a forage before giving them quarters, to annoy the enemy and maybe make them come out of their lines. He sent rather large detachments to advance toward Kingsbridge while Mr. de la Fayette and 2000 men marched along the right bank of the North River, descending the Jerseys. He marched on Staten Island which we hoped would abandon the island at the sight of the American troops before Kingsbridge. The enemy didn't budge. The forage was done with peace and tranquility and the desired success. Mr. Washington returned toward West Point where he established part of his army in its quarters, the rest at New Windsor on December 1. Mr. de la Fayette also came to take his quarters.

December
Effect of Our Presence in America

There you have the account of our first campaign. The north of America was peaceful for some time. Behold a great change occurred in view of the affairs of our allies before fame had our great public feats to publish. Fire and steel sometimes decide the fate of empires. Our presence remains a fortunate promise of the latter. Already the prejudices against us are three quarters overcome. The example, the urbanity, the popularity of our brave general won the hearts of the former Englishmen. We have revived their spirits; we

49 Jeremiah Wadsworth (1743-1804) was an American sea captain, merchant and statesman from Hartford, Connecticut who was suspected of profiting from his position as a government official charged with supplying the Continental Army. Washington trusted Wadsworth, and his reputation ultimately withstood these accusations. After the Revolution, his investments in American banking secured his family a large fortune.

50 John Carter (1730-1819) was a member of the Committee of Safety in 1774 and served as lieutenant and captain in the Connecticut militia.

have reaffirmed the shaky idea of independence; we have not chased the enemy since our arrival but they have conquered nothing nor attempted anything. Their influence diminishes; the fear which they produced is dissipating. Thus, we foresee a happy outcome. Behold pleasant indicators. Could we be more useful than we have been, more than we are now? What a change in the political balance have we not effected by our conduct alone? There has been no bloodshed, but could we have done better without fighting, could we have done something else without other means? I ask it but I leave it for others to judge but I believe it difficult.

Mr. de Monteil Chief of Squadron

Mr. de Guichen, on leaving the West Indies, had left Mr. de Monteil[51] there as commander of the fleet with eight vessels and with orders to come join the Chevalier de Ternay if requested. Mr. de Monteil received some dispatches but did not come. His conduct was examined. He responded that he did not have the numbers which the Chevalier de Ternay felt compelled to write him about.

Our General Makes a Reconnaissance in Connecticut

Mr. de Rochambeau continued to nourish the hope that the second division would arrive. The quarters in Newport, already being cramped enough, he conducted a reconnaissance in the region around New London to see where he might make camp if this division arrived. He left Newport on the second for this purpose and returned by Lebanon where he visited the quarters of Lauzun's hussars.

L'Hermione and *la Surveillante* which had gone out with l'*Amazone* captured a 300-ton English merchant ship of on their cruise and brought her to Boston where they released her.

51 François-Aymar, baron de Monteil (1725-1787) commanded the French fleet in the West Indies in 1780 and 1781. He assisted the Spanish during the Siege of Pensacola of 1781, and served under Admiral François Joseph Paul Comte de Grasse during the campaign of 1782.

Tarleton Beaten by Sumter

The American and British troops continued the campaign in the South. A large British detachment commanded by Sir Colonel Tarleton[52] was recently beaten by the others under General Sumter.[53] The Americans killed 150 British, captured as many prisoners and then forced Lord Cornwallis to retreat to Charleston. His army was greatly reduced from illness and the extreme heat of the end of the summer weather. This general also did not enjoy good health himself. These circumstances merged with a plan recently adopted by the British government to send reinforcements to this province or to form establishments in Virginia which had only a few militiamen for her defense.

The British Send a Detachment to Virginia

Clinton ordered Brigadier General Leslie[54] and a strong detachment which embarked and set sail for the Chesapeake Bay. Leslie landed at Portsmouth on the Elizabeth River. He wanted to march from there to join Cornwallis and to put General Greene's[55] army between them; but, as I said above, part of Cornwallis's advance guard was defeated by several militia colonels and he retreated. Leslie then deemed his plan impracticable. He made a few incursions in the country, re-embarked and set sail for Charleston where he rejoined Cornwallis.

Arnold Boards with 1500 British to Divert This Province

After this failed initiative, Arnold the traitor proposed to Clinton and said that since he wanted to make a diversion in Virginia and to establish a foothold there, that, after landing, he would take charge of burning and killing everything and that he only asked for a detachment of 1500 men to do so. Clinton wanted to see what he was capable of and

52 British Lieutenant Colonel Banastre Tarleton(1754-1833)commanded a corps of light cavalry and was noted for his ruthless brutality. One of his sobriquets was "Bloody Ban."

53 Brigadier General Thomas Sumter (1734-1832) nicknamed the "Gamecock," a soldier in the Colony of Virginia militia and a brigadier general in the South Carolina militia. Perhaps his greatest military achievement was his partisan campaigning which contributed to General Cornwallis's decision to abandon the Carolinas for Virginia.

54 Brigadier General Alexander Leslie (1731-1794) commanded the British troops at the Battle of Harlem Heights. He replaced Cornwallis as commander in the South in 1782.

55 Major General Nathanael Greene (1742-1786) commanded the Congressional forces in the South. His leadership is viewed as instrumental in wearing down the British forces in the Carolinas.

Lieutenant Colonel Banastre Tarleton

National Park Service, Colonial National Historical Park, Yorktown Collection

granted his request. But what shameful testimony did his infamy engender when almost all the officers refused to march under his orders—a well-deserved reward for the traitor that he is, even despised by those to whom he is useful. Authority constricted goodwill. Arnold embarked, arrived at Portsmouth on December 7 and signaled his arrival soon afterward with ravages and arson.

Major Talmadge Takes Fort St. George
Major Talmadge Takes Fort St. George on Long Island

Mr. Tallmadge[56] major of Sheldon's[57] American regiment of dragoons in Connecticut, reconnoitered Long Island and requested General Washington for permission to make an expedition there. It was granted. The major commanded 60 men who embarked aboard two boats. He landed at Long Island and marched toward Fort St. George where there were 50 men to defend it. It was dawn. He divided his men, made two feints and a real attack. This plan succeeded. He captured the fort and took everything that was inside at his discretion.

This fort defended a small beach or cove on the shores of which the enemy had some stores of considerable forage. The major torched it as well as a vessel at anchor. He returned with all his prisoners without having a single man killed. This major Tallmadge was a very active and intelligent man and was very useful to Mr. de Rochambeau to receive intelligence of the enemy.

These sort of raids by the Americans were often repeated until now in the course of this war. One fine summer night, British General Prescott[58] was taken from his camp on this island and brought to prison by a man named Barton[59] from Providence and major of a Rhode Island militia regiment.

56 Major Benjamin Tallmadge (1754-1835) was a American military officer, spy master and politician. George Washington appointed him director of military intelligence after Nathaniel Sackett was relieved of his duties.

57 Colonel Elisha Sheldon (1740-1805) commanded the 2nd Continental Light Dragoons, known as "Sheldon's Horse. The town of Sheldon Vermont is named in his honor.

58 Brigadier General Richard Prescott commanded British troops in Rhode Island. He was captured by Colonel William Barton and exchanged for General Charles Lee.

59 Colonel William Barton (1748-1831) planned and led a raiding party of 38 men and six officers in five whaleboats on the night of July 10–11, 1777. They attacked British headquarters and captured Major General Richard Prescott.

Mr. de Rochambeau Goes to Boston

Mr. de Rochambeau, who had not yet seen Boston, left on the 10th accompanied by the Chevalier de Chastellux and Mr. de Choisy to go see this city, the cradle of independence of the United States.

Death of the Chevalier de Ternay
The Baron de Vioménil Sends Me to Boston

During his absence the Chevalier de Ternay died of a putrid fever with which he had been ill for only eight days. On the morning of the 14th, the command of the fleet passed to Mr. the Chevalier Destouches who commanded le *Neptune*. The Baron de Vioménil sent me to Boston to bring the news of our admiral's death to Mr. de Rochambeau. This mission made me see this vast continent for the first time. Very deep snow covered the ground. My horses became tired after a few leagues. Mine very rudely rolled on my body and remained there unable to get back up. My batman fortunately soon saved me. I was not hurt and I arrived at Seecamplain[60] at the tavern of a very kind man who took charge of my tired horses and procured two others with a mounted guide for the night. I passed Dedham, Wrentham, Attleboro, to Roxbury[61] and arrived at Boston at 5 a.m. on the 15th.

Mr. Hancock, Governor of the State of Massachusetts Bay

I found my general at Mr. Hancock's,[62] governor of the state. This man is one of the true sons of liberty, for whom nothing deterred the beginning of this revolution. He is one of those who contributed the most to ignite it. Without a transcendent spirit, he has the necessary brilliance which characterizes a statesman, strength of wit and justice so necessary to make a wise or forceful decision as the case requires. He saw the enemy among his properties. He saw his house occupied, his silverware and furniture under the power of the British, part of a large fortune in England, without anything to compensate for his desire to eradicate tyranny, the joyful and flattering idea of liberty. He did not command the

60 This is probably "Seachonk Plain" or "Seekonk Plain," now the town of Seekonk, MA.

61 The sequence of travel from Newport would have been Attleboro, Wrentham, Dedham, Roxbury, Boston.

62 John Hancock (1737-1793) served as President of the Continental Congress and a signer of the Declaration of Independence.

armies but his example, his writings made thousands join ranks under the flags. He was president[63] of Congress and is governor of the state of Massachusetts for the second time.[64]

Mr. de Rochambeau was very much grieved by the death of the Chevalier de Ternay with whom he got along in perfect harmony. This event made him leave Boston sooner than he planned. He invited Governor Hancock for breakfast and set out to arrive at Newport. I was not able to accompany him. My horses were too tired. The French consul loaned me others with which I wandered through the city and environs. It is very large, very beautiful and well-built. Almost all the houses are brick. It could pass for a first rate city in France.

Roxbury is a very fine village two miles from this city. The sea bathes both sides of the road from one to the other at high tide. On approaching Boston, this spit of land called the neck, becomes wider and forms a rather vast plateau. Boston is built on part of it, which makes it very difficult to capture by land. The port and the harbor are very spacious, but the entrance is difficult because of the mud flats and the 23 islands.

The Americans built Fort William to defend the harbor. Here were placed the canons of the *Somerset*, a 74-gun British ship which perished on this coast in 1778 when Admiral Howe came to Newport to assist the city attacked by Mr. d'Estaing.

General Washington's First Action

The English dominated the city. They had a large garrison for its defense and a navy in port. They evacuated the city, having no other enemy in mind than General Washington. General Howe, brother of the admiral, had neglected to take possession of a height called Bunker's Hill which commands the harbor. He did not think it was possible to march there because of the marshes surrounding it. Mr. Washington, camped near the city, set up chandeliers[65] on the marshes in a single night and had his whole army and his artillery cross. After this incredible work in a single night, he cannonaded the British fleet which was at anchor and in the harbor at dawn. Admiral Howe sent word to his brother that if he did not evacuate the city, he would leave all alone and that he would then have to escape as best he could. There was a cease-fire granted for the evacuation on condition that the enemy would

63 This note is in the manuscript: "These two places read: one in Congress by the members who compose it, the other in the General Assembly of each state. They are triennial and no president or governor can continue unless reelected."

64 Ibid.

65 Chandeliers are large and strong wooden frames used instead of a parapet. Fascines are piled on top of each other against it to cover workmen digging trenches. Sometimes, they are only strong planks with two pieces of perpendicular wood to hold the fascines.

not touch a single property and would not take anything from the city. This memorable action of General Washington in 1776 was the first blow he attempted. All his camps, all his positions near Boston could not have been better selected or militarily chosen. The few moments I had to visit this city did not permit me to go see them but I saw the plans and often heard speak of them to Mr. de Rochambeau who approved them all.

I departed again on the evening of the 15th. I traveled all night, passing through the places I described above and I arrived at Newport the morning of the 16th to give an account of my mission to Mr. de Vioménil. There are 75 miles between Boston and Newport.

Funerary Honors rendered to the Chevalier de Ternay

Mr. de Rochambeau who slept en route only arrived the night of the 16th. The Chevalier de Ternay had been buried that morning. From the hour of his death to that of his burial, his ship fired every half hour. The land troops took their weapons and fired three musket volleys.

His Character

This admiral was not mourned by his officers, his fleet. He commanded harshly, was not very approachable, dry and reserved. Without making any big mistakes, he never distinguished himself in command. The only action that he is noted is saving some vessels from disaster after the unfortunate Battle of the Marshal de Conflans in 1759.[66] He was annoyed by merchants of shoddy goods when he received command of Ile de France[67] and Bourbon[68] and convened a council of war. His battle at the Bermudas, his conduct at Chesapeake Bay lost him the confidence of his fleet. Their tears, their regrets did not accompany him to the grave. Very few followed his cortege. The accompaniment of a few was indecent enough.

66 Louis de Brienne de Conflans d'Armentières (1711-1774) oversaw the landing troops in Scotland for an invasion of England in 1759. His flagship, the *Soleil Royal* ran aground, without his knowledge, within only a few cable lengths of the English fleet. He realized his danger at dawn, sailed to *Le Croisic* where he embarked on the French vessel *Héros* and returned to evacuate and burn his flagship.

67 Mauritius.

68 Réunion.

The Chevalier Destouches Assumes Command of the Squadron

The Chevalier Destouches assumed command at a rather critical time. The ships needed repairs, there were few resources, not a cent in the navy's chest nor in the army's. Both made loans and borrowed at 25% interest as our expenses quadrupled due to the lack of help from France, the lack of news from …

Custom in England and America

I noticed a custom in England and North America on the 25th, Christmas Day which we do not know. That is to wish "good Christ mass" merry Christmas just as we wish each other happy new year on the first day of the new year, but one does not replace the other.

The 26th, six merchant ships from our convoy belonging to Mr. de Montieu[69] set sail for France. Mr. de Baudoin[70] Lieut. Col. succeeding to Lauzun's Legion embarked aboard two ships along with Mr. Mayer, ambassadorial secretary of Mr. Gerard from Strasbourg who was an extraordinary minister to the United States before Mr. the Chevalier de la Luzerne was appointed Minister Plenipotentiary. Mr. Mayer was charged with copies of dispatches for the court. He departed on the *Amazone* with the Chevalier de la Pérouse.

69 Jean Joseph Carrier (Carié) de Montieu was one of Pierre-Augustin Caron de Beaumarchais's preferred suppliers.

70 Louis Gabriel de Baudoin was a French Navy officer and captain. See Quintin, Danielle, and Bernard Quintin. *Dictionnaire Des Capitaines De Vaisseau De Napoleòn.* S.P.M, 2003.

Campaign of 1781

Introduction

Lauberdière began this section with a comparative discussion of New Year wishes. He recounted Brigadier General Morgan's defeat of Colonel Banastre Tarleton's forces at the Cowpens and the mutiny of the Pennsylvania line. General Henry Clinton, informed of this action, sent two spies with very attractive offers, promising employment and money if their leaders came to New York. The sergeants declined the offers, stating they were not traitors to their country.

Admiral Arbuthnot stationed his fleet at Gardner's Bay to better observe the movements of the French fleet. Benedict Arnold made several incursions in Virginia and established himself at Portsmouth. Lauberdière mused Virginia, one of the largest, loveliest and richest states of the United States, was so apathetic and weak that a traitor and a weak body of 1500 men could pillage with impunity. The government requested assistance from the Chevalier Destouches's fleet. Captain de Tilly and a few ships reconnoitered the coast and her anchorages and attempted to capture Arnold's ships. This excursion captured the 50-gun Romulus, coming to take command of this area, and 500 prisoners.

Captain de Tilly's success prompted Congress to renew its insistence to the Chevalier Destouches for the relief of Virginia. Lafayette marched to Virginia with 1500 men to join the Baron de Vioménil. Slow preparations delayed the fleets launch until March 8. During this time, the frigate Astrée arrived in Boston with 15,000 francs, carrying the first dispatches and the letters the army received since their departure from France a year earlier.

Lauberdière recorded the praise and reception General Washington received during his visit to Newport. The American leader inspected the army and examined their works. General Washington complimented Rochambeau and the entire army on their fine appearance and discipline before returning to his headquarters at New Windsor.

Admiral Arbuthnot set sail in pursuit of the Chevalier Destouches. The two fleets engaged each other in the Battle of the Chesapeake, after which the French fleet returned to Newport.

Lauberdière recounted the Battle of Guilford Courthouse and recorded his thoughts about naval superiority being crucial in this war.

The frigate Concorde arrived in Boston on May 8. The ship carried the Viscount de Rochambeau and the Count de Barras, who was appointed commander of the fleet and successor to the Chevalier de Ternay. Lauberdière summarized some of the dispatches carried by this frigate.

During this period, 3000 troops arrived at New York from England. Another 2000 at Charleston, SC and eight British ships of the line appeared off Newport.

These events did not deter General Rochambeau from leaving for Wethersfield, Connecticut to meet with General Washington. After the conference, Rochambeau wrote to de Grasse, explaining the Americans' disastrous state of affairs, their meager resources, and what had to be done. Rochambeau imparted the liberty to go to the location he thought of greatest import for the success of his plan.

The army prepared to depart. Many small vessels assembled at Newport to transport the men and their baggage to Providence. Brigadier General de Choisy remained at Rhode Island with 100 men per regiment. Lauberdière stayed behind, convalescing. He received several wounds in a duel—most likely stab wounds from a sword in the arm, torso or leg. At this point, the young Frenchman waxed nostalgic while recording his impressions upon arrival at Newport. He wrote his observations of Newporters' civil life, the different religions in Newport, a Quaker bee, a work party similar to a quilting bee, a Quaker wedding, products unique to Rhode Island, its port and harbor, public buildings, and on Mr. Mrs. and Miss Champlain.

The army departed Providence when Lauberdière was well enough to travel. The fact that the entire military force waited until this young man was well enough to travel highlights his importance. He described the organization of the army for the march and indicated which regiment camped at which location each day of the march and usually gave the distance travelled. Generally, Lauberdière did not include maps of the march and the camps. The maps of Rochambeau's cartographer, Louis Alexandre Berthier, have been reproduced in The American Campaigns of Rochambeau's Army, *translated and edited by Howard C. Rice and Anne S.K. Brown (Princeton, NJ, 1972), vol. 2.*

Lauberdière often described the locations and recorded his impressions of the countryside, terrain and the people. When they were in proximity of previous battlefields, such as White Plains, and the Bronx. General Rochambeau and his staff chose to visit some of these battlefields, and Lauberdière recorded his notes about the actions.

When the army arrived at Phillipsburg, it occupied a very strong position on the left of the American camp. They camped there for an extended period, giving the soldiers time to rest, and the officers to plan their strategy—whether they would besiege New York or march south. Lauberdière described his impressions of the Continental Army and noted some false alarms which caused panic in both armies and several minor actions in the area, such as attacks at Kingsbridge, Tarrytown, Valentine's Hill, Morrisania, Throg's Neck, the forts on Manhattan, Mamaroneck, Dobb's Ferry, etc.

The presence of the allied forces alarmed General Clinton, despite being twice as strong. He seemed more afraid of being attacked than the allied forces had the means or the desire to do so.

General de Choisy, tired of the inactivity at Newport, planned an attack upon Fort Lloyd at the end of Huntington Bay. Faulty information neccesitated a hasty retreat back to Newport.

In August, the French were foraging at New Rochelle and Eastchester where the residents vacillated to whoever was more powerful in the area.

The frigate Concorde, from Admiral de Grasse's fleet, arrived in Newport on August 15 carrying news that he was heading to the Chesapeake Bay. General Rochambeau met with General Washington who expressed reluctance to abandon New York for a move south. Rochambeau countered Washington's arguments, and the two leaders came to an accord. However, Admiral de Barras wanted to stay in Newport and planned an expedition to the Penobscot.

The French built bread ovens at Chatham as a decoy. As it takes several days to build a bread oven and quite a bit of time to make enough bread to feed an army, making the ovens was an indication that the Army planned to spend quite a bit of time there.

Lauberdière described the towns and the people along the way. He gave a rather long description of West Point and Stony Point. By comparsion, he gave only brief accounts of the battles that occurred in battlefields they passed by: Trenton, Princeton, Brandywine, Germantown, Red Bank, Mud Island. He described the grand reception the French and Americans received upon entering Philadelphia and remarked upong the defenses built there.

News of Admiral de Grasse's arrival in the Chesapeake brought great joy to the generals and Congress, reanimating the morale of the soldiers. They resumed their march to Head of Elk (Elkton, MD), boarding as many men as possible. The rest of the army marched south to Yorktown. Ordered to Williamsburg, Lauberdière informed Lafayette of these new developments, and to stayed to serve temporarily as his aide-de-camp.

The army arrived at Williamsburg on September 25, immediately planning the siege of Yorktown. Lord Cornwallis strengthened his defenses in response. Lauberdière gave an extensive day by day description of the works undertaken, the capture of Tarleton's Legion at Gloucester and of the ultimate British capitulation of Yorktown.

Supplementing Lauberdière's text are the articles of capitulation and issues of several American newspapers, such as the Pennsylvania Packet and the Pennsylvania Journal, with articles about the surrender. An issue of the Gazette Françoise, the first known service newspaper published by an expeditionary force is also included (The Gazette Françoise was printed on a printing press which the French brought to Newport). It is generally thought that only seven issues and a supplement were published. However, the issue included here is numbered 93 and is the only known copy to survive.

Lauberdière also includes a poem about the Count de Rochambeau, a letter from the President of Congress to the Count and a resolution of Congress.

General Washington dispatched Colonel Tench Tilghman, one of his aides-de-camp, immediately after the surrender, to bring Congress the news. The next day, he issued general orders in French and English congratulating the French officers and the armies for the victory. He released all the prisoners and ordered divine services performed in the several brigades and divisions the following day, recommending all troops not on duty should attend.

Lauberdière provides a summary and an extract of a dispatch from Lord Cornwallis to Sir Henry Clinton about the surrender, along with his commentary.

Count William des Deux Ponts departed to bring the news to France. Admiral de Grasse left for Martinique while Rochambeau had the troops refill the trenches and destroy the redoubts connected to it.

Lauberdière concludes the campaign of 1781 with his thoughts and observations about the operation, and what was happening in Gibraltar and the West Indies. Resolutions of the Congress for their gratitude to the French and reconnaissance reports of the positions at Portsmouth and of the British works in this part of Virginia are also included in his journal.

The Diary

January 1781
Happy New Year Wishes

Each country, each style, each usage, each custom. When we only know our own country, the neighboring people, we are surprised to find different customs, different practices which don't resemble each other. That's what happened to us and our allies every day, but they found us silly the first New Year's Day. In England and in America, when two men meet the first time in the day, they extend their hand and shake it saying to each other "how do you do" sometimes even in a very strong manner as a sign of cordiality.

Two friends, a father and a son who had not seen each other for 10 years would not express their joy, their tenderness, differently at their first encounter. Finally, the men never embrace. How astonished were the inhabitants of Newport when, on January first, they saw most of the soldiers of all the regiments mingled, embrace each other in the streets and resume embracing each other again. Many officers did the same as a sign of friendship, interest. Men, women, children came to the windows to be joyful witnesses of this new and unusual spectacle for them.

The soldiers were held to the strictest discipline. The inhabitants had feared to see us living in their city, always imbued with false ideas, false prejudices about our principles, about our customs. They slowly began to become aware of their injustice regarding us and of the odious calumnies of the British. While they occupied the city, the women did not dare to appear in the streets at night without fear of being attacked. Today, the most just confidence, the firm assurance that any abuse would be severely reprimanded and punished gave them confidence. Each officer is hosted at his host's house who loves him dearly.

The Frenchman is the same everywhere. No other country possesses the charming art of making one loved and desired when he wants. His humor, his gallantry, sometimes ridiculed by other people, always finds itself rather pleasurable, unappreciated by one gender. It is the same in all countries. The thoughtfulness, the attentions, even the compliments, whether true or false, seduce. They are always in season with him. Our manners first surprised the Americans. Our kindnesses and our politeness soon won them over. They quickly recognized our superiority in this matter. We promise them, we already gave them a few balls. They saw with pleasure Mr. de Rochambeau build a grand and large barracks near his quarters destined to assemble together all the officers to prevent gaming and to save wood which was rare and expensive. The women reckoned correctly. The general promised to give them a ball every eight days for their pleasure and that of the garrison.

Passages of Bristol and of Howland's Ferry Protected and Defended

Idle time in quarters needs to be filled. Amusing his garrison is always the best means a general might take in a city. We then easily forget the difficulties that the service and distance can have. Mr. de Rochambeau regularly mounted his horse every day. He visited the pickets. He often went to see the works of a large fort which the Rhode Island Regiment and the American militiamen were constructing at the top of the island, at four leagues or 12 miles from Newport. This fort commanded and dominated two main passages to go on the continent: that of Bristol's Ferry and that of Howland's Ferry. It could cannonade enemy vessels that might attempt to capture the island. It could protect our retreat north in the event we were forced to abandon our entrenched camp and to retreat to the continent.

Morgan Defeats Tarleton in Carolina

The mild temperature of the winter climate in the Carolinas allowed the armies to operate while ours were inactive. There were frequent skirmishes, encounters of parties. Brigadier General Morgan with 200 men of the Maryland line and 600 militiamen defeated

1200 regular troops commanded by Colonel Tarleton on the 7th.[1] Half of his forces were cavalry which put Morgan at a great disadvantage as he was in the plain. He separated his men into different detachments and ranks and created a small reserve. Tarleton's cavalry attacked in disorder and without bearing in force anywhere. Morgan had 70 or 80 horses from Washington's[2] dragoon regiment charged part of Tarleton's cavalry in the rear and put it to the rout. His infantry retreated. Morgan pursued a little as he was in the plain and the cavalry and the enemy cavalry could rally. He killed over a hundred English men. Tarleton had two fingers of his right hand cut off. Two hundred of his men were also wounded and 500 taken prisoners. He lost two field pieces, two flags, a hundred dragoon horses, 35 wagons and 800 muskets. This could be called a complete rout and there is nothing to flatter the vanity of the British.

Mutiny of the Continental Army

A revolt of Washington's army erupted on the 18th which could have become of much greater consequence if, by his prudence and firmness, he did not quell it quickly.

There are funds to pay the American army, that is to say there are resolutions from Congress and from each state in particular which require the states and the state the counties that compose it, to give the voted amount to the maintenance of the regiments which they have in the army. The appointment of the officers and the soldiers always suffered much in return or rather were not paid for a long time. We saw, in all the states, some agents, some sutlers enrich themselves at the expense of the army. Each state, independently of the taxes in specie which it was required to raise, the state was also required to send a certain quantity of flour, beef, pork, salt, and rum to camp, but none of these articles were neither paid nor collected precisely. The legislative power was not executed at the same time. It had no power, no support such that it paid whoever it wanted

1 Daniel Morgan (1736–1802), an American pioneer soldier and politician from Virginia, commanded a corps of riflemen and is widely considered one of the most gifted battlefield tacticians of the American Revolutionary War. He served in Benedict Arnold's expedition to Québec, the Saratoga campaign and the Philadelphia campaign but resigned from the army in 1779. He returned to the army after the Battle of Camden and led the Continental Army to victory in the Battle of Cowpens. He later commanded troops during the suppression of the Whiskey Rebellion (1791–1794).

2 Lieutenant Colonel William Washington (1752–1810), a distant cousin of George Washington, served as a cavalry officer of the Continental Army and participated in a number of notable battles in the Carolinas during the campaigns of 1780 and 1781. He held a final rank of Brig. Gen. in the newly created United States after the war.

but the unfortunate army was totally naked. Three quarters of it were almost reduced to starvation half of the time.

Fifteen hundred men of the Pennsylvania line, tired of the harshness of this sort of life, this ingratitude of their fellow citizens, left their quarters on the 18th with arms and baggage and went 30 miles from quarters at New Windsor, regardless of the threats of General Wayne[3] who commanded them. They threatened to take him with them if he persisted in his speeches demanding to arrest them. They chose one of their sergeants to lead them and camped near Morristown.

Sir Henry Clinton Seeks to Contain a Party

General Clinton who was informed of this action had a good opportunity to attract them to the King's side. He sent two spies with very attractive offers for their leaders if they wanted to come to New York, promising employment, money. He himself sent troops from Staten Island to be ready for any eventuality. The sergeants began by having the spies arrested. They have since been hanged. The sergeants responded to Clinton that they did not want to accept his offers, that if he himself advanced to force them, they would show him that they were not traitors to their country.

Response of One of the Leaders

The American general Howe[4] was sent from New Windsor to make them return to their duty. He beseeched them without success. They said they had no intention of deserting to the enemy, that they only wanted to force their ungrateful nation to recognize their past services and to appreciate such good men as they, that they only demanded pay that was due them for such a long time and the assurance of better treatment in the future. He offered a sum to the sergeants who arrested and delivered the spies. They wanted nothing more.

3 Anthony Wayne (1745–1796) served as a Continental Army officer and statesman. His military exploits and fiery personality quickly earned him promotion to Brig. Gen. along with the sobriquet "Mad Anthony".

4 Major General Robert Howe (1732–1786) served as a Continental Army general from NC, the only Maj. Gen. in the Continental Army from that state. He also played a role in the colonial and state governments of North Carolina, serving in the legislative bodies of both.

General Washington has the Militiamen Return to Duty

Eight days passed thus. General Washington, having tried all means unsuccessfully, went to find them himself without escort and almost without any retinue. He showed how much confidence and love are often more effective than all the threats and punishments. He spoke to them as a true general, explained their duties to them, promised them what he could offer, and finally succeeded in winning them over. The most seditious, the leaders of the mutiny, however were severely punished.

Shortly after these troubles were appeased in the Pennsylvania line, the same thing happened in the Jerseys. Fortunately, this mutiny had no consequences, other than opening the eyes of the various states for a more exact accounting of what they taxed. The army was paid for some time.

Position of Admiral Arbuthnot at Gardner's Bay

Admiral Arbuthnot, to better observe the movements of our fleet, stationed his fleet at Gardner's Bay located on the North point of Long Island at the beginning of winter. From here he often sent some of the vessels and frigates which cruised two or three days off Rhode Island and often approached close enough to count our vessels in the harbor. Several of them which appeared on the 21st were greeted with a very strong wind during the night. The *Bedford* was dismasted, the *America* was forced out to sea and the 74-gun *Culloden* was beached at Montauk Point on the Long Island shore.

L'Hermione and la *Surveillante* which were returning from Boston received the same blast of wind. They had no damage and arrived at Newport on the 23rd.

Arnold's Successes in Virginia
Congress Writes to the Chevalier Destouches

Arnold was still in Virginia. He had made several incursions and had established himself at Portsmouth after having burned some very large tobacco warehouses there. This city is located on the Elizabeth River not far from its mouth in the James River. In this vast country, where the English only possessed a few places or ports on the coast, it was indispensable to them to always maintain a large number of ships to facilitate all their offensive expeditions. Arnold brought with him a 50-gun ship, two frigates and many transports.

Virginia is one of the largest, one of the loveliest and richest states of the United States. It was one of the first that took up arms at the beginning of the Revolution and which dismissed its governor Lord Murray Dunmore. A spirit of apathy reigned among the people and the government of this state which only furnished one or two incomplete regiments to General Greene's army. And it was unbelievable to see a weak body of 1500 men commanded by a traitor establish itself to pillage with impunity a region which could muster a large body of militia. Congress felt the importance of removing him. The first plan it adopted was to begin by burning or capturing his fleet to cut off his retreat. It wrote to Mr. Destouches to ask him what he could do to achieve this end.

State of his Fleet
He detaches Mr. De Tilly with Several Vessels

The Chevalier Destouches's fleet was not in the best shape, even though it had always remained in port since our arrival in America. The crews were incomplete, illnesses had greatly weakened many sailors. Despite that, he wanted to give Congress proof of his good will. It was the first time that the French would be employed offensively in the service of the United States. With all the secrecy that such an expedition demanded, Mr. Destouches ordered Mr. De Tilly,[5] Captain of the 64-gun *l'Eveillé* and the frigates *la Surveillante* and *la Gentille* to prepare themselves to set sail in a few days along with the 14-gun cutter *la Guepe* to capture Arnold's ships if possible. Mr. de Tilly was charged with the mission to reconnoiter the coast and her anchorages.

February
Mr. De Tilly Sets Sail

His small fleet set sail on February 9. It was opposed by very bad weather which separated it. It rallied and arrived at the entrance to the Chesapeake Bay on the 14th except for la *Guepe*, of which we had no intelligence. Arnold's vessels went up the Elizabeth River at the sight of Mr. de Tilly. They dumped their water and managed to escape. Mr. de Tilly's vessels drew more water than the enemies' and could not follow them. His expedition should have been a quick attack. He could not maneuver as they. The principal object lost, he decided to gather some intelligence on Arnold's position, on the anchorages in Lynnhaven Bay and he anchored at the mouth of the James River. Eight small enemy

5 Armand Le Gardeur de Tilly (1733–1812) was a French admiral serving in the West Indies. He captured the British frigate *Minerva* off Saint-Domingue in 1778. He served in de Ternay's fleet in 1780 and captured the British vessel *Romulus* on February 19, 1781. He distinguished himself in combat with Admiral Arbuthnot's fleet on March 16, 1781 and took part in the battles of St. Kitts and the Saintes.

privateers arrived to enter it by a ruse, disguising themselves as British or by force. All eight were captured.

He Sinks the 50-gun Ship *Romulus*

Mr. de Tilly prepared himself to go out of the Chesapeake Bay when he received intelligence of a large ship. It was the 50-gun *Romulus* which was coming to take command of this area. Mr. de Tilly gave her chase and soon caught up with her. He made the usual signals of identification and fired a cannon shot. The English immediately prepared for battle.[6]

The British are very brave but they only fight well when the forces are equal or when they have superiority. I heard it said to Captain Gayton[7] who commanded the *Romulus* that he did not see how a captain would needlessly risk the lives of a number of brave men under his command against a superior force when their loss seems evident. Our Navy has not always been successful. It has not always served as it could have or should have, but, during this war, if honor is the guide of all our sailors, we are different from the English in this way. Have we not seen la *Capricieuse* commanded by Mr. de Ransanne[8] attacked by two superior frigates, fight and sink rather than surrender; *La Belle Poule*, the *Junon*, *la Surveillante* fight against 64-gun ships for two and three hours?

Mr. de Tilly captured 500 prisoners in this expedition. He sent many to the American guard at Yorktown. He could not bring his prizes. He left them at Hampton except for the *Romulus* and returned with this ship on the 23rd.

The Chevalier Destouches gave the command to Mr. de la Villebrune,[9] who commanded la *Gentille* and this frigate was given to the Chevalier de Launay Tromelin,[10] the ship's lieutenant aboard l'*Ardent*.

6 February 19, 1781.

7 Commodore Clark Gayton (1712–1785) was an admiral in the British Royal Navy serving in the American Revolutionary War and in the West Indies. He was succeeded by Sir Peter Parker as commander of Jamaica station. His health was very poor in his last years.

8 Lebreton de Ransanne (1743–) was a lieutenant de vaisseau in the French Navy.

9 Jacques-Aimes Le Saige (Chevalier de la Villebrune) was a commander of French naval forces at York, Virginia. He was Lieutenant de Vaisseau and Commanding Officer of Le *Romulus*. He later joined the Count de Barras's squadron from Newport to reinforce Count de Grasse and took part in the operations at Yorktown.

10 Maurice Boudin de Tromelin de Launay (1740–ca. 1815) lieutenant de vaisseau in the French Navy.

The 14-gun Cutter ***La Guepe*** Separates on the Mud Flats
La Guepe was lost near Cape Charles in Pursuit of a Small British Privateer

The Chevalier de Maulevrier[11] who commanded this cutter managed to save most of his crew with great difficulty. He could not give his news. He was believed drowned for a long time. He was rather fortunate to bring all his people back to Newport in a journey of 300 leagues by land.

L'Astrée's Arrival at Boston

Mr. de la Pérouse, commanding the 40-gun frigate *Astrée* arrived in Boston the 28th, after a crossing of 63 days. We did not have a single cent in the treasury for quite some time. We lived day by day by borrowing at exorbitant interest rates. He brought us 15,000 francs, the first dispatches and the first letters which we received since our departure from France. In the course of a year how many things occur, that interesting things happen 1500 leagues from home. We fear, after a lapse of time, of learning about the loss of a brother, a friend. We tremble on opening a letter. We feel, more than ever, the sacrifices that separation demands.

New requests from Congress to the Chevalier Destouches
He Prepares to Leave with his Entire Fleet

After Mr. de Tilly's successful expedition, Congress renewed its insistence to the Chevalier Destouches for the relief of Virginia. Mr. Destouches had not yet arrived there due to lack of resources and because he had no knowledge of the Chesapeake Bay. Mr. de Tilly gave him sufficient intelligence on this matter, about his success and about the *Culloden*, from Arbuthnot's fleet, having almost matched our forces to those of the British. Mr. Destouches no longer vacillated and he prepared to go out with his entire fleet to go occupy the Chesapeake Bay, intercept all aid to Arnold and to capture his vessels.

Mr. de Rochambeau Boards 1200 Men

I say to interrupt all assistance because Virginia, without its own defenses, was going to get out of the state of distress in which Arnold put it. Mr. de Rochambeau had just boarded

11 Édouard Charles Victurnien Colbert, comte de Maulévrier (1758–1820), was the commander of La *Guepe*.

on the vessels a detachment of grenadiers and light infantry, 600 infantrymen and 140 artillerymen with cannons all under the command of the Baron de Vioménil.

Mr. de la Fayette Marches to Virginia With 1500 Men

Meanwhile, General Washington sent Mr. de la Fayette by land with a detachment of 1500 American light infantrymen who were already on the march at this time. Mr. de la Fayette was to join the Baron de Vioménil in Virginia.

Departure of the Fleet
March

The fleet was slow in its preparations and provisioning for the departure. The winds became excellent for getting underway and even more so because they prevented Arbuthnot, stationed at Gardner's Bay, from putting a vessel to sea. Not enough effort was made. We were not ready. Mr. Destouches didn't sail until 6 p.m. on the eighth with a very fresh northeast wind which promised a successful enterprise.

General Washington Arrives at Newport
He Receives the Same Honors as the Marshals of France

The officers and soldiers were again encouraged, before their departure, by the presence and laudatory compliments of General Washington. It had been a long time since Mr. de Rochambeau had engaged him to come see the body of troops who were destined and who burned with desire to fight under his command. It was this opportunity which he chose. He arrived the day that the Baron de Vioménil's troops boarded. Mr. Destouches sent his canoe which brought him aboard his vessel the *Duc de Bourgogne* where Mr. de Rochambeau had gone to receive him and the other generals. There, he had a conference with our admiral. He then went ashore. All our troops were under arms forming a double rank from the landing to Mr. de Rochambeau's quarters where his lodging had been prepared. The battery of Fort Thomany Hill[12] fired. He was, in everything, received (under orders of the court) with the honors due to the marshals of France.

The actions, the life of a public man fill us with admiration while we do not know him. It is difficult enough to express the feelings which fill us, when we see him for the first time, after hearing his praises for so long.

12 Tomini, now Miantanomi Hill.

General George Washington

Independence National Historical Park

His Praise

North America is a large book in which we read, at every moment, something to the glory of General Washington. Who other than him could have been placed at the head of this nation with the same success? No less a good political administrator than a good general, he has gone to visit all the regions of the 13 states since the beginning of the revolution. A heroic courage, a virtue, a patience proven by the most vexatious adversities, his talents, his actions, the unanimous approval, even from his enemies, everything concurs to rank him among the greatest men. He is the father and idol of his soldiers. Finally, whoever does not like him is forced to at least esteem and admire him.

His Portrait

He is very tall in stature. He has a noble air, a fine face. His temperament is cool but mild and affable. His demeanor is easy and inspires confidence. He often has the impression of thought depicted on his face.

The State Addresses Him

He had never come to Newport. He received noticeable expressions of joy and pleasure, that his presence caused to the inhabitants of the city and to the army. The state addressed him, the city was illuminated and, during his stay, we gave him celebrations which a large number of Tories attended.

He Visits our Workshops and Examines our Works

Mr. de Rochambeau had him examine all our new fortifications. He did not fail to ask our engineers to instruct him about what he did not know about the artillery. The light construction of the carriages especially gave him the greatest pleasure and he had many conversations with the leaders of this body and Mr. de la Chaise[13], captain of the workers, relative to his instruction in this area. It is in the little things that sometimes we can see the truly great man, the man for whom vanity has no appeal. This observation was noticeable to everyone when we saw General Washington, general in chief for six years, publicly receiving lessons from subaltern officers.

13 Jean de la Chaise was the foreman at the manufacturer of the carriages.

His Departure

He gave the most flattering compliments to Mr. de Rochambeau and to the entire army on their fine appearance, the fine dress and discipline of the troops, and after having seen them in as much detail as time permitted, he took his leave on the 13th to arrive at his headquarters at New Windsor. The troops lined up along the road.

Arbuthnot Sets Sail and Goes in Pursuit of the Chevalier Destouches

Despite all the precautions we took to prevent any vessel from leaving the port before and after the departure of our fleet, we were too much surrounded by Tories, enemies, for Admiral Arbuthnot at Gardner's Bay to not be promptly informed of the departure of Mr. the Chevalier Destouches. The British had repaired, with incredible effort, the damage from the storm of January 21. They were ready to sail. The winds changed at 10 in the morning. Arbuthnot immediately got underway and pursued Mr. Destouches. The latter had left Newport in stormy weather. The winds became even stronger at sea and separated his fleet which did not rejoin him until the night of the 14th, 48 hours ahead of the enemy, giving him meanwhile a fine field, but the American pilots he had aboard made him take too much distance to avoid the coasts. Arbuthnot, less fearful, or knowing better, cut them and arrived at the mouth of the Chesapeake Bay in enough time to close the passage to the French. It was the morning of March 16 as a thick fog was clearing and as the winds permitted Mr. Destouches to enter the bay that the two fleets met.

Battle of the Chesapeake The Chevalier de Medine's Fine Maneuver

Mr. Destouches then realized that his expedition had failed and he was only concerned with preserving the honor of his ensign in the face of a superior enemy. He made several maneuvers which extended, leaving the wind to the enemy, to conserve the use of his lower battery as the weather was rather bad and the sea rough. About one o'clock in the afternoon, the lead vessels found themselves within pistol range. The battle began, the wind in the rear. The fire was very intense for an hour, after which that of the British relented, either because they had some guns dismounted or they lost many men. Ours continued, especially that of the *Conquérant* which fell, having had to deal with the lead

14 Virginia Capes, March 16, 1781.

vessels of the enemy which twice broke the helm, rendering her unable to maneuver under fire of their warships. The 90-gun *London* and the 74-gun *Roebuck* pursued him and might have captured him without the maneuver of the Chevalier de Medine[15], commander of the *Neptune*, who came to take the *Roebuck* from behind and fired three volleys in this position. This vessel was obliged to come to and to withdraw from battle, towed by a frigate.

Admiral Arbuthnot Leads to the Chesapeake Bay

The fire ceased on both sides at 3 o'clock. Mr. Destouches then gave the signal to come about on the enemy, but the *Conquérant*, badly damaged and with 108 men killed and wounded, responded to the signal that he could no longer maneuver. Mr. Destouches, already weakened in the action, felt he had one vessel less. Moreover, not knowing the enemy's condition, he abandoned the idea to resume the battle. Arbuthnot, who had the wind, decided not to pursue him. He himself had three vessels entirely disabled. He set sail for the Chesapeake.

Council of War

Mr. Destouches convened a council of war on board his ship which decided to return to Newport. Mr. de Cheffontaine, captain in second of the *Conquérant* and Mr. de Kergus, ensign, were killed. The 17th, the *Hermione* was detached to Philadelphia to inform Congress about the results of the sortie of our fleet.

Our Fleet Returns to Newport

The night of the 26th, we had not received any intelligence nor any about Arbuthnot when a signal was sent at the end of the Neck. Several vessels. Everyone thought it was the British coming at us, profiting from the absence of our navy. Mr. de Rochambeau consequently made the necessary arrangements to receive the enemy well. He had some troops march to the end of the Neck, etc. . . . But the frigate la *Surveillante*, on advancing, made signals of identification and calmed every anxiety.

15 Chevalier Charles René Magon de Medine (1763–1805) was a French contre-admiral. He was killed in 1805 the Battle of Trafalgar while commanding the ship-of-the-line *Algésiras*. For his sacrifice his name appears on the Arc de Triomphe in Paris.

Not a single ship captain thought enough to praise the detachments of our army that they had aboard. Mr. de la Clochetterie,[16] de Marigny, [Chevalier] de Medine and de la Grandière[17] also deserve much praise for the manner in which they fought on March 16.

Marquis de la Fayette Goes to Head of Elk

While Mr. de Vioménil was aboard the *Duc de Bourgogne*, Mr. de la Fayette, unimpeded from marching because of the wind, had arrived at the head of the Elk River which empties at the north of the Chesapeake Bay. To save himself from another long march by land, he had assembled many small vessels at this place and had his men board with great care. He then set sail and descended the bay; but the French, unable to arrive first, were not the masters. Mr. de la Fayette fortunately learned about the outcome of Mr. Destouches's sortie and battle soon enough. He went back up the Chesapeake and promptly reached the port of Annapolis where he was soon blockaded by two 20-gun British vessels, the *General Monk* and the *Hope*. He armed two strong cannoneer shallops on which he placed two 18-pounders which he found at Annapolis. The British couldn't respond, not having any artillery as strong, they were obliged to raise anchor and never appeared again. Mr. de la Fayette then departed Annapolis and had his boats placed in a secure location at Head of Elk. He then resumed marching by land to arrive in Virginia to oppose whatever advances Arnold might make.

Battle of Guilford Courthouse

Lord Cornwallis, in Carolina, was reinforced with a large detachment which had embarked at Cape Fear and joined him at Charleston. He then marched toward General Greene and reached him on March 15 at Guilford Courthouse. Of all the American generals, Greene is the most military and the best tactician. He made excellent deployments at Guilford but, right from the beginning of the action, neither the number of his troops which were a little stronger than those of the enemy, nor the advantage of a good position could prevent the militiamen he placed in the front line from retreating. Despite his efforts,

16 Jean-Isaac Chadeau, Sieur de la Clochetterie (1741–1782) served as captain of *La Belle Poule* in 1778. He became commander of the *Jason* in early 1780 and fought at the Battle of Cape Henry and the Battle of Saint Kitts, particularly distinguishing himself in the former engagement. He died in 1782 at the Battle of the Saintes commanding *L'Hercule*.

17 Charles-Marie de La Grandière (1729–1812) served as captain of *Le Conquérant*. He remained faithful to the king at the beginning of the French Revolution, refusing any new promotions and retired from the service.

he could not rally them. He passed them in the woods between a few Maryland troops and the British guards. Both sides suffered much bloodshed in a very tough battle in which they both demonstrated great courage. However, Greene, abandoned by part of his men, was forced to retreat. Lord Cornwallis held the battlefield. His loss in men was similar to that of the Americans—very considerable. The latter also lost four pieces of cannon.

The Victor Retires with Little Advantage

This is the only advantage Lord Cornwallis drew from his victory. Marching toward Greene, he advanced too rapidly. He could not advance a single step for lack of provisions. He was forced to march 100 miles and withdraw to Wilmington, capital of North Carolina.

Cornwallis Marches and Retreats Again

The desire to fight made him march again toward General Greene some time later. The latter, finding himself weaker, risked nothing to the fortunes of war. He knew the area and its lack of resources.

April 1781

He prudently retired on the *Roanoke*. Cornwallis was even obliged to withdraw to Halifax for lack of provisions.

He Advances to Virginia
Conduct of Carleton and Simcoe
Junction with Arnold's Troops

General Greene had manoeuvered well until then, but seeing his enemy moving away, he abandoned the area, leaving it without defense. Cornwallis had left a strong garrison at Charleston and feared nothing. He advanced toward Virginia. Pillage and murder accompanied his march. He had a vanguard of dragoons and light infantry under the command of Colonels Tarleton and Simcoe.[18] They committed all sorts of depredation and made themselves hated. Instead of changing minds to the government, as he boasted upon

18 Colonel John Graves Simcoe (1752–1806) was a British Army officer who sought to form a Loyalist regiment of free blacks from Boston. Instead, he was offered the command of the Queen's Rangers. He was first Lt. Governor of Upper Canada from 1791 until 1796 in southern Ontario and the watersheds of Georgian Bay and Lake Superior.

entering Virginia, they made the British reputation detested. Lord Cornwallis joined Arnold's corps at Petersburgh. He had been reinforced by a detachment under General Phillips[19] bringing his army to between 8 and 10,000 men. He had lost many on his march.

Recall of the Traitor

Arnold did not know Lord Cornwallis. Foreseeing that the latter, loyal and frank, would not like a man of his character, he requested to be recalled and given permission to go to New York which was granted without delay.

Weak Defense of Virginia

Virginia's only defense then was the corps under Mr. de la Fayette and a few militiamen commanded by Governor Nelson[20] and General Muhlenburg.[21]

Naval Superiority is Crucial in this War

L'*Hemione* returned from Philadelphia on April 7. The British had no port in the interior of the country and all those they possessed on the coast were very distant from each other. They needed many ships and transports for all their expeditions. Naval superiority is therefore indispensable to successfully engage in warfare in America. What a difference of

19 Major General William Phillips (1731–1781) was a renowned artilleryman. He took part in the recapture of Fort Ticonderoga, where he stated, "Where a goat can go, a man can go. And where a man can go, he can drag a gun." He was part of the Convention Army until he was exchanged for American Gen. Benjamin Lincoln in 1780. While on his way to link up with General Cornwallis, he contracted either typhus or malaria, becoming so ill Arnold lead his men. He died at Petersburg, Virginia, five months before the surrender at Yorktown.

20 Thomas Nelson, Jr.(1738–1789) was an American planter, soldier and statesman from Yorktown, Virginia. He represented Virginia in the Continental Congress and was its governor in 1781. He signed the Declaration of Independence as a member of the Virginia delegation and fought in the militia during the Siege of Yorktown. According to legend, he urged General Washington (or, in some versions, the Marquis de Lafayette) to fire on his own home, the Nelson House, where Cornwallis had his headquarters, offering five guineas to the first man to hit his house.

21 Brigadier General John Peter Gabriel Muhlenberg (1746–1807) was a Lutheran clergyman, Continental general and politician. His unit was first posted to the South, to defend the coast of South Carolina and Georgia. He was made a Brig. Gen of the Virginia Line, commanding that brigade at Valley Forge. He saw service in the Battles of Brandywine, Germantown, and Monmouth. After Monmouth, most of the Virginia Line was sent to the far south. He commanded the first brigade in Lafayette's Light Division at the siege of Yorktown.

resources are found at Rhode Island or New York. In addition to eight ships of the line, they have 40 and a few warships and more than 300 transports. They also receive two packet boats from England to Newport each month. We have eight ships of the line of less strength, two frigates and about 30 transports deployed in the name of the King. These transports have just received the order to depart for Saint Domingue. Our resources were few; they will be diminished even more.

On the 15th, all our merchant ships set sail escorted to the latitude of Philadelphia by *la Surveillante* and *l'Hermione.*

Newport Warehouses Emptied

Curiosity alone had not brought General Washington to Newport in the month of March. He had had frequent conversations with Mr. de Rochambeau and they had made a plan for the campaign without making it definite. Our general had not received any order from the court. He could not foresee the politics of the cabinets in Europe in the event we might march. The probable plan was that the march would be directed toward New York. The season was advancing, so we began to empty the Newport warehouses and to transport the materiel by water to Providence. The siege artillery and the munitions also went at the same time.

The Staff of the Army Reconnoiters the Route to New Windsor

Mr. de Béville[22] went to Providence to see the new camps and marched from there to New Windsor with two assistant quartermasters to reconnoiter suitable locations along the route for camping, the means of survival, transport, etc.

The Army Remains in Quarters

While the season was still good for camping, Mr. the Count de Rochambeau preferred to leave the troops in their quarters. To make them leave would not have served any useful purpose. Our tents weren't very good and we didn't have many resources to repair them.

All our forts were stripped of their artillery which was transported to Providence before the end of the month.

22 Pierre-François de Béville (b. 1721) entered French service in 1744 and attained the rank of brigadier in 1778. He served in Rochambeau's army as maréchal général de logis (Quartermaster General, March 1780) and maréchal de camp (Camp Marshal, December 1781). He returned to France in 1783 and retired from active service.

May 1781
Arrival of the Concorde at Boston

The frigate la *Concorde* commanded by Mr. de Tanoüarn,[23] ship's Lieutenant, arrived in Boston on May 8 with Mr. the Count de Barras,[24] and the Viscount de Rochambeau[25] on board as passengers. Mr. de Barras was appointed commander of the fleet and sent to take the command of the Chevalier de Ternay. By the return of this envoy, we were very pleased to receive news of the imminent arrival of a second division which we awaited for so long and which was promised to our general. Instead of reinforcements which would have allowed him to operate offensively with certainty, we learned of the Count de Grasse's[26] departure from Brest but for the Windward Isles on March 21 and that only the 50-gun *Sagittaire* and a few transports with 600 recruits would be sent to us.

Extract of the Dispatches Received by This Frigate

The dispatches from court gave no plan for the campaign. They said to remain in Newport with the Navy. You would make a useful diversion in that the British would be separated from their troops at New York and would be forced to always maintain a certain number of vessels there. If during the course of the campaign you see an opportunity to make an expedition to Hudson's Bay to draw the English business agents there, you could use a few troops and a few vessels. These plans were far from accommodating the need

23 Louis-Marie, Chevalier de la Tanouarn, was captain of the French frigate *Concorde.*

24 Admiral Jacques Melchior, Comte de Barras (1719–1793), succeeded Admiral de Ternay as commander of the French fleet in America. He is best known for his service during the American War of Independence, especially during the Yorktown Campaign.

25 Donatien-Marie-Joseph de Vimeur, vicomte de Rochambeau (1755–1813), was the son of General Rochambeau. He served as an aide-de-camp to his father. He participated in an unsuccessful campaign to re-establish French authority in Martinique and Saint Domingue in the 1790s. He was later assigned to the French Revolutionary Army in the Italian Peninsula and was appointed to the military command of the Ligurian Republic. He was appointed to lead an expeditionary force against Saint Domingue in 1802. He was captured aboard the frigate *Surveillante* by a British squadron at the surrender of Cap Français and returned to England as a prisoner on parole. He remained interned for almost nine years and was exchanged in 1811. He returned to the family château where he resumed the work of classifying the family's growing collection of maps which his father had begun.

26 Admiral François Joseph Paul Comte de Grasse (1722–1788) played a decisive role in the Yorktown campaign. After this action, he returned to the Caribbean with his fleet. British Admiral Rodney decisively defeated and captured him at the Battle of the Saintes in 1782. De Grasse was widely criticised for this loss and he demanded a court martial upon his return to France in 1784. Its verdict acquitted him of fault in the defeat.

which America still had to strike and to bring mortal blows to the enemy. The entire South, since Lord Cornwallis's march, could be considered under British domination. However, the war was excessively burdensome and costly and began to tire this nation which continued to live in the hope of seeing all the plans they were harboring for Henry Clinton and Lord Cornwallis succeed, plans which were no less than the total reduction of America for this campaign. They flattered themselves that, in marching, a large number would flock to their colors. They saw the French inactive at Rhode Island. General Washington's army was very weak, very incomplete compared to what it should have been after the last resolutions of Congress to raise recruits which had produced no results. Mr. de la Fayette had only 2000 men at most against 8 or 10,000 in Virginia. Greene's army was in no better state than the rest and could not undertake anything because of the lack of resources. The American troops were neither paid nor clothed nor well-nourished. Everything had the air of annihilation on the one hand. Everything took a new life and promised success on the other.

The court of France was convinced that as long as it would not send men to help America, England would not send any either. Consequently, acceding to the demands of our general would increase the desolation in this unfortunate country and the consequences that war entails. She gave Congress the freedom to draw on letters of exchange for the value of five or six million which would cover its needs and furnish something to pay soldiers.

Arrival of Troops at New York and Charleston

The two courts of France and England certainly had not communicated with each another as 5000 men arrived from England at the same time, 3000 at New York and 2000 more at Charleston.

This circumstance caused a lot of discussion in Congress. The event gave Mr. de Rochambeau a bad cause to defend. He was obliged to plead before Congress, to show the intentions of the King, to make offers of the greatest devotion to the interests of the 13 states. He had been charged to say, upon his arrival, that he was only the vanguard of a much larger body which France would send to help them. As he was badly treated on this account and with little leeway granted to him, he still made plans. He wrote to General Washington to ask him to hold a conference in which he would participate and in which they would decide together and agree on a definitive plan.

The Enemy Appear off Newport

The enemy appeared off Newport on the 18th with eight ships of the line. Illness and the battle of March 16, had reduced the crews of our vessels a little. Mr. de Barras requested Mr. de Rochambeau for 700 men to complete them, preparing himself to go fight if the British wanted to undertake anything.

Conference at Wethersfield

This circumstance did not prevent the general from leaving for Wethersfield in Connecticut, the place Mr. Washington indicated for their meeting.

This general had no other goal in sight, had no other plan than the siege of New York. He believed the passage was vulnerable with naval superiority. Mr. de Rochambeau, who had veteran sailors, was not of his opinion and saw clearly that New York could not be taken with the available forces. All our operations depended on the navy and on the location where Mr. the Count de Grasse would choose to pass the winter. They then had to decide on one location rather than on another and to be ready for any eventuality. The evacuation of Rhode Island by the French was decided and their junction. Their march toward the American army was determined at this time.

There were only three places we could act offensively: New York, Virginia where Cornwallis was and Charleston. The first of these cities was defended by a garrison more numerous than the two armies, French and American. It also had the advantage of a very strong position which is very easy to defend and a harbor whose entry could be defended by a small number of vessels. Charleston had almost the same inconveniences for us and was 300 leagues farther away. We learned from intercepted letters from Lord George Germaine to Sir Henry Clinton that the latter had firm orders to occupy a post in Virginia. Consequently, strong or weak, we would certainly find an enemy to fight. This location was more important than all the others because the area was open and almost without defense. That is the one that Mr. de Rochambeau preferred. He knew, from his dispatches, that Mr. de Grasse had orders to come pass the winter in this region. The location had to be determined early to operate successfully because it had not yet been agreed upon.

27 May 21, 1781.

Admiral François Joseph Paul de Grasse

Independence National Historical Park

Dispatch to Mr. de Grasse

After the Wethersfield conference, Mr. de Rochambeau wrote to Mr. de Grasse and explained the Americans' disastrous state of affairs, the meager resources they had, what had to be done etc. He detailed the strength of the posts of which I spoke, the probabilities of successful attacks in the various locations and gave him the liberty to go to the one he thought of greatest import for his plan. He also asked him for 3 or 4000 men for landing troops, as the islands didn't need any during the winter, and for 1,200,000 francs in silver. Some had just arrived for us at Boston but the transport would have been too difficult and too long to arrive in time. A long march, everything required for a campaign required enormous expenses. Everything has to be foreseen when one commands. Mr. de Rochambeau charged the *Concorde* with these important dispatches and she set sail immediately for Martinique where Mr. de Grasse was.

The American Rhode Island Regiment is Surprised in Quarters

The 14th of this month, part of the American Regiment of Rhode Island which was in quarters near Pines Bridge on the Croton River was surprised by a band of Delancey's[28] refugees. Colonel Greene, who was with us at Newport, had gone to visit their quarters with his major. They were killed along with part of their men.

The Fleet has Orders to Return to Boston

In the event Rochambeau's army made a movement and evacuated Rhode Island, Mr. de Barras had orders to withdraw to Boston to [anchor] his fleet in safety. Wherever the combined armies might act, wherever Mr. de Grasse might go, in accord with Mr. de Rochambeau's plan, the Point of Rhode Island was a much better station for the fleet than that of Boston in that a junction was much easier to execute as this place is much closer and there are much better breezes to sail from Newport. We were obliged to leave all our heavy artillery and the greatest part of our ammunition at Providence. Mr. Barras, on leaving Newport, was then unable to bring them to us as needed.

Council of War Aboard the *Duc de Bourgogne*

To cover his conduct and that of Mr. de Barras in opposing the orders of the court, Mr. de Rochambeau called two councils of war on board the *Duc de Bourgogne* where he explained the reasons above. It was proposed to decide what would be the best location for the fleet to guard, the most advantageous in case Mr. de Grasse went somewhere that we would have to join him, and for us for our artillery. This same fleet covered enemy endeavors. Everthing was debated and it was decided that our navy would not budge and a detachment of 4 or 500 infantryman would be left behind for its safety.

28 Brigader General Oliver de Lancey (1718–1785) was a a merchant and a senior Loyalist officer in America He and his brother James raised and equipped the three battalions of DeLancey's Brigade, consisting of 1,500 loyalist volunteers, from the Province of NY. They served primarily on Long Island.

The 700 men who were embarked to complete the crews of the vessels in case the fleet was obliged to fight debarked on June 3.

The fourth and the sixth, the hussars and Lauzun's infantry who were quartered at the end of the Neck were ordered to abandon their post and leave for Lebanon where the greatest part of the Legion was located.

The *Sagittaire* and a Small Convoy Arrive at Boston

On the ninth, the 50-gun *Sagittaire* which had left Brest with Mr. de Grasse on March 22, arrived at Boston with a few transport vessels containing 600 recruits sent to us and some effects for the King's warehouse. Being offshore with this flotilla, an atrocious storm arose. Two ships of its convoy perished on the coast.

The Army Leaves Newport

To avoid two days of march for the troops, a rather large quantity of small vessels was assembled at Newport to transport them and their baggage. The two brigades boarded at 10 and 11 a.m. and set sail for Providence.

Mr. de Choisy Commands at Rhode Island

Mr. de Choisy, Brigadier, was appointed to command the detachment of 100 men per regiment who remained at Rhode Island. This detachment was composed of the weakest of our men because they wouldn't have to act as much as the rest of the army. The state of Rhode Island also decided to assemble 1000 militiamen under the command of Brigadier General Miller and to send them to Newport for the safety of the island and the protection of our vessels but the absence of the enemy decreased the Americans' zeal and activity. Mr. de Choisy never had more than 300 to command and they were very poorly armed.[29]

29 Brigadier General Nathan Miller (1743–1790) was an American shipbuilder and merchant from Warren, RI. He was a delegate from that state to the Confederation Congress in 1788. Although reappointed to the Congress in 1789, he did not attend that year.

June 1781

Mr. the Count de Rochambeau personally left on June 12 with the headquarters to go to Providence where he arrived the same day. The troops were camped a short distance from the city.

Upon receiving news of the arrival of the *Sagittaire*, we sent some officers to Boston to conduct to Providence the recruits who arrived from France. They arrived on the night of the 15th and were immediately divided and put on subsistence in the regiments. Those who had been recruited in France only sent their worst men with furnishings in a pitiable state. Mr. de Rochambeau sent 200 of the weakest and invalid to Newport after the long crossing they had made and he ordered Mr. de Choisy to send an equal number to the army. This [illegible] was done the 16th and the 17th.

I remain at Newport because of a grievous wound received in a duel with the Marquis Dubouchet[30] Brigade Major of the army who was also seriously wounded.

I could not follow Mr. de Rochambeau to Providence. We are sometimes exposed in the world to the event which prevented me, without having the least reproach to make. I was grievously wounded on the 10th by a brigade major of the army whom I likewise reduced to keep it small for a time. The best of things of this nature is always very disagreeable but if it is possible to draw a sort of satisfaction in regard to the public, I certainly proved it on this occasion! The matter in which I conducted myself previously, afterward and during this type of combat so new to me, brought me the most marked praises and expressions of interest from all my comrades and of all the general officers and superiors! My antagonist meanwhile conducted himself as a very brave man but he wronged me repeatedly which drew the blame of everyone and which forced him at all the amends that I could demand!!! My state of health was dangerous for several days but, soon after, I found myself well. I could leave my room and witnessed, in the city, the regrets on the departure of the French.

On the Departure of the French army from
Newport Rhode Island May 1781
Waked by the music's martial band I rode
to see the troops depart
Their looks bespoke their last repose
while anguish rends their hearts.

30 Probably Louis II du Bouchet de Sourches, 3rd marquis de Sourches (1711-1788), who served as an officer of the French monarchy.

And as they pass each weeping fair
in sighs their wishes sends
for inward truth bids them declare
they wish them for their friends.

Their pleasing form & gentle air
alas! too well approved:
a modest blush forbids declare
with how much truth me have!

No more we seek with nicest care
our ornament to place;
no more in curls or plated hair
decked with becoming grace.

Our grand parade no more is seen
Decked with red, or white *Soissonnais Regiment
the waving plume lappels of green *Saintonge Regiment
no more to bless our sight

The charms of music's power resignd
our evening Levees too
Where wit & sense with lustre shined
alas! To all we bid aDieu

by Miss Momford[31]

When we arrived at the island of Rhode Island, few French officers could speak English which was an obstacle even more so to conquer the type of antipathy that every Englishman or English descendent has for the French and the innumerable and unfounded prejudices which the British had insinuated to the credulous Americans against us until they contracted their alliance with France, an alliance which, at that time, was forced only by necessity!! Strict discipline established among our soldiers, the acts of kindness which we made, gradually won over to us the minds of those estranged from us. We lived without difficulty and without animosity toward the inhabitants. First, our money greatly seduced them. We paid very exactly everywhere and the first purchases of every type we made cost us dearly.

31 The poem is in English, followed by a French translation.

Newporters' Civil Life

Newporters are from a gentle society and in the year that I spent with them, I never had the least argument or altercation in a family or even in a group. The young people have much freedom and they rarely consider it! While they are not married, they take great care of their appearance but, almost immediately afterward, they often neglect it. Their only ambition is to capture their husbands, to prove their tenderness. The latter, on their part, are extremely faithful. In gatherings, we rarely see them apart which makes women lovable in France and in every country. The desire to please does not guide them in this country and the men once married, are only concerned about their business, their commerce.

Clubs are generally not followed very much or interesting. They differ very much from us, at least on one of the most important points for the happiness of their marriage. We hardly see an unhappy man in America because a young man's and a young girl's desire and inclination make them decide to get married. Neither interest nor fortune count for anything in this matter. That can make them happier than us who daily see victims rather than lovers dragged to the altar to mouth oaths in which their heart neither has nor can have any part. Here the simple promise is almost as solid, almost as strong as the public act. The young lovers begin by studying themselves for a long time. Once they know each other and have seen each other every day, sometimes for two or three years, they get engaged to each other. When circumstances put off marriage even more, often because of lack of money, settling etc., then the young man works, trades, makes overseas voyages and often they marry only four, five or six years after their engagement. The young girl, sure of her lover, is no longer involved with anyone else. Her heart is given; she no longer seeks to please. I saw two children born at Newport whose father and mother were only engaged. Their birth was declared legitimate. The parents are not obliged to give up anything for the children they marry. Often, the young spouses are very uncomfortable, but they are in love. Even if, in fact, they are not happy, they believe they are. That's the main point.

The Inhabitants in America are Happy

I was always imbued with the principle which I believe natural for those who have never seen other peoples, who have never lived under another government than their own—that nowhere does anyone live as happy. The French government, that of the 13 states is well-enough known that I will not speak of it. But it happens that what we call the people in France approaches the mildness and the pleasure of life of that in America. It is free and does not depend on anyone with talents. Everyone can hope to participate in government. There is no legal system to annoy or vex them, no duties to pay. His small portion of land is his. He is master to dispose of it. The inhabitants of the seaside towns are involved in ocean trade, have more activity than those in the country who are lazy and indolent. If they harvest to feed their families that's all they want. Animal life of what we call planters or farmers is excellent. They only eat corn bread which they prefer to wheat. They cook and bake both poorly. The base of their beverage is rum which they mix with water. They sometimes add some nutmeg to this beverage which had the name of grog and now is called toddy. One has to be accustomed to it to find it tasty.

Different Religions in Newport

There are five different religions in Newport that are all freely practiced by the wise and just law of tolerance, Anglicanism, Presbyterianism, Anabaptist, Quaker and Jewish. Each sect has its temple or meetinghouse and individual ministers. The children often are not required by their parents to adopt their religion. However, the Anglicans have a type of scorn for the others. At a certain age, they are sent to be instructed in the principles of all. They go hear the different ministers preach and they decide on the one that influences them the most or for the cult that they believe the best. It also happens, as a result, that they often do not know themselves what they are.

Quaker Bee

The Quakers form an association and they differ from the others in that all the society accepts and agrees to what is acceptable. This sect is very widespread in North America since William Penn settled here in 1681 after King Charles II of England gave him a piece of land which he named after himself, Pennsylvania, and where he founded Philadelphia. The Quakers, being distant from all types of business by their statutes, are lazy and indolent. Their mores are mild but their manners crude. They do not take off their hats, never greet, speak familiarly [illegible] with everybody. All the peoples are their friends. They constantly pray for general peace and concord. They are horrified by blood and are never soldiers. They tried to conciliate the British and the Americans in this conflict. They were not vexed by either one but the latter, however, forced them to pay their taxes for the support of the war. They are very somber, speak little at home or elsewhere and even less at the meetinghouse or place of assembly unless in this last place they have no fear of inspiring loss of spirit.

They gather for worship twice a week. Sometimes they are in meditation or in very deep silence for the two or three hours which their meetings last and they leave without speaking. If, by chance, a man or a woman from their community, regardless of age, believes [illegible], he rises. If it's a man, he removes his hat and speaks about a subject related to their belief such as a passage from the Bible etc. They affect a trembling voice everywhere in public which gave them the name Quakers. George Fox of the dissenter party in England, son of a silk worker, founded the sect in 1642. He preached true [illegible] in public. He was completely flogged different times [illegible] a few proselytes and went to Holland where he made many. They are not baptized, [illegible] that the Christ was baptized by John but never baptized himself.

Marriage Ceremony

I once assisted at one of their marriage ceremonies. The friends (that's how they always call themselves) gather at their meeting as [illegible]. Those who are inspired or believe they are speak. If there are none, after two hours of profound and annoying silence, the secretary of the [assembly] says to the betrothed that they may get married. Then the future husband arises, takes the right hand of the woman and recites this formula in a loud voice: "My friends, I take you all to witness that I choose such a woman for my wife and I promise always to be faithful to her and to love her until death." The woman [repeats] the same words and then they go sign the contract. So that it bears greater authenticity, all those present, without exception, can go sign. After [the ceremony] is finished, the spouses leave the [meeting] first, their eyes lowered and in silence, and they all go home to eat. This seems more like a funeral than a wedding.

It is very easy to distinguish a Quaker or a Quakeress externally. The latter never groom their hair as all the women in America, even those deep in the country. They wear them very short under small bonnets of fine linen without folds which are tied under the neck with a little cord. None of them have the hair tied, do not powder it, never dance or sing. Their appearance is always serious. Their head is always covered with a large hat without hooks.

Catholicism is the only religion which is not tolerated even though some exist in Maryland. The Americans believe that an infinite number of scruples should stop us at each step. . . . They were badly mistaken. The life of a French soldier is not very much like that of the convent and what they thought to find in in us, we have found among them. It would be impossible for an American to sing, dance, play an instrument or even cards, or go to some show on Sunday. They go to church morning and evening at times. The reading of the Bible, which each family possesses in a large folio, occupies the rest of the day. The same thing exists in London and in England with this difference: that if the English do not play, they go to the cabaret or to the girls.

A few years ago, nobody would go on a voyage, would never dare mount a horse on Sunday. But in fact of religion, customs or usages, war makes them pass and raises many difficulties which is what happened.

Everybody knows the English way of life so it is useless to talk about it here, since that of the Anglo-Americans resembles it in everything. However, the latter, not having lived much with the Europeans, follow several ancient customs more than the English do today.

Products Unique to Rhode Island
Age of Newport

Rhode Island is the smallest of the 13 united states of America. It abounds in pasture lands, in excellent cattle, and all kinds of fowl. Her coasts provide a very abundant and a large variety of excellent fish. Rhode Island was called the garden of America before the war, [not] because of the abundance of fruit but because of the [large] number of lovely country houses and the gardens which decorate them. All the roads were bordered. The island is generally flat, except the part of the Neck where there are only rocks. The air is very healthy and pure and the blood can be no braver. Newport, the capital of this island, was built in 1642. Before the British took possession of it in 1776, it flourished and was one of the largest cities in North America.

The winter of 1779 to 1780 was so bitter that the British, unable to penetrate onto the continent, cut down all the wood on the island without reservation and destroyed almost everything built of wood and almost 400 houses in the city and environs. The city is longer than wide. It extends along the port. It has a road which is a quarter league long. As in most of the northern states, the houses are built of wood. The levels are low. They are [warm] in winter, cool in summer. In these houses, there is no distribution of apartments which are the delight of ours. They are all built on the same plan, but they and the furniture are neat and well-maintained which ours cannot match.

Its Port and Harbor

The port is very fine and large but only the small vessels can enter. The frigates and warships, especially, remain in the harbor which is probably one of the most spacious and finest in all of America.

Public Buildings

There are three public buildings in Newport: the city hall, the court house and the marketplace which is very fine and a library where there is a rather large number of volumes, but it does not contain any research and it lacks a large number of excellent works.

Mr. Mrs. and Miss Champlain

Before leaving Newport, I want to pay tribute to its gratitude once more. The [wound?] which I received attracted the general interest of the army but it was also shared by almost all the inhabitants. However, I must single out Mr. and Mrs. Champlain and Miss Peggy Champlain, their eldest daughter. This young and charming person enjoys the advantages of the most exquisite and the most uniformly pretty face that I have seen in America, the simple and mild manners of the new continent which the customs of the people, education and the desire to please give to attractive and lovable women. I met her early. She gave me English lessons and I gave her French lessons which she came to speak rather well. The departure of the army and that of my general's house, having left me without support, I was amply rewarded by the generous and constant care of this lovable family, by those of Miss Champlain, to which I was particularly sensitive. Beauty never loses the rights—her memory will always be present to me and my wishes will accompany her unceasingly. My regrets at leaving her were as real as sincere. My recovery, although not perfect, was well-enough advanced that I then decided to bid her adieu which cost me dearly and I left to rejoin the army on June 23.

March to New York
June 1781

The Army had departed Providence when I arrived.[32] It was camped at Waterman's Tavern to the east of the town near the road which it was to follow. It had made a stop of six days at this camp during which we could acquire everything that was necessary for the march. The large baggage was put in storage and remained at this site along with the siege artillery and a detachment of this body. The general assigned to each company a wagon drawn by four oxen to carry the soldiers' tents and the officers' equipment. The field artillery was drawn by horses and, as we were earlier very discontent with the service and the negligence of the teamsters, we made a deal with them in which they agreed to supply the horses, repairs to the hitches and the ironwork for two dollars per day during the campaign.

The general divided the army into four divisions for the ease of marching and for supplying them. They would march at a day's interval one from the other. A division of artillery was attached to each one of them, a certain number of staff officers, of the

32 The army began the march out of Newport on June 18. They marched in four divisions, spaced a day apart.

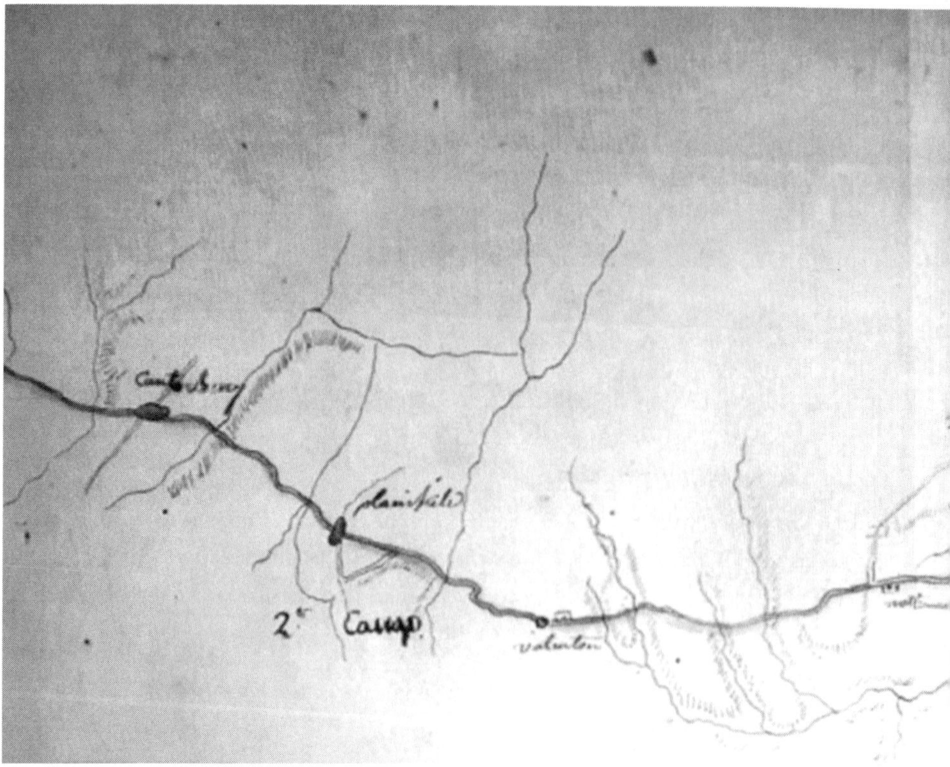

Louis de Lauberdière's drawing (facing pages) of the route of march from Providence, Rhode Island, to Canterbury, Connecticut, showing camps 1 and 2, June 18–21, 1781.

Bibliothèque Nationale

headquarters, of the Corps of Engineers . . . Mr. de Rochambeau marched with the first, Baron de Vioménil commanded the second, the Count de Vioménil the third and Mr. the Count de Custine the fourth.

The Duc de Lauzun was at Lebanon with the Legion. He was ordered to form the left column and to march parallel to the first division at eight or ten miles distance.

All the orders having been issued, Mr. de Rochambeau began to march on the 18th with the Bourbonnais division and camped at Waterman's Tavern, 15 miles.

The 19th, this division camped at [Plainfield] 15 miles. The same day, the Royal Deux Ponts division arrived at Waterman's Tavern.

The 20th, the first division went to camp at Windham, 15 miles. The second camp at Plainfield and the division of Soissonnais arrived at Waterman's Tavern.

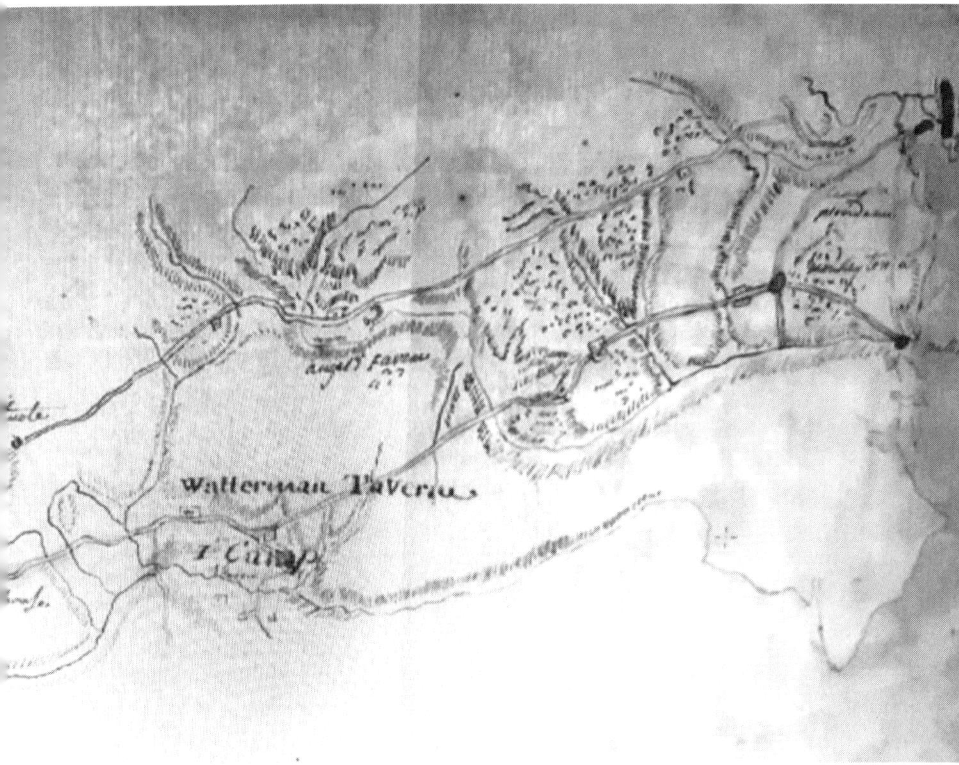

The 21st the Bourbonnais division left its camp at Windham and camped at Bolton, 18 miles. The Deux Ponts division camped at Windham, that of the Soissonnais at Plainfield, the Saintonge division departed Providence and camped at Waterman's Tavern.

The 22nd, the Bourbonnais division came to camp at East Hartford, 13 miles. The Deux Ponts division at Bolton, the Soissonnais at Windham, the Saintonge at Plainfield.

The 23rd, the first division rested at East Hartford, the headquarters crossed the Connecticut River and set up camp at Hartford itself. The same day, the Deux Ponts division arrived at camp at Hartford. The Soissonnais were camped at Bolton and the Saintonge at Windham.

Finding myself much better from my wound, I left Newport the same day to rejoin the army. I took the road to Bristol Ferry to go to Providence. A ferry generally means any sound or river that one needs to cross by boat on which horses and vehicles can board. The boat is called a ferry boat; the boatman ferry men. There are many ferries in America. Almost all the rivers are very large and very [illegible] and there is almost no way to build a bridge from Newport to Bristol Ferry. There is a ferry to Bristol itself, there are two [illegible] rather fine place east. It is located near the Newport harbor. It can now contain about 100 houses all built of wood like those at Newport. The British in command of

Rhode Island made an incursion under the command of General Grey[33] on May 25, 1778. They torched many houses and ravaged the area. This odious and horrible means was, along with the carnage, the only ones which they employed since the beginning of the war to subdue a people who had enough strength and courage to take up arms against them! This destructive means can only alienate, only arouse spirits. The Americans are beginning to want nothing to do with the English except the language. They prefer the state to which their enemies reduced them to a better condition under the yoke of tyranny.

Warren is four miles from Bristol and is, in some ways, almost as large. Her location is rather favorably selected. The name Warren will always be dear to the Americans. The first general of this nation to have been killed by the English in the cause of liberty, at the beginning of the Revolution, was General Warren[34]. Boston was his birthplace. He practiced medicine there and was also noted for his many virtues. He was one of the first to take up arms. His courage equaled his strength of spirit and his death caused universal regret.

I stopped briefly in Warren and then took the road to Providence which is 12 miles. It is made in the middle of much forest and we cross a ferry, a little smaller than the one at Bristol, which is only one mile from the city.

Providence is the second city of the state of Rhode Island and has about three to 400 houses. It is situated between two hills: one in the open, the other to the east which make it very hot in the summer and cold in winter. The northwest winds often blow on the hill to the east. There is a very fine college where there are no longer any students since the war. Its location, in a pure and healthy climate, induced our administration to take possession of it to send part of our sick from Newport.

There is a little river at Providence whose mouth forms a fine port for commerce. Warships and frigates can go up and, at 4 miles, it empties into the Patuxet River or channel. The inhabitants of this city, like those at Newport, engage in commerce with the West

33 Major General Charles Grey (1729–1807) was one of the more successful British army leaders. He commanded the 3rd Brigade at the battles of Brandywine Germantown and Monmouth. He led raids at New Bedford on September 5–6, 1778 and the night attack at Old Tappan, NJ, which came to be known as the Baylor Massacre. He was appointed commander-in-chief of the British troops in America, but hostilities ended before he could take command. He earned the nicknamed "No-flint Grey" after the Battle of Paoli. Grey reportedly ordered his men to remove their musket flints during a night advance, ensuring they would rely only on the bayonet.

34 Joseph Warren (1741–1775) was an American physician who played a leading role in Patriot organizations in Boston during the early days of the American Revolution. He was commissioned a major general in the colony's militia on June 16, 1775. Rather than exercising his rank, he chose to serve as a private soldier the following day and was killed when British troops stormed the redoubt atop Breed's Hill.

Indies where they bring horses, cattle, wood for construction. They also conduct the slave trade.

I did not notice any produce foreign to France in the state of Rhode Island. Its [climate] is the same as that of Flanders.

The 21st, Lauzun's Legion departed its camp in Lebanon, formed the left column and came to camp at East Hampton.[35]

The 22nd, they crossed the Connecticut River, made camp at Middletown where they rested on the 23rd.

The 24th, the two divisions of Bourbonnais and Deux Ponts rested at East Hartford. They [crossed] the baggage and artillery of the Bourbonnais division at the Hartford Ferry. The Soissonnais division arrived at the East Hartford camp. The Saintonge division departed Windham and made camp at Bolton. Lauzun's Legion rested at Middletown.

I left Providence without regret the same day because I knew nobody and the tavernkeeper with whom I lodged, profiting from the necessity of the French to travel, charged me triple the usual price. I took the road to Waterman's Tavern. This route is covered with thick woods. The land is full of rocks and hills but the valleys are very fertile. There is a rather large number of houses and settlements.

When the English came to settle in this part of America, it was probably only a vast forest where one could barely find a few clearings. They themselves and their descendants managed to make their land interesting, by work and effort, in a span of 150 years.

Agriculture was thriving as they hunted or, as the rest of the conquerors of America, killed the natives. It took a rather large population to bring them to the current state. Tolerance produced this result. All religions being allowed: English, French, Danish, Dutch, German, everything was acceptable; all built churches. An individual arrived and seized, or bought, at a very good price, a parcel of land considered until now a wasteland. He burned or cut down all the wood and, after four or five years of work, peacefully enjoyed a rather large settlement. Their descendents or successors continued. They searched in the forests and found a location that appealed to them. They first began by cutting down the small trees which they did not discard. They cut the ends and stacked them one on another to construct the walls of their first hut. They put a covering of kindling between each log, some earth and a roof suitable to the rest of the structure. Once completed, they bring some cattle and finish it little by little. We see many of these types of nascent settlements emerging from these wild retreats where there are only a few roads barely cleared. There are no wild or ferocious beasts in these forests. Rabbits and squirrels

35 East Hartford.

are plentiful. They are not as heavy as those in France. Theirs are grey and generally well endowed and long.

These forests are all filled with fine trees which the Americans still take for granted because they are plentiful, but they will soon realize their value for the construction of vessels. There is a type of oak, called willow oak or weeping oak, whose leaves resemble exactly those of this tree. It cannot be mistaken because of its bark and acorns.

Almost all the fruit trees are in open wind. The fruit is not bad but the variety is small and sparse.

There are several species of birds indigenous to this country which are unknown to us. The red bird or cardinal, the bluebird and the mockingbird. The feathers of this latter one have nothing unusual but its song is remarkable in that it resembles that of the jay in our forests. It imitates all the other birds, often being mistaken for them. It's natural song is very pleasant.

I dined at Mr. Waterman's and was shown the site of the camps which the troops had occupied on the road near the tavern. The Americans don't have our custom of giving their taverns names which they keep. They are always designated by the name of the owner. Many of their dwellings don't even have a name. This could be cause for travelers' mistakes if changes occur and signs made between ten and twelve years could be of no use. Most of the names could have been changed. It's 15 miles from this site to Plainfield which is in the state of Connecticut and located on a hill whose dominant location would be equally good against an enemy who would enter either the state of Rhode Island or that of Connecticut. Thirty or 40 houses make up the neighborhood.

Headquarters were set up [in] the forward camp abutting a forest and the left on the Canterbury Road. This latter location will soon become renowned as the city which bears this name in England. It is 5 miles from Plainfield. The tavern called Township bears the name of the town as do many others. Sometimes we travel a quarter of an hour without doubt that we are there. One should never reckon or count the distances to the meetinghouse or to the courthouse. There are often no houses in the neighborhood or near one another. A greater population would bring the properties closer together and increase the number of buildings. There are eight or 10 houses at Canterbury. I [illegible] and I passed a fairly pleasant evening with a country squire who came to this place to see the French army. How great would his astonishment have been if he had arrived in time? I can only judge by his appearance when he saw me. He had a preconceived idea of the French which after I assured many times that I was one, he didn't want to believe me, telling me that I could only be Scottish, that I was [too] white for a Frenchman, that the people of this [town] were not usually so polite, so well behaved as I seem to be. . . . I responded that my freshness was not surprising because I was only 20 years old and that all my compatriots had the same kind manners for everyone, even for the English when they were their prisoners. He told me that it would be very easy, when he returned home, to deceive his neighbors about what they thought of us, that he was happy to give us justice and that he always wanted to forget the false notions he had of us. We left very good friends.

On the 25th, the Bourbonnais division and the headquarters departed Hartford and East Hartford and made camp at Farmington, 13 miles. The Deux Ponts and the Soissonnais divisions rested at East Hartford. The baggage and artillery of the Deux Ponts division crossed the East Hartford ferry. The Saintonge division came to camp at East Hartford and Lauzun's Legion left its camp at Middletown and took the one at Wallingford.

I departed Canterbury the same day on my way to Hartford by way of Scotland, a little place emerging where nature is still wild. Some rather high mountains, woods, ravines, rocks—that is what we see on this route. It is only 5 miles from there to Windham. This little town is built halfway up a hill and is surrounded by woods. It can have between 100 and 160 houses. Headquarters was set up and the camp posted a mile from the foot of the mountain in a fine field facing a little river. I stopped at Windham a few moments and took the route to Bolton which is 18 miles away. This area is very wooded, hilly and rocky. There are few houses. There are 10 or 12 at Bolton and a meetinghouse. All the inhabitants of this region are Presbyterians. Their ministers are highly regarded, very respected and always dressed in black and wear large wigs of imitation white hair to give them even more importance. After staying at Bolton, I took the road to Hartford which is 11 miles. This route offers nothing of interest. Approaching East Hartford, the land becomes more level. This location is situated a mile from the Connecticut River. It crosses a stream which gives water to the camp. It consists of a few houses and a meetinghouse. I did not [stop] and immediately passed the Hartford ferry [where] I slept.

This city is the capital of Connecticut. It can contain three to 400 houses. The roads are not paved and are very wide. The courthouse, where the general assemblies of the state are held, is quite large and lovely. The Connecticut River which runs through it, flows from north to south and empties into the sound at New Haven. Ships of 80 to 100 tons can sail up to Hartford. The largest ones stop at Middletown. The state of Connecticut abounds in pastures where there are cattle of great beauty. Wheat is grown. The flour is sent to the West Indies. The inhabitants like it just as well if they don't prefer cornbread. They are all Presbyterians. It is this sect which populated the four states of New England: New Hampshire, Massachusetts Bay, Rhode Island and Connecticut. Simplicity, kind manners prevail everywhere in these regions. War is a cruel scourge whose full weight they all feel, but, in their families, nothing troubles them. They all seem happy. They are very faithful to their commitments, to their word. They never deceive in their [illegible]. They are all fairly generally slow and lazy. The peaceful New Englander, inhabitant of New England, peacefully cultivates his field. He only seeks the comforts of an easy life, without outdoing or surpassing his neighbor. Ambition does not devour him.

We often find beauties, lovely girls in the country. They bring their flocks to pasture. They truly fulfill the idea we have of the shepherdess and which we no longer find in Europe except in the pastorals and in the poets. Their hair is always coiffed and their daily labors do not harm the cleanliness which they always maintain on their clothing. Finally, happiness seemed to be the destiny of these regions before the war. But: Oh Europeans! You have discovered a vast continent and you have polluted it with your trash. You have established colonies whose care and whose customs produced every joy! You would still change one and tarnish the other. Already the emigrants of all nations abound. We see angry fathers of families, desperate mothers, badly mistaken girls arriving here. Luxury, European customs are introducing themselves. But I'm stopping. And I leave a picture which pains me to paint and which I never want to finish.

On the 26th, the Bourbonnais division went from the Farmington camp to that at de Baren's Tavern,[36] 13 miles. The Deux Ponts division camped at Farmington. The baggage and artillery of the Soissonnais division crossed the Hartford Ferry and together with the Saintonge division rested at the camp of East Hartford. Lauzun's Legion camped at Oxford.

On the 27th, the Bourbonnais division camped at Breakneck, 13 miles. The Deux Ponts division camped at Barnes's Tavern. The Soissonnais division left East Hartford and went to Farmington. The Saintonge division rested. Its baggage and artillery crossed the Hartford Ferry and Lauzun's Legion departed Oxford and made camp at West Stratford.

I was not totally recovered. I had made fairly long marches the preceding days. I and my baggage spent the 26th at Hartford to rest with my retinue. I resumed travel on the 27th to go to Barnes's Tavern. The banks of the Connecticut River are very inviting. West Hartford is 5 miles from Hartford. A few houses comprise this location. The goodness of its soil and its cultivation make it notable. Farmington is 8 miles from here, built in a very pleasant valley. The continuity of houses of this fine town extend more than a mile. A stream passes by here which makes all the pastures and fields very abundant. There is a rather high mountain to the east from which we can see perfectly the beauty, loveliness and richness of the soil of this little enclave between two mountains. I knew an old man of 93 years from this place who told me «my father was the first Englishman to settle here. A thick forest covered the outskirts which you see. A brother who is 97 years old and I helped him build a house where you see me. We worked hard. Other colonists came to share both our hardships and our labors. I saw [born] all those who exist today. They seem to be all my children.» The discourse and the great age of this respectable Connecticutian filled me with

36 Barnes's or Barn's Tavern.

admiration and veneration. Anyway, I left him and took the road to Southington. I crossed a very lovely town. We see a large number of houses along the route, proving its goodness.

Southington is very well-situated and gives its name to a township or fairly extensive territory. Barnes's Tavern is 4 miles away. A few houses built near a brook form a group with the tavern. I found the Baron de Vioménil whose tokens of goodness and interest about what happened to me at Newport touched me very much.

On the 28th, the Bourbonnais division broke camp at Breakneck and went to Newtown, 18 miles. The Deux Ponts division camped at Breakneck. The Soissonnais left Farmington and came to camp at Barnes's Tavern and the Saintonge division at Farmington. Lauzun's Legion rested at West Stratford.

I left Barnes's Tavern the same day to rejoin my general at Newtown. A few miles from Barnes's is [West?] Mountain dominating the entire Southington valley. There are few vistas so rich and pleasant as that of West Hill. The town then becomes much less interresting, is very wooded and hilly. We cross the Mad River, so named because of its course amid the rocks the stones, and we arrive at Waterbury, a place of about 50 rather fine houses. A pretty large creek, called the Waterbury River,[37] passes by here and empties into the Stratford River. Waterbury is dominated by a mountain with a lovely view. Breakneck is 5 miles from Waterbury. It comprises two or three houses situated in the lowland. The whole area is hilly and covered. The roads are terrible and difficult. I found nothing of interest there, except for a very pretty young American girl who looked very much like the queen of France after a brief nap. I took the Newtown road. Two miles from Breakneck there is a large marsh. Woodbury is 7 miles further. It is a town of about 20 well-situated houses. The town is good despite being high and low and rocky. The roads are very difficult for baggage and artillery trains. Three miles beyond that, we cross the Stratford River, which has two other names, on a bridge called Carleton's Bridge. It is made of wood and sits on piers of stone. Newtown is 5 miles further and we can only arrive there by very bad roads that are very covered. The area is not bad.

Mr. De Rochambeau sought only the comfort of his troops at the different camps he took as far as Newtown. The land where we are headed, being filled with Tories and refugees and evil people, he sought to position himself more militarily. He detached the grenadiers and light infantry and brought them forward of the camps covering Newtown on a dominating hill generally the key to the area. There is a rather large marsh at the base of this mountain with very difficult and muddy banks which covered the front of the camp of the grenadiers and light infantry. It is near this marsh that I saw a superb tree called a tulip

37 Naugatuck River.

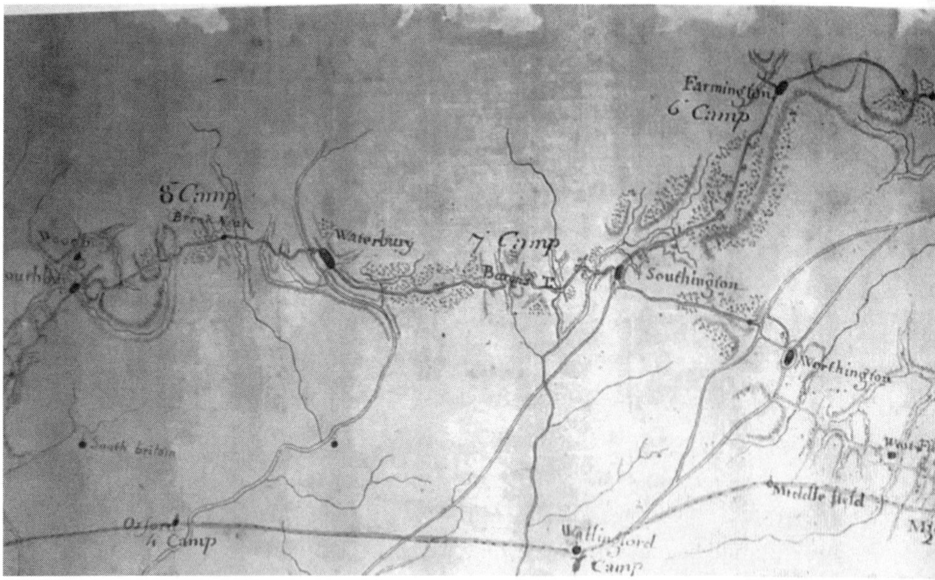

Louis de Lauberdière's drawing (facing pages) of the route of march from Windham, Connecticut, to Southbury, Connecticut, showing camps on the route to and from Yorktown, Virginia, June 21-30, 1781.

Bibliothèque Nationale

tree for the first time. Its flowers resemble so much a tulip that it was given the name. It grows very high and straight. I saw some 60 or 80 feet without a single branch.

On the 29th, the Bourbonnais division rested in camp at Newtown. That of the Deux Ponts arrived there. The grenadiers and light infantry of this division were posted in front with those of the Bourbonnais. The Soissonnais division camped at Breakneck and that of the Saintonge at Barnes's Tavern. Lauzun's Legion remained at West Stratford, 6 miles from Newtown.

On the 30th, the Bourbonnais brigade remained at the Newtown [camp]. The Soissonnais division came to join the Saintonge division and camped at Breakneck. The Legion remained at West Stratford.

General Washington had not yet left his quarters. His army was not strong and he did not want to take risks before joining with the French army. Seeing it approach, he decided to signal this junction with a cannon salute. New York was always the object of his desires. He soon adopted everything that could expedite her capture. He learned very recently that Delancey's corps of 600 refugees had departed the island of New York and set itself up at

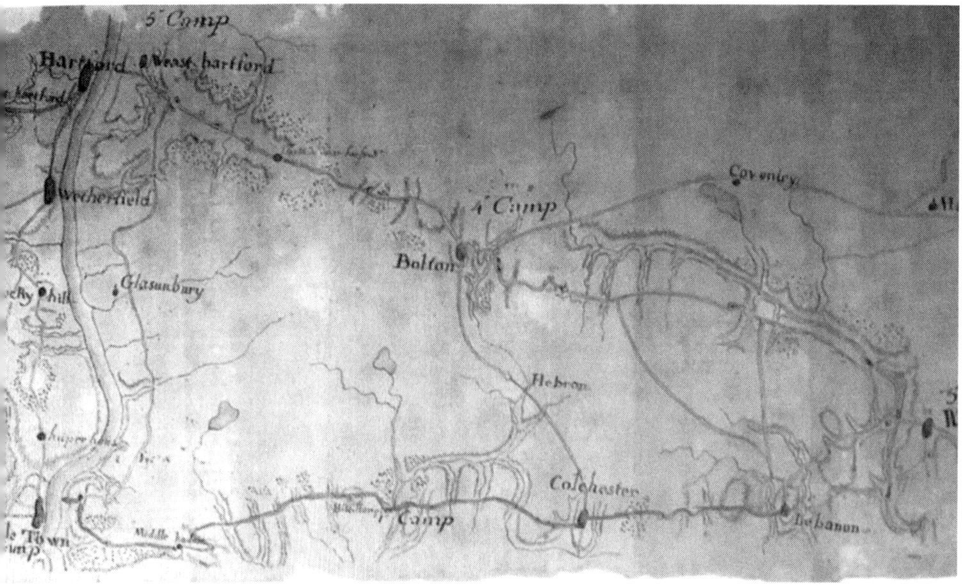

Morrisania. So he dispatched Colonel Cobb,[38] one of his aides-de-camp, to Mr. de Rochambeau to ask him to advance in a hurry toward White Plains to surprise Delancey's corps. It was the key to the island and the English land position. Mr. De Rochambeau saw many problems with this plan. His [plan] was to follow the route to Peekskill, to cross the North River[39] and to establish himself in the Jerseys which would put him at arm's length of New York if Mr. de Grasse would arrive and give him enough advance [notice] to march to Virginia and if this admiral would take a position at the Chesapeake Bay. The provisions however were secure on the Peekskill road and the resources were lacking to bring them to other places. Despite all these reasons, he wanted to prove his goodwill to General Washington. He saw that some of the obstacles could be overcome with some effort. It was already 5 p.m. He immediately gave orders to depart the following morning, dispatched an aide-de-camp to Lauzun's Legion to have it march and gave the quartermasters urgent

38 David Cobb (1748–1830), a physician was a member of the Massachusetts Provincial Congress in 1775, and Lieutenant Colonel of Jackson's regiment in 1777 and 1778. He served in RI and NJ, was General George Washington's aide-de-camp. He was appointed major general of militia in 1786. He served as a U.S. Congressman for Massachusetts's at-large congressional seat.

39 Major General Benjamin Lincoln (1732–1810) was involved in three major surrenders during the war: his participation in the Battles of Saratoga contributed to John Burgoyne's surrender of a British army. He oversaw the largest American surrender of the war at the 1780 Siege of Charleston, and, as George Washington's second in command, he formally accepted the British surrender at Yorktown.

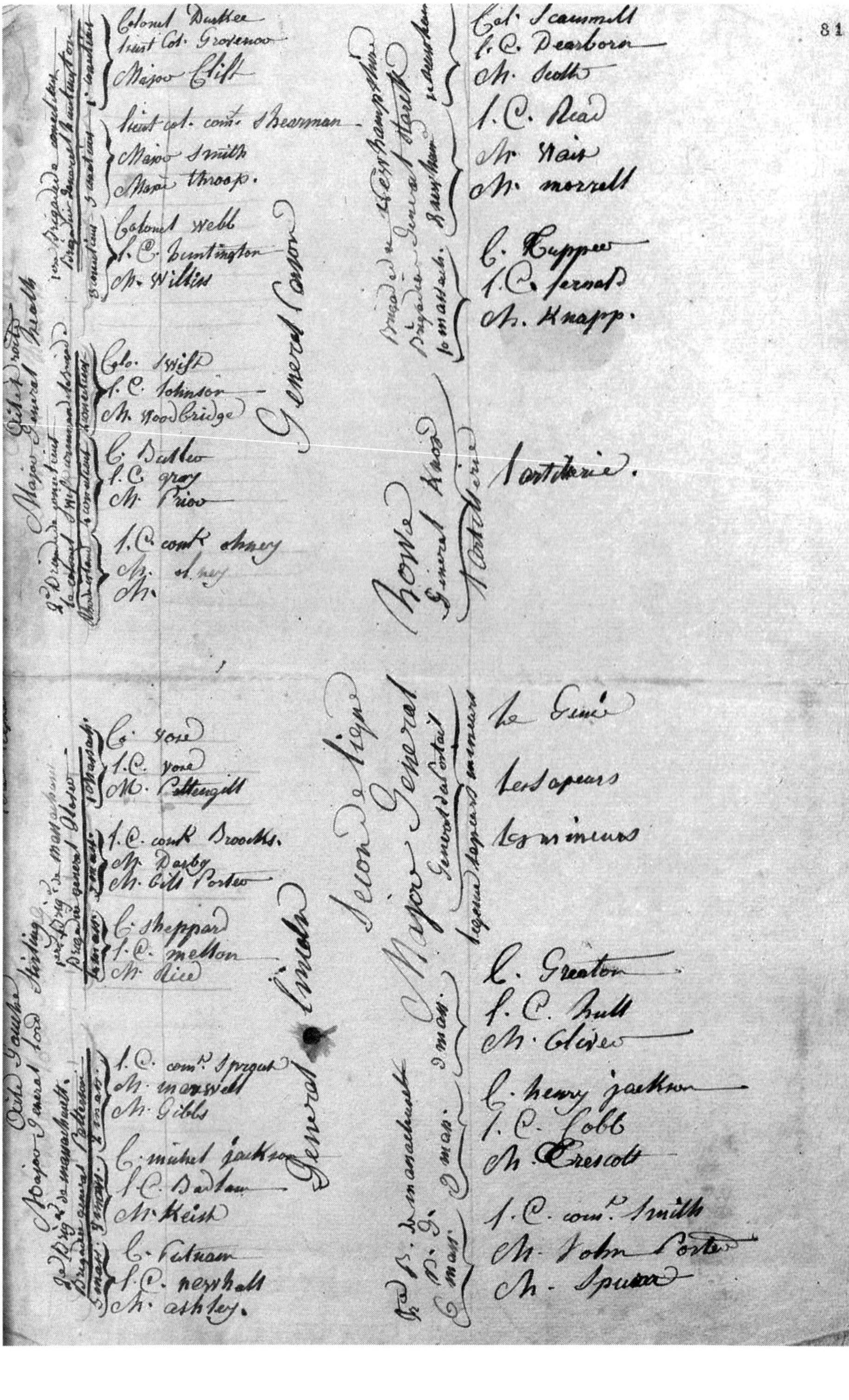

(Facing Page) A loose page found inside Louis de Lauberdière's journal that appears to be the organization of the Continental Army, as he understood it, at New York. *Bibliothèque Nationale*

orders for food. Everything we had then arrived by convoy from Hartford with great difficulty. The further away we went, this service became more difficult and needed to be more supervised. Bread rations were short but a bit more meat and cornmeal were allotted.

General Washington would personally lead a large corps to Kingsbridge to distract the enemy from General Lincoln and Lauzun's Legion and Sheldon's American dragoons camped in this region who were to march toward Morrisania.

In addition to marching in divisions, Mr. De Rochambeau had the army march by brigades to be a greater force. This order was necessarily a rest for the Saintonge division. One had to overlook this consideration because rest was almost absolutely indispensable for each division because of the extreme difficulty of the roads we took and to repair all the wagons, baggage etc.

July

Newtown is located halfway up a hill. It could contain 70 or 80 houses. Woods abound in this area.

The Bourbonnais regiment left the camp at Newtown on July 1 and camped at Ridgebury, 18 miles. Lauzun's Legion continued to form the left column and arrived at Ridgefield. The Soissonnais division camped at Newtown and that of the Saintonge left Breakneck to arrive there.

On the second, the first brigade left the camp at Ridgebury and went to Bedford, a few miles away. Lauzun's Legion entered into the right column and also came to Bedford, 17 miles. The Soissonnais division and that of the Saintonge, which did not camp at Newtown, formed the second brigade and came to camp at Ridgebury.

The Duc de Lauzun only refreshed his cavalry and rested his infantry at Bedford. He received his latest instructions and departed with Colonel Sheldon under his command to go to Morrisania. Brigadier General Waterbury,[40] who commanded the militia in this area, was supposed to support him. They found themselves very close to Kingsbridge at 3 a.m.

General Washington, on the other hand, made his move. Lincoln had embarked and descended the North or Hudson River to then land on New York Island, near Fort Washington. All the plans were thwarted. A British frigate stationed off the northern end of the island prevented General Lincoln from passing, forcing him to land his men. Mr.

40 Hudson River.

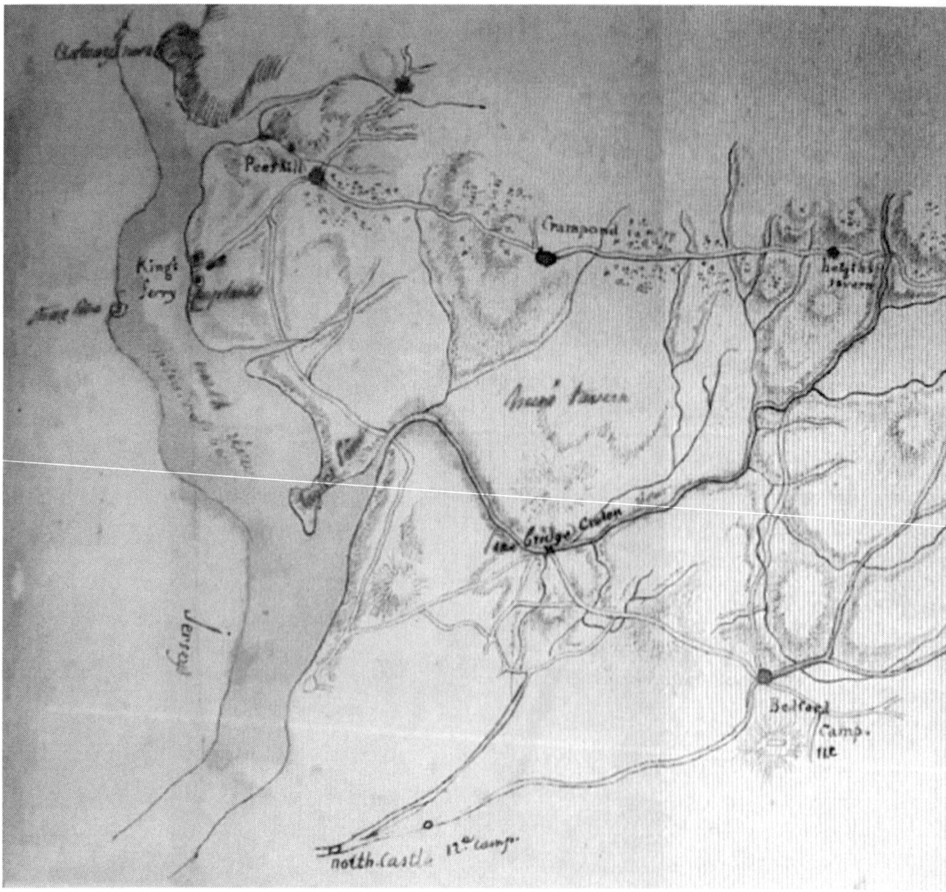

Louis de Lauberdière's drawing (facing pages) of the route of march from North Stratford, Connecticut, to Peekskill, New York, June 29 – August 24, 1781.

Bibliothèque Nationale

Washington did not abandon his plan. He marched his men toward Kingsbridge by land but he was not any more fortunate in this place.

As luck would have it, eight to 900 enemy troops came out at 3 a.m. to forage. They discovered General Lincoln and immediately received help. They fought and killed many Americans who, through Lincoln's fault, made a feint. General Washington, who had the rest of the troops advance a few miles from there, retired and went to camp at White Plains, 3 miles from Dobbs ferry. The Duc de Lauzun could do nothing and was forced to follow the Americans' movements. He also retired and camped 4 miles from General Washington on the left bank of the Bronx River, after having made his legion travel more than 40 miles without eating or drinking.

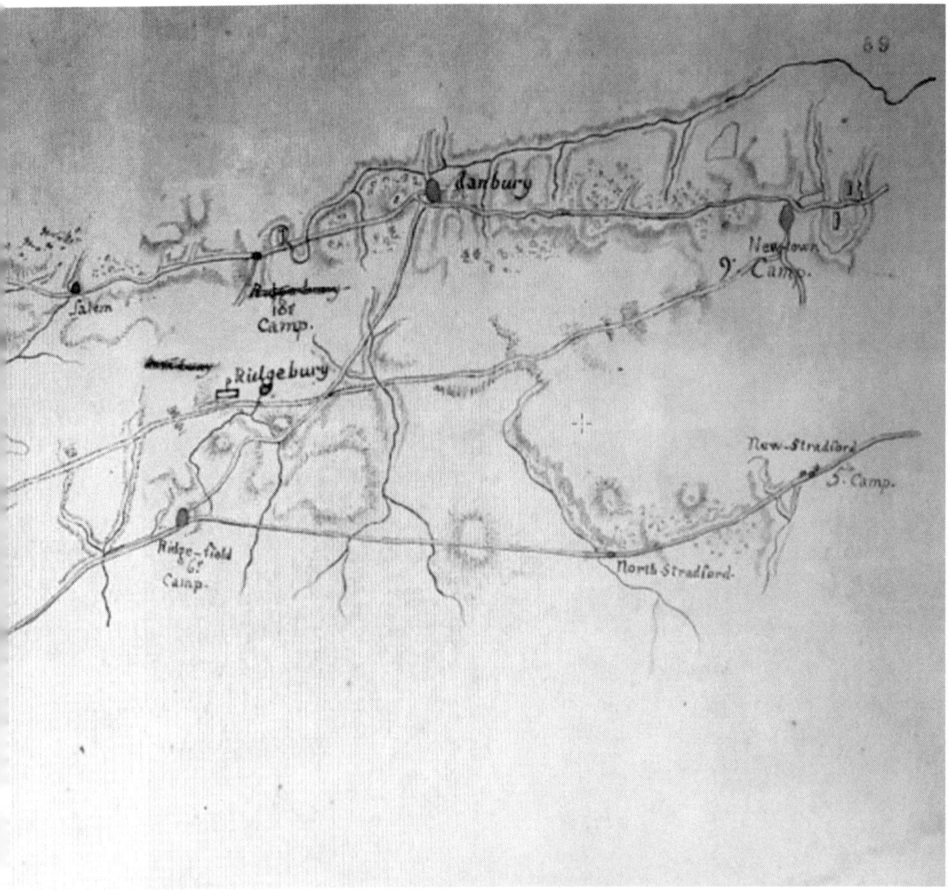

Mr. De Rochambeau also made a movement. He camped at North Castle on the third, 5 miles from the camp at Bedford. The second division departed Ridgebury and also camped at North Castle, 23 miles. The position which our general took was very strong and became even more so by the one which he had the grenadiers and light infantry occupy in front of the camp.

North Castle is only four or five houses located near a rather long marsh. It is not natural and the water remains there only by dikes which are placed against it. All this region which is part of the state of New York much resembles all of Connecticut. In other words, it is very full, covered and hilly. There is much forage, but, despite that, large armies would find it difficult to survive. Surprises should not be common nor easy, as it is almost impossible to travel anywhere except along well-traveled roads which are easy to guard. The long and ruinous English neighborhood entirely demolished this region. The Tory refugees are in such great numbers that the inhabitants never go out unless armed. Those who decide to stay at home are pillaged and robbed by both friend and foe. Also, almost all the houses are abandoned. In the others, there are only miserable women.

The fourth and the fifth, the army did not move. They repaired the damage of a long and arduous march. General Washington came to camp on the fifth. We honored him. He agreed with our general that the army would march the following day toward Phillipsburg, where the Americans were camped, to effect our junction with them.

Arrival at Phillipsburg

The morning of the sixth, the army broke camp at North Castle to go to Phillipsburg, 20 miles. We marched in one column. This day was trying for the troops because of its length and the extreme heat. A few miles from his camp, General Washington sent some staff officers of his army to our general to lead him through a very difficult region. However, we arrived. General Washington's demonstration of joy upon seeing us join him was very moving. His army was camped at the White Plains. I think the name comes from the color of the flowers that cover the soil throughout the fine season. The Americans occupied a very strong position which General Washington and Mr. de Rochambeau came to inspect for us to camp on the left. All this region, despite being called White Plains, consists of groves of wood, ravines and hills. Mr. de Rochambeau placed himself on an impregnable one. Our left extended toward the road to New York on which we took good posts which were entrenched. The summit which the camp occupied absolutely commanded the whole region. Our front was cut by deep ravines with unique difficulties. Our right was against a creek or brook on which we established communications between both camps.

The same day, Lauzun's Legion left the position which it occupied after its march toward Morrisania and came to camp on the left flank of the French camp two miles on a hill called Chatterton Hill with the Bronx River in front and on the left.

It is in this very position that General Washington, abandoned by part of his army, was attacked by General Howe with an army twice the size of his on October 28, 1776. Mr. Washington contested the battlefield for some time before he was finally obliged to yield to greater numbers. He crossed the Bronx in haste and retreated. This battle is called the battle of White Plains.

The various positions which were reconnoitered and the length of the march prevented the troops from camping early. When they had all arrived, Mister Washington, who had his army take up arms proposed to Mr. de Rochambeau to go see it which he accepted. Lethargy still prevailed in the other states. Despite the resolutions of Congress of the preceding year, the army which should be at least 26,000 men consisted of a corps of 4000 infantrymen at most. We found them in battle in front of their camp. A glance gave me great pleasure not because of the appearance and uniform of the regiments, for, at present and since the beginning of the war, they are practically all naked. But I remembered their great accomplishments and I could only see, with a certain admiration, that it was with these same men that General Washington so gloriously defended his country. The officers were in the uniform which their regiments were supposed to wear. They are armed and salute with the espontoon.

The corps of sappers and miners seemed very fine. It is not part of the artillery; it is under the command of the officers of the Corps of Engineers. The latter corps does not yet have a single American. It is entirely composed of French engineers, some of whom were sent with the King's approval, the others came voluntarily to offer their services.

The regiments which should be of 600 men barely had 250. They lacked many officers who had not yet rejoined even though the army had left its quarters and was on the march. Marriage is a state in America. Even bachelors enjoy little respect. Almost all the officers in the army are married and they often ask permission to return home regardless of what the army or their particular regiment is doing. They do not return until their leave is finished. In that regard, they differ greatly from our officers and even our soldiers who would not do likewise under similar circumstances. Love and pleasure created the spirit of patriotism and duty among them until now. I have seen several who, knowing very well that their regiment was marching, rejoined it at the expiration of their leave. But stopped three or four days wherever they enjoyed themselves at their friends or acquaintances. In general, our allies are lazy and they don't like to be inconvenienced.

After the review, we were at headquarters. I did not have a very good idea. At the time of the order it is always very numerous and all the general officers arrive promptly. There is always a table set up on which there are some glasses and several bottles of either wine or rum. . . . to refresh anyone who has need and which are always found in great number among the Americans. Their custom, upon meeting, is to extend the right hand and to shake it. I have several times admired General Washington's patience and goodness who has the kindness to give it thus each day to 80 or 100 people who come to see him. It is the true, such is the state of the Republic where everyone has a voice. Those in office have to agree with the majority.

Everything about General Washington bears a particular character. It is easy to recognize his aides-de-camp and the officers who see him most frequently by their tone and their deportment. His aides-de-camp have the rank of major. They always number six, in addition to a secretary who is an officer—great and wonderful tents always stretched at his quarters, eight baggage wagons lined up alongside, a battalion of foot guards and a company of 60 dragoon guards never leave him and are always camped near his tent. Very fine horses at his picket remove every semblance of pettiness and meanness from Mr. Washington's headquarters. There is no pomp of a marshal of France when orders are given but rather all the grandeur, nobility and, at the same time, the simplicity due to a general of a poor republic.

The Americans are camped in the English manner in two parallel rows of tents. Under arms, they are in two [ranks] by height. In good weather, they put their muskets in front of their tents on a wooden stand and they bring them in during the night or when it rains. This custom is subject to many inconveniences.

The entire country from Providence to the North River differs very little. In other words, it is very wooded, full of hills, boulders and ravines. It abounds in pastures and cattle, especially Connecticut which provides the finest. The inhabitants are fairly brave and good soldiers. Patience is one of their virtues. All those who live along the seashore are not very supportive of the American cause because they fear the neighboring English and the refugees of Long Island. The militias of the four northern states are the best in America as they have always demonstrated. The inhabitants are more industrious than those in the South even though they work very little.

Philipsburgh is located 17 miles from New York and three from the North River. This region draws its name from Mr. Phillips, a rich landowner, now at New York. There are only a few sparse houses on this land which is excellent. This fertile land is almost a wasteland today due to the lack of hands. The ravages of war and the looting of the refugees are the cause of these disasters. There are many pastures. The country is extremely covered and difficult. All the valleys are abundant.

For some time, we drew our provisions partly from the north of the state of New York and partly from Connecticut. The rapidity of our marches demanded the most active and the most vigilant care on the part of the administration. Hartford still served as the storehouse but, as the convoys arrived only with great difficulty from a distance of 115 miles, we soon established new ovens at Tariton,[41] 6 miles from camp. The administration selected this site on the North River in order to receive flour by water. Mr. de Rochambeau disapproved of this plan because he thought the enemy, masters of the river, would pay attention to a settlement whose destruction could only harm us much, as we were already short of provisions, and bring them a sort of satisfaction. In addition, he would have to force the quartermasters to imitate the Americans who promptly construct ovens with stones, never bricks, everywhere they camp.

On the eighth, General Washington passed the allied army in review. He began with the Americans which gave us great pleasure to see. There are some very handsome men in

41 General David Waterbury (1722–1801) served as a Brigadier. General in the CT militia and was assigned to the northern department. He was captured at Valcour Island and remained a prisoner for four years. After his release in October 1780, he commanded a brigade in General Washington's main Army in the summer of 1781, becoming part of the Yorktown campaign.

all their regiments. We also see Negroes and mulattos. They are in the ranks by seniority. This method presents a very bad impression and harms the fine appearance of a troop because it occurs frequently—a tall man between two short ones, a short one between two tall ones—The regiments of Massachusetts Bay and Connecticut seemed the finest to me.

From the Americans, the general passed to the French. We had only one day to repair the damage of the march. Even so, the troops appeared in the finest dress. Mr. de Rochambeau positioned himself in front of the white flag of his senior regiment and saluted General Washington. Almost all the officers of his army, having dismissed their troops, accompanied him. Our general received his highest compliments on the appearance of his troops. It is true that, without any choice, on our departure from France, all those we had were superb. It is also very different to see troops well-aligned, well-dressed and of equal height and to see others which don't have any of these advantages.

Mr. de Choisy still remained at Newport with Mr. de Barras's[42] fleet. Tired of the inactivity of his detachment, he requested some information about the coast of Long Island, hoping to make an attack there. At the very end of little Huntington Bay is Fort Lloyd about which he received some apparently attractive but false information. He had 300 men, half French and half American, board at Newport to go take and destroy it. He put the detatchment under the command of Baron d'Angely, in the French service but who had no commission in the army. He came to America as an aide-de-camp to the Baron de Vioméenil. Baron d'Angely left on the 12th with a frigate and some transports and arrived in front of Fort Lloyd the same day. He landed without opposition, but he found some in the fort which was better garrisoned than we thought. Either because the attacks were poorly conducted and led or because other causes moved the moons[?] further away, he could not take hold on the island or he would soon have lacked provisions. He would also have had to fight reinforcements. His expedition was only a raid where much strength was needed. He therefore re-embarked and returned to Newport with as much glory as when he left.

Everything between the armies at the Phillipsburg camp passed without anything remarkable. Our untiring general spent every day on horseback to study and know the area perfectly. He often visited his posts and was, in this way, assured of the regularity and punctuality of service. He set the example to maintain communication between the two armies. Every day, he invited several American officers to his table. General Washington also had several French. Mr. de Rochambeau went precisely at the time of orders to receive them from Mister Washington. This great man sought, on every point, by his extreme

42 Tarrytown.

kindness and foresight, to diminish what passive obedience might disgust an old general. He consulted him often and had come from so far to put himself at his command.— As for all the other officers of the army, he was governed by the court. The American would always have the command over the French as to rank and seniority.

Tarrytown

On the 15th, reconnoitering Tarrytown on the banks of the North River, we saw a British frigate heading up river. We could not yet determine her intention. The settlements at Tarrytown attracted the enemy's curiosity as Mr. de Rochambeau predicted to his quartermasters. The frigate approached Tarrytown about 10 p.m. to land some men. They planned to destroy, pillage and burn but they were impeded by the conduct and the bravery of a sergeant and a guard of the Soissonnais Regiment. With a handful of men, they put up such a fire on the enemy boats that they kept their distance far enough from land that nobody could land. The night was very dark and the camp could hear the cannon and musket fire perfectly, because the wind carried the noise and the echo of the mountains repeated it. These two causes made it difficult to determine the distance and the location and we believed we were being attacked.

Consequently, the Marquis de Laval, colonel of the Bourbonnais Regiment, who was the most senior officer in camp at this time, had the general beat without any orders whatsoever. It was agreed that the artillery would fire two cannon shots in case of alarm. At the beating of the general, the artillery fired and effectively alarmed everybody. It was then about 11:30 at night. Mr. de Rochambeau was in bed. The intelligence that there were some vessels in the river made him guess what it might be and did not draw his attention. The general woke him to go bring order. He quickly went to the camp where he found everybody under arms and he had everybody return promptly.

Beating the general is a frightening thing at night. Those who don't know what is happening almost always experience confusion, disorder and fright. Darkness seems to increase the danger, if there is any, and decreases thought when the alarm surprises us, so to speak, into jumping make me think that it requires great prudence to put one's men under arms at night by means of the general. It requires however that we be warned in enough time but the activity of the leaders, the aides-de-camp promptly sent everywhere with orders can reenforce the sound of the alarm and establish more confidence. We have several examples in the war of 1757, Clostercamp, among others, where we were almost surprised and where the enemy was defeated.

The Marquis de Laval certainly merited the strongest reprimand for acting without orders.

General Washington immediately sent some artillery to Tarrytown, but under a false alarm that the enemy had destroyed and burned it, he had it return.

An American galley left Tarrytown to go down as far as Dobbs Ferry which is 3 miles from Phillipsburg, blundered among the enemy vessels and was taken. She was loaded with some uniforms for the American dragoons of [unintelligible] and 10,000 rations of bread for the French army. This blow affects us a bit. We only live day to day and the soldier's ration of bread had to be reduced, an unfortunate necessity which was blunted a bit by giving him more meat.

Both sides had a few men killed at Tarrytown. The Americans regretted very much the loss of one of their officers who lived near this place and brought several men. He dove in the water in front of the enemy boats and was mortally wounded.

The morning of the 16th, Mr. de Rochambeau sent 4 12-pounders to Tarrytown under the command of the Chevalier de Neurisse.[43] They were in the battery by 10 o'clock and fired on the frigate which was sailing away.

The 17th, we constructed another battery as close as possible to her last anchorage. Our gunners fired a dozen balls at her. She moved above Tarrytown and anchored at Haverstraw Bay. We should not be surprised to see a frigate cruising like this in a river. It is thus in America with almost all those that empty into the ocean. The North or Hudson, often three quarters of a league wide, is very deep everywhere so a vessel of 50 guns can sail it as far as Albany.

Haverstraw Bay

The 18th, the enemy landed some men near Haverstraw Bay. Without doing any more havoc, they pillaged and burned some fine houses in their usual manner and then re-boarded.

Mr. Washington, who always had an expedition against New York in mind and would have good reason to do so if it were within our means, had already proposed to Mr. de Rochambeau to reconnoiter it. As the departure of the enemy frigate left the crossing of Dobbs Ferry free, they crossed the river on the 19th accompanied by only two engineers. They followed the right bank of the Hudson River all the way to Paulus Hook located on the seashore. Passing by old Fort Lee, they noted that the British occupied five or six camps on York Island with about two battalions each which were generally fairly well situated.

43 Baron François Marie d'Angely (1735–1808), served as aide-de-camp to Antoine- Charles du Houx, baron de Vioménil, in Rochambeau's army. He emigrated in 1791 and undertook a spy mission in 1793 for William V of Orange-Nassau.

They saw the different forts very well. They noticed that they [the British] recently moved a lot of earth, apparently because of our junction with the Americans. They also took intelligence of the coast and the landing sites. They re-crossed the North River the same day and returned to headquarters.

Mr. Hartmann,[44] Lieutenant of hussars in Lauzun's Legion, went on patrol the night of the 19th to the 20th and encountered a patrol of Delancey's refugees. He advanced to recognize them and was killed by gunshot. He mounted a very fine horse. This animal, frightened by the gunshot and the fall of its master returned very quickly, fleet of foot, and arrived at Lauzun's advanced post. The night was very dark. The sentinel cried out but nobody could respond. The poor animal was fired upon and struck by two balls which killed it.

The 20th, the British frigate which came up to Haverstraw Bay went downriver. Mr. Washington, when making camp, foresaw what the enemy might do. He had a fort constructed at Dobbs Ferry where he placed several cannons. The river being more narrow at this location, it provided a good field to fire to advantage. Mr. de Rochambeau consequently had mortars brought over, under the command of Mr. de Verton.[45] Lieutenant of Artillery and the pieces of the Chevalier de Neurisse which had already fired on her. The frigate was perfectly saluted as she passed. She was at good cannon range. The mortars ignited her twice. The frightened crew immediately released their prisoners. The unfortunate ones, profiting from the confusion on the vessel, dove into the water and swam to shore but only two of about 20 were fortunate enough to attain it and to give us these details.

The entire and perfect reconnaissance of York Island was interesting whether we wanted to attack the beach or whether it served to provide a change for the enemy or to make them constantly fear whether we would attack elsewhere. Our generals had voluntarily undertaken it right from the first days of the junction of the two armies but it is good to remark, in passing, that any man who commands is often mastered by the circumstances. I have already observed this several times. The public is always ready to blame rather than to praise and it often condemns a soldier's conduct or his actions often without any consideration or understanding of the facts or its causes. In his place, he would have always marched, done everything, attempted everything. That's what we often hear and which few people contradict. Yet there exists a more pressing need before which everything gives way and which frustrates the plans of a general. Wherever he goes, he must assure provisions. The need to eat is a daily need.

44 Bernard de Neurisse (1736–) was a artillery officer in the Auxonne Regiment.

45 Jacques Hartman (ca. 1745–1781) served as a sublieutenant in Lauzun's Legion.

Since our arrival at the camp at Phillipsburg our provisions were so short that, with all the effort imaginable, we could not succeed in putting more than a daily ration of bread in the soldiers' pack. The rapidity of our marches rendered service very difficult and it became even more so by the difficulty of gathering the resources of the land. However, on the 17th, we reached the desired location and orders were issued for a night march. About 5 p.m., such detestable weather arose, such abundant rain, that it was realized we could do nothing and everything in camp was countermanded.

Three thousand French and 2000 Americans received orders to keep themselves ready to march on the night of the 21st. The French detachment was under the command of the Chevalier de Chastellux and was composed of the Bourbonnais brigade, the battalion of grenadiers and light infantry of the Soissonnais brigade commanded by Mr. De Charlus,[46] of Lauzun's Legion and a division of artillery. The retreat served as the general and the troops marched immediately afterward. The 2000 Americans formed the right, the brigade of the Bourbonnais the center, Lauzun's Legion and the battalion of grenadiers and light infantry of the Soissonnais and the Saintonge the left. General Washington and Mr. de Rochambeau put themselves at the head of all. We had 17 miles to travel to arrive off York Island. Our march was necessarily slow during a fine but dark night across woods and barely blazed roads. Absolute silence reigned everywhere. About midnight, the right and center columns joined at Valentine's Hill to form a single column. We still had 4 miles to march. The troops resumed the march for, although we neither wanted to surprise nor attack, we wanted to arrive early and to seize an advance position not in the open.

We arrived at Kingsbridge at daybreak on the 22nd without the enemy having any awareness of our movement. Nobody had any idea that we wanted to capture a fort called number eight on this side of Harlem Creek and the Kingsbridge redoubt on the island. We would not have found any resistance nor lost any casualties as they were both weakly defended. However, we had no expectation of taking, at the risk of the lives of a few men, that which we should not nor want to guard. Our generals only wanted [illegible] to capture a good position and to mount their posts.

46 Jacques Philippe de Verton (1756–ca. 1820) volunteered in the Auxonne artillery regiment in 1772. He was promoted to lieutenant in 1777 and came to America with Rochambeau's army. He was wounded Yorktown and promoted to captain in 1787. He emigrated in 1792 and took part in the Quiberon expedition. He retired to Eu as Battalion Chief under the Restoration. He made frequent fruitless requests to be promoted but was made a Baron instead in 1820. While his exact date of death is unknown, it is likely ca. 1820, when his voluminous correspondence suddenly ceased.

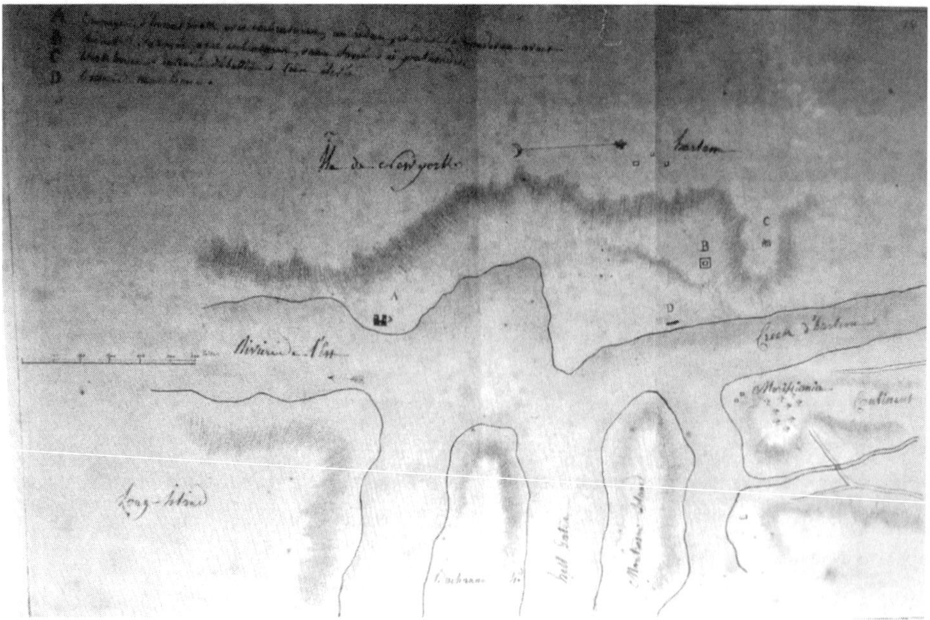

Louis de Lauberdière's drawing of Morrisania and part of Long Island, July 6, 1781.

Bibliothèque Nationale

Morrisania

A mile from York Island, the Duc de Lauzun and his Legion took the road to Morrisania, hoping to surprise Delancey's corps of refugees who were quartered there. But this band of bandits fled into the woods at their approach and boarded some longboats which took them to York Island or Two Brothers.[47] However some of them who stayed behind were taken prisoners.

From Fort Independence, built by the Americans in 1776 when they were still masters of New York, we can still see very well the most advanced works of this island which it dominates. It is there that the generals and engineers directed their reconnaissance after they crossed a muddy creek to turn and see these same works in reverse.

47 Armand-Charles-Augustin Le comte de Castries de Charlus (1756–1842) served as colonel en second of the Saintonge Regiment in 1780. He was quartermaster general of the cavalry in 1784, camp marshal and inspector of cavalry in 1788. He emigrated at the end of 1790 and served in the army of the Princes in 1792. At the end of the year, he raised a regiment in his own name, at the expense of England, which served in Portugal in 1797. He resided in England until 1814 when he was made a Peer of France and given the rank of a Lieutenant General. He was employed until the end of 1818.

As groups of people always draw cannon and musket fire very unnecessarily, our generals ordered their aides-de-camp to leave them alone.

Our arrival soon gave the alarm to New York and we soon saw General Clinton appear. Despite being twice as strong as us, he continued to demonstrate that he was more afraid of being attacked than we had the means or the desire to do so. He promptly had men cross over to this side of Harlem Creek and a few dragoons who scattered themselves, firing at everything they saw move. The Chevaliers de Damas and de Vauban[48] wanted to burn a charge with them, as much as I, aide-de-camp to Mr. de Rochambeau, wanted to charge them. We were only three and we had the satisfaction of making five or six flee several times. We fired our pistols at them several times but without success. That gave us the idea of charging them with saber in hand if we could overtake them. We engaged them a little before and we were routed by other British dragoons from whose hands the legs of our horses saved us. Fortunately for us, because none of us was at our post and, if we were captured or wounded, we would have been told «too bad for you. What were you doing there?» We rejoined our general whom we found driven in a coach near Fort Independence with his spyglass in hand.

Passing out of range of Fort number eight and following the bank of Harlem Creek, our generals advanced from the side of Morrisania, the southernmost part of the continent opposite York Island. There are few works in this area; there is no landing site on the island whose shores are sloped and more elevated than on the continent. Morrisania was even more interesting to explore than the rest. While we were no less than 2 miles away from the neighborhood of the refugees that the Duc de Lauzun swept in the morning, we saw two large boats which crossed to York Island upon our approach.

A certain number who still could not find place on the barges remained on shore. General Washington had his dragoon escort with him whom he ordered to run between the Chevalier de Damas, the Baron de Closen, the Count de Vauban, Mr. Berthier, a staff officer, Mr. Mullins, captain of the army guides, and me to request Mr. de Rochambeau to join the American dragoons which he granted to us. We soon caught the refugees. They were all taken, killed or wounded. Harlem Creek is very narrow in this location. There was a battery on the opposite shore, at Mr. Morris's house, which we had not seen before and which made a lively fire on us along with the refugees who had just landed. But as we were a small number, separated and running after them, none of us was harmed. Only the Chevalier de Damas had his horse killed under him. This volley was warmer than our generals expected and compelled them to have the head of a column, which marched

48 A pair of small islands located in New York City's East River, at the eastern entrance to Hell's Gate, between the Bronx and Rikers Island.

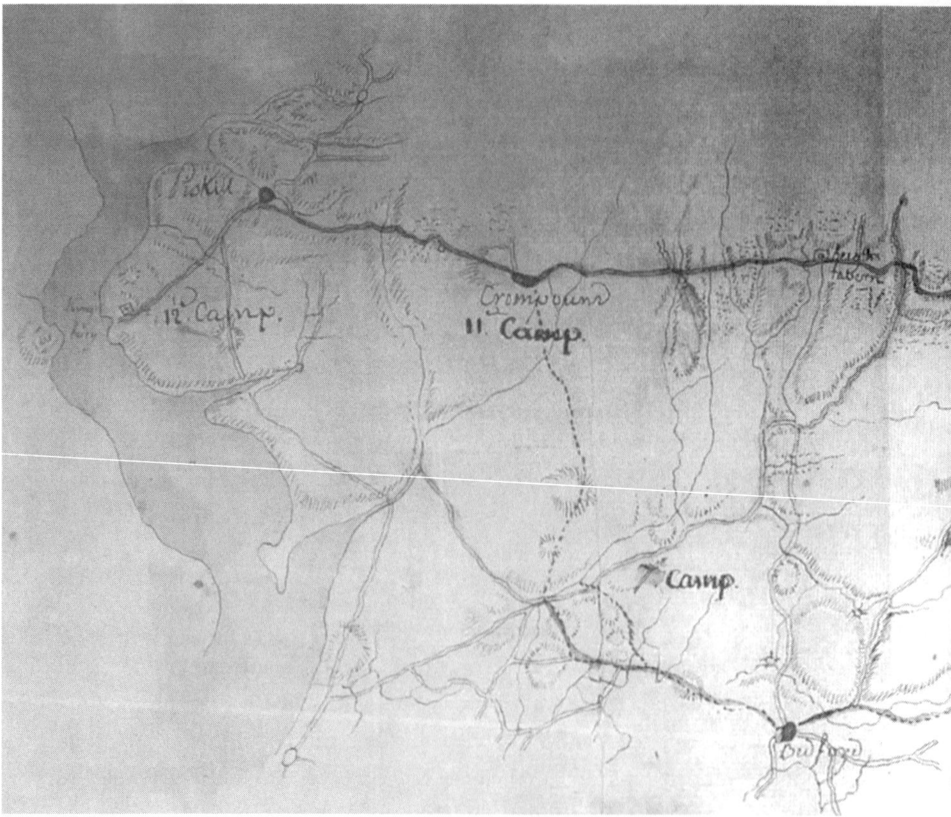

Louis de Lauberdière's drawing (facing pages) of Frog's (Throg's) Point (lower right on next page) and part of Long Island, New York, July 23, 1781.

Bibliothèque Nationale

alongside them, advance to draw the enemy's attention and share their fire which continued for some time but without success.

After this little expedition, we released our prisoners to the Americans and we retook the road to camp which was 10 miles away. We arrived at 8:30 p.m. and we were very happy to find a frugal meal under an apple tree. We did not leave any scraps. Our general had us on horseback for 25 hours without letting our cook get down, so to speak. We had an appetite. Everyone had marched without baggage. The troops slept in bivouac.

On the 23rd, we remounted the horses early to complete the reconnaissance of York Island located the mouth of the North River which separates it from the continent. The west bank also separates into two branches and forms Staten Island or the Island of States which by its great proximity to that of York in fact where a part of the defense is along the land and sea sides. The east bank is called Harlem Creek. It empties into an arm of the sea

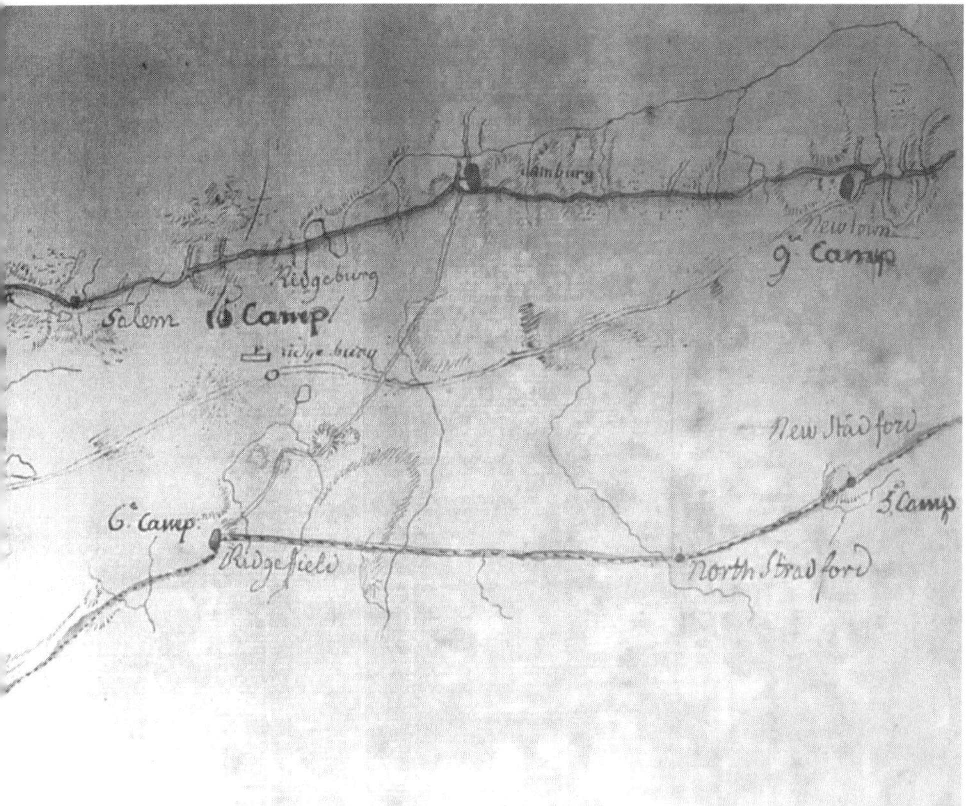

called the Sound which separates the island of York and that of Long Island a short cannon range apart. The tip of the latter is where the enemy constructed very good defensive works. Whether we come from the interior of the island or from the sea, it entirely commands New York. It is therefore clear that to successfully attack this place, one would have to be master of the works on Long Island, force the pass and get within cannon range of the city which is even more difficult for warships. At the entrance to the harbor, there is a bar that they cannot cross easily. The risk of this passage increases considerably more when it must be undertaken under fire from the land batteries. It would also require a fleet which is absolute master of the sea. All these obstacles, all these considerations should have rendered the idea of a siege foreign to the Americans and their commander who was certainly aware that the enemies were all English, Hessians and refugees who could put 16,000 men under arms while we could only turn out 8 or 9000.

In spite of all this, the reconnaissance could be useful if only to serve as a diversion. It was done in detail and it is with this in mind that our generals went toward Frog's Neck from whence we can see Long Island perfectly. We passed by Westchester on the morning of the 23rd. It is a small town which has only one road. It is located in a fine country, very

Louis de Lauberdière's drawing of the northern part of
New York island (Manhattan), July 21, 1781.

Bibliothèque Nationale

level and pleasant, three miles from the Sound. We crossed a small section of the sea dry shod. We arrived at Frog's Neck on the other side. The whole coast of Long Island on the opposite shore from this spit of land is raised and the width of the Sound at this point, about 500 toises.[49]

49 Jacques Anne Joseph le Prestre, Comte de Vauban (1754–1816), served as one of Rochambeau's aides-de-camp and was sent back to France with the general's dispatches in 1782. He was promoted to colonel and second in command of the régiment d'Agenoris. On June 13, 1784, the duc d'Orléans, whose chamberlain he was, made him Col. in command of the régiment d'infanterie that took his name and knight of the order of Saint-Louis. He emigrated to Varennes, going to Ath, then Koblenz, where the comte d'Artois made him his aide-de-camp. He then went to England and joined the Quiberon expedition in spring 1795. He was arrested in 1806 and held prisoner for an extended period.

We were cannonaded a long time by guard vessels stationed on this coast and which fortunately caused us no fear and no harm. We then took the road to Westchester. The little arm of the sea which we crossed on a ford at low tide was filled with water and blocked the passage. A small bark was fortunately found nearby. It served to cross the men. About 100 of our horses swam across. Several American dragoons even dared to cross with their horses. No accident occurred. The Morrisania side was poorly reconnoitered the previous evening. Our generals applied themselves again. The vessel which fired on us the previous day again gave us heavy fire, fortunately with no greater success. We also took a few more prisoners. Our generals then returned to camp, recalled all their piquets and countermarched to return to Phillipsburg. Mr. Washington left Colonel Scammel of the light infantry for the rearguard.[50] The British did not detach a single man to pursue us. Our march was quick and everyone returned to camp by 11 p.m. We did not lose a single man in this reconnaissance.

Defenses of York Island

I already spoke of the state and of the defense of the south of York Island. I only have two words to say about what we observed at the north of this island.

The northernmost post is a quasi-redoubt which can contain 60 or 80 men and which has two embrasures directed toward Kingsbridge which is half musket range distant.

Behind this redoubt, on a very steep hill or boulder on the North River is Cox Hill Fort near which the enemy constantly maintain a frigate on guard to observe everything that could come down the river or enter Harlem Creek whose banks are muddy. The officer on guard at this fort was a Hessian who recognized our generals and who did not want to have them fired upon when they approached to recognize him.

Fort Tryon is located south of Cox Hill on the west bank of the river. Fort Laurel Hill is constructed on the east and about the same height. These two forts command a gorge which must certainly be crossed to penetrate the island. This gorge is further closed by a line of redans, batteries and abatis behind which the communication between Forts Tryon and Laurel Hill is assured.[51] Continuing to the south is a height absolutely commanding all

50 Colonel Alexander Scammel (1742–1781) served as a Continental officer from MA under Gen. John Sullivan. He succeeded Timothy Pickering as Washington's adjutant general on Jan. 5, 1778. He was wounded near Yorktown on September 30, 1781 and died a few days later (Oct. 6) in Williamsburg, Virginia. As a colonel, he was the highest-ranking American officer killed during the Siege of Yorktown.

51 Abatis, or sharpened branches, were usually placed outside fortifications pointing toward the enemy and were intended to slow or disrupt an assault.

of the works I just talked about, on which the Americans raised a fort in 1776 which they named Fort Washington. The British did not neglect this important work. It is always well-garrisoned and supplied with cannons. The map will give a better understanding of the strength of this position which is not easy to capture because there are very few landing sites. In addition to these fortifications, New York is surrounded by earthworks.

The only real way to capture this place is to have a navy master of the sea and to attempt to capture it from Long Island with an army on land. The tip of this island, which faces New York, commands the city which would not be tenable without Long Island. But in addition to the suitability of this position, the enemy continue to surround it with earthworks. It is even said that, since our junction with the American army, they want to separate the tip of Long Island from the rest of the island by a canal which would extend from the Sound to the ocean.

The American troops marched in good order and silence for this reconnaissance. This was the first time that I saw them under arms. I found them quicker than our troops. It is true that it was very hot. Our soldiers were loaded and dressed very warmly for the summer. The Americans, on the contrary, only have a type of shirt or camisole and long pants.[52] Their misery is at such a point that three quarters of them have no shoes. Their provisions embarrass them little. We actually give them a bit of cornmeal which each soldier uses to make his own bread. Each man is also furnished with a small woolen blanket which he takes with him everywhere. This method is good in a country where the cool evenings rapidly follow burning heat. The haversack of the American soldier, not being full, provides a light assistance which we could not give our troops for fear of increasing an already heavy load.

The dragoons of General Washington's guard are finely mounted. During the reconnaissance, they were divided into small troops which greatly cleared the march of our generals. They jump over hedges, barriers and ditches. Their weapons consist of a pair of good pistols and a long straight saber which they always have in hand. This gives them great facility of movement. They wear a cap of boiled leather furnished with a little chain and covered with black bear skin. At a glance, they are very military. They have no other clothing than a jacket.

The reconnaissance of the 22nd completed, under enemy cannon fire with all the attention we could devote, promptly drilled the [unintelligible] and the politics of the largest number of our warriors. The thickest veil still covered the eyes of everyone, which was the purpose of our operations. The arrival of Mr. de Grasse in our waters, the place where he was supposed to arrive, could only lead to one conclusion. The New York newspaperman,

52 Long pants, or overalls.

Mr. Rivington,[53] a witty man, but paid by the British government to create the news, inserted in his pages an article with emphases where he spoke of our large post off New York and of our retreat accomplished with all imaginable haste. General Clinton meanwhile was not so easily convinced that we only knew how to flee. He wrote, without delay, to Lord Cornwallis in Virginia, enjoining him to send part of his troops to New York because he feared being attacked during the campaign. Three thousand recruits which he received from Europe about the same time did not quell his fears or prevent him from repeating his orders to Lord Cornwallis.

The latter, who commanded 8 or 9000 men in Virginia, had no other enemy to fear or to fight than the Marquis de la Fayette who was at the head of 2500 and a few militiamen. He was 24 years old, loved, respected, even by his enemies, full of experience beyond his years, and successfully played the role of another Fabius.[54] He had sustained several small combats with honor, not wanting to engage in general actions. All his enemy's maneuvers however only attracted him in order to destroy him in a single blow. Feeling his inferiority, the latter retreated on purpose and in good order, gained time, covered as best he could what he wanted to defend, harassing, ceaselessly annoying his enemy and refusing to let himself be trapped.

The British government had conceived the most flattering hopes of this campaign. Her generals nursed the hope of defeat and total surrender of the southern states. It was essential that the Royal Navy have a safe place of refuge in this region. A very formal order was given to select it. Portsmouth seemed worthy of attention to Arnold. Its position at the entrance to the bay and on the Elizabeth River convinced him to strengthen his position there, but this post had the inconvenience of only being able to accommodate vessels of 50 guns or less. The few enemies that he had to fight gave him the freedom to go where he wanted. He crossed the James River and penetrated the countryside, which he ravaged and had relinquished his command when Cornwallis appeared. The British, under the orders of the latter, of Simcoe and Tarleton made their name despised. They returned to Williamsburg by successive movements, followed closely by Mr. de la Fayette.

53 James Rivington (1724–1803) was an English-born American journalist who published a Loyalist newspaper in the American colonies called *Rivington's Gazette*. Detractors called it *The Lying Gazette*. Some scholars in the 1950s determined that despite all outward appearances, Rivington was a member of the American Culper Spy Ring.

54 Quintus Fabius Maximus Verrucosus (ca. 280–203 BC) was a Roman statesman and general of the third century BC. He employed a delaying tactic against Hannibal's forces during the Second Punic War. Facing an outstanding commander with superior numbers, he targeted the enemy's supply lines and accepted only smaller engagements on favorable ground, rather than risking his entire army on direct confrontation with Hannibal himself. He is regarded as the originator of many tactics used in guerrilla warfare.

General Clinton continually repeated his order to Lord Cornwallis to send him some troops and then to keep himself as best he could in the hope that he would choose to put the navy in safety. Cornwallis had crossed to Yorktown. He did not command [?] Portsmouth which convinced him to march there. He left Williamsburg to go to Jamestown where he embarked. Mr. de la Fayette, arrived with his small body of troops almost at the same time. The British had already begun to board when they sighted him. A certain number of troops hid themselves behind hedges and only showed a very few to protect the boarding. Mr. de laFayette placed General Wayne's Pennsylvania Regiment before them with the firm order not to attack as long as he personally was their leader. Moreover, [illegible] the position of the enemy. Their number diminished noticeably. General Wayne thought it was a good time to fight and attacked. Those of the enemy who were prone on the ground arose then. Wayne was repulsed with loss. He lost two pieces of cannon. Mr. de la Fayette who, with reason, expected success on this occasion, arrived in time to repair the damage and to retreat.

Portsmouth did not suit Lord Cornwallis's purpose. He re-embarked a short time later and returned to Yorktown where he began to entrench.

The French made no movement until the 31st. At this time, a forage was ordered at Mamaroneck on the Sound 10 miles from camp. Mr. de Rochambeau ordered a fairly strong escort under the command of the Chevalier de Bressolles,[55] Lieutenant Colonel of the Bourbonnais Regiment, to protect the forage party. He did not want them to do any hunting as they almost always did in the previous war because in this way, there is no strength anywhere. He had all the routes guarded by good pickets and retained a reserve to strike anywhere the enemy appeared in force. The only ones we had to fear in this region were Delancey's refugees which remained very quiet.

Mamaroneck is one of the finest towns that I've seen in the North. Forty or 50 houses in the neighborhood make up the town. It is occupied by the French. The Sound is 4 miles wide here.

August

On August 3, we foraged in the same manner at New Rochelle. It is a fine village which gets its name from La Rochelle where the inhabitants and those of Mamaroneck departed to come settle here after the revocation of the Edict of Nantes in 1685. Their descendants now speak a broken French. They are not strongly attached to the American cause,

55 Chevalier Gilbert de Bressolles (1739-1810) of the Bourbonnais Regiment left the unit at the end of 1791. He did not emigrate during the French Revolution.

certainly because of the nearness of the English. It is excellent land with an area of 20 miles, almost completely owned by two or three rich individuals such as Messrs. Phillips, Morris and Delancey. The uncertainty of the outcome of the war made them side with the British because, as enemies, they feared having them as neighbors; as friends, they saved their possessions from ravage and pillage. They had no difficulty making the tories their vassals. Part of Delancey's band of refugees lived in this area at East and West Chester, toward Morrisania and as far up as Harlem Creek. They are all pillagers and thieves. The illegitimate gains they make in this way are very great. They sell very dearly all the cattle they catch to the butchers of New York. This is why the Americans call them cowboys or cow stealers. They are not concerned when they meet.

Our patrols discovered a British fleet of 32 ships, the largest of which had only two masts, in the sound on the 5th. We observed their movements in fear that they might land some men. Their purpose seems to be a reconnaissance and a burial of forage, but, fortunately, we had taken what was available in this area two days earlier.

The 7th, we foraged at Eastchester, 11 miles from camp. This distance was a little far for the forage to be secured if the enemy appeared in force. Mr. Count de Rochambeau had a battalion of grenadiers and light infantry march, in addition to the usual escort, with two field pieces under the command of the Chevalier de la Valette,[56] Lieutenant Colonel of the Saintonge Regiment.

The 10th, we foraged again at Eastchester. The battalion of grenadiers and light infantry was under the command of Mr. de Bressoles. A detachment of Lauzun's hussars captured a patrol of refugees. Our foragers were no longer harassed.

We foraged again around Eastchester on the 14th. The detachment of 600 men was under the command of the Count St. Maisme du Muy,[57] camp master, commanding the Soissonnais Regiment. We captured a few refugees. Everything else went very peacefully.

56 Chevalier Charles-François Chaudron de la Valette (1731-) served as lieutenant colonel in the Saintonge Regiment. Despite his "lesser" rank, he was entrusted with the command of the rearguard after the capture of Yorktown and during the retreat. He was left at Yorktown with 600 men and the siege artillery while the rest of the army went ahead. He rejoined the bulk of the army at Baltimore.

57 Jean Baptiste Louis Philippe de Felix d'Ollière, comte de Saint-Maisme then du Muy (1755-1820) served as colonel in the Soissonnais Regiment, barely 19 years old when promoted. His services at Yorktown earned him a letter of satisfaction from Marshal de Ségur, the Minister of War, and the cross of chevalier de Saint-Louis. He was promoted to camp marshal in 1788. He became lieutenant general in 1792 and given command of the seventh military division. Falsely accused, at the National Convention on October 3, 1792, for inciting civil war at Avignon, he was cashiered on January 26, 1795. This was overturned and he was later reinstated. He was named inspector general of infantry troops for the Sambre and Meuse Army in 1796. He participated in the Egypt expedition of Napoléon Bonaparte. He was retired in

Great order prevailed during all the forages. They taught us how much inexperience could often be detrimental. Our artillery especially needed many lessons in this matter. Not a single soldier, nor any teamster knew how or wanted to reap. Not a single one knew how to prepare a kit or to load a wagon carefully. The cavalry had no ropes nor scythes such that, in the first two forages, we were a little annoyed by an enterprising enemy. If we were obliged to hurry, for lack of time, part of the two bodies and several officers headquarters and of the army headquarters would have lost their horses due to lack of provisions. Some were poorly managed, some were lost by the foragers, some were left behind by negligence and ignorance of resources. Firm orders, a bit of experience and need promptly corrected the errors committed.

Mr. the Count de Rochambeau received information about the arrival of the frigate la *Concorde* at Newport on the 15th. She was sent from Martinique by Mr. de Grasse in response to the dispatches which Mr. de Rochambeau sent to him by the same frigate in the month of April. The admiral was sending it to our general only after carefully considering the plan of the campaign which was sent to him and after resources became available. He agreed that he would begin to embark as many troops as he could on board his navy's vessels and go to the Chesapeake Bay for the immediate relief of Virginia. He would also exert himself to bring 1,200,000 francs which were requested of him and he would arrive in the Chesapeake Bay before the end of August.

Change of Plans

Mr. de Rochambeau immediately went to General Washington to inform him of this satisfactory and important dispatch. General Washington who always had New York in mind did not seem very satisfied, not because the expedition to the Chesapeake did not seem important to him, but he thought that the capture of New York would put an end to the war. He believed in the possibility of this great enterprise but knowing the almost invincible repugnance of the troops from the northern states to go south, he feared that none would follow him. Mr. de Rochambeau countered all these objections forcefully and with knowledge of the facts. He finally told him that matters were too far advanced to back out, that he was determined to march, come what may, with the body of French which, united with the troops promised him from the islands, would be sufficient numbers, that he ignored his own glory and that he only had the common good in mind.

December 1815 due to his advanced age. He was named a Peer of France in 1815 and was noted for his patriotism and wise opinions.

He insistently requested that he come personally to Virginia where he would find Mr. de la Fayette with 2000 men, that militiamen would be sent, that he would know of all ways and by all means to form the largest army corps and that he would always serve with great pleasure under his command.

General Washington agreed and preoccupied himself only with how to convince his troops and to bring as many of them as possible with him.

Mr. de Rochambeau had another obstacle to conquer in the conduct of Mr. de Barras who wanted to stay in Newport. This admiral had also received some letters from Mr. de Grasse, by way of the *Concorde*, where either by deference or because he believed him strong enough to be master of the sea, he responded that he followed his instructions and that he would leave him master of the sea. Mr. de Barras's was not very pleased to go serve under the command of a younger Navy officer and, as commander of the fleet, he was recently promoted to lieutenant general. He took the ball and left there to notify Mr. de Rochambeau that he planned an expedition to the Penobscot and that he intended to bring the detachment of 400 men that Mr. de Choisy commanded at Newport.

We can imagine Mr. de Rochambeau's astonishment by the impossibility of acting that this reduced us to. First, the American army had no siege artillery numerous enough or in good enough condition and all of ours was left at Providence with three quarters of our munitions of war and the ocean was our only route to have it arrive in time. Second, we also knew that Admiral Hood[58] was due to arrive at New York and would join Admiral Graves with 20 ships. We also knew that Admiral Digby[59] was expected along with Prince William Henry,[60] the son of the King of England, with six vessels which could arrive at any moment, that [joined] with the Rhode Island fleet Mr. de Grasse would only have a superiority of two vessels which could not guarantee success.

Mr. de Rochambeau consequently dispatched the Count von Fersen, one of his aides-de-camp, to Mr. de Barras, to inform him that he knew perfectly well the contents of the instructions the Chevalier de Ternay gave him as well as those he received since then as he had copies that indicated the purpose and main objective of the Rhode Island fleet's mission was to provide direct assistance to America and that the commander should only

58 Admiral Samuel first Viscount Hood (1724–1816) was sent to intercept Admiral de Grasse off Martinique after the capture of Saint Eustatius in January 1781.

59 Admiral Robert Digby (1732–1815), was second-in-command of the British Channel Fleet in 1779. He helped organise the evacuation of some 1,500 Loyalists to the small port of Conway in Nova Scotia. The settlement transformed the tiny village into a town, which was renamed Digby in 1787.

60 Prince William Henry, Duke of Gloucester and Edinburgh (1743–1805), was the son of King George III.

act in concert with General Washington and him, that when there was nothing planned, he could attempt to make an expedition to the North, but that was no longer the case as two councils of war were held aboard his ship to decide the course of action, that, in addition, if he continued in his plan, he forbade Mr. de Choisy to board. Mr. de Barras understood the importance of the matter and the weight of the reasons. He made a similar response to our general and told him that he would have the munitions, the artillery etc. loaded without delay and that he would leave immediately afterward to join Mr. de Grasse.

General Washington, who had not yet seen our troops drill, saw the Bourbonnais regiment drill on the 16th. The two companies which comprised it were perfectly instructed and dressed.[61] The Marquis de Laval commanded it. There was a great gathering of the curious and American soldiers who showed me neither their astonishment nor their praises. General Washington told Mr. de Rochambeau that he would never fear to confront the enemy with such troops.

Chatham

Awaiting the response from Mr. de Barras, Mr. de Rochambeau did not remain idle. He had already given orders with the utmost secrecy for the necessary supplies for a march to Philadelphia. But to assure that our movements were not interrupted, we had to give the enemy a diversion and to make them fear for New York. Mr. de Villemanzy,[62] Commissioner of War, was charged with making a bakery at Chatham in the Jerseys with great preparation and fanfare but at the least expense. This village is only 4 miles from Staten Island. Mr. de Rochambeau confided his plan to Mr. de Villemanzy which was really only to send the army to Trenton by making a settlement at Chatham.

He acquitted himself perfectly well of his charge. He searched for bricks as far as the mouth of the Raritan off Staten Island where he was cannonaded.

Calculating people, indiscreet tongues are not rare in the army. It was essential to throw them off track. Everybody believed that the purpose of the maneuvers they observed was the siege of New York. The officers around our general were not better

61 Here, "dressed" means formed for drilling, rather than clothing.

62 Jacques-Pierre Orillard de Villemanzy (1751–1830) was a French war commissary responsible for arranging army supplies. He arranged to be a prisoner of the enemy during the Reign of Terror. After being exchanged, he became chief commissary in the French Army of Italy led by Napoléon, who was impressed by his performance. He continued to serve as a senior commissary to Napoléon's armies until 1809, when he retired and was made a Senator and later a Count of the Empire. After the Bourbon Restoration of 1814 he was made a Peer of France. His name is on the Arc de Triomphe among those of Napoléon's generals.

[informed]. It was necessary to take the Inspector of the Army into his confidence for provisions. This one had confided too much to his subordinates who assured several of my companions and me that the army would not go to Chatham because they had orders to supply them as far as Trenton but once there, our guesses were lost. We especially feared that the enemy might hear rumors of our departure from the camp at Philipsburg and bring vessels to King's Ferry to block our crossing the North River. This would have thrown us way off course and lost a lot of time. The army staff, in any case, had opened different routes and lines of communications at Phillipsburg. Finally, our generals agreed and set the date of departure for the 18th. The order of march was established in three columns.

General Washington took command of the left column. He passed by Tarrytown, filing the length of the North River and arrived at King's Ferry in two days. He could only bring the Rhode Island Regiment with him which had been with us for a long time on this island, only one regiment of Canadians commanded by Brigadier General Hand.[63] The same language united them with us, as his battalion of guards and part of his staff, but he received news that upon crossing the North River, he would be joined by two regiments from the state of New York coming from Albany and which would descend the river in flatboats. Mr. Washington left 3000 men at the camp of Philipsburg under the command of General Heath to serve as a rearguard and to cover West Point while we were gone.

The center column commanded by the Viscount de Vioménil was composed of the second battalion of grenadiers and light infantry with the reserve artillery, the large baggage. It took the route of Pines Bridge,[64] one day's march ahead of the rest of the body of French. It was hoped that this way the rest of the army, marching more slowly could go from Phillipsburg to King's Ferry in two days, but many unforeseen obstacles upset this plan.

We marched in retreat. Consequently, the army had to form the rear guard with its baggage. To march more lightly and with less encumbrance, we decreased several wagons per regiment. Despite the firmest orders, the wagons left behind were the ones that were overloaded and many broke at the outset. These minor events delayed the rest of the column. All the structures built to house the provisions had to be emptied at this time, but the quartermasters discovered a shortage, having, by laziness or by negligence, left behind a large store of flour which Mr. de Rochambeau saw and feared that it would fall into the hands of the enemy if it were left behind. He sent Damas to Tarrytown in search of wagons to remove the food so it took a long time before the army was ready to march. It began to

63 Brigadier General Edward Hand (1744–1802) commanded one of the two brigades of light infantry in the Continental Army in August 1780. He replaced Alexander Scammel as adjutant general of the army in 1781. Later, he was a member of several PA governmental bodies.

64 Yorktown Heights, NY.

move at 5 p.m. It was led by a recently and poorly conceived communication or it was continuously halted by the baggage train. Some terrible weather arose, a heavy rain and instead of the 19th, the army arrived at North Castle[65] only on the 20th at 5 a.m. 20 miles. The inspector of the army was strongly reprimanded for the lack of services which he oversaw.

The difficulty and fatigue of the night, the innumerable repairs compelled Mr. de Rochambeau to rest at North Castle on the 20th. He ordered frequent patrols on the rears to reassure himself that the enemy was not following us.

We broke camp on the 21st to go to Hunt's tavern. Eight miles from North Castle, we crossed the Croton at Pines Bridge. This river is fordable almost everywhere and empties into the North River at Taylor's Point.

The column of artillery (center) entered the right one at the Croton crossing. Hunt's Tavern, where the general made camp, is 4 miles further. The second battalion of grenadiers and light infantry and the legion camped in a very fine location 3 miles behind to always face the enemy. This land is very rocky and hilly. Mr. de Rochambeau did not stop at Hunt's Tavern. He took the route to Peekskill where he found General Washington. The troops he had brought had filed at King's Ferry 4 miles further and their number increased through the arrival of two regiments of the state of New York which had come down the river in flatboats.

The March South

The French army marched to King's Ferry on the 22nd, 16 miles. The headquarters halted at Peekskill. The American army was already on the other side of the river. The artillery and Lauzun's Legion crossed the same day.

The King's Ferry crossing is more than a big half league wide and is defended by two forts: that of Verplanck's Point or Fort la Fayette on the eastern bank and Stony Point on the west. The enemy should have tried to prevent our crossing by sending one or more vessels to block it. They could have also sent some troops to harass us during the division of our forces. To defend against these nuisances, as soon as the American artillery crossed the river, General Washington placed them along the shore on a hill where they could fire with advantage on any vessel which might appear. The departure from Phillipsburg was done in great secrecy. It is possible that despite the great quantity of wit and badly intentioned fear

65 Mt. Kisco, NY.

which abounds in this region Mr. [Clinton] was misinformed and he took General Heath's[66] corps for the entirety of our forces and that, for this reason, he was compelled to not budge, come what may. We sent off everything that we could, in great haste, to King's Ferry. The Rhode Island Regiment was very useful to us. Almost every soldier in this corps is a good sailor. They divided our soldiers aboard their boats, which we know our soldiers would not have been able to maneuver without risk for the passengers and whatever cargo. Some platforms were built of good beams on two flatboats which could carry across two cannons on their carriages or a loaded wagon. A small sail oriented and some men in each boat ferried everything. Most of the horses and the cattle swam across. The troops boarded specially made longboats capable of carrying 60 or 80 men at a time.

Peekskill could comprise some 30 houses. It is built on the banks of a creek which empties into the North River. All the inhabitants of this town and the surrounding area are very loyal to the cause even though the proximity of their armies ruined almost all of them. In the midst of this very hilly land, covered and filled with rocks, they enjoyed abundance before the war. All the valleys produced excellent wheat and many pastures. And they conducted an extensive trade in cattle and salted goods with New York on the North River.

The Americans always have large warehouses at Peekskill. We established a hospital and a depot there for everything which we left along the route since leaving Providence. The British came from New York and attacked it in 1777. They pillaged and burned.

The 23rd, the wind became very strong and almost standing to cross the river. Only the munitions and provision wagons crossed that day. The bad weather did not prevent Mr. de Rochambeau, who had never seen West Point, from boarding a boat to go visit this Boulevard of American freedom. General Washington came to Peekskill landing to accompany Mr. de Rochambeau. I also followed him along with the Count de Vauban.

August 1781

Nothing is finer, more majestic, more stunning to see than the course of the North or Hudson River. It gets its name from the point on the horizon where its source begins. It made its bed among steep rocks[67] whose peak is only covered by a bit of foliage and very high hills. A few miles upriver from Peekskill, there is a large hill called Anthony's nose. A

66 General William Heath (1737[–1814) was a farmer, soldier, and political leader from MA. He served as a major general in the Continental Army and as commander of the Eastern Department. After the war, he was a member of the MA Convention that ratified the US Constitution in 1788. He served in the state Senate 1791–1792, and as a probate court judge. He was elected the Lieutenant Governor of Massachusetts in 1806 but declined the office.

67 Palisades.

short distance from there, still upriver we see the ruins of Fort Montgomery,[68] constructed by the Americans and which General Clinton captured in the month of October 1777. It was constructed at the mouth of a small creek on which they built a bridge to communicate with Fort Clinton on the other side of the creek. They were both captured by assault and it was after this loss that the Americans began the first earthworks at West Point to prevent the British from advancing any further and to secure open communication between the northern and the southern towns.

Fort Montgomery had a very long vista on the river. The Americans, who now dominate the river, have only a very weak guard with one fieldpiece to warn about what is happening on the river which is more than one league wide here. It is very well-directed and its course often winding because of the mountains above and a few miles from Fort Montgomery. There is a very high one called Sugarloaf[69] on the left bank. It effectively forms a scarp. Mr. Washington who made us observe the uniqueness, which nature was pleased to accumulate and to vary in this area, did not forget to show us the house of Mr. Robertson[70] where he was to breakfast with Arnold the day of his treason, the landing where the traitor embarked to escape just punishment for his infamous action. We soon lost the despicable idea of the traitor. We turned our eyes away from where he lived to discover the ones which he prepared to surrender. We travelled 4 more miles and arrived at West Point. We found Major General McDougall,[71] commander of this important post. He was on the river bank with his principal garrison officers to receive our generals who were saluted with 13 cannon shots.

As I already mentioned, the course of the North or Hudson River is North and South. An enormous mass of rocks forms the right bank at this location which is called West

68 This note is in the manuscript: "American general killed in the expedition to Canada. American governor of the state of New York."

69 The name appears in English with a French translation.

70 Colonel Beverley Robinson (1721–1792), was a soldier and wealthy New York colonist. He sought to remain uninvolved at the onset of the American Revolutionary War, but eventually relented. He formed the Loyal American Regiment in 1777 and commanded that unit throughout the war. He is known for his work with the British secret service during the war, particularly regarding Benedict Arnold's treason, as Arnold used Robinson's home as his headquarters.

71 Brig. Gen. Alexander McDougall (1732–1786) was an American seaman, merchant, and a Sons of Liberty leader from New York City before and during the American Revolution, and a military leader during the war. He served as a Maj. Gen. in the Continental Army and as a delegate to the Continental Congress. After the war, he was the president of the first bank in the state of New York and served a term in the New York State Senate.

Point.[72] This wild place which was only inhabited by wild beasts seemed to the Americans suitable for the defense of the river. They found a superb esplanade at the top of the boulder where eight battalions would drill, where the main works are constructed today. That's where the garrison is camped, where the magazines are built, where the reserve artillery is located.

West Point, in its present state, is equally good to defend against land troops or against ships. Nature, which already accomplished much at this location, was also very well supported by art. I will first talk about the defense of the river. West Point forces it to make a turn almost at a right angle. Opposite the North face, is Constitution Island which changes the course. A very strong chain stretches from West Point to Constitution Island. It is supported at various distances by large beams which block the whole width of the river in such a way that an enemy vessel wanting to cross would necessarily be stopped because it is forced to turn at the point where the river forms a detour and its course changes and decreases. After the turn, it no longer has the strength nor the power to make any effect on the chain. Moreover the crossing would be attempted only at great risk. Constitution Island is well fortified and supplied with cannons and the rock of West Point is steep and defended by good and plunging batteries.

The main fort at West Point is called Fort Clinton. It is situated at the extremity of the point and its fire would be equally good against a vessel going upstream or after it turned. It was constructed in 1778 after the capture of Fort Montgomery. The Americans first called it Fort Arnold. It was then very extended and required many men to defend it. Since then, the French engineer Mr. Duportail[73] reduced it to what it is now and gave it the name of Fort Clinton. There are good casemates inside to enclose the garrison. It is well-fraised[74] and has good moats around it. On the parapet, there are some very tight palisades which rise and fall at will, the pivot of which is on the side of the scarp. They are left down when the enemy is far away; the cannon is out of range. They are raised if there is an attack, which raises them six more feet and allows time to fire many musket shots, to launch bayonets; the [floor] is covered with boards.

Above West Point, Fort Putnam is constructed on the summit of a steep rock. It is very large and is the only work at West Point which is covered in masonry.

72 The name appears in English with a French translation.

73 Brigadier General Louis Lebègue de Presle Duportail served as Washington's chief engineer. He was responsible for the defenses of Philadelphia, Valley Forge and Yorktown. He was founder and first Commandant of the US Army Corps of Engineers.

74 Fraise are sharpened stakes built into the exterior wall of a fortification to deter attackers.

Brigadier General Louis Lebègue de Presle Duportail

Independence National Historical Park

The brief time we had did not permit us to go see the other forts. There are five strong redoubts on the same bank as West Point. Their positions are very well selected and they defend all the approaches to this now famous rock.

Moreover, General Washington had four works built on the east bank. They command the whole region. They defend the roads of Pines Bridge and Peekskill and cover Fishkill where the Americans have large warehouses. All these fortifications did not cost the state a shilling. Mr. Washington had them constructed amidst the rumors and troubles [by] the soldiers who were neither clothed, nor paid, nor well [fed] but [by] the love which his army brings him, the respect he enjoys, his patience was more unshakable than the rocks which he fortified and his triumphs were the reward of his virtues and his labors.

The town of West Point is called Highland.[75] In my view, I have not seen any rocks and mountains so steep. They are all of fairly large [illegible] without any of them being very dominant. An intelligent and active commander must live in a post with great security against enemy [attacks]. There are only paths to advance; the troops would not march easily and would experience very great difficulty by wagon. The enemy were so convinced of this characteristic that they despaired of ever gaining anything by it. They used deception which fortunately did not succeed any better.

We dropped the probe in front of West Point at 175 fathoms without finding the bottom. After having seen everything in this area which might interest us as soldiers and as site-seers, we re-embarked to go down river and go to King's Ferry. Our general received a 13-gun salute from the artillery. Mr. Washington had ordered that the guns be pointed to the side where the mountains would echo the sound. The echoes repeated each cannon

75 The word appears in both English and French.

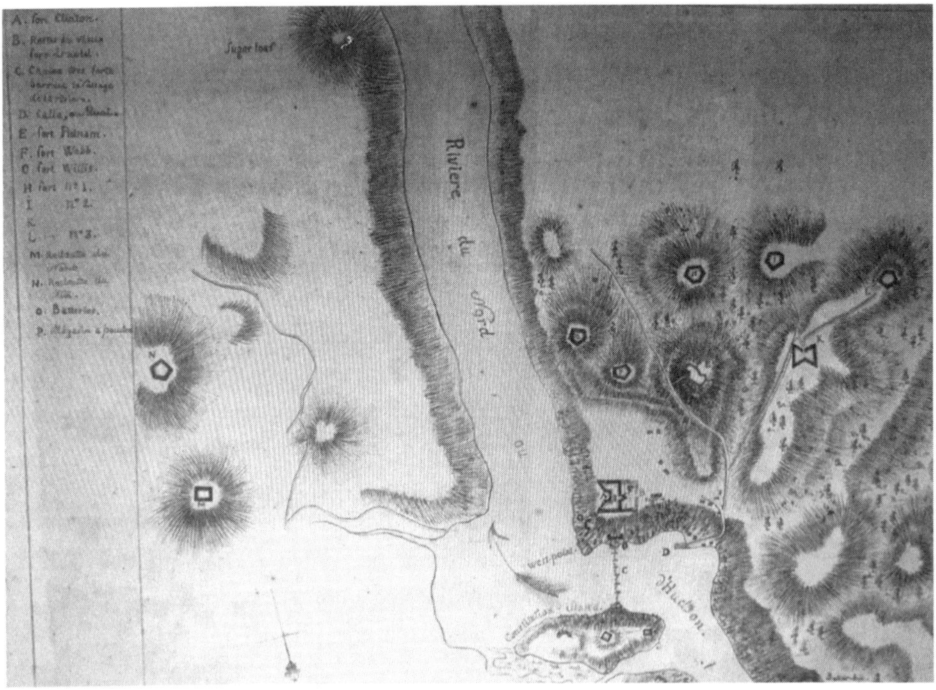

Louis de Lauberdière's drawing of West Point, 1779 - 1781.

Bibliothèque Nationale

shot a hundred times. We were then in the middle of the river. A somber glance and, everything majestic and unique to the area, along with the sonorous music which accompanied our departure, produced an indescribable effect on us.

After having traveled 10 miles on the water, we arrived at King's Ferry. It was 4 o'clock in the afternoon. We thought it prudent to approach General Washington's quarters, that we had lodged 2 miles away at the house of the infamous Mr. Smith who had received Arnold and Major André for their interview. This house is located in a charming location which commands a rather extensive valley which is bordered on the front by the river.

On the right bank, the fort of Stony Point defends the King's Ferry crossing. The British captured this fort and kept it until 1778 when General Wayne attacked it with a Pennsylvania brigade. He had under him Mr. de Fleury,[76] of Lieutenant Colonel

76 François Louis Teissedre de Fleury (1749–1799), was a French volunteer and engineer captain in the Continental Army. He led one of the attacking columns at Stony Point in July 1779. Congress awarded him a medal for being the first attacker to enter the bastion and capturing the British flag. Granted leave to return to France later that year, he returned to fight

Rouergue's[77] company who was serving with the Americans and is now major of the Saintonge Regiment, to whom he conferred the main attack. It was pursued vigorously and Mr. de Fleury was the first to enter on July 16. The Congress had a gold medal struck for this occasion on which is engraved Fort Stony Point. It was presented to him as a gift and he wears it at the boutonniere with the permission of the king of France.

The fortifications of Stony Point were destroyed after Mr. de Fleury's action. Today it is only a square redoubt which can contain 60 men. It is very well fraised. It is constructed at the summit of a rock which itself has its base on a another with an even more extensive surface in such a way that it can see the enemy from a distance, but once the enemy arrive at the foot of the large rock, [they are under cover]. At the center of this little fort, a [cabin] was built for the garrison. The ground floor is [illegible] where seven or eight large containers of water are always replenished so as to have a 20[-day] supply in case of attack. We enter by a hidden entrance cut into the rock and this hidden entrance is covered by a traverse.

Colonel Livingston commanded this post when he wanted to fire on the boat which transported Arnold when this traitor fled and deserted a homeland which he had [served] well until that time, to embrace an unjust cause, to live in [shame] and scorn, even from those who corrupted him.

The Bourbonnais regiment crossed the river with all its baggage on the 24th. We have no idea of the foreseeing and intelligent activity [illegible] on the part of the officers of the staff of the Army [illegible] the crossing of a large river like the Hudson. It is true that they were perfectly supported. The officers of all grades and classes, everybody worked with the same zeal, with the same hope to then see the enemy up close. The French camp was located on a hill [near] Haverstraw Bay and not far from Mr. Smith's house.

Even though the Soissonnais regiment was sent to camp at Verplanck's Point, Mr. de Rochambeau saw himself more and more pressed by the weather and was delayed by unforeseen accidents and bad weather since his departure from Philipsburgh. He decided to leave the camp at Haverstraw Bay on the 25th with the Bourbonnais regiment and preceeded by Lauzun's Legion. We made 15 miles and camped at Suffren. This place is in

---

at Yorktown. Back in the French army, he held commands in India and the Indian Ocean until 1790 when he returned to France. He was badly wounded early in the French Revolution and resigned. The De Fleury Medal is awarded to outstanding members of the United States Army Corps of Engineers.

77 Chevalier Charles-François Chaudron de la Valette (1731-) served as lieutenant-colonel in the Saintonge Regiment. Although he had only the rank of Lt. Col., he was entrusted with the command of the rearguard after the capture of Yorktown and during the retreat. He was left at Yorktown with 600 men and the siege artillery while the rest of the army went ahead. He rejoined the bulk of the army at Baltimore.

New York State. It was covered with woods like the rest of America but it was cleared by industrious Swedes and Dutch workers who settled there and who changed it into a very fine field.

General Washington and his troops were at the head of all the French forces and camped 2 miles on the other side of Suffren on the Pompton road.

The same day, the entire Soissonnais regiment crossed the North River and camped at Haverstraw. The boats in which two regiments of the state of New York came down from Albany were put aboard specially made wagons. They left immediately to take up the rear of the column of the Americans' baggage.

The Bourbonnais regiment broke camp at Suffren on the 26th. One mile from this place, we crossed the Ramapo, a small river which empties into the North River and makes the boundary between the states of New York and the Jerseys. We entered this province and took the Pompton meetinghouse road. We crossed the Pompton River and camped at Pompton. 15 miles. Going away from the banks of the North River, the land becomes flatter and level. It is well-cultivated and almost entirely inhabited by people of Dutch origin.

The Soissonnais regiment came from the Haverstraw camp to take the one at Suffren.

The American column, to be closer to New York, took the left road, a few miles before Pompton and camped 4 miles from the French.

The Bourbonnais regiment left Pompton on the 27th and camped at Whippany, 16 miles. It is a village which comprises 13 houses in the midst of an excellent town. Near this place are are all the properties of Mr. Livingston,[78] a man equally noted for his knowledge and his virtues, who enjoyed the highest regard under the British domination and who always supported the Americans governing the state of New Jersey since the independence.

The Soissonnais regiment left the camp at Suffren the same day and camped at Pompton.

While we were at Whippany, General Washington still forming the left column, came very close to Staten Island for a demonstration and camped on a very large front on a height where the enemy could see him perfectly from its island. Mr. Clinton believed so much that they had come to attack him, he was far from imagining that we were going two hundred and fifty leagues farther, that he crossed 2000 men to Staten Island to oppose the Americans. He was not the only one who made false assumptions about the allied army when it began to march. Secretum meum mihi,[79] that is Mr. de Rochambeau great principle

78 William Livingston (1723–1790) was the first governor of NY. He was also a signer of the US Constitution.

79 My secret is mine.

in war. Mr. Washington, the Count de Chastellux and he were the only ones to know the objective of the campaign. He never lets himself be discovered and each of the officers around him learns only what he wants them to know.

The Bourbonnais Regiment left Whippany and the Soissonnais brigade arrived there on the 28th.

Mr. de Rochambeau, who was very comfortable [illegible], left Whippany on the 28th and gave the command to the Baron de Vioménil. He preceded the army at Philadelphia by a few days to observe along the route, especially at Trenton to see if he could find the means to embark the troops on the Delaware to shorten the march by a few days. Mr. Washington also left his camp near Chatham to go to Philadelphia the same day. The departure of our generals clearly indicated that New York was not the real purpose of the preparations. Meanwhile, to deceive the enemy, the Americans remained camped near Chatham and in view of Staten Island while their heavy artillery filed off behind them. Our movement was also covered by this means.

The Americans remained in camp on the 29th but the Bourbonnais Regiment left Whippany to go to camp at Bullion's Tavern. 13 miles. Morristown is a lovely little town 4 miles from Whippany in a hilly region full of military installations and noted for its winter quarters which General Washington took despite the enemies in 1777.

The Bourbonnais Regiment camped at Somerset Courthouse on the 30th, 13 miles. The Soissonnais Regiment marched to Bullion's Tavern where it camped.

The Bourbonnais Regiment departed Somerset on the 31st and camped at Princeton 18 miles. The Soissonnais Regiment came to occupy the camp at Somerset Courthouse. Seven or 8 houses make up this place.

I had not followed Mr. de Rochambeau to Philadelphia. He did not need six aides-de-camp to travel very slowly. The Baron de Vioménil received intelligence of the enemy from the Americans the night of the 30th to the 31st. He sent for me and confided them to me to bring them to Mr. de Rochambeau. I left Somerset early on the 31st and arrived at Princeton where I halted 18 miles. This town, the second in the Jerseys, is very famous today since General Washington surprised three British regiments there on January 2, 1777 eight days after the affair at Trenton. He was camped on the right bank of the Delaware. He crossed the river during the night of the first to the second with his army below Trenton to deceive Lord Cornwallis who was at Trenton. He left all the fires of his camp burning and arrived near Princeton without being discovered. Colonel Mawhood[80] who commanded this town happened to have received the order to bring the 17th and 55th

80 Lieutenant Colonel Charles Mawhood (1729–1780) commanded the British army at the Battle of Princeton.

regiments to Maidenhead,[81] on the road from Princeton to Trenton, the same day. He had just left when he met General Washington's vanguard. He had them reconnoitered and saw that he had to deal with the entire American army. He had left the 40th Regiment at Princeton to guard the warehouses and munitions. That's why, fearing that they would fall into the hands of the Americans, he changed course and to take his chances although he was weaker.

He took a position upon the heights from whence he cannonaded the American army which was forming. He then had the 17th regiment attack the head of one of the columns and routed it. General Washington succeeded, with great difficulty, in rallying the troops which, in turn, slowly pushed back the enemy who were fleeing from all sides. A large number were killed or wounded. Washington entered Princeton with the rest. He made the 40th Regiment lay down their arms at a very fine college.[82] He received word, a short time later, that Lord Cornwallis was marching from Trenton to pursue him. He left to march on Brunswick where the fleeing men withdrew. His rear guard was leaving Princeton as Cornwallis's vanguard was arriving. He found some troops at Brunswick and they contested the crossing. Lord Cornwallis pressed him closely near the latter which forced him to cross the Millstone River at Kingston and to enter Morris County where he established his winter quarters at Morristown. The land is very good [unintelligible] and Mr. Washington could draw all sorts of provisions from it.

There could be 88 houses at Princeton. The location is pleasant. Its college is fine and has the title of university.

I left this town after refreshing my horses and in passing by Maidenhead [illegible] place on the route, I arrived at Trenton [12] miles from Princeton.

Trenton is the largest in the Jerseys and could be called the capital. It is on the Delaware which, by reason of its usual course, is so wide, so deep in this place. There are rocks that prevent going back up.

General Washington surprised this city guarded by a brigade of Colonel Rail's[83] Hessians on December 25, 1776. He was encamped on the right bank of the Delaware to cover Philadelphia. He crossed the river at McKonkey's Ferry during the night of the 25th, 9 miles from Trenton and advanced in two columns. The left, where he was personally, took the route to Pennington through the woods. The right followed the river bank, and was put under the command of General Sullivan. Sullivan arrived first. He encountered no resistance and captured the lower town at a bridge over a little creek to cut off an enemy

81 Lawrenceville, NJ.

82 Princeton University.

83 Johann Gottlieb Rall (ca. 1726–1776) commanded the Hessians at Trenton.

retreat. Mr. Washington arrived a little later. He placed cannons at the top of the streets and, after a very weak resistance, made the Hessians lay down their arms. Only a few escaped and joined Colonel Donop[84] at Burlington by fording the creek as General Sullivan had possession of the bridge. Colonel Rall was killed. Mr. Washington gave General Irvine[85] a division to better surround the city. He ordered them to cross the Delaware below Trenton. The ice blocked him and he did not arrive.

Colonel Rall had neglected to take possession of and to fortify the places outside the city which should have assured his safety. After this expedition, Mr. Washington re-crossed the Delaware and Lord Cornwallis came from Brunswick to occupy Trenton.

This was the first defeat that the British Army suffered in America.

I crossed the Delaware at Trenton. The right bank is the border of Pennsylvania, the left that of the Jerseys. I skirted the river and passed by Bristol which is 10 miles from the Trenton ferry. It is a very small place. The Delaware is more than 2 miles wide. On the bank opposite Bristol we can see Burlington, a large village known for its saltworks.

Two miles from Bristol, we crossed the Harmony River[86] ferry which is a little river which empties into the Delaware. And 5 miles further in the township of Bensalem in Bucks County is the Red [Lion] Tavern. I crossed Pagan Creek,[87] made another 13 miles and arrived at Philadelphia at Mr. the Chevalier de la Luzerne,[88] Plenipotentiary Minister of France to the United States, where I found Mr. de Rochambeau to whom I gave the dispatches which the Baron de Vioménil entrusted to me that morning. Some people pretend that American horses are worthless for the service. Mr. Dubourg[89], who accompanied me, and I can testify that we covered 21 leagues, on the same horses during a six hour march.

84 Colonel Karl Emil Kurt von Donop (1732–1777) had been a personal aide-de-camp of the Landgrave. He led the Hessians in an attack on Fort Mercer.

85 James Irvine (1735–1819) was commissioned a brigadier general of PA militia in August 1777 and assumed command of the 2nd PA Brigade. After the war, he held the rank of major general in the PA militia from 1782 to 1793.

86 Neshaminy Creek.

87 Possibly Frankford Creek.

88 Chevalier Anne-César de la Luzerne (1741–1791) was minister of France to the United States.

89 Jacques Barbeu-Dubourg (1709–1779) was a French doctor, botanist and philologist. He was one of Silas Deane's main contacts in France. He was also a writer, translator and publisher known for translating Benjamin Franklin's work into French and for inventing a gentlemen's umbrella fitted with a lightning conductor.

September

September 1, the Bourbonnais Regiment, preceded by Lauzun's Legion arrived at [Trenton]. The Soissonnais came from Somerset Courthouse to camp at Princeton.

Our general's plan was always [unintelligible] the Philadelphia crossing for the troops for the rapidity of the march, to prevent desertion... To make them [illegible] the Delaware as far as New Castle which is only 15 miles from Head of Elk[90]. There were not enough ships at Trenton to execute this plan. That's why Mr. the Count de Rochambeau immediately sent an order to Mr. de Vioménil to cross the Delaware at [unintelligible] and to prepare himself to then march to [Philadelphia] by way of a ford located near Trenton facilitated the execution of this order for Mr. de Vioménil to [cross] his artillery and baggage.

The Bourbonnais Regiment, at the head of Lauzun's Legion came to camp at the Red Lion Tavern on the 2nd. 17 miles. The Soissonnais division arrived at Trenton where it crossed the Delaware with its artillery and baggage.

Everything which relates to war and all the places stained with the blood of our allies are of interest to the French. That is why, the same day, Mr. de Rochambeau, whom I accompanied, had us see the battlefield of Germantown which is 6 miles from Philadelphia. Mr. Washington took it upon himself to give us a detailed account of the battle on the site. If he were supported by his generals, he would deserve a place aside of the greatest captains this day.

The British, after their defeats at Trenton and Princeton, seeing that they could never enter Philadelphia by the Jerseys, attempted another route. General Howe embarked in the month of June 1777 and left Sandy Hook to go to the Chesapeake Bay and debarked at Head of Elk. The Americans were essentially occupied with the defense of Philadelphia. They constructed formidable earthworks on the river to block the route to a fleet while Mr. Washington, who had left his quarters at Morristown, arrived within a day's march from the British to cover this great city.

After the unfortunate Battle of Brandywine on September 11, he withdrew, picking up the pieces of a shattered army before victorious troops. He was obliged to evacuate Philadelphia and to take a strong position at Skippack Creek 16 miles from Germantown. There he was reinforced with a few troops from Peekskill. On September 23, 1777, General Howe crossed the Schuylkill at Fatland Ford and made his entrance into Philadelphia with Lord Cornwallis and some troops, while the largest part of his army marched toward Germantown, a village 2 miles long, almost entirely built and inhabited by Germans. The

90 Elkton, MD.

British Army covering Philadelphia was camped toward the middle of the village, cutting it in two. The left extended toward the Schuylkill, the right was against a deep ravine. In this position, Mr. Washington decided to surprise them in camp.

He left his camp the night of October 3 and marched two main columns, one where he was in person and commanded by General Sullivan was to attack the British center. The other commanded by General Greene was to attack the right. Two other columns of lesser importance consisting of militia commanded by General McDougall and another general were ordered to [march] through the woods, turn and attack their right [flank] and rear. Mr. Washington marched all night and arrived at the enemy's outer pickets at 4 a.m. They retreated to the main army which got under arms. The ground was contested for some time but at [the end] General Sullivan's victorious column repulsed [illegible] and penetrated as far as the center of the village and [without] doubt would have entered the other camp except for the bravery and presence of mind of Lieutenant Colonel Musgrave[91] who, seeing his men routed, threw himself and five companies inside a fine stone house, one of the only ones in Germantown, which the [left] of the British right wing abutted. From there, they gave lively fire on the Americans who decided to capture [or] burn the house.

First they fired four field pieces to little effect. The Chevalier Duplessis- Mauduit,[92] an officer of the French artillery in the American service, then proposed to General Washington to go [there] or to lead 100 volunteers. The risk was great. His plan seemed too rash and unappealing. Meanwhile however, he insisted and was granted permission. He found only 27 men. Colonel Laurens[93] became the 28th. Mr. Duplessis dared to march to the house with this handful of men. He sent a man to search for some straw in a [illegible] which was very near the house, with torch in hand at one of the windows while Colonel Laurens tried to break down the door with an ax. They soon became aware of their vain efforts, looking around and seeing their men stretched out on the square. They decided to

91 Lieutenant Colonel Thomas Musgrave (1737 – 1812) commanded the 40th Regiment of Foot in the Philadelphia campaign. He distinguished himself in the defense of the Chew house at Germantown on Oct. 4, 1777. He went to the West Indies as quartermaster-general in 1778. He returned home to England, in 1781, as aide-de-camp to the king and Lt. Gen. of Stirling Castle. He also served in India.

92 Thomas-Antoine de Mauduit du Plessis, or Thomas Duplessis or Thomas-Antoine du Plessis-Mauduit (1753–1791), was a lieutenant of artillery who distinguished himself at Brandywine, Germantown and Monmouth, which gained him a promotiom to rank of lieutenant colonel.

93 Colonel John Laurens (1754–1782) served as General Washington's volunteer aide from Sept. 1777 to March 1779 and September to Nov. 1781, often serving as secretary and translator. He fought at Brandywine, Germantown and Monmouth. He is best known for his criticism of slavery and his efforts to help recruit slaves to fight for their freedom as U.S. soldiers. He was killed in the Battle of the Combahee River on Aug. 27,1782.

retreat which they executed by marching very slowly in reverse, not wanting to turn their back on the enemy. Mr. Laurens then received a contusion on the shoulder. However, he rejoined General Washington with Mr. de Mauduit and a soldier. After this action, they wanted to summon the commander to come. The Chevalier de Mauduit was asked to go make the proposal. He excused himself because he did not speak good English; an American officer then took it upon himself to perform the duty, with a flag of truce in hand and accompanied by a drummer. It didn't seem that either one would be killed on the spot. It is thus that happiness often accompanies one (Mr. de Mauduit is proof) and often flees the other.

While Sullivan's column amused itself at the house, General Greene, who got lost in the woods in a thick fog, arrived; but instead of surprising the enemy, he found them in battle. He was never able to put himself in line and was even broken. General McDougall who was supposed to turn the right flank, also got lost and did not appear at all. General Washington, having received intelligence that Lord Cornwallis was arriving from Philadelphia with fresh troops in great haste, made the prudent choice to retreat. His troops were very tired. He put his cavalry on the summit of a dominant hill during the battle while his artillery and his infantry marched behind. The enemy did not dare follow and he peacefully returned to camp at Skippack Creek.

His plan was superb, his dispositions well done and, if the attack was made in unison as ordered, he would certainly have defeated the enemy who even admitted it themselves. Part of their camp was plundered and overrun. I believe, along with several very knowledgeable people, that if Mr. Washington had left on the left the house which he had attacked, he would have captured this same house which he could have done under cover of musket fire and that he would have thus fallen on the enemy's rear and very few would have escaped and so many less than all [unintelligible] instead in front of General Sullivan's column.

Arrival at Philadelphia

The entire city of Philadelphia awaited the arrival of the [illegible] corps with great impatience. They shouted loud praise from the windows along the route he was supposed to take.

Lauzun's Legion and the first brigade left the Red Lion Tavern on the 3rd, to arrive there. 13 miles. The troops halted at the entrance to the city where Mr. de Rochambeau rejoined them. He entered Philadelphia at their head in the grandest parade and which was very necessary to capture the attention of the advisors of our allies. The drums, the music, Lauzun's hussars especially, but even more so, the Duc de Lauzun's magnificently dressed runner, attracted gazes and attention. All the members of Congress were on the top step of the court with Mr. Mackean,[94] president of this assembly, at their head. They gave us infinitely [illegible]. Mr. de Rochambeau saluted the president and had his troops parade near him. Mr. McKean was dressed in a suit of black velvet in the middle of summer. Little accustomed to receiving such an honor, he asked our general if he should return the salute. Mr. de Rochambeau responded, saying that the King saluted him with his troops when they passed in review. [After] passing before Congress, they were between the Schuylkill and the road to Germantown, 1 mile from Philadelphia. The Chevalier de la Luzerene gave us a very large [ball] where he entertained a rather large number of pretty women. The minister arrived [illegible] at a very thorny time and he is [illegible] to fill a place with general approval. I think the greatest compliment we can give him is to say that a minister of a great king to a poor republic is equally proper to represent the republic, in fulfilling all his duties with dignity, amidst the pomp of the court of France. His personal merit, popularity and finally the qualities with which he is endowed both as a social man and as a public man soon won him him all the hearts of Philadelphia.

On the 4th, the Viscount de Vioménil arrived at the head of the second brigade of the French army in the same order and was no less admired than the first. Congress demonstrated, in particular, the greatest pleasure with our general.

While the French attracted the attention of the Philadelphians, the American army did not remain inactive. It remained camped visibly enough on the heights a few miles from Staten Island and once we were near Trenton, freed of its artillery which continued to travel and which had descended the Delaware, it proceeded long days and arrived at Trenton when the French marched into Philadelphia. It found boats at Trenton. The flatboats in which two regiments of the state of New York descended the North River, which served us in the crossing and which we put on wagons, were also very useful on this occasion. Many soldiers boarded them and, during our stay at Philadelphia, they passed wide of the city, descending the Delaware, to arrive at New Castle which is only 15 miles from Head of Elk.

Pennsylvania is one of the finest provinces of the 13 United States both for its size and for the fertility of its soil. In our other states, agriculture is not so far advanced. This rich region owes its actual splendor to the large number of industrious and hard-working Germans who [illegible] and who vexed by their little princes enjoyed the pleasures of a free life and previously not exempt from troubles, worries, [illegible] rights and their posessions.

94 Thomas McKean (1734–1817) was a signer of the Declaration of Independence. He served as Chief Justice of Pennsylvania from 1777 to 1799. He was elected president of Congress on July 10, 1781. He is also known for holding many other public positions. Keap Street in Brooklyn, though erroneously spelled, was named in his honor.

William Penn founded this colony in 1681. He began by making an alliance with the [Americans], his neighbors. This is the only treaty between the savages and the Christians which was not sworn to and which was not broken, at least during his lifetime. The new sovereign was also a legislator of Pennsylvania. He established very wise laws, none of which were changed after him. The first is not to mistreat anyone on the subject of religion and to consider anyone who believes in God as a brother. [After] he established his government, many American merchants came to populate his colony, the fields of the region, rather than flee to the [forests]. They got along so sensibly with the pacifists who [illegible] and came in droves to ask Penn to receive them as his subjects. This was a very novel sight: a sovereign to whom everyone spoke familiarly studied, to whom they spoke hat on head. A government without priests, [illegible] without arms, citizens all equal, neighbors [illegible] jealousy, William Penn could boast [of having] brought on earth the golden age of which we speak and which probably existed only in Pennsylvania. Things changed very much since his death [which occurred] in London in 1718 when he went to request new benefits for Pennsylvania commerce. The sect, of which we could call him the leader [of which] George Fox was the first in 1642 weakens every day in America. Throughout the land the dominant religion, when it does not persecute at length, swallows the others. The Quakers cannot be members of Congress nor employed in any public office or hold any office where they would have to swear an oath because they do not want to swear. They are reduced to the necessity of earning money by commerce. Today no one likes to be shunned from general society. Children, enriched by the labors of their fathers, want to enjoy them, receive honors, wear buttons, repaired hats, sleeves, powder. They want to dance, sing, amuse themselves. They are almost embarrassed to be called Quakers and they become Presbyterians, Anglicans etc. to be in style. At Philadelphia, their birthplace in America, their society no longer dominates.

This large and beautiful city founded by William Penn is the capital of Pennsylvania and could also be called that of North America. It is built on the Delaware, the length of this river and should have extended to the Schuylkill according to the first maps of its founder. All the houses are fairly high and built of brick. All the streets are laid out in a line, very wide and have sidewalks on both sides for safety and convenience. Those that follow the river are more than a long quarter league and are cut perpendicularly by other very long roads.

The Delaware is very wide at Philadelphia even though it is 100 miles from the ocean; 64-gun ships can go up river. Navigation isn't easy because of the frequency of berms.[95]

95 Chevaux-de-frise are obstacles consisting of horizontal poles with projecting spikes to block a passageway. They were used on land and modified to block rivers to enemy ships.

The court house where Congress assembles is a rather large building, without a very fine architecture. An academy was established in this city. In general, every European, every foreigner who arrives in the city cannot help but be struck by her beauty, her grandeur, her population, the environs when one stops to think that everything one sees is the work of a hundred years. This marvel could only be accomplished with the help of tolerance, only under the protection of a wise government which attracted the emigrants of all the nations.

We can still see, near this city, the line of fortifications with which the British encircled it when they occupied it and which extended from the Schuylkill to the Delaware.

Amidst the acclamation of the people, Mr. de Rochambeau was not however without worry. He had not yet received any news of Mr. de Grasse. We were marching toward the Chesapeake Bay and he knew that Admiral Hood had left New York to go there. Time would become precious. That's why he decided to have the first division of his army depart from Philadelphia on September 5 to camp at Chester. 15 miles. As this place is located on the Delaware, Mr. de Rochambeau wanted to go there by water in order to go see the old fort at Red Bank and that of Mud Island.

The Americans, evacuating Philadelphia, had kept these two essential posts to intercept the course of the river. They sank some ships and chevaux-de-frise in the middle. They were constructed in the form of [illegible] with strong pieces of wood joined together by large beams. A large quantity of rocks was placed in the middle, enough to make them sink a little below the water level and give them solidity.

They presented three strong iron points on the tips, capable of piercing any vessel opposing it. At the base, they were attached one to the other and completely blocked the river. The left was against the fort at Red Bank and the right at Mud Island. In front of this line, there were many small armed vessels and two floating batteries. Their largest vessels withdrew to the protection of the fort of Red Bank.

After the Battle of Brandywine, General Howe having marched to Philadelphia, his brother, the admiral, departed the Chesapeake Bay and entered the Delaware where he went as far as New Castle. He detached two 64-gun vessels in front: the *Vigilant* and the *Augusta* and the 22-gun *Merlin*.

The Americans constructed Fort Mifflin on Mud Island, named after a general known much less for his military exploits since the war than for his partisan spirit and animosity toward General Washington. Much work had been done on Fort Mifflin but the parapets were not very high because the island is very low, marshy and almost at sea level.

The British decided to attack Red Bank by land on October 22, 1777 while the *Augusta* and the *Vigilant* fired on the American vessels and Fort Mifflin.

General Washington, having observed the courage and intrepidity of the Chevalier de Mauduit-Duplessis at the Battle of Germantown, then assigned him the defense of Red Bank. This one found the extent of the fort much too great for the number of men (280) he had to defend it. Being both an artillery officer and an engineer, he reduced the fortifications. They were barely finished when Colonel Donop and 2100 Hessians crossed the Delaware and arrived at Red Bank. Before the attack, he sent an officer under a flag of truce who spoke these arrogant words: "the King of Great Britain orders his rebellious subjects to lay down their arms, otherwise they can expect no quarter."

Mauduit jumped on the palisades and responded he would make them repent their insolence and gave them a signal to withdraw. He reentered his fort and the attack began a few minutes later. It was badly conducted on the part of the Hessians, who attacked by an entering angle. They were repulsed three times with loss and it is especially at the crossing of the abatis, where Mr. de Mauduit let them approach by design, that many were killed. He discerned Colonel Donop perfectly by the military decorations and medals he wore in the attack and by the courage he showed. He received two musket balls in the abatis.

The fall of their leader disconcerted the soldiers. They retreated, leaving 700 of their men and many officers at the place. Many had penetrated the moat and were captured. After the attack, de Mauduit visited his battlefield. Many Americans were already around Colonel Donop who was not dead and who demanded his sword. He never wanted to give it to them. De Mauduit appeared and as he spoke poor English, Colonel Donop asked him who he was. The other responded "a French officer and I command the fort.» «In that case," resumed the colonel. "I surrender this weapon to you and put it in the hands of courage and honor." The Chevalier de Mauduit had him taken to the nearby house of a Quaker and gave him all the care in his power for three days. Colonel Donop was very much connected to Mr. le Comte de Saint Germain,[96] then Minister of War in France. He gave Mr. de Mauduit a letter in which he requested his old friend to reward his merit. After giving his prisoner his greatest respect, Mr. de Mauduit grieved his loss. The colonel died on October 25.

The Chevalier de Mauduit is today Captain of Artillery and Regimental Adjutant of Artillery for our army. He was with Mr. de Rochambeau when we were at Red Bank. He had not revisited this post since his fine defense. As soon as we were on the bank, he ran as fast as he could to see if a stone and a small inscription which he put on the colonel's tomb four years earlier was still there. He found it and could not help shedding a few tears. I speak today with so much more pleasure of the Chevalier de Mauduit as we both served in the same army and bonded in friendship. It was he who wanted to serve as my second in the particular affair I had on June 10.

96 Claude Louis, Comte de Saint-Germain (1707–1778), served as French war secretary (1775 to 1777). His efforts to install Prussian-style discipline into the French Army was unpopular.

During the attack on Red Bank, the *Augusta* and the *Merlin* also gave a very warm fire on the American vessels and batteries. The large number of sunken vessels and the chevaux-de frise had changed the channel. Moreover, Mud Island was surrounded by beams such that the two British ships sank. Fort Mifflin and the batteries then redoubled their fire. They succeeded in getting aboard the vessels which became the prey of flames despite the best efforts of the British to save them, the Americans soon had the satisfaction of seeing them both explode. On November 11, the British sent a sloop of war and the *Vigilant*, which they abandoned and on which they left only twenty-four 24-pounders, up river between Hog Island and the continent, in a narrow passage. The fire of these vessels which were retaking Fort Mifflin was so lively that the Americans could not respond. They had many men killed and they evacuated a short time later.

Lord Cornwallis landed at Billing's Port[97] with a very large detachment on the 18th. The Chevalier de Mauduit was then obliged to evacuate Red Bank on the 21st. He broke the trunnions[98] and spiked the cannons which he could not bring. The Americans burned almost all their remaining vessels and brought the rest to Burlington.

The line of chevaux-de-frise no longer being defended, the British entered and succeeded in destroying some on November 24 after great effort. The vessels returned to Philadelphia. After they abandoned this city Mr. Duportail refortified FortMifflin but this work is not yet finished.

After the capture of Mud Island, General Washington took a position at Whitemarsh a few miles from Philadelphia which he made impregnable. From there, he hoped to strike some new blows against the enemy who were outside their lines; but they reentered, forcing him to cross the Schuylkill on December 9 and take his famous camp at Valley Forge where he quartered his army and passed the winter of 1778.

After having seen Mud Island, we were at Billings Port which is only 4 miles away. Before undertaking anything on Mud Island, the British became masters of this post which was not yet perfect. British Colonel Sterling[99] embarked at Chester with two battalions and marched. The Americans did not expect him. They burned what they could and spiked their cannon. This fort is very extended at present. It would require 400 men to defend it.

97 Billingsport, NJ.

98 Two pieces of metal sticking out of the sides of an artillery piece. They serve to hold the artillery piece on the carriage, allowing it to be raised or lowered as needed. The trunnions are generally as long as the diameter of the cannonball and have the same diameter.

99 Colonel Thomas Sterling (1733-1808) commanded the 42nd Regiment or Royal Highland Watch at the battles of Trenton and Princeton.

There are cannons. The channel is dominated by its fire and all the vessels which go up the Delaware are required to come show their papers.

From Billing's Port we re-embarked to go to Chester. General Washington who had rejoined his troops at the head of ours promptly countermarched with an express from Mr. the Count de Grasse whom he met, to advise Mr. de Rochambeau that this admiral had arrived in the Chesapeake Bay on August 26 with 28 ships of the line and that he brought 3200 men from the islands and that he took 2 24-gun British frigates upon entering the bay and the packet boat *Queen Charlotte* bringing Lord Rawdon to England. It was he who commanded at Charleston while Mr. Cornwallis was in Virginia.

It is not easy to describe the display of joy of the two generals on this occasion. It was soon communicated to the entire army and we immediately dispatched an aide-de-camp to Congress which was no less moved along with the entire city of Philadelphia. From this moment the goal, the purpose of the march was no longer a secret. Everyone forgot past hardships in the hope of an imminent and brilliant future. Each soldier revived and demanded to march and all the epithets that they could give to a general who hopefully would soon be defeated were added to the name of Cornwallis.

Cornwallis Fortifies Yorktown and Gloucester

This general, as I said above, not having found at Portsmouth what he wanted for the safety of the British Navy came to take possession of the posts of Yorktown and Gloucester. The first is on the right bank and the second is on the left bank of the York River. Sir Henry Clinton, erroneously believing that he would be attacked, ordered Lord Cornwallis to send him 2000 men. The final dispatch arrived about the same time as Mr. de Grasse. Lord Cornwallis's departure from Portsmouth preceded the arrival of this admiral by only a few days. As soon as he anchored in the bay, he sent the 74-gun *Triton*, the 50-gun *Experiment* and a frigate to capture the James River, the 64-gun *Vaillant* and the 74-gun *Gloire* that of York to prevent anything from escaping. At this moment, Cornwallis's loss was limited only to a pilot, for if the *Gloire*, commanded by the Baron d'Escars, had one aboard, he would have gone up the York River where the fleet and flotilla which had brought Cornwallis were and captured all of his artillery which had not yet been landed.[100]

This first preparatory movement of much greater ones, was followed by the landing of the Gatinois, Tourraine and Agenois regiments and 200 volunteers commanded by the

100 Baron Viscount d'Escars served as captain of the French frigate *Gloire*.

Marquis de Saint Simon,[101] the Marquis de la Fayette's camp marshal, who, at the approach of Lord Cornwallis, withdrew to West Point, an excellent post at the junction of the Pamunkey and Matepony[102] rivers which formed that of York from where he observed the British and had just departed. He camped near the Chickahominy River and marched to Williamsburg where Mr. Saint Simon came to join him. Although a simple colonel of dragoons in the service of France, Mr. de la Fayette took command over Mr. de Saint Simon because he was senior major general in the service of the United States.

Mr. de Rochambeau and Mr. Washington left Chester on the 6th to arrive at Head of Elk. The Bourbonnais Regiment and Lauzun's Legion marched to Wilmington. 14 miles. The Soissonnais division left Philadelphia to go to Chester.

Our generals doubled the day only to hasten to the most effective means of getting them to Virginia promptly. The ocean seemed to be the shortest, the least tiring and the least expensive route. They gave orders to assemble as many ships as possible and hurried to Baltimore to have them arrive.

I did not accompany Mr. de Rochambeau at Head of Elk. I was with his son to see the battlefield of Brandywine.

This battle with the British, within musket range of a few regiments of militia, is the first one of the campaign of 1777. As I said, General Howe, despairing of entering Philadelphia through the Jerseys, embarked on the fleet of Admiral Howe his brother, entered the Chesapeake Bay and arrived near Head of Elk. General Washington's plan was to fight him at the landing site. He arrived too late and only marched as far as Relly's Creek[103] 10 miles from Head of Elk. From one place to another, he stayed in front of the enemy and ended up withdrawing behind them on the left bank of Brandywine Creek where he positioned himself on a hill commanding the creek, a ford called Chadds Ford.[104]

General Howe camped on the right bank of the Brandywine and seized a good position from which he observed the Americans. On September 11, the British general

101 Claude Anne de Rouvroy, Marquis de Saint Simon Montbleru (1743-1819), commanded an expeditionary force of 2000 men. They came to America in Sept. 1781 and served primarily at Yorktown, where he was shot in the leg but refused to leave the lines until the British army surrendered. During the French Revolution, Saint-Simon, a royalist, fled France and settled in Spain. He was made a general of the Spanish army and later led Spanish troops against Napoléon. Captured by the French in 1808, he was sentenced to death for treason, but Napoléon commuted his sentence to life imprisonment. He was released when Napoléon fell from power in 1814 and he lived in Spain for the rest of his life.

102 Mattaponi.

103 Ridley's Creek.

104 The name appears in both English and French.

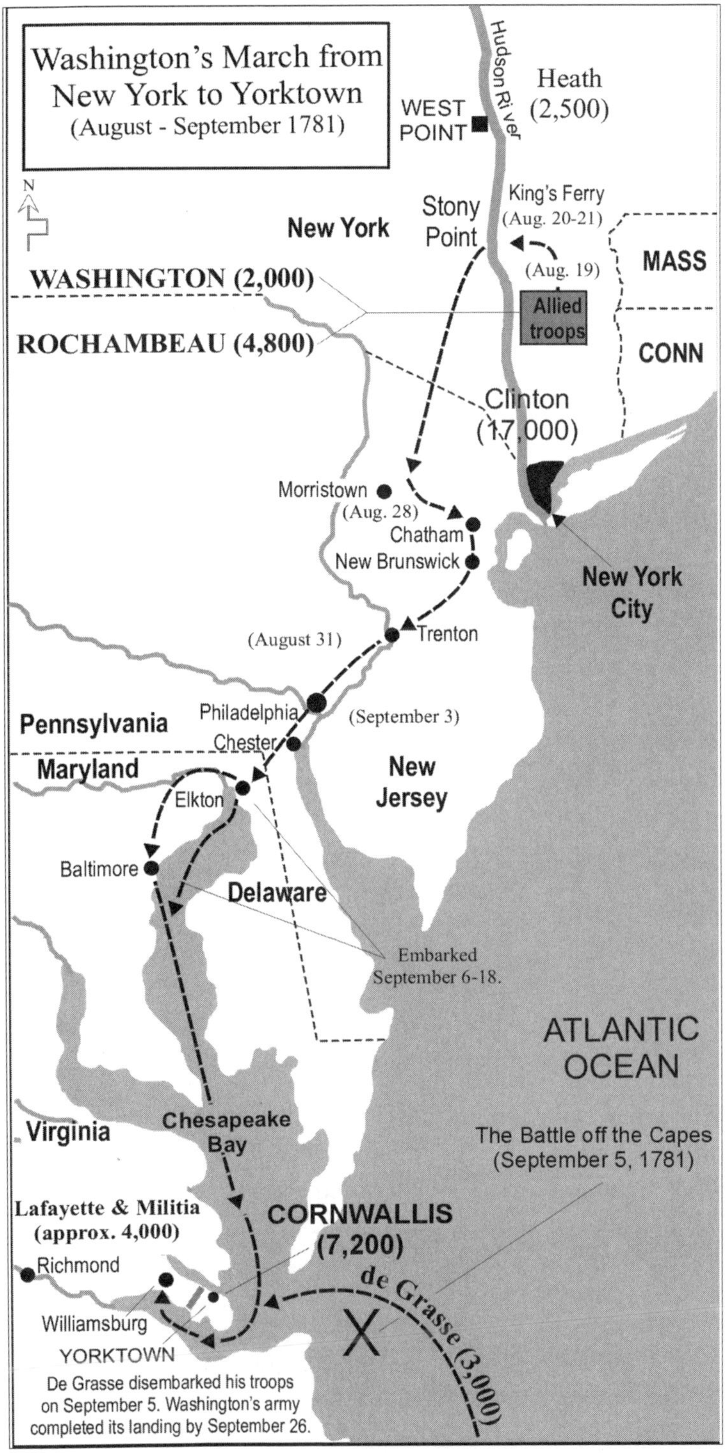
Washington's March from New York to Yorktown (August - September 1781)
N
Hudson River
Heath (2,500)
WEST POINT
King's Ferry (Aug. 20-21)
Stony Point
New York
(Aug. 19)
MASS
WASHINGTON (2,000)
Allied troops
ROCHAMBEAU (4,800)
CONN
Clinton (17,000)
Morristown
(Aug. 28)
Chatham
New Brunswick
New York City
(August 31)
Trenton
Philadelphia
(September 3)
Pennsylvania
Chester
Maryland
New Jersey
Elkton
Baltimore
Delaware
Embarked September 6-18.
ATLANTIC OCEAN
Virginia
Chesapeake Bay
The Battle off the Capes (September 5, 1781)
Lafayette & Militia (approx. 4,000)
CORNWALLIS (7,200)
Richmond
de Grasse (3,000)
Williamsburg
YORKTOWN
De Grasse disembarked his troops on September 5. Washington's army completed its landing by September 26.

decided to force the ford. Mr. Washington had small fortified posts there which defended it. The action began with a lively cannonade ordered expressly to attract the attention of the Americans. During this time General Howe was having Lord Cornwallis turn their right with a detachment of 5000 men who crossed Brandywine Creek 7 miles above Chadds Ford. However, this movement could not be accomplished without General Washington noticing it. He had 3000 men under the command of General Sullivan march by his right. They marched 3 miles through hilly and wooded countryside and took a position commanding Birmingham Church. The routes they took to arrive there were narrow and bad. His artillery was delayed a bit and he did not have enough time to put it in place before being attacked. Lord Cornwallis placed his artillery near Birmingham Church and had it fire immediately. It was a signal for General Howe who had General Knyphausen's[105] Hessians attack Chadds Ford. The little pickets which General Washington placed on the opposite side of the creek were forced back and the Hessians crossed the creek. The departure of General Sullivan changed the order of battle a bit and the Americans corrected the first plan poorly; they were shaken; it was impossible to rally them and they fled everywhere.

The Count Cornwallis, in attacking General Sullivan, turned his left with a column of grenadiers. They climbed one side of the hill that General Sullivan selected to place his cannon. When this artillery, delayed by the difficulty of the roads, arrived on the other side, they did not have any difficulty to capture it. Sullivan defended himself for a long time despite that but he was finally obliged to yield. He retreated in fairly good order, pursued closely, and rejoined General Washington who retreated to Chester.

Mr. de la Fayette, who commanded a corps of light infantry under General Sullivan, was wounded in the leg during the retreat. It appears that the Americans were fleeing heavy fire because the trees are pierced by a large number of balls at the place where he was wounded.

All the land is very wooded and difficult and, after Philadelphia, more hilly than the rest of Pennsylvania.

After having seen Brandywine, I went to Wilmington. It is a little bit above the city that the creek empties into the Delaware.

Wilmington is located on this river. It is well-built. All the houses are brick and they form only one large street which is fairly long. I don't believe this area is very healthy, as the banks of the Delaware are very marshy above and below.

105 General Wilhelm von Knyphausen (1716-1800) commanded the Hessian troops. He returned to Europe and became military governor of Cassel. He died in 1800 as the result of an eye surgery.

Lauzun's Legion and the Bourbonnais division departed from Wilmington on the 7th, made 22 miles and camped at Head of Elk. The Soissonnais division left the camp at Chester and arrived at the one at Wilmington.

Newport is 4 miles from Wilmington. It is already a rather large village and well-built. There's a creek 4 miles further which empties into the Delaware which we cross on a bridge called Christian's Bridge. It is 2 miles away from Christian's Village which is located in a fine place and contains some 30 houses. We cross Ridley's Creek 2 miles from this location which is 10 miles from Head of Elk.

Elk town[106] is located a mile from the river and contains 30 or 40 houses. General Washington and Mr. the Count de Rochambeau, having seen that they would not be able to embark all their troops, busied themselves to find the means to allow as many as possible to go by sea. They sent to Baltimore to collect as many ships as possible.

The Americans who descended the Delaware from Trenton to New Castle preceded the French and had already arrived at Head of Elk a day before them. Some rumors arose among them that reached their general and made him aware that several officers raised their voices. They threatened nothing more than to let him to go to Virginia alone. Mr. Washington used his prudence and usual spirit of conciliation to bring the malcontents around, to make them return to duty; but the most powerful means he used was that of the French purse.

Mr. de Rochambeau learned from some of Mr. de Grasse's dispatches, brought by the cutter *Serpent*, that the admiral had 1,200,000 [livres] aboard for him. That's why he loaned General Washington 180,000 livres, the only money he had left, with which the Americans received one month's pay and assurances for their future needs. These unfortunate troops usually were neither paid nor clothed and often badly nourished. They were going away from a climate and region that they knew. They thought they needed to assure themselves of fleeting comfort, but the moment of an almost certain victory toward which they were marching never should have been part of the rumor.

Mr. de Rochambeau had, at this moment, so much greater facility than before to save the Americans in addition to the 12,000,000 francs brought from Havana by Mr. de Grasse, he had just learned of the arrival of the *Resolue* at Boston with 1,800,000 livres for the French. Col. Laurens, son of the president, who was sent to France to request any possible assistance, also arrived on this frigate with 3,000,000 for the United States and a sufficient quantity of cloth to dress 12 or 15,000 men.

All the ships at Head of Elk could only hold 50 or 60 men each, at most. Many were of lesser capacity. With all the searching and activity possible, we could not find enough, in all

106 Elkton, MD.

the little neighboring ports of the bay, to transport all our troops. That's why Mr. de Rochambeau soon decided to send them by land, most of them to Baltimore and Annapolis under the command of the Baron de Viomenil. He left a detachment of 1500 men, consisting of all the grenadiers and light infantry, Lauzun's infantry and the artillery to embark at Head of Elk under the command of Mr. de Custine.[107] Lauzun's cavalry, all the baggage formed a separate column which had orders to march long days and to go to Williamsburg by land. Mr. Collot,[108] Quartermaster General of the Army was ordered to conduct them.

This marching order was determined on the 8th, that the first division remained in camp and that the Soissonnais arrived there from Wilmington.

The artillery had already marched to the landing and was already working to dismount their trunnions and to board the bombs, cannonballs etc.

The pear was ripe and the time was getting more precious every day. Our generals respectively gave orders and saw to everything that was necessary for the embarkation, the march were busy to get to la Fayette's army. General Washington, being a Virginian, knew well the resources of his state and promised Mr. de Rochambeau that they would easily find the means to make 60 to 70 miles a day. Mr. de Rochambeau could only [send ?] him Mr. de Fersen and Damas, two of his aides-de-camp. In order to rejoin them as quickly as possible, the Count de Vauban and I requested to embark with Mr. de Custine and we remained at Head of Elk. The generals departed the night of the 8th and Mr. the Baron de Viomenil marched with most of the army to go to Baltimore on the 9th. On our part, we worked, with every possible effort, for our embarkation. After an inspection of the galleys which were to transport us, it requires a sense of duty or rather the desire to avoid a hard march to risk ourselves on pontoon boats, some lacking masting, others leaking water everywhere, many more commanded, operated by a single Negro.

The 10th was employed in the same manner as the preceding day. We made soundings by boat 6 miles from Head of Elk to Plum Point where Mr. de Custine had his detachment march on the 11th. Vauban and I were very useful to him in all the work that such a

107 Adam Philippe Comte de Custine (1740–1793) was a general in charge of the French troops that opened the first parallel at Yorktown. He returned to France and rejoined his unit in the Royal Army. Later, he was elected to the Estates-General and served in the subsequent National Constituent Assembly as a representative from Metz when the French Revolution began. The Committee on Public Safety's Revolutionary Tribunal attacked Custine through his publication and found him guilty of treason on August 27, 1793. He was guillotined the following day.

108 George Henri Victor Collot (1750-1805) served as Governor of Guadeloupe. He is best known for his expedition down the Ohio and Mississippi rivers in the spring and summer of 1796.

precipitous embarkation necessarily requires and done with so few resources. We lacked provisions at one time, making us fear for the crossing. We had no wool. Mr. de Custine, Mr. des Deux Ponts, the Duc de Lauzun, Vauban and I gave our purses with which Mr. Blanchard,[109] principal Commissioner of War provided for the needs as much as the region allowed. Gaiety, desire, hope prevailed on this occasion but officer or soldier, nobody was comfortable. The Americans were under the orders of the French commander. The Rhode Island Regiment and a regiment of the state of New York were destined to board the flatboats, which had already been so useful to us, and to row down the bay.

The morning of the 12th, all the detachments embarked and we set sail at 5 p.m. The navigation of the Elk River being difficult and the night dark, we anchored near Back Creek in sight of the only courthouse, the landing site of General Knyphausen and the Hessians in 1777 when General Howe entered Pennsylvania.

At dawn on the 13th, we we got under way with a favorable wind. We rounded Turkey Point early, which is the northernmost point of the Chesapeake Bay and we continued on our way until nightfall when the sea became very rough. Three quarters of our galleys were loaded with bombs, cannonballs and overloaded with soldiers and did not have a single foot above the waterline. All the conductors understood the need for prudence. They all agreed to hug the shore and anchored near Annapolis. Mr. de Custine, with whom I embarked, wanted very much to be the first to reach Mr. de Grasse's fleet, to speak with him, to learn where he would land his detachment, to oversee the necessaries. He wanted to brave the bad weather in his boat. He did not join the flotilla at Annapolis but a short time later by fear and luck we were obliged to drop anchor in the middle of the bay.

Mr. the Count de Rochambeau and General Washington received an express from Mr. de la Fayette, along the way, advising them that the British fleet had appeared off the capes, that Mr. de Grasse had gone out and that they had seen two British frigates in the bay. Not knowing the outcome, fearing to expose his troops aboard, General Washington dispatched Colonel Humphrey,[110] one of his aides-de-camp, to stop loading, until further orders, anything which needed to be loaded anywhere he found it. Colonel Humphrey arrived at Annapolis the same evening as our flotilla and executed his orders.

109 Claude Blanchard (1742-1803) was Commissary of War until 1793. He is often confused with another Blanchard, who was also a Commissary of War. He died at the Hôtel des Invalides on May 11, 1803.

110 Lieutenant-Colonel David Humphreys (1752–1818) was aide de camp to George Washington, a secretary and intelligence agent for Benjamin Franklin in Paris, American minister to Portugal and then to Spain, an entrepreneur who brought Merino sheep to America and member of the Connecticut state legislature. He was a poet and author. He was one of the writers called the Hartford Wits. He wrote the first sonnet known to have been written in America about the time independence was declared.

We ran great danger in the bay several times. The sea was very rough and the surf could be disastrous for us because we were loaded with bombs and cannonballs. And, at various times, they all rolled onto the same side and we were two fingers from perishing in this position. We came about and packed ourselves against one another 60 grenadiers of the Saintonge Regiment. We had them all sit on the bombs to keep them safe.

The morning of the 14th, we resumed sail. We had a very favorable wind and we encountered the *Romulus*, la *Gentille* and several other vessels dispatched by Mr. de Grasse to go to Baltimore or Annapolis to get the troops commanded by the Baron de Vioménil.

The 15th, we arrived rather early at the foot of the bay where the navy was anchored in view of Capes Charles and Henry, between two banks called Middle Ground and Horse Shoe. We had dinner on board the *Ville de Paris* where Mr. the Count de Grasse informed us of the details of a battle he fought on the 5th with the British commanded by Admirals Hood, Graves and Drake who had 21 vessels. When they appeared, Mr. de Grasse had 1800 men less on board all his vessels which he sent ashore for different services and for [l'équade]. Despite this great void in his crews, he had the vessels of his navy cut their cables and he set sail with 24. The four others remained at the entrance to the York and James Rivers to prevent anything going to the enemy or escaping. His vanguard reached the British rear guard and attacked it vigorously. The engagement was partial. Only twelve of his vessels were engaged. The *Pluton*, commanded by Mr. Dalbert de Rioux, the *Diademe* by Mr. de Montéclerc, the *Auguste* by Mr. de Bougainville[111] particularly distinguished themselves. The enemy did not believe the sides equal. They hugged the wind closely and sailed away. The two navies remained in sight without engaging for five days. During this time, Mr. de Barras with the Rhode Island fleet which sailed far to the east then to the south to encounter nothing from New York, arrived in the bay on the 10th and Mr. de Grasse reentered the 11th, captured the British frigates *Iris* and *Richmond* which were those that so intrigued our generals during the fleet's sortie and were seen cutting the buoys. Mr. de Barras also captured two vessels on his voyage from Newport to the Chesapeake.

The British lost many men in the battle of the 5th.[112] No longer able to hold on [illegible] the 74-gun *Terrible*, they set it on fire and also had five vessels totally disabled.

111 Louis Antoine de Bougainville (1729–1811) was a French admiral and explorer. A contemporary of the British explorer James Cook, he took part in the Seven Years' War in North America and the American Revolutionary War against Britain. He gained fame for his expeditions, including circumnavigation of the globe in a scientific expedition in 1763, the first recorded settlement on the Falkland Islands, and voyages into the Pacific Ocean. Bougainville Island of Papua New Guinea as well as the Bougainvillea flower were named after him.

112 Battle of the Virginia Capes or Battle of the Chesapeake.

A few hours after our arrival at Mr. de Grasse's navy, Mr. de Custine dispatched me to Williamsburg to inform Mr. de la Fayette. Mr. Blanchard, Commissioner of War, also came with me to work without delay on everything under his responsibility. We had only 50 miles to travel to arrive at Williamsburg, but I experienced that the sea is not always the quickest and the safest route for an aide-de-camp. With four rowers and an American boat which took on water, we threw overboard everything we couldn't keep on board. We departed from the town of [illegible]. We were thwarted by the wind, a very rough sea for our light skiff and we entered the James River which, despite its great width, is surprisingly difficult to navigate because of the oysters banks there. I failed four times in the middle of the river. I spent two nights and a day in the boat in the bay with a piece of bread and a jug of water. The fever took Mr. Blanchard and we didn't arrive at Williamsburg until the 17th.

General Washington and Mr. de Rochambeau were there since the 15th. Upon receiving the account which I gave them of what happened to us since their departure from Head of Elk, Mr. de Rochambeau sent the Count de Fersen to Annapolis to have the grenadiers and light infantry come down the bay and prepare the boarding of the Baron de Vioménil on the navy vessels.

During all the time of our marches in the states of New York, the Jerseys, Pennsylvania, the secret of the expedition was so well kept, the demonstrations before New York so well and so realistically conducted that the plan of our generals was never suspected by Clinton. He never advised Lord Cornwallis. The latter had no suspicion and only the arrival of Mr. Washington and Mr. de Rochambeau who passed in review the troops of Mr. de la Fayette and those of Mr. de Saint Simon the same day and the news of the imminent arrival of the French and the dangers which he had to fear was brought to him by a Williamsburg Tory called Hubbard.

On the 18th, our generals embarked aboard the *Queen Charlotte*, which was stationed in the James River, to go in search of Mr. the Count de Grasse and to concert their operations.

During their absence, we experienced a great shortage of provisions which was not surprising in a region with no supplies and where the British Army pillaged, ravaged and camped for some time. Mr. Nelson, current governor of Virginia, used all his credit, all the means in his power to promptly provide for a shortage which increased hourly in proportion to the number of people who continued to arrive. We needed wagons and horses. Mr. Nelson procured some and even gave some of his own. In the end, he spared no care, no effort, no avenue and we saw him do everything which can be expected of the most zealous patriot.

On the 19th, Mr. de Choisy, who was on board the *Experiment* in the James River with the [400?] men he commanded at Newport, landed and rejoined Mr. de la Fayette.

It was at this moment that I had a wonderful opportunity to know the young general. Mr. de Rochambeau being absent, I spent several days with him and followed him everywhere as his aide-de-camp. I observed him much and I soon experienced all the feelings that great accomplishments, which precede or don't wait for age, can inspire: the great knowledge of his duty, the moderation, the unusual modesty, the most perfect kindness. How wonderful it is, at his age, to be a successful emulator of Cornwallis, of him who always made the Americans tremble. It is rare to leave one's country at 24 years of age, to go to an almost unknown shore, and, in such a short time, to attract general support and the greatest regard of an entire vast country and at a time when the local state of affairs of the country, the nature of the conflicts which cause them to take up arms, offer each individual the means of distinguishing himself. The memory of the Marquis (for that is the way the Americans call Mr. de la Fayette) will pass from generation to generation and the first word which every veteran soldier who served under him will teach his young son to pronounce will be his name.

The French grenadiers and light infantry and the troops of General Washington embarked at Head of Elk, arrived in the James River from Annapolis on the 22nd and landed.

Camp at Williamsburg

They came to camp at Williamsburg on the 23rd at which time our generals returned from the *Ville de Paris.*

They were 8 miles from Williamsburg at the mouth of Queens Creek on the 24th. From here we can see very far up the York River to observe any enemy movement on this river.

The Baron de Vioménil arrived the same day, from Annapolis, on board the *Romulus* with most of the French troops. They all landed on the 25th and came to camp at Williamsburg on the 26th.

Lord Cornwallis could not have learned calmly about all the preparations. We learned, from a deserter that he captured 400 Negroes who worked day and night. They cut down the pine trees which surrounded York to block the way and to make abatis. He employed 1800 workers continually at these works.

The 64-gun *Triton* and the 64-gun *Vaillant* and the frigate *Railleuse* were still in the York River. Cornwallis sent fire ships toward them during the night of the 26th. They were diverted with difficulty. When they came very close, many sailors, frightened at the approach of danger, jumped in the shallops instead of working. Many others jumped in the water and most of them drowned. But the greatest misfortune that occurred was the brawl which the *Triton* caused when she came alongside the *Vaillant.*

Our field artillery, embarked at Annapolis, was landed at the same time at College Landing near Williamsburg.

In addition to the post at York, the enemy were masters of Gloucester on the left bank of this river. They had constructed many earthworks for its defense.

To prepare for the investment, Mr. Washington requested Governor Nelson to have 800 militiamen march there. They mustered promptly under the command of Brigadier General Weeden who was ready to march at the first order. Lauzun's cavalry had also arrived in the area and camped at North Creek.[113] Mr. de Rochambeau had the infantry of this corps parade along with Mr. de Choisy to command the entire siege in this difficult area. There were also under his command 800 garrison troops whom Mr. de Grasse landed from the vessels.

Governor Nelson placed himself aside of us at the head of 1200 militiamen. Finally, everything we could expect of the troops camped since the 27th, was a day of rest for everyone after the fatigues which we all experienced by land or by sea.

Lord Cornwallis, on his side, did not remain inactive. He put everything in motion for a strong defense. It is surprising that he did not send out some parties, some reconnaissance to observe us.

At dawn on the 28th, the allied army composed of 5000 Americans of the Continental Army, 1200 Virginia militiamen and 8000 French marched for the siege of York. The Americans, as nationals, were at the head. There are 12 miles between Williamsburg and York and this route is covered with woods. We could have taken several excellent positions, which were very long and difficult to capture, for its defense, but we found no opposition there, either because Cornwallis did not expect us that day or because he did not want to advance from the main body at his location.

York County is enclosed in a peninsula formed by the James and York rivers and the Chesapeake Bay. All its exits were guarded by the navy. The town of York itself is difficult to approach and is enclosed between two muddy creeks one of which flows above and the other below the town. There are only two exits by land. One leads to Hampton at the base of the peninsula; the other goes to Williamsburg which we held.

113 Brigadier General George Weedon (1734–1793) served as a lieutenant under George Washington in the French and Indian War, mainly assigned to garrison duty in western Virginia. Thomas Jefferson wrote the Statute of Religious Freedom, the very first document of its kind to acknowledge government recognition of religious tolerance, in Weedon's Tavern in January 1777. He was made a lieutenant colonel and second in command to Hugh Mercer in 1775. He was promoted to colonel in 1776 and succeeded Mercer in command of his regiment. He was promoted to brigadier general upon Mercer's death at Princeton in 1777. He fought in the Battles of Trenton, Brandywine, and Germantown. He resigned in 1778 and went home to VA to lead a brigade of the state's militia at the request of Governor Thomas Jefferson. He led his militia unit in the Yorktown campaign, where his brigade repelled Colonel Banastre Tarleton at Gloucester Point.

Siege of Yorktown

Four miles from York, in the woods, the Americans took the right and the French the left for the siege. We were only discovered 1 mile from the place when a few enemy patrols fired at the head of our advance guards. The Baron de Viomenil, at the head of the grenadiers and light infantry, took favorable ground behind which Mr. de Rochambeau placed the rest of his troops. Caution was needed on the roads, barely cleared, in the woods. We pushed our lead pickets, from place to place, to within 50 paces of the enemy.

Our three divisions shared the ground from the York River to just aside of Secretary Nelson's house. The Americans extended from this point to the banks of the lower York. The siege on the French side was complete at 4 p.m. The troops were exhausted. There was an excessive and burning heat and, if we were attacked, we could not draw on any part of the division from the islands. Three quarters of the soldiers of the companies which composed it had fallen along the roads from the heat. Although they were accustomed to scorching heat, they were not like ours, to be endured in long marches under the haversack.

The Americans were not able to finish their siege the same day. They had to cross a marsh where the British had cut all the causeways. It was also guarded by a strong detachment of Tarleton's cavalry. A few cannon shots which Mr. de Rochambeau had fired at them soon dispersed them. He withdrew into York and crossed to the Gloucester side. Mister Washington then approached the marsh and used the rest of the day and all night to reestablish communication on the marsh. He spent the 29th there and completed the siege of the place.

On the Gloucester side, Mr. de Choisy and all the troops under his command performed the same operation as the allied army on the 28th without the least opposition.

During the night of the 29th to the 30th, the enemy evacuated the three works on Pigeon's Hill which they left in very good condition. Our patrols noticed it at dawn, and Mr. de Rochambeau had the Bourbonnais grenadiers and light infantry occupy it without delay. They were supported by their regiment which approached and camped nearby.

Two of these works were two redoubts, squared, fraised and palisaded. One could contain 100 men, the other 60. They were completely enclosed by the gorge. The third was not yet finished. There were some platforms for two pieces of cannon which, at the first appearance of the Americans, killed two of their men. Governor Nelson had a militia detachment march to capture it and work to close it.

Lord Cornwallis, having observed that our advance posts were supported by large bodies, when he saw them very close, feared that we might capture these redoubts by force. That convinced him to evacuate them and to withdraw to the main body of the place. But, in doing so, he committed a serious error because they were located at the head of a marsh which we could not cross. He must have known the position and the importance of his

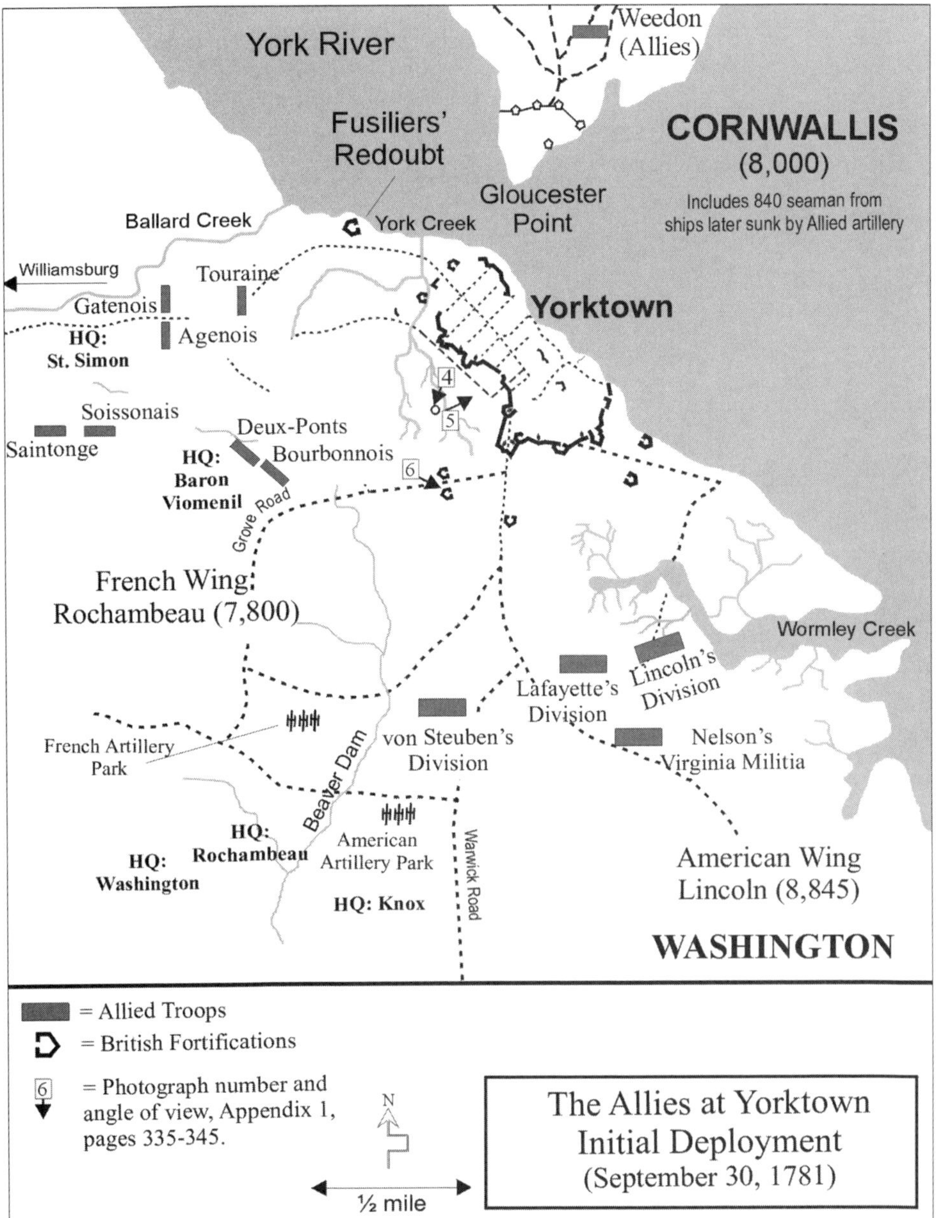

posts which, being in good condition, would have obliged us to open the trench in front. This would have delayed us about eight days. Secondly, in a siege, one should never decide to tighten defenses until the last minute.

General Washington and Mr. de Rochambeau spent the entire day of the 30th reconnoitering the works on the left of the enemy, on the side of the lower York.

The Marquis de St. Simon was ill at the time of the investment. The Viscount de Vioménil took command of the island division which held the French left. In front of this left, the enemy had a post on a hill which the Viscount de Vioménil captured. There was a cannonade and a few musket shots which killed one of our soldiers and wounded another. Mr. de Brouillet, Second Captain of the Agenois Regiment had his thigh broken by an exploding mortar shell.

October 1781

During the night of September 30 to October 1, a French detachment and most of the American militiamen were busy constructing communication trenches between the redoubts and other works to prevent sorties and to facilitate the approaches. Until now, the enemy only fired on those who advanced near their location out of curiosity or out of duty. They began to make a continuous fire on the workers but fortunately without effect. They only killed one man that day.

Colonel Scammel of the light infantry and one of the finest officers of the Continental Army went out to reconnoiter and was taken prisoner. After his surrender, a British officer fired a pistol into his kidney and killed him. The Americans greatly regretted his loss.

We almost lost Mr. de Rochambeau who, during the reconnaissance, took a map from his pocket. He was on foot on a small hill, his legs spread apart. A ball was fired which buried itself more than 2 feet in the ground between his legs. The Baron de Closen and I were holding his map.

The 2nd and 3rd, our workers continued the works already begun. The enemy continued an incessant fire on them to which we could not respond. Our siege artillery and ammunition were not yet landed. Mr. de Barras had brought them from Rhode Island and the vessels which had them aboard had just gone up the James River as far as Tribel's Ferry,[114] 8 miles from Yorktown. Mr. de Rochambeau had the landing accelerated for which the flatboats which had already given us so much service since the North River were

114 Trebell's Landing. Trebell's offered more direct access to the primary road networks operating between Carter's Grove and other prominent points on the peninsula. It was designated by Thomas Nelson as the operational headquarters for the Virginia Navy beginning in September 1781. Once it was expected that Washington would move south to invest Cornwallis at Yorktown, Nelson directed Commodore James Barron to assemble his fleet and gather small boats at Trebell's. This was the designated landing site for supplies, food and stores collected throughout Virginia and transported along the various waterways. Nelson also directed the Virginia State line and militia to guard these stores at Trebell's. As a result, it became the predominant landing site for French artillery.

very useful. Governor Nelson procured horses to transport our artillery to them along with those of our crews which had not yet arrived.

In camp, our soldiers did not remain idle. The engineers had them work nonstop making gabions, fascines and saucissons.[115] If, on our part, we took all the precautions necessary for the attack, Lord Cornwallis forgot nothing for the defense. From the time we arrived, he had greatly increased his earthworks.

On the 4th, Mr. Collot arrived with the column of equipment which we awaited with great impatience to use the horses to transport our artillery.

We received intelligence of the enemy from a dozen Hessian deserters who came to find us.

On the Gloucester side, Mr. de Choisy wanted to take a position closer to the post than that which he already had. He received intelligence along the route that Colonel Tarleton was having his cavalry forage and that he was supported by the infantry. He prepared to harass the foragers and gave the order to Mr. de Lauzun who marched there with his hussars. His infantry and General Weeden's militiamen were supposed to follow him.

Tarleton, before being overtaken, had time to arrange his wagons and to prepare for battle with 250 horses. He placed his infantry at the edge of a wood on his [unintelligible]. Mr. le Duc de Lauzun's march was a little delayed by his infantry. Seeing that it wasn't arriving, he placed 50 horses on his right and 50 on his left to cover his flanks. He charged the until now invincible Tarleton with a squad so vigorously that a melee ensued for some time. Our hussars finally broke through Tarleton who retreated to his infantry in great haste. Mr. de Lauzun pursued him but, when he approached the British infantry, they made a very lively fire on him. Mr. de Choisy sent him an order to withdraw. This was the first action where his corps found itself, since its creation, in addition to the demonstrations of his hussars' bravery. This is one which belongs only to Mr. de Lauzun.

After receiving the order to retreat, which he did, he himself being the rearguard of his corps, he saw one of his hussars still engaged with three British dragoons. He ran to his assistance, saber in hand, disengaged him and brought him back to his troop.

Mr. de Lauzun had three men killed, eight wounded. Tarleton left 15 men on the battlefield, had about 20 wounded and 10 taken prisoners.

After this action Mr. de Choisy, free of movement, took an excellent position one great mile from Gloucester. He captured all the roads and, as it was possible that Cornwallis might want to cross the York River and force him to flee, he withdrew.

115 Gabions are cylindrical baskets made of wicker and filled with earth for use in building fortifications. Fascines are long bundles of sticks tied together, used in building earthworks and in strengthening ramparts. Saucissons are long fascines, from 18 to 21 feet and 10 or 12 inches in diameter.

Lord Cornwallis had sunk a large number of vessels all around York to defend the approach on the river side. He still had a fairly large number and many boats with which he could attempt a landing at Gloucester and then escape. To quell even the idea of it, Mr. de Rochambeau greatly desired one of Mr. de Grasse's vessels to go above York to command the river and to intercept any crossing. He wrote some dispatches about the subject and sent me to bring them to Mr. de Grasse aboard the *Ville de Paris*. I left at 9 o'clock the night of the 4th and traveled 25 miles to Hampton. I found the little boat of the *Expériment* in this port. I boarded it to descend the James River and to enter the bay. This damned sea was never favorable to me. Beaten by a wind which was too strong for my frail boat, I spent the entire day of the 5th and part of the night to make 20 miles. After having fought the wind for a long time, I was fortunate enough to reach the *Victoire*, the lead vessel of the navy. I climbed aboard extremely tired by need and seasickness. I found something to compensate for what I had suffered in the kindnesses of Mr. d'Albert Saint Hyppolite, captain of this vessel. The sea became calm and he gave me the means to get aboard the *Ville de Paris* where I arrived at 1 a.m. on the 6th. Mr. de Grasse was ill. However, I requested him to send me away as soon as he could. His dispatch finished, he sent me aboard the *Glorieux* to ask Mr. the Baron d'Escars for his vessel's boat for my return. I was very happy to meet this brave sailor who spoke to me thus: tell Mr. the Count de Rochambeau, "Sir, his Majesty's vessel le *Glorieux* is ready to go above York at the first signal. Despite the general fear and rumors, she would attack the enemy land batteries and fire ships." This speech was so much nicer from his lips. Except for two or three captains of vessels out of 36, all the others had distanced themselves from this mission. Mr. de Grasse himself seemed to me only very mildly in favor. I arrived at Hampton very fortunately. From there, I went very promptly to give an account of my mission to my general.

I found him giving orders to open the trench which was to occur that same day, the night of the 6th.

During my absence from the 4th to the 6th, the enemy had maintained a continuous fire [illegible] on our workers. The French were more fortunate than the American militiamen who only lost a few men.

Our artillery had exerted an untiring effort in landing its pieces and ammunition and soon had everything brought to the park.

Lord Cornwallis, seeing his hour had come, so to speak, no longer wanted useless mouths in his place. He sent away more than 300 Negroes, negresses or little Negroes (who had been stolen), all naked and without a single piece of bread. This characteristic of inhumanity was preceded by thousands of other stronger ones during the course of the campaign. Not knowing what harm to do to the Americans, the British captured many of their Negroes whom they inoculated and let them run throughout the region in this condition. Many died as well as whites who were infected with the disease. They captured a pregnant woman near Portsmouth and hanged her with this inscription: «You will no longer give birth to rebels.» Theft, rape, murder, arson followed their path everywhere in Virginia. Let us then try to bring peace to this unfortunate province and may our courage awaken since we hold her enemies two fingers from their perdition.

General Washington had never conducted a siege and could not have any knowledge of this matter other than what he might acquire through careful thought. Even though he was commander-in-chief, Mr. de Rochambeau took the direction of the siege which he already conducted from his bed. The months of August and September are very unhealthy in Virginia because of the extreme heat and it is not rare to see part of the inhabitants attacked by a fever called ague in this season. The harshness and difficulty of the life which Mr. de Rochambeau led the previous two months caused him to come down with it almost as soon as he arrived at York. Despite the weakness this illness causes, he was busy every day when it left him only an hour or two for tasks. The little strength he had remaining, he spent reconnoitering the enemy works to give direction to the parallels. General Washington and the principal American and French engineers came to report twice a day. One received his advice, the others his orders. Finally, everything was in order and ready for the opening of the trench. On the night of the 6th, 1600 workers from both armies were commanded to perform this duty. On the French side, they were supported by the Bourbonnais and Soissonnais regiments commanded by Mr. the Baron de Vioménil.

Yorktown is half surrounded by deep ravines and by a muddy and impassable creek which begins at Pigeon Hill near the center of town and runs a little above York into the river of the same name. The enemy had guarded the crossings established on this creek with redans[116] and other little works. And, at its mouth on the left bank, they constructed a picketed star fort with a good moat and two rows of abatis. It could contain from 150 to 200 men. Inside the fort, there was good covering to shelter its defenders from bombs. The banks of the York River near the fort are very steep and the British vessels anchored between York and Gloucester were under its protection.

Mr. the Count de Rochambeau wanted to make only one feint on this side and decided the real attack would be on the enemy's left. The feint was entrusted to the Touraine Regiment which was to furnish the workers and the guards.

Mr. the Marquis de Saint Simon, on landing, gave the command of a small body of 200 volunteers drawn from the three regiments that he brought to his brother, the baron. They were ordered to always remain entrenched with the Touraine Regiment. A little before the end of the day, one of these volunteers deserted to the enemy and gave them intelligence of the preparations for the opening of the trench which he saw on this left. At nightfall, all the

116 A redan is a V-shaped earthwork usually projecting from a fortified line.

workers, supplied with gabions, fascines and tools marched through the woods in silence and arrived at 100 toises from the star fort. Their right was against one of the branches of the muddy creek of which I spoke; their left at the York River. The enemy, informed, kept a very lively and sustained fire on the workers throughout the night and almost nobody would have been victim if Mr. de Saint Simon had placed an advance picket of grenadiers of the Touraine Regiment with more foresight and less in view of the enemy. There were at least 10 killed and several wounded needlessly.

The trench of the true attack, which began near Pigeon's Hill and extended all the way to the edge of the lower York River, received only a few cannon shots. We can even say that the opening of this parallel was taken from the enemy by surprise and that they were not aware of it. We had only three wounded.

We opened a battery on our left, on the bank of the river, that same night to fire simultaneously on the vessels and the star fort. Mr. de la Loge, a promising young bombardier officer was killed by a shot from a long-barrelled musket.

The aides-de-camp rarely perform the same duty as the troops in the trench. Both for our satisfaction, our instruction, and to silence any rumors on this matter, we requested Mr. de Rochambeau to allow us to spend 24 hours in the trench for two entire days. He granted the request very willingly as he was ill and confined to bed. He ordered us to always have a horse ready to leave the trench and to inform him of anything new happening there, both on the right and on the left.

The day of the 7th to the 8th, the trench was relieved by the Saintonge and Agenois regiments under the command of Mr. the Chevalier de Chastellux. I went to this trench. We labored to improve the works of the previous evening. The battery on the left, of 2 24-pounders, 2 12-pounders and 6 mortars, was advanced with such activity that it was ready to fire on the morning of the 8th. But Mr. de Rochambeau did not want her to do so in order not to attract enemy fire on only one, because the batteries of the grand parallel were not yet ready. We opened the batteries of the true attack and we began four redoubts linked to the parallel to increase its defense and to prevent enemy sorties. We had 9 men killed and one wounded.

The day of the 8th to the 9th, the trench was relieved by the Gatinois and Royal Deux Ponts regiments posted under the orders of Mr. the Marquis de Saint Simon. We completed the trenches and worked with the greatest activity on the batteries of the grand parallel. The enemies continued their fire, killing and wounding a few men.

The day of the 9th to the 10th, the trench was relieved by the Bourbonnais and Soissonnais regiments under the command of the Viscount de Vioménil.

The two battalions of the Touraine Regiment and Saint Simon's volunteers alternated to relieve our left. From this location, we thought we saw the enemy unload more cannon and bring it to the star fort. This action compelled Mr. the Count de Rochambeau to have

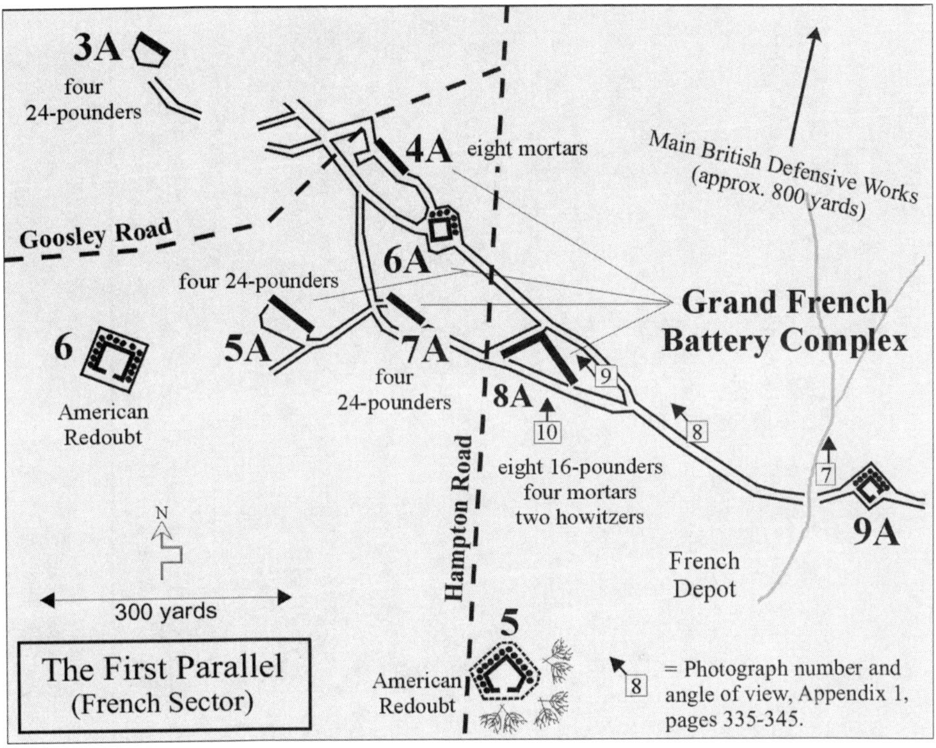

us fire on the vessels to chase them away despite his intention to have all the batteries play on them together. Two 24-pounders which we substituted for 2 18-pounders produced the desired effect. In order to distract the enemy's attention, the battery on the right of the Americans also began to fire on their earthworks.

The morning of the 10th, all the batteries of the parallel fired. Lord Cornwallis, having observed that we had not fired a single cannon for several days, took this occasion to encourage his troops, saying that he was informed that we had no siege artillery and that all our efforts would be vain. His and their astonishment must have been great, as he was hardly able to respond after two hours of our firing.

From the 10th to the 11th, the trench was relieved by the Saintonge and Agenois regiments under the command of Mr. the Baron de Vioménil. Our batteries continued their fire with remarkable success.

It was not even probable that Lord Cornwallis would attempt to cross to the Gloucester side to escape from the poor front where he found himself engaged. Before going any further, he now had to defeat Mr. de Choisy who was very well positioned. His plan of escape pleased him but it was fleeting. Mr. Count de Rochambeau would have wanted one or two of the Count de Grasse's vessels to go up above York to block the river and to remove any concern from that side. Our general, seeing that the admiral wasn't

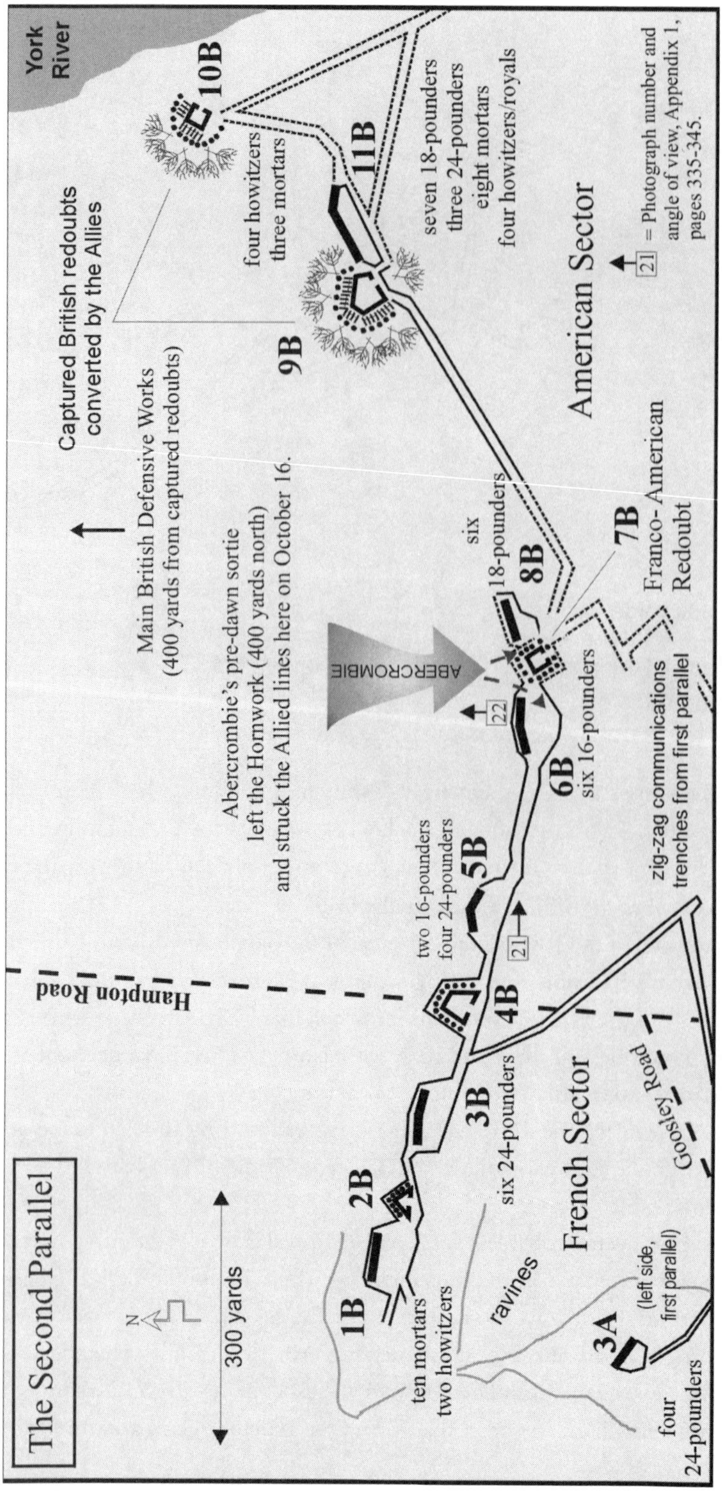
The Second Parallel
N
300 yards
York River
Hampton Road
Captured British redoubts converted by the Allies
Main British Defensive Works (400 yards from captured redoubts)
Abercrombie's pre-dawn sortie left the Hornwork (400 yards north) and struck the Allied lines here on October 16.
ABERCROMBIE
1B
ten mortars two howitzers
2B
3B
six 24-pounders
4B
two 16-pounders four 24-pounders
5B
21
6B
six 16-pounders
22
8B
six 18-pounders
7B
Franco- American Redoubt
9B
four howitzers three mortars
10B
11B
seven 18-pounders three 24-pounders eight mortars four howitzers/royals
3A
(left side, first parallel)
four 24-pounders
ravines
French Sector
American Sector
Goosley Road
zig-zag communications trenches from first parallel
21 = Photograph number and angle of view, Appendix 1, pages 335-345.

making a decision, decided to destroy British ships if he could. Most of them were within range of the cannons at the battery on our left. I brought his orders to the artillery commander to have some grills brought up to heat some cannonballs and fire red hot balls.[117] This arrangement produced success a few hours later. We set fire to the 50-gun ship *Charon* and two other large transports. Fortunately for the enemy, there was no wind. The other vessels, to avoid spreading the fire as we had hoped, cut their cables and retreated to the Gloucester side where they remained since. It was a fine evening. The vessels were still on fire and illuminated the river. The large number of bombs in the air, the noise of the cannon of the place and of the siege guns produced a spectacle and a combination which we rarely see and which is hard to describe.

The night of the 11th to the 12th, the trench was relieved by the Gatinois and the Royal Deux Ponts regiments under the command of the Chevalier de Chastellux. That night, the second parallel was opened and we were as happy as at the opening of the first. In other words, our workers were not harassed and the enemy killed very few men. We might even think that they would not notice our new works to raise the batteries of the first parallel until the next morning. They continued to fire above the second. They could do so only because they were constructed on small hills dominating the ground of the second parallel.

From the 12th to the 13th, the trench was relieved by the Agenois and the Saintonge regiments under the command of the Viscount of Vioménil [and] the Bourbonnais and the Soissonnais under the command of Mr. the Marquis de Saint Simon. We completed the works of the previous evening and we began the redoubts and the batteries of the second parallel. We had three men killed, two officers and 12 soldiers wounded

From the 13th to the 14th, the trench was relieved by the Saintonge and Agenois regiments under the command of Mr. the Viscount of Vioménil. We continued to work on the redoubts and the batteries begun the previous day and evening.

The Chevalier de Mauduit-Duplessis, who twice tried unsuccessfully to set fire to the abatis of the enemy's works on the right succeeded that night. These abatis were reinforced and made with strong branches and the tops of green pine trees so that they burned very little. The hardy action of the Chevalier de Mauduit is no less meritorious even though it was contested by his corps out of jealousy and aggravation. I was present and owe him this testimony. We had 25 soldiers wounded and 6 killed.

The day of the 14th to the 15th, the trench was relieved by the Gatinois and Royal Deux Ponts regiments under the command of the Baron de Vioménil.

Two detached works from the body of the place were deemed capable of being attacked successfully. Mr. de Rochambeau added four companies of grenadiers to guard

117 Also called hot shot.

the trench and decided to attack these redoubts. General Washington ordered Mr. de la Fayette to attack the one on the right even though it had no trench. The one on the left was given to the Baron de Vioménil under whose command were placed the Count William de Deux Ponts, the Baron de l'Estrade,[118] Lieutenant Colonel of the Gatinois, and the companies of grenadiers and light infantry of this regiment and that of the Royal Deux Ponts. The Baron de Vioménil put a few sappers at the head of this detachment to open a passage in the abatis and to cut the fraises. The enemy began firing at a distance of 150 toises. We did not respond with a single musket shot. The march was rapid. The Baron had the charge beaten and penetrated the redoubt. We did not have any need for ladders. The same zeal, the same bravery animated the commander and the soldiers and we took the work sword in hand. There were 160 men to defend it. We only took 73 prisoners. The rest jumped over the parapet (the redoubt being closed on the side of the place) when the first French grenadiers entered. The vanquished demanded quarter which was granted them. Berthelot,[119] captain in second of the Gatinois grenadiers was killed. Colonel the Count William, the Baron d'Estrade were wounded; Mr. de Sireuil,[120] captain of the Gatinois light infantry had his leg broken on the parapet. The Chevalier de Lameth,[121] Assistant Quartermaster General, who went there as a volunteer received two musket shots in the knees. We also had 102 soldiers killed or wounded.

Mr. de la Fayette was equally pleased at the head of the Americans. The work he attacked contained only 60 men. Mr. de Gimat,[122] Major of the Viennese Regiment and the

118 Claude Aimable Vincent de Roqueplant baron de L'Estrade (1729-1819) was lieutenant-colonel of the Gâtinais regiment. He was promoted to Camp Marshal in 1788 and lieutenant-general in1792. He was chosen to command troops to subdue Lyons in Sept. of 1793 but he refused because of his infirmities. He retired on October 13, 1793.

119 Augustin Clement de Berthelot chevalier de Villeneuve (1750-1781) served as captain of the Gâtinais Regiment (Royal Auvergne). He died in 1781 from wounds received at Yorktown.

120 Jean-Jarlan de Sireuil (?-1781) was the fourth ranking captain of the Gâtinais Regiment (Royal Auvergne). He was wounded at Savannah and Yorktown. He died of his wounds at Williamsburg on Dec. 20, 1781.

121 Alexandre-Théodore-Victor, comte de Lameth (1760-1829) served as one of Rochambeau's aides-de-camp. He was elected to the Estates General and advocated for the abolition of clergy privileges. He became colonel of the fifth Regiment of horse guards in 1791 and camp marshal in 1792. He accompanied Lafayette on his flight and was imprisoned until 1797. He returned to France in 1799, became prefect in 1804, lieutenant general in 1814 and Peer of France in 1820.

122 Jean Joseph de Gimat de Soubadère (1747–1793) served as lieutenant colonel in the Continental Army. He served at Lafayette's side at Brandywine, PA, Gloucester, NJ, and Barren Hill, PA. He returned to France in 1779) and commissioned a major in the Viennois regiment. He was awarded the Cross of the Order of Saint Louis (1780) and returned to America with

colonel of a regiment of American light infantry, received a musket shot in the foot. The Americans lost or had 40 men wounded.

To draw the attention of the enemy on our left, Mr. de Rochambeau ordered a feint at this place which was to be done a little before the main attack and one at the center for the same purpose. The first was done too early. We had only two men wounded. The one in the center was done too late and after the redoubts were taken. It was commanded by Mr. de Custine, who had 12 Soissonnais light infantrymen killed by his own fault.

The Baron de Viomênil immediately had the captured works joined to the second parallel by communication trenches. The Bourbonnais Regiment was sent as reinforcement to guard the trench.

The day of the 15th to the 16th, the trench was relieved by the Soissonnais and Agenois regiments under the command of the Chevalier de Chastellux.

Mr. de Marin,[123] captain of the grenadiers of the Soissonnais Regiment, had his jaw and thigh broken by bombs as he entered the trench. He later died from his wounds at Williamsburg.

At nightfall, we questioned an enemy deserter about what was happening at the place. He told us that he had seen some preparations for a sortie. The commander of the trench thought this was false information and did not make any new arrangements to welcome them. The enemy, numbering 400 men, appeared about midnight. They fell upon a picket from the Agenois Regiment. Overconfidence doomed the captain. The British passed themselves off as Americans, captured the captain and fell upon his detachment which they didn't spare. They then entered a battery and spiked four 16-pounders. The Count de Saint Maisme-Dumuy approached the battery with his grenadiers and a few companions of his regiment from the trench. The Chevalier de Chastellux hastened there with his reserve and repulsed the enemy with loss. They also spiked two pieces of cannon in the American battery but were also repulsed. Our artillerymen unspiked their pieces with some effort and they resumed playing the 16 with all the other batteries of the parallel. More precaution, defiance and vigilance on the Chevalier the Chastellux's part would have prepared for the disaster of this night. The small number of men we had for the various duties obliged them

Lafayette. Washington named him commander of a light infantry regiment on Feb. 17, 1781. He left Philadelphia for France on indefinite leave on January 4,1782. His discharge from the Continental army was dated Nov. 3,1783. He was put in command of the colonial regiment of Martinique. He was governor of Saint Lucia from June 21, 1789 to June 3, 1792, when he left the service of the French revolutionary government. He was commanding a force of 1100 émigrés at Martinique when he was mortally wounded.

123 Jean-Baptiste de Marin (1737-1781) served as captain of the grenadiers of the Soissonnais Regiment. He was wounded at Yorktown and died of his wounds at Williamsburg on Nov. 14, 1781.

to spend three, four and five nights in a row and these unfortunates slept in the trenches almost standing up. The officers were equally tired. The report of the deserter should have kept everybody on the alert.

From the 16th to the 17th, the trench was relieved by the Gatinois and the Saintonge regiments under the command of the Marquis de Saint Simon. Our boats continued their fire with the greatest success. The enemy fire decreased noticeably because of the large number of pieces we dismounted for them. Mr. de St. Simon was wounded in the leg by a long-barreled musket shot.

From the 17th to the 18th, the trench was relieved by the Bourbonnais and Royal Deux Ponts regiments under the command of the Viscount de Vioménil.

British Surrender

Lord Cornwallis and his engineers, carefully considered the dilapidated condition of their position and the garrison, the ever increasing effect of our batteries, many of which enfiladed the enemy works and realised that they would be open and vulnerable from all sides. He sent a flag of truce to propose a 24-hour cease-fire, requesting that both sides appoint commissioners for the capitulation of the posts at York and Gloucester.

He was given only two hours for the cease-fire and before an interview of officers appointed on both sides. He was asked to send his proposal in writing to the American lines at the end of the two hours. Mylord sent his proposal at the appointed time with the request for a continuation of the cease-fire during the night, on condition that neither side would work to repair the earthworks. The request was granted.

Mr. Washington responded to Mylord and laid out the definitive basis on which we could establish a treaty of capitulation: the one given to the American garrison at Charleston in the month of May 1780. Lord Cornwallis agreed and requested, in return for the state of defense in which he surrendered the post of Gloucester, that he be given the sloop of war *Bonetta* at his complete disposition, without being searched or inspected, to carry his dispatches to Sir Henry Clinton with the persons whom he judged proper to send to New York and who would be included in the capitulation.

Both armies then appointed officers who assembled at Mr. Moore's house to draw up the articles of capitulation. The Viscount de Noailles and Colonel Laurence[124] were

124 John Laurens.

appointed for the allies, Colonel Dundas[125] and another officer for the British. All together they debated the articles of capitulation part of the day and night and it was signed only on the morning of the 19th of October.

Articles of Capitulation

Settled between his Excellency General Washington, Commander-in-Chief of the combined Forces of America and France; his Excellency the Count de Rochambeau, Lieutenant-General of the Armies of the King of France, Great Cross of the royal and military Order of St. Louis, commanding the auxiliary Troops of his Most Christian Majesty in America; and his Excellency the Count de Grasse, Lieutenant-General of the Naval Armies of his Most Christian Majesty, Commander of the Order of St. Louis, Commander-in-Chief of the Naval Army of France in the Chesapeake, on the one Part; and the Right Honorable Earl Cornwallis, Lieutenant-General of his Britannic Majesty's Forces, commanding the Garrisons of York and Gloucester; and Thomas Symonds, Esquire, commanding his Britannic Majesty's Naval Forces in York River in Virginia, on the other Part.[126]

ARTICLE I. The garrisons of York and Gloucester, including the officers and seamen of his Britannic Majesty's ships, as well as other mariners, to surrender themselves prisoners of war to the combined forces of America and France. The land troops to remain prisoners to the United States, the navy to the naval army of his Most Christian Majesty. Granted.

ARTICLE II. The artillery, arms, accoutrements, military chest, and public stores of every denomination, shall be delivered unimpaired to the heads of departments appointed to receive them. Granted.

ARTICLE III. At twelve o'clock this day the two redoubts on the left flank of York to be delivered, the one to a detachment of American infantry, the other to a detachment of French grenadiers. Granted.

The garrison of York will march out to a place to be appointed in front of the posts, at two o'clock precisely, with shouldered arms, colors cased, and drums beating a British or

125 Thomas Dundas was a British politician who sat in the House of Commons from 1763 to 1794. Later raised to the peerage as Baron Dundas. He was responsible for commissioning the *Charlotte Dundas*, the world's "first practical steamboat."

126 The text and spelling of these articles is drawn from the English version, except for one notable change noted in Article IV.

German march. They are then to ground their arms, and return to their encampments, where they will remain until they are despatched to the places of their destination. Two works on the Gloucester side will be delivered at one o'clock to a detachment of French and American troops appointed to possess them. The garrison will march out at three o'clock in the afternoon; the cavalry with their swords drawn, trumpets sounding, and the infantry in the manner prescribed for the garrison of York. They are likewise to return to their encampments until they can be finally marched off.

ARTICLE IV. Officers are to retain their swords.[127] Both officers and soldiers to keep their private property of every kind; and no part of their baggage or papers to be at any time subject to search or inspection. The baggage and papers of officers and soldiers taken during the siege to be likewise preserved for them. Granted. It is understood that any property obviously belonging to the inhabitants of these States, in the possession of the garrison, shall be subject to be reclaimed. Granted

ARTICLE V. The soldiers to be kept in Virginia, Maryland, or Pennsylvania, and as much by regiments as possible, and supplied with the same rations of provisions as are allowed to soldiers in the service of America. A field-officer from each nation, to wit, British, Anspach, and Hessian, and other officers on parole, in the proportion of one to fifty men to be allowed to reside near their respective regiments, to visit them frequently, and be witnesses of their treatment; and that their officers may receive and deliver clothing and other necessaries for them, for which passports are to be granted when applied for. Granted.

ARTICLE VI. The general, staff, and other officers not employed as mentioned in the above articles, and who choose it, to be permitted to go on parole to Europe, to New York, or to any other American maritime posts at present in the possession of the British forces, at their own option; and proper vessels to be granted by the Count de Grasse to carry them under flags of truce to New York within ten days from this date, if possible, and they to reside in a district to be agreed upon hereafter, until they embark. The officers of the civil department of the army and navy to be included in this article. Passports to go by land to be granted to those to whom vessels cannot be furnished. Granted.

ARTICLE VII. Officers to be allowed to keep soldiers as servants, according to the common practice of the service. Servants not soldiers are not to be considered as prisoners, and are to be allowed to attend their masters. Granted.

127 The English version used the term side-arms. The French version specified only swords which were the side-arm officers wore rather than bayonets, tomahawks, knives, pistols, etc.

ARTICLE VIII. The Bonetta sloop-of-war to be equipped, and navigated by its present captain and crew, and left entirely at the disposal of Lord Cornwallis from the hour that the capitulation is signed, to receive an aid-de-camp to carry despatches to Sir Henry Clinton; and such soldiers as he may think proper to send to New York, to be permitted to sail without examination. When his despatches are ready, his Lordship engages on his part, that the ship shall be delivered to the order of the Count de Grasse, if she escapes the dangers of the sea. That she shall not carry off any public stores. Any part of the crew that may be deficient on her return, and the soldiers passengers, to be accounted for on her delivery.

ARTICLE IX. The traders are to preserve their property, and to be allowed three months to dispose of or remove them; and those traders are not to be considered as prisoners of war.

ARTICLE IX response. The traders will be allowed to dispose of their effects, the allied army having the right of preemption. The traders to be considered as prisoners of war upon parole.

ARTICLE X. Natives or inhabitants of different parts of this country, at present in York or Gloucester, are not to be punished on account of having joined the British army.

ARTICLE X response. This article cannot be assented to, being altogether of civil resort.

ARTICLE XI. Proper hospitals to be furnished for the sick and wounded. They are to be attended by their own surgeons on parole; and they are to be furnished with medicines and stores from the American hospitals.

ARTICLE XI response. The hospital stores now at York and Gloucester shall be delivered for the use of the British sick and wounded. Passports will be granted for procuring them further supplies from New York, as circumstances may require; and hospitals will be furnished for the sick and wounded of both garrisons.

ART. XII. Wagons to be furnished to carry the baggage of the officers attending the soldiers, and to surgeons when travelling on account of the sick, attending the hospitals at public expense.

ART. XII. Response. They are to be furnished if possible.

ART. XIII. The shipping and boats in the two harbors, with all their stores, guns, tackling, and apparel, shall be delivered up in their present state to an officer of the navy appointed to take possession of them, previously unloading the private property of the officers which had been on board for security during the siege. Granted.

ART. XIV. No article of capitulation to be infringed on pretense of reprisals; and if there be any doubtful expressions in it, they are to be interpreted according to the common meaning and acceptance of the words. Granted.

Done at Yorktown, in Virginia, October 19th 1781. Signed George Washington, Le Comte De Rochambeau, Le Comte De Barras, Cornwallis, Thomas Symonds.

Mr. de Grasse, not enjoying good health, was obliged to remain aboard his ship. Mr. de Barras, the most senior officer of the navy after him, signed the capitulation in his stead.

At the appointed time, the designated American and French detachments took possession of the redoubts of York, after which the victorious army was put in order of battle in two lines facing each other. The Americans were on the right, to see the besieged parade. The two major generals of the allied army remained at the end of the line to be ready to receive the flags and to lead the vanquished on the field where they were to lay down their arms.

Lord Cornwallis was, or feigned being, ill and did not appear at the head of his troops. He was replaced by Brigadier General O'Hara who, in passing before General Washington, handed him his sword which the American general returned to him. The reputation of these British, of their leader, so boasted in America, the hardships we endured, the sweet pleasure of seeing them finish by our success made us feel charmed by the glance of our enemies parading between us. The British seemed discouraged; the Germans, on the other hand seemed very serious and passed in better order than their allies. They knew (and certainly very wrongly) that they were not loved, and that they served with distaste and said loudly that they were basely and heartlessly sold by their princes. During the entire siege, 70 Hessians deserted and gave us excellent intelligence of the state of the garrison.

The capture of the posts of York and of Gloucester procured for the United States the deliverance of Virginia and of almost all the southern states and 7350 prisoners, not counting 1000 or 1200 sailors, a 36-gun frigate, several cutters, 80 transports, half of them sunk (but easy to refloat) half on the water, belonging to the French navy by the surrender. The bulk of the land army was 15,000 men but the long marches, the hardships, the battles fought with General Greene in Carolina reduced it to half. The famous Tarleton and his light dragoons, numbering 300, were included in the number of prisoners. We also took more than 400 horses, 280 pieces of cannon, 18 flags 9 to 10,000 muskets. . . .

Immediately after the surrender, General Washington dispatched Colonel Tench Tilghman, one of his aides-de-camp to Congress to bring them the news. Mr. the Count de Rochambeau appointed the duc de Lauzun to bring the news to the King. Colonel Humphrey, another of General Washington's aides-de-camp was selected to bring the flags and the details of the siege and, on the French side, the choice fell on the Count William des

Deux Ponts. Mr. de Rochambeau, independently of any particular considerations he might have had, preferred these two officers because they were the only ones who had seen action during the siege. He was acting justly and wisely and this conduct was generally approved by the army. However, the voice of a few malcontents arose without warrant or justification. Mr. de Charland, son of Mr. de Castries particularly distinguished himself in this manner and Charles de Damas, one of my comrades who repaid, in bad faith and ingratitude, the friendship which our general showed him.

Mr. de Lauzun embarked on board the *Surveillante* and set sail on the 22nd.

Such was the end and the fate of Lord Cornwallis after seven campaigns in America where he had nothing but victories. He contributed the most to General Howe's success and he personally won several battles. He was well-liked by his troops whose hardships he shared with much courage and pleasure.

He was full of ardor and the pleasures of campaigns always showed as did particular actions [which were] dictated more out of animosity against the Americans. Either coupled with the resources at his disposal or calculated according to the probability of the outcomes, he always relied on the hope of victory and never anticipated enough the consequences of a failure. He hurled himself without examining anything. His final campaign proved it well when, after going 100 miles to engage in the battle of Guilford Courthouse[128] where he remained master of the battlefield, he was obliged to retreat a much greater distance to survive. This forced retreat did not make him any wiser, as he believed he needed to fight General Greene again camped on the heights of the Santee River. He lost some men there and although victorious, he could not pursue his victory for lack of provisions, having once again marched without precaution. Finally, after many marches and counter-marches and having his army march more than 3,000 miles since the battle of Camden, won in October 1780 over General Gates, his plans, those of his court and the contrivances of our general put him into our hands after a sequence of events. Against Mr. the Count de Rochambeau, he forgot the maxim which is to never ask how many are they but where are they? to beat the charge and to charge. He never gave enough credit to the Americans who are brave and that is what Mr. de Rochambeau taught him at York (because he was said to be ill) the day of the signing of the capitulation. My Lord was humble and kind.

Our general consoled him, pitied him, encouraged him and engaged him especially to appreciate and even like Mr. Washington who must inspire his enemy by his life and his actions, his feelings.

128 March 15, 1781.

The Americans were very vexed by the surrender. They hoped to be able to avenge, in an assault, the tyranny or, should we say, the cruelties which they experienced from the English during the war. The French are always friends of the vanquished. Kindness was the guide for our conduct toward them. The last cannon shot was, so to speak, the signal of friendship. The letter of Lord Cornwallis, appended here, will certify this even more, than the dinners we gave them and whatever I might say.

It is common enough, in the American armies, that, in giving a report of a victory either to Congress or to any leader, the general makes some note of almost every officer either out of justice or to please them or out of politeness or rather because, in a republic, all men are equal after a war and one must always make friends and make everybody indebted. The day after the surrender, Mr. Washington, in paying his compliments to the truth, for everybody had served well, gave his thanks to the army in the orders. I place this piece here to show the sentiments of this great man and as a most honorable testimony to the officers named here.

Extract of general's orders 20th October 1781:[129]

> The general congratulates the Army upon the glorious event of yesterday.
>
> The generous proofs which his most Christian Majesty has given of his attachment to the cause of America must force conviction on the minds of the most deceived among the enemy, relatively to the good consequences of the alignments, and inspire every citizen of chosen states with sentiments of the most unalterable gratitude.
>
> His fleet the most numerous and powerful that ever appeared in these seas commanded by an admiral whose fortune and talents insure great events.
> An army of the most admirable composition both in officers and men, are the pledges of his friendship to the United States and their cooperation has secured us in the present signaled success.
>
> The general upon this occasion entreats his excellency Count de Rochambeau to accept his most grateful acknowledgments for his counsels and assistance at all times.
>
> He presents his warmest thanks to the generals Baron de Vioménil, chevaliers the Chastellux, Mr. de St. Simon, Vicount de Vioménil, and Brigadier General Choisy who had a separate command for the illustrious manner in which they have advanced the interest of the common cause.

129 Written in French and English.

He requests that Count de Rochambeau will be pleased to communicate to the army under his command the high sense he entertains of the distinguished merits of the officers and soldiers of every corps and that he will present in his name to the regiments of Gatinois and Deux Ponts the two pieces of brass ordnance captured by them as a testimony of their gallantry in storming the enemy's redoubt on the night of the 14th instant when every officer and man so universally vied with each other in the exercise of every soldiery virtue.

The general's thanks to each individual at merit would comprehend the whole army, but he thinks himself bound however by affection, duty and gratitude to express his obligation to Major Generals Lincoln, La Fayette and Steuben for their dispositions in the trenches,

To General Duportail and Colonel Kerenez, for the vigor and knowledge which were conspicuous in their conduct at the attack, and to General Knox[130] and Colonel d'Aboville[131] for the great care and attention and hardship in bringing forward the artillery and stores and for their judicious and spirited management of them in the parallels.
He requests the gentlemen above mentioned to communicate his thanks to the officers and soldiers under their respective command.

Ingratitude which the general hopes never to be guilty of, would be conspicuous in him, was he to omit thanking[132] in the warmest terms his Excellency Governor Nelson for the aid he has derived from him and from the militia under his command to whose activity, emulation and courage much applause is due. The greatness the acquisition will be an ample compensation for the hardships and hazards which they encountered with so much patriotism and firmness.

In order to diffuse the general joy through every breast, the general orders that those men belonging to the army who may be in confinement, shall be pardoned, released and join their respective corps.

130 Brigadier General Henry Knox (1750–1806) was chief of artillery in the Continental Army. He also served as the first US Secretary of War from 1789 to 1794.

131 François Marie comte d'Aboville (1730-1817) organized the French corps of artillery. He commanded the French artillery at Yorktown. He became colonel of the artillery regiment of Metz in 1782, camp marshal in 1788, inspector of artillery in 1791, commandant of artillery of the northern Army in May 1792 and lieutenant general in Sept. 1792. He was imprisoned at Soissons on Nov. 1, 1793 and released on April 8, 1794. He was recalled to service on June 13, 1794 and became first Inspector General of artillery on January 5, 1800. He fulfilled various military functions under the Empire and became a Peer of France in 1814.

132 The letter a in the word thanking is slightly darker than the rest of the word but it has a dot above it. The original word was probably "thinking" and corrected to "thanking."

> Divine service is to be performed tomorrow in the several brigades and divisions.
>
> The Commander-in-Chief earnestly recommends that the troops not on duty should universally attend with that seriousness of deportment and gratitude of heart with the recognition of such reiterated and astonishing interpositions of Providence demand of us.

The prisoners departed for their destinations on the 22nd and they were escorted by the Virginia militia.

The *Bonetta* set sail the same day for New York with Lord Sutton, Lord Cornwallis's aide-de-camp, on board whom he entrusted with his dispatches for Sir Henry Clinton. Before giving an account of this dispatch, we should say that a little time before Yorktown, Admiral Digby arrived at New York from England with three ships of the line. He had on board Prince William Henry, son of his British Majesty. General Clinton was then preparing to embark troops to come rescue Lord Cornwallis. Admiral Digby took command of the naval forces at New York. The embarkation of the land troops under Clinton's personal command was done promptly and he appeared in sight of the Chesapeake capes on the 25th with 25 vessels and transports. His plan was to try to force the passage on three sides, hoping that the transports would still put many men ashore in the confusion. But before beginning anything, he received word that Cornwallis had been captured. The French navy was then too well situated. He soon decided that it was impossible to attempt anything. However, he remained in view for several days.

It is then that General Clinton received Lord Cornwallis's dispatches of which I will give an extract:

> I have the mortification to inform your Excellency that I have been forced to give up the posts of York and Gloucester and to surrender the troops under my command by capitulation on the 19th instant as prisoners of war to the combined forces of America and France.
>
> I never regarded this post in a very favourable light, but when I found I was to be attacked in so unprepared a state by so powerful an army and artillery, nothing but the hopes of relief would have induced me to attempt its defense, for I would either have endeavored to escape from Gloucester to New York by rapid marches immediately on the arrival of General Washington's troops at Williamsburg or I would, notwithstanding the disparity of numbers, have attacked them in the open field, where it might have been just possible that fortune would have favored the gallantry of the handful of troops under my command. But being assured by your Excellency's letters that every possible means would be tried by the navy and army to relieve us, I could not think myself at liberty to venture upon either of those desperate attempts. Therefore, after remaining for two days in a strong position in front of this place, expecting to be attacked, upon observing that the enemy were taking

> measures which could not fail of turning my left flank in a short time, and receiving on the second evening your letter of the 24th of September informing me that the relief would sail about the 5th of October, I withdrew within the works on the night of the 29th of September, hoping by the labor and firmness of the soldiers to protract the defence until you could arrive. Everything was to be expected from the spirit of the troops, but every disadvantage attended their labor. We continued the works under enemy fire and our stock of entrenching tools, which did not exceed 400 when we began the works in August, was now much diminished.
>
> The enemy opened the trench on September 30." Here he details everything which occurred from that time until he thought it prudent to surrender. Then he continues "Under all these circumstances I thought it would have been wanton and inhuman to the last degree to sacrifice the lives of this small body of gallant soldiers, who had ever behaved with so much fidelity and courage, by exposing them to an assault, which, from the numbers and precautions of the enemy which assured their success.
>
> I therefore proposed to surrender, and I send your Excellency the copy of the correspondence between General Washington and me and the articles of capitulation. I sincerely regret that I could not obtain a better one, and I have neglected nothing to alleviate the misfortune and distress of both officers and soldiers. The men are well clothed and provided with necessaries and I trust will be regularly supplied by the resources and attention of the officers who are permitted to remain with them.
>
> The treatment in general that we have received from the enemy since our surrender has been perfectly good and proper; but the kindness and attention that has been shown to us by the French officers in particular, their delicate sensibility of our situation, their generous and pressing offers of money both public and private has really gone beyond what I can possibly describe and will, I hope, will be felt in the heart of every British officer whenever the fortune of war should put any of them into our power.

He [Cornwallis] then praises the bravery and good conduct of his troops and says "A successful defense, however, in our situation was perhaps impossible, for the place could only be reckoned an entrenched camp, subject to enfilade in many places, and the ground in general so disadvantageous that he extended his fortifications only to protect the navy; that the hardships, the illness of his troops, the wounded reduced them to 3,200 men fit for duty against 8000 French, 7000 American and 500 militiamen (General Washington could only bring 2000 men with him," who, joined with the 2000 which Mr. de la Fayette commanded in Virginia made four and 1200 Virginia militiamen under the command of Governor Nelson totaling 13,200 men besieging instead of 20,000 which Lord Cornwallis cites here.

This letter needs a few comments because although my Lord indicates himself the reasons of his conduct, he places, with reason, the blame for almost everything on Clinton to whom he says that without his orders and his promises, he would have tried to escape and go to New York. This sentence which figures well in a letter seems too advanced to whomever would face the facts of the events and would know the area a little. When my Lord would only find weak opposition in the body which Mr. Choisy commanded at Gloucester, his plan would always appear chimeric and impracticable when we think that he had 200 leagues to travel in enemy territory, that he had a large number of rivers to cross, many of them 2 or 3 miles wide and that consequently fleeing without resources, we would soon have trapped and harassed him. This fine plan, however, was costly, was tried by my Lord. After the surrender, he once made me honor to speak to me to tell me that he expected at the same time to leave all the poor marchers at Yorktown to surrender and recommended the sick and the wounded to General Washington and leave without baggage.

Thus, he would not have escaped with more than 2 or 3000 men and he might have been forced to replay the scene of Burgoyne at Saratoga and to ground arms in the field. (Lord Cornwallis requested to surrender on October 17. It is very extraordinary to note that this is four years after the surrender at Saratoga which occurred on October 17, 1777.)

The plan which my Lord speaks of, in his letter, to march to Williamsburg was much better, but he should have done so when Mr. de la Fayette joined Mr. de St. Simon and occupied this place with 5000 men. We could blame him for not harassing us at the beginning and during the siege, but his biggest mistake was abandoning his exterior works, before which we would have been forced to open a trench and be restricted in the body of his place without reserving any place to shelter his garrison or to put those not in service out of harm's way.

General Washington's plan and certainly that of Mr. Rochambeau, who surveyed the British Army and the resources after the capture of Yorktown, was not to limit his conquests there. On leaving Carolina, my Lord left only 1500 men at Charleston because he hoped that as he advanced through Virginia, the people would bend and receive the yoke. He could not foresee, after his past victories, what would be his sad and unfortunate demise in America. The poor reputation of Colonel Balfour,[133] commanding at Charleston, and the

133 Lieutenant Colonel Nisbet Balfour (1743—1823) was one of General Cornwallis' most trusted officers. He was severely injured in the Battle of Bunker Hill (Breed's Hill). Balfour also participated in the battles in Elizabethtown, Brandywine, and Germantown. Promoted to Lt. Col. of the 23rd Regiment of Foot in 1778. He accompanied Cornwallis to Charleston where he sometimes served as commandant. He was promoted to major general in 1793, colonel of both

weakness of his detachment assured [the success of] almost any attack against him. Consequently, our two generals arrived in the Chesapeake Bay on the 23rd, on board the *Ville de Paris*, to confer with Mr. de Grasse and to convince him of the utility of this enterprise which, if it succeeded, would capture the entire south of the United States and would concentrate the British forces at the single place of New York. I must repeat at this time that Mr. de Grasse only came to the Chesapeake Bay, only brought 3000 men from St. Domingue, only brought 1,200,000# in silver at the simple request and on the promise of Mr. de Rochambeau's plan. He himself had operations underway in the West Indies with Mr. the Marquis de Bouillé to whom he had (supposedly) promised to return at the beginning of November. So when Mr. de Rochambeau proposed the Charleston expedition to him and to bring his army to besiege it, that he would protect, he totally refused. The entreaties and the reasons deduced by the two generals were useless. They took leave of Mr. de Grasse and returned dissatisfied at being forced to not have the resources at their disposal to operate and to be constrained to take their winter quarters.

Embarkation of the Troops

Mr. de Rochambeau immediately gave orders for the embarkation of the troops from the West Indies under the command of Mr. de St. Simon.

On the 28th, the Count William des Deux Ponts, going to France to bring the details of the siege and the state of their graces the Duc de Laval,[134] Count Charles de Damas, the Count de Charlus[135] and a few other officers on board the *Andromaque* set sail, but, in the offing at Cape Henry, they discovered the navy under the command of Admirals Digby and Hood and were obliged to reenter the Bay. They probably remained at this station only to

---

the 93rd Foot and the 39th Foot in 1794 and served in the war with France. He served in Parliament from 1790 to 1802.

134 Anne-Alexandre-Marie-Sulpice-Joseph de Montmorency, 2e duc de Laval (1747- 1817), a lieutenant general of the King's armies. He was made Peer of France in 1814 and promoted to Lt. Gen. four days later.

135 Charles Eugène Gabriel de La Croix, marquis de Castries, baron des États de Languedoc, comte de Charlus, baron de Castelnau et de Montjouvent, seigneur de Puylaurens et de Lézignan (1727-1800) was named governor of Flanders and Hainaut shortly after the peace of 1763. He was made lieutenant captain of the company of Scottish police and commandant of police from 1770 until his retirement in 1788. He was named Secretary of State of the Navy on Oct. 13, 1780 on the recommendation of his friend Jacques Necker. He remained in this post until Aug. 24, 1787. He was made a marshal of France in 1783. He reorganised the fleet and had a new naval strategy adopted that led to French naval successes in the American War of Independence. He died in 1801 at the home of his old enemy Charles William Ferdinand, Duke of Brunswick, now his friend.

spy on the movements of Mr. de Grasse, but seeing that he was not leaving and suspecting some plans against Charleston, they set sail to this place on the 29th to land 1500 men.

At the same time, General Washington divided the few troops he had. General Greene, who was still in the Carolinas, had suffered much and needed help. Mr. Washington sent him Major General Sinclair[136] with Brigadier Generals Wayne and Gist[137] with the Pennsylvania and Maryland lines, making a body of 1500 or 1800 men. He himself personally marched with the troops which he brought from the Jerseys, Rhode Island and the state of New York to rejoin the body which he left at Phillipsburg near New York under the command of General Heath and then take his winter quarters.

On the 30th, Mr. de Rochambeau visited those which he would set up at Hampton for Lauzun's Legion. This little town, situated 25 miles from York near the mouth of the James River in the Chesapeake, gives its name to the harbor which is rather fine despite having suffered an attack by the traitor Arnold when he first commanded the army in Virginia. It is still rather fine. The houses are lined along the two main shores and are well built. Mr. de Rochambeau was still 4 miles away on the seashore at a house called Sheldon's house, named after its owner where he established an observation post overlooking capes Charles and Henry to alert about anything that might appear in the offing or in the bay between these two capes which form the entrance.

November

On November 1, the Gatinois, Touraine and Agenois regiments together with the artillery division which Mr. the Count de Grasse had brought from St. Domingue was were all boarded on their respective vessels. The admiral then only awaited a favorable wind to set sail. The seven vessels of the Rhode Island fleet commanded by Mr. de Barras continued to be numbered among the grand fleet which, with this addition, consisted of 36 vessels

Mr. de Grasse left for Martinique on November 4 to join Mr. de Bouillé, General Commander of the Windward Isles, with the intent of then forming together an expedition on Barbados. The *Andromaque* left for France the same day.

136 Major General Arthur St. Clair (1737-1818) served in the British Army during the French and Indian War and as an aide-de-camp to General Washington. After the war, he served as President of the Continental Congress and then governor of the Northwest Territory in 1788. He commanded the American forces in what was the United States's worst ever defeat by the American Indians in 1791, dubbed "St. Clair's Defeat."

137 Brigadier General Mordecai Gist (1743–1792) joined the southern army under Nathanael Greene. He was given the command of the light corps when the army was remodeled in 1782.

Mr. de Grasse left the *Romulus* in the York River under the command of Mr. de Villebrune[138] and the frigate l'*Hermione* and the *Diligente* commanded by the Chevalier de la Touche[139] and the Chevalier de Cléonard[140] with all the prizes captured from the British before and at the surrender of York.

Immediately after the surrender of this place, Mr. de Rochambeau ordered the trench refilled and the destruction of the redoubts connected to it. He thought about setting up his quarters only after his return from Mr. de Grasse's navy and he opted to make a new plan for the fortification and defense of York. He kept a few of the British ones, had the others razed and put a wide and deep ravine in front of his lines which Lord Cornwallis had filled in. The Soissonnais regiment immediately began these works. The York area was assigned to it. Williamsburg was assigned to headquarters, to the Bourbonnais Regiment and a battalion of the Royal Deux Ponts Regiment. The second battalion of this Regiment was assigned to camp at Jamestown, former capital of Virginia and the first settlement of the Europeans in this country. Before the British occupation, we could see some fine houses which suffered the fate of buildings which they occupied, that is to say they were partly destroyed. Jamestown is 7 miles from Williamsburg and is located on an island only 3 miles long. As it is very marshy, it is presumed that, for this reason, it has not grown as much as the rest of the region.

The York River is formed by two rivers, the Pamunkey and the Mattaponi, which change their name to the York River at their junction. This area offers a very good location that is easy to defend called West Point. That's where the siege artillery and the munitions of war were located, in the interior of the town 25 miles from York. The season was advancing and the weather was becoming harsh but the destruction of the town of York prevented us from entering quarters. Even though we are soldiers and must still sleep on straw when there are no enemies to fight, shouldn't we at least shelter ourselves from the ravages of the weather? Many of the houses were beyond repair because of the bombs and

138 Servant Paul le Saige de Villesbrune (1747-1782) was captain in the Agenais Regiment. He fought at Pensacola and Yorktown and was killed at St. Christopher.

139 Louis René Madeleine Le Vassor de Latouche-Tréville (1745-1804) commanded the frigate *Hermione* from 1780-1783. He became a prominent figure of the French Revolutionary Wars and of the Napoleonic wars. He was imprisoned during the Reign of Terror and eventually freed by the Thermidorian Reaction. He returned to the Navy after a long period of unemployment, took command of the Flottille de Boulogne, where he repelled the Raids on Boulogne organised by Nelson. He then served in the Saint-Domingue expedition which compromised his health. After his return, he took command of the fleet in Toulon.

140 Chevalier Robert Sutton de Clonard (1751-1788), a French naval officer of Irish descent, served on the *Glorieux* under Captain vicomte d'Escars and took command of the *Diligente* on September 12, 1780, on the orders of the Comte de Grasse.

cannonballs. A battalion and a half of the Saintonge Regiment was assigned to camp and barrack at and in the neighborhood of Half Way house, so that Hampton made the right of our quarters, Half Way House, York and Williamsburg the center, all the way to Jamestown which made the left. They occupied 44 miles. Everything being ready the troops arrived on the 16th and departed the camp at York to arrive there respectively.

Conclusion of the Campaign of 1781

Thus ended the campaign of 1781 for the French, begun without resources, sustained with courage and ended so gloriously. Never did a general have to take on as much as Mr. de Rochambeau in this campaign because he acted against the orders of the court, because he gathered all his resources to himself, because he was denied everything which [unintelligible] to conduct the war for good. Everything which France could promise him for well-thought out and calculated plans on the very sites. Cabals, intrigues, false politics, detractions from merited reputations what you have seen at the British surrender at York?

When we have begun a war solely to give liberty to a country, to create a new power by weakening its rival, how can we send troops 1500 leagues away, to leave them on their own, to support everything which is necessary for its main purpose and forget them, so to speak. That is the situation in which Mr. de Rochambeau found himself. I agree that we could have delivered great blows to England at other places than North America. I agree that the ruin of its merchant fleets, the capture of Jamaica were mortal blows if they were executed. But why use 50 vessels for the blockade of Gibraltar which, once taken (which I don't believe), would give Spain only a rock and would not weaken England? The idea of American independence irritates this power. She sent 60,000 to this unfortunate country which they settled in detail. She consumed her treasures. She was always abused by her generals. She always flattered herself for taming 1500 miles of coastline and from 150 to 200 inland. Is that possible? She experienced the opposite and Mr. de Rochambeau proved it physically by the capture of Cornwallis's army.

Let us not then doubt that this event will bring peace. It is glorious for more than one and if Mr. de Rochambeau had conceived everything, made everything work, we should say to Mr. the Count de Grasse's praise that he supported him well, served him well and without him we could undertake very little. We did not even have a cent when he arrived and we did not have enough troops. The gratitude of the French should extend to the governor of St. Domingue who released troops under his command for us to send them to

Mr. de Solano,[141] the Spanish governor who allied himself with the assistance Mr. de Grasse sought to bring us. The Touraine Regiment which could do nothing without his participation, even to the women of Havana who joined together and sent us some money when the merchants of St. Domingue refused. The orders were well given, the marches well-planned, but it is fortunate that Aeolus was half in our favor and that by a very rare event, all our resources arrived from the four corners of the globe at the same time and at the same place. If anything would have gone awry or, better said, to actively oppose our plans, it was General Clinton with 12 to 14,000 men at New York, against our little corps.

He let us cross the North River peacefully and traverse the Jerseys without foreseeing any consequences. Let us only speak of the successes. They will be assigned in the history books. Our general covered himself in glory because, in deploying the talents of a soldier and a minister in this campaign, he triumphed over the avowed and armed enemies of the state and he will certainly rise above those who act silently and who are at Versailles. It is much sweeter for me to retrace everything which could serve to his praise, that linked to him by the bonds of blood, I am no less so than by those of gratitude and by the deepest feelings of esteem and admiration for both his military and civic virtues.

After the capture of York, Congress rendered him the same testimony and I join here an extract of its resolution and its [regitrance].

Resolutions of the United States in Congress assembled the 29 October 1781

Resolved

That the gratitude of the United States in Congress assembled, be presented to his excellency the Count de Rochambeau, for the zeal and courage with which he seconded and advanced the progress of the allied army against the British garrison in York and Gloucester.

Resolved

That the United States in Congress assembled, will cause to be erected at York, in Virginia, a marble column, adorned with emblems of the alliance between the United States and his Most Christian Majesty; and inscribed with a succinct narrative of the surrender of Earl Cornwallis to the allied army under the command of General Washington, Commander in Chief of the combined armies of America and France, the Count de Rochambeau,

141 Don José de Solano y Bote Carrasco y Díaz, Marquess of Socorro (1726–1806), commanded a Spanish squadron during the Anglo-Spanish War. He came to the aid of Louisiana governor Bernardo de Gálvez in March 1781 in the Siege of Pensacola. He was promoted to lieutenant general in 1782 and became the General Captain of the Armada in 1804.

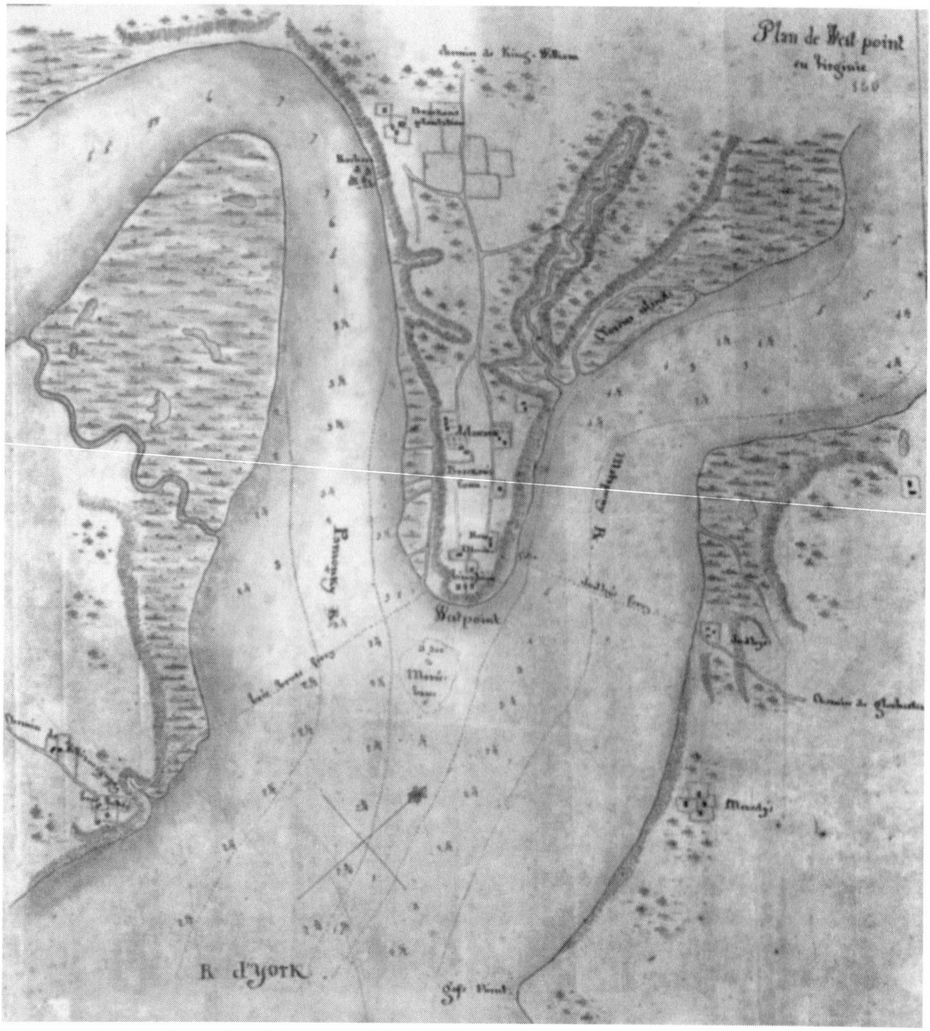

Louis de Lauberdière's map of West Point at the junction of the Pamunkey and Mattaponi rivers in Virginia, October 9, 1781.

Bibliothèque Nationale

Commander in Chief of the auxiliary troops of his Most Christian Majesty in America, and the Count de Grasse, Commander in Chief of the French navy in the Chesapeake Bay

Resolved

That two pieces of the field ordnance, taken from the British army under the capitulation of York, be presented by the Commander in Chief of the American army to Count de

Rochambeau; and that they be engraved to say that Congress presented them in consideration for the part he had in effectuating the surrender.

Extract of the minutes, Charles Thomson, secretary

Upon arriving at Williamsburg, the French received almost the same kind of reception from the Virginians as they did when they landed at Rhode Island. The disasters which the war entails, the encampment of the armies had alienated part of the inhabitants who sought refuge in the interior of the country. They owed the French the salvation of their country, the preservation of their goods, of their property. Despite that, Virginia a flourishing colony, rich, inhabited, founded by the English government on more aristocratic than republican principles, still nursed at her breast many friends of England who, profiting from the circumstances, were of one party or another depending on who was stronger. They wanted to extend the freedom for which her true zealots fought without engaging in anything to cooperate in this great work. They finally refused lodging to the soldiers and to receive among themselves those who came to shed their blood for them.

It is true that this question and the enactment of the Stamp Act was one of the first causes of the revolution but we could not nor should we ever be involved in a proscription of this type. We had all the hardships in the world to provide for our barracks, our camps, and we had to take the greatest precautions to neither harm nor anger anyone and to change the indifference, not to say the hatred, and to change them into friendship. Strict discipline, the assurance of payment, personal kindness changed their preconceived minds and a few days after the arrival of the headquarters and of the Bourbonnais Regiment, the inhabitants of the town joined together to give us a feast to cement our union. The feast was brilliant; nothing was lacking and, from then on, we occupied ourselves more with seeking and the means to entertain our allies. Mr. de Rochambeau began and announced that he would give two balls each week. His example was soon followed in each camp where everyone endeavored to rest from the hardships they had experienced.

December

In addition to the post at Charlestown,[142] the British also had that of Wilmington in North Carolina. At the approach of General St. Clair and of the detachment he was bringing to Greene's army, they evacuated and retreated by sea to Charleston. After Admiral Digby's arrival at the Chesapeake, Clinton sent reinforcements of 1300 men to

142 Charleston, SC. Charles Town, or Charlestown, was renamed Charleston in 1783.

Louis Armand de Gontaut-Biron,
duc de Lauzun

Independence National Historical Park

Charleston. Despite this assistance after the junction of St. Clair, General Greene left the Heights of the Santee where he was camped, made a rapid movement on this place, approached to 6 miles and forced the enemy to abandon several redoubts or posts without hardly firing a musket.

Lauzun's Legion was camped at Hampton. Toward the end of December, Mr. de Rochambeau received several dispatches from General Greene who asked him to march his army to Carolina and Georgia to make an assessment of the places still held by the British. Mr. de Rochambeau did not consent to General Greene's request, as he lacked the resources and did not want to risk his army in a land ravaged by war in the middle of winter. However, he responded that he would still be disposed to maneuver with him when he found an object of definite utility and to prove that he would cooperate more voluntarily to his operations, he would have his vanguard march to the Carolinas to Charlotte Courthouse and from there he would be in range to bring assistance if he found himself either pressed or pursued by the enemy.

Mr. de Rochambeau took the pretext of the scarcity of forage for displacing Lauzun's Legion and he ordered Mr. Dumas, assistant quartermaster general, to go set them up. Dumas experienced many difficulties and was even summoned to the General Assembly of the state of Virginia to account for his actions. Mr. de Rochambeau ordered him to appear in person. Dumas had no difficulty in proving that he acted only in conformity to the care of the town, that he respected the properties and that only evil citizens and worried minds could complain. Dumas found praise and gratitude where his accusers wanted to see him either punished or admonished. But such was the spirit of the Virginians, even of the administration of this great state, that the virtuous and brave Governor Nelson who had been so helpful to us at the beginning of the siege, who gave us his horses, his slaves, his wagons, who even commanded the militia, was denounced to this same assembly for having (so-called) illegally pressed a few horses for service either for his troops or ours and for having acted thus against the title of a free man, an independent landowner who bears and wants to respect each American. For every excuse, the governor cited his exemplary

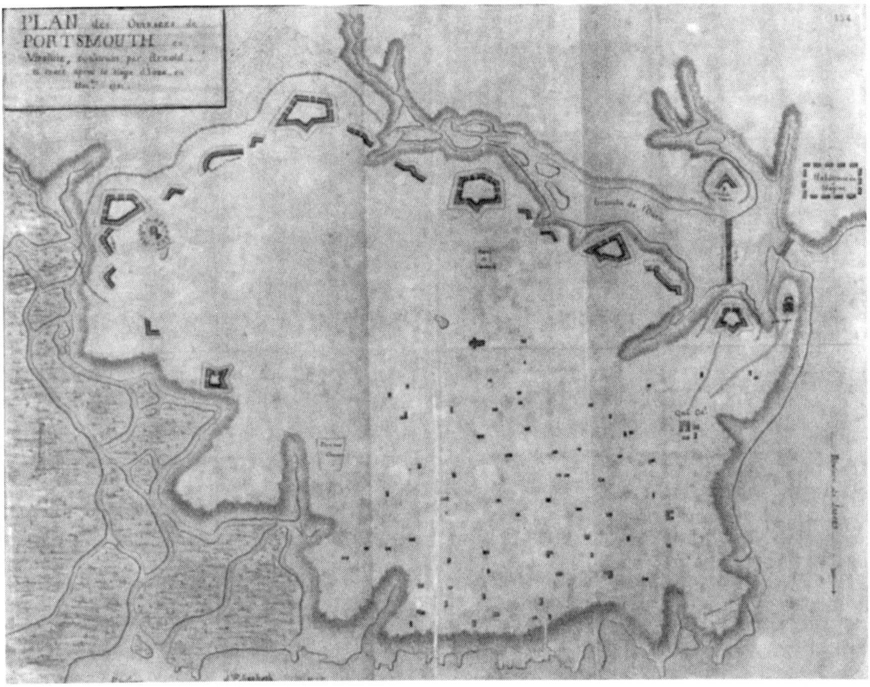

Louis de Lauberdière's map of the defenses of Portsmouth, Virginia, constructed by Benedict Arnold and razed in November 1781 after the siege of Yorktown.

Bibliothèque Nationale

---

conduct for every true patriot, the pressing needs of the armies, the importance of the conquest and the necessity of neglecting nothing for the service on such an occasion. His excellent reasons were poorly rewarded. The governor then made a fine speech in which he related the happy, shining moments of his administration. He reproached his fellow citizens for their ingratitude, made them feel, for the future, the thoughtlessness of their conduct in his regard and resigned from office for future peace.

This little digression might serve to understand the minds which we had to deal with daily, the difficulties required to have the smallest detachment march. What a conciliating, political mind Mr. de Rochambeau must have had. He, a general of an army come from a distant country where the mere will of the king often becomes law, where everyone bends, receives the yoke in his name or under his orders without respect, without consideration, for their properties, business affairs, and often the condition of the citizens.

Meanwhile, the Americans, sooner or later, will feel the view of an executive administration vested with no power. The legislature makes very good laws, very wisely passed but not supported by authority. It is rare that a resolution of Congress, or the General Assembly, has its entire execution because in the state of freemen where the last,

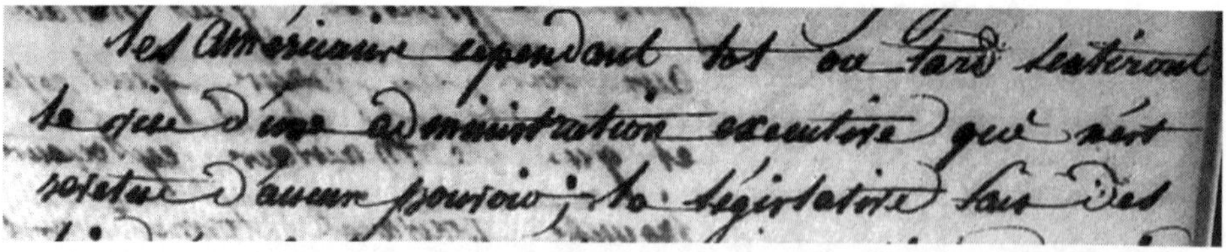

les Americains cependant tot ou tard sentiront
le [illegible] d'une administration executive qui n'est
revetue d'aucun pouvoir; la legislature sans des

the least affluent citizen, wants to live, he recognizes no one above him and often forgets what he himself has signed, that which is agreed upon by his representative or member of this same general assembly of his state and, from there, to Congress.

Campaign of 1782

Introduction

The winter of 1782 brought reorganization of the Continental Army. The sick and wounded from the French regiments, after the siege of Yorktown, embarked on the sloop Bonetta. *British cruisers, stationed at the mouth of the great rivers and at the entrance to the Chesapeake Bay, captured these poor unfortunates. The prisoners languished in the dismal holds of floating British prison ships. One of the sufferers managed to get a letter to General Rochambeau, detailing the abysmal conditions. In a display of magnanimity, General Henry Clinton agreed to the release of the prisoners before the end of January.*

The frigates Hermione *and* Déligente *headed to America, as part of the reserves. torms cast the* Déligente *upon a reef; she sank with half of her crew. 2 miles south of Cape Henry, VA.*

Exhausted from the previous campaign, and beset with bad weather, the armies rested. Admiral de Grasse operated in the Windward Isles. The French foiled a British attempt to capture St. Christopher (St. Kitts). Admiral Hood surrendered his post at Brimstone Hill St. Kitts Feb. 10. The British still held Charleston, SC and Savannah, GA, leading occasional sorties into the hostile countryside. General Washington spent the winter in Philadelphia; his French allies in the vicinity of Williamsburg, VA.

Lauberdière focused on the Jamaica expedition in April. Peace talks began in Paris on April 12, with the formal negotiations beginning September 27.

The French departed from their camp in Williamsburg, joining General Washington at Philadelphia on July 1. Lauberdière specified the order of march, the dates and the camps each regiment occupied, as he did on the march south. This time, his descriptions of the places and people focused on the changes since their last visit. Some of these accounts are lengthier than the ones on the march south. As this journal was intended for his personal use and not for publication, his observations about the people and lack of culture are sometimes quite caustic, particularly those about Martha Washington in a rather long account of the French sojourn at Mount Vernon.

While at Annapolis, the French troops paraded before the governor of Maryland and conducted firing exercises in early August. A negligent soldier fired a cartridge with ball, seriously wounding a woman spectator in the thigh.

There is a lengthy account of the Asgill affair in June and of the junction of the French and American armies at Peekskill where Lauberdière describes the grand scene of both armies parading before each other.

The frigates Aigle *and* Gloire *departed Rochefort at the beginning of August to bring dispatches and specie to pay the army. The* Aigle *ran aground in the Delaware Bay and risked losing the payroll trying to escape from a fleet of British ships. The* Gloire *managed a narrow escape.*

The French army made a prolonged sojourn at Crompond (Yorktown Heights, NY) in September and October. As they prepared to depart, an unusual incident of the war occurred. The miller on whose property the French had encamped, convinced the local sheriff to arrest and hold General Rochambeau until the miller received restitution for the property his men had damaged. The general ordered a committee of his officers to assess the damage. They determined that the miller was demanding three times what the damaged property was worth. Rochambeau paid half of the price, indicating the surplus as a goodwill measure.

Upon reaching New London, General Rochambeau and his retinue visited the sites of Forts Griswold and Trumbull. On September 6, 1781 Benedict Arnold attacked these sites, in a failed attempt to distract the allied armies, and draw them away from the march to Yorktown back to New England.

When they arrived at Newport, Lauberdière visited many of the acquaintances he made in the town during the winter of 1780. After a brief stay, the French continued their march to Providence, and then to Boston. From Boston, they planned to board vessels headed to Jamaica, to cooperate with the combined Spanish attack against the British possession. Lauberdlière described the general sadness of the army and the inhabitants at the time of their departure.

Lauberdière accompanied General Rochambeau to Philadelphia, where he was to take a frigate to return to France. The Chevalier de Chastellux and his aides-de-camp, Mr. de Béville and several staff officers of the army such as Mr. de Choisy took the same route on different days with the same intent. Lauberdière described how the Philadelphians adopted French styles in clothing and grooming and dancing since his last visit and how French currency greatly improved the economy.

As General Rochambeau and his officers prepared for departure, they learned of the capture of the American frigate South Carolina *by British cruisers at the mouth of the*

Delaware Bay. The British apparently received word of Rochambeau's departure as well; doubling their surveillance in an attempt to intercept and capture him.

The preliminary articles of peace were signed on November 30 with an effective date of January 20, 1783. However, ratification of the articles of peace did not take place until April 15, 1783.

The Diary

January 1782

Up until the glorious time of the capture of York and the preceding union of the French Army with that of Washington, the American troops, although very brave and who had served well, had only an imperfect idea of this European discipline brought to such a high point today and which makes the beauty of an army. In their affairs, the Americans found models which they copied quickly and which they tried to emulate. They worked at it throughout the entire campaign but during winter they occupied themselves with giving a new form to their military, re-founding its principles or to arrive at this goal and to lighten a small part of General Washington's burden. Congress created the post of Minister of War and two secretaries or commissioners to give a new sanction and importance to this part of the Constitution. General Lincoln, a very brave man, devoted to his country, to liberty but unlucky in war was Congress's choice for the first of these positions. The position of Minister of Foreign Affairs was also created at the same time and Mr. Livingston was appointed.

Colonel Laurens, son of the president, imprisoned in the Tower of London for so long, was sent to France the previous year to solicit aid, directions, money and cloth to clothe the army. His mission was very successful and he had brought back 3,000,000# in specie at the beginning of October 1781 and something to clothe 15,000 men. For the first time in 7 years, the American soldiers were to be clothed. Each state was to recruit and complete the regiments, at the same time, was also charged with clothing them.

The French regiments from the islands had, at the time of their departure from the continent, left some sick and wounded at York. Mr. de Rochambeau had them embark on board the sloop *Bonetta* which had been loaned to Lord Cornwallis to rejoin their regiments at St. Domingue or at Martinique. The British still maintained cruisers at the mouth of the great rivers, at the entrance to the Chesapeake. The *Bonetta* was captured at her landing and

Brigadier General Benjamin Lincoln

Independence National Historical Park

taken to New York. The unfortunate prisoners, still recovering, were put in the holds of the vessels [unintelligible] for English prisons. Malnourished, untreated, some of them died. One of them found the means to send a letter to Mr. de Rochambeau who, justly angry at the treatment given to his prisoners after the very different one he had given to Lord Cornwallis, he, in turn, wrote to Mr. Clinton and sent the Chevalier du Bouchet[1] to him, under a flag of truce, to reclaim his prisoners. This officer, after a voyage during which he did not have to praise the treatment of the British general, returned to York with the unfortunate remnants of the crew and the soldiers who were passengers on the *Bonetta*.

February

The frigate *l'Hermione*, under the command of Mr. de la Touche, was sent to France about February 2, with the Baron de Vioménil and the Chevalier de Lameth, sufficiently recovered from his wounds, on board. The frigate *La Déligente*, commanded by the Chevalier de Clonard, also received orders to set sail and to go in reserve with *l'Hermione* up to a certain latitude. The weather was ferocious [unintelligible], snowy. The coastal pilot of the *Diligente*, whatever the Chevalier de Clonard might say, refused to approach too close to

1 Denis Jean Florimond Langlois de Mautheville, marquis du Bouchet (1752-1826) was promoted to major in the American Corps of Grenadiers on the battlefield of Saratoga on October 7, 1777. He served as Gen. Rochambeau's aide de camp became a Lt. Col. and chevalier de Saint-Louis in 1783. He was admitted to the order of the Cincinnati in 1784 even though he was not a Col., one of the requirements. He attained that rank and then rank of adjutant general in 1791. He took command of the 21st infantry regiment which he left the following August to join the Prince de Condé at Worms. He was promoted to Brig. Gen. in 1794. He returned to France in 1802 when amnesty was granted to the émigrés. He resumed his service in 1809 and was named Camp Marshal in 1814. He retired the following year.

land and lost her on the reefs, 2 miles south of Cape Henry. The rear of the frigate was almost instantly under water, and the sea very rough. The bitter and biting cold put the crew and all hands in this cruel situation in danger of all the horrors of a shipwreck. Clonard had rafts made and exerted himself to set up a shuttle to the land. Many of the sailors succumbed to the violence of the cold and the effort required to board the boat. After infinite effort, Clonard, who also began to row, reached land and by this means of communication managed to save those who the water, cold or hunger had spared. Half of the crew perished. Everything aboard was lost and the Chevalier de Clonard returned to York where he immediately became dangerously ill.

While the armies, which the weather on the continent reduced to resting and inactivity, refreshed themselves from the preceding campaign, the Count de Grasse and the Marquis de Bouillé operated successfully in the Windward Isles. Mr. de Grasse's first plan was to make an expedition on Barbados. He attempted it several times, having superiority over Admiral Hood, but the winds always unleashed themselves against him. Seeing the moment that the enemy might receive aid from Europe, he decided to besiege St. Christopher to prevent it. Mr. de Bouillé put himself at the head of this expedition and landed very fortunately with almost 10,000 men. The Chevalier de Grasse took an advantageous position from which he could easily protect the siege, land munitions of war and cannonballs and place himself above the enemy. Hood, cunning Hood, appeared. Mr. de Grasse set sail to give combat. If the French Navy had done its duty, Hood would have been crushed. The engagement was partial; many of our vessels were not engaged despite repeated signals to arrive on the enemy. Hood escaped and fled but with the intent to return soon.

Mr. de Grasse should have seized this moment to demote some captains and to punish laziness and insubordination. He did not do it. He probably had the desire but not the courage. The following will show that he had cause to regret it.

A few days after his battle, he set sail to get water at xxxx, a provision which he was on the verge of lacking. Hood seized the moment and came to capture the anchorage of his enemy near St. Christopher. He immediately landed 1500 men to create a diversion and to attempt to take the land. The Chevalier de Fléchin[2], Second Colonel of the Touraine regiment, who found himself within range of the landing, took command of 400 men and, with this handful of men, marched to the enemy, made his attempt fruitless, defeated him, repulsed him and covered himself in glory.

2 Charles-François-Joseph comte de Flechin de Wamin (1744-1801) served as a colonel-en-second in the Régiment de Touraine. He became camp marshal in 1791 and emigrated to serve in the army of the Princes in 1792.

Meanwhile, Mr. de Bouillé advanced the siege with vigor and surrounded the fort on Brimstone Hill [illegible]. A young man of 23 named Thion[3] a soldier of the Touraine regiment gave uncommon heroic displays of courage during the siege. He carried some bombs in a battery. A cannonball took his right arm. He took his knife and completely cut off his arm which still held a little something to bandage himself — a soldier must perform his duty— took the bomb with his left hand and still risked losing it marching to the battery.

Hood abandoned his position at the approach of Mr. de Grasse whose maneuver of the fleet was blamed. The enemy, despairing of being saved after a fine defense on the island in general and at fort Brimstone Hill, chose to surrender on February 10.

General Greene, always active, did not lose any opportunity to profit from the enemy's few mistakes or negligence, still confined at Charleston. The winter passed in mutual observation and there were only a few small engagements during which the victories sometimes varied. The British held the post of Savanna, the capital of Georgia, and occasionally conducted missions from there to the countryside. General Greene sent General Wayne to oppose them during the month of March.

General Washington, who never left his army since the beginning of the war, passed the most rigorous months of the winter at Philadelphia to recover from the fatigues of the campaign. There, he found the reward of his labors. It was neither money nor promotion but the general and pleasant support of his fellow citizens, the blessings of the people, the unanimous agreement and the yearning for gratitude, and every heart toward him. It is a triumph which does not have the appearance of what we find in the pomp of the pride of heart, but is much better appreciated when virtue alone, the love of good, guide us and when patriotism is strongly understood. These are the distinctive qualities of General Washington as a business leader.

He left Philadelphia on March 8 to go to Newburgh on the right bank of the North River to set up his headquarters in order to be ready to follow all the parties which might request his help and guidance and particularly those for clothing the troops and their adequate instruction which Baron de Steuben worked at and oversaw. He had served with the Prussian troops and Congress appointed him Inspector General.

The French at Williamsburg and in their other quarters, more than 200 leagues away from any enemy, spent the winter mildly and peacefully with people whose character is

3 Jean Claude Thion (1763-) was a private in the Régiment de Touraine. He distinguished himself during the capture of Brimstone Hill, on the island of St. Christopher on January 20, 1782. He was ordered to carry bombs from the magazine in the trenches to the batteries. On one of his trips, a cannonball cut off his right arm which only hung by a tendon. He borrowed the knife of one of his comrades, cut the tendon, had the bomb replaced on his left shoulder and carried it to the battery before having his wound dressed.

based on these two qualities. Mr. de Rochambeau made a couple of trips in the neighboring mountains. We occupied ourselves courting a large number of pretty and lovely Virginians, entertaining them. We often hunted with some inhabitants who had excellent dogs. A few armed sloops of war which we had in the York River were cruising in Chesapeake Bay for the protection of American commercial coastal navigation. Unity, good intelligence, even friendship reigned among us and our allies. Nothing unusual happened while our life our ideas varied a little by the arrival of the frigate l'*Emeraude* from France at Newport on March 24. It was the first news from our country since the siege. The arrival of our letters and the ministerial dispatches partly alleviated our hopes. The previous campaign was fine, rare, pleasant, excessively tiring. Nobody was well rewarded and everyone was discontent, rumor widespread. General Mr. de Rochambeau (treated himself in a mediocre manner) was obliged to force several officers to accept favors which we can say as half fact that Mr. de Ségur[4], Minister of War, had granted.

We received intelligence at a distance of about 1500, 2000 leagues from the metropolis. We rarely receive news. We must then anticipate events, foresee them and plan ahead. The official dispatches contained only a few compliments on the past, but treated the political part lightly.

March 1782

There was nothing foreseen, nothing decided, nothing certain for what remained to be done, no date for manoeuvers against the enemy in Europe or elsewhere which nevertheless have some influence. And for the resources, the probabilities need to be planned with the distant operations. War was being waged, and was continuing for the freedom of America and the weakening of England. And it was always the body of troops which should and only they who had contributed. They were neglected, even forgotten. They were refused the resources, employed uselessly elsewhere and considered as accessories in the general mass of affairs. Then let us rest again, as in the last campaign, on

4 Philippe Henri, marquis de Ségur (1724-1801), a marshal of France and Minister of War under Necker. He was appointed to the command of an infantry Regiment at 18 and served under his father in Italy and Bohemia. He was wounded at Roucoux in Flanders in October 1746 and lost an arm at Lauffield in 1747. He succeeded his father as Lt. Gen. of Champagne and Brie in 1748. He fought at Hastenbeck, Crefeld and Minden in the Seven Years War and was taken prisoner at Kloster-campen in 1760. He became a marshal of France in 1783 and resigned from the ministry of war in 1787. He was imprisoned in La Force during the Reign of Terror. After his release, he was reduced to considerable straits until he received a pension from Napoléon in 1800.

the talents, the wisdom, the foresight of our general and, having nothing to do on our continent for the moment, let's look at the affairs of France in the Windward Isles.

Jamaica Expedition
April 1782

The Jamaica expedition was already attempted very ineffectively. It was evident that to decide the outcome of the war and to bring England to recognize American independence, we had to exhaust her and to give her strong blows. The most effective were those which destroyed the source of its riches, of her commerce. We cannot wage war without money. Our affairs in India were entrusted to Bailli de Suffren,[5] an active man, stern, capable, intelligent and who acted successfully. Mr. de Sartine was no longer Minister of the Navy and this department had fallen into the hands of the Marquis de Castries. Convinced that speed in operations, in armaments, is one of the principal sources of success over devoted enemies, when they are well understood, and forewarned, Mr. de Castries had armed all the vessels which were to escort a convoy of all sorts of munitions and troops to reinforce Mr. de Bouillé since the month of December. This armament was put under the command of Mr. de Guichen, Lieutenant General. At the same time, Mr. the Marquis de Vaudreuil[6] received the command of four vessels which were to go to Cadiz. An intrigue changed the destination of the two commanders. Mr. de Vaudreuil obtained the one which should have gone to reinforce Mr. de Grasse and that is the first source of the reversal which this unfortunate admiral tried to [unintelligible].

The British, still surprised by the successes and the victories of the preceding campaign, regardless of the activity they put into their posts, could not reinforce their navy in the West Indies before two months. But having received intelligence of the preparations of France, they had Admiral Kempenfelt[7] go out with 12 vessels. He cruised off the coast of

5 Admiral Pierre Andre de Suffren de Saint Tropez (1729-1788) was part of Adm. d'Estaing's squadron operating on the coast of North America and in the West Indies in 1778 and 1779. In 1780, he was the captain of the *Zélé* in the combined French and Spanish fleets which captured a great English convoy in the Atlantic. He engaged in four actions against Sir Edward Hughes off the coast of India and Ceylon (Sri Lanka) in 1782.

6 Louis-Philippe de Rigaud, Marquis de Vaudreuil (1724-1802) served as was second in command of the French Navy during the American Revolutionary War. During the French Revolution, he and other naval officers, forced their way into the Palace of Versailles on the night of October 5–6 to protect the royal family. He then emigrated to London in 1791. Upon returning to Paris in 1800, he was granted a Naval pension by Napoléon.

7 Admiral Richard Kempenfelt (1718–1782) was Capt. of a fleet of twelve ships of the line with orders to intercept the French fleet under the comte de Guichen. He is best known for his

Ushant and waited several days for his prey. The occasion to pounce on them did not delay. Mr. de Guichen and de Vaudreuil set sail on December 8, 1781. Against all the rules of a fleet escorting a convoy, Mr. de Vaudreuil left his behind immediately after they set sail. Mr. de Guichen signaled him to put to sea. Mr. de Vaudreuil ignored this repeated advice. Night fell. Kempenfelt appeared, set sail and fell on Mr. de Vaudreuil's convoy. He captured part of it, dispersed the rest and captured a 64-gun ship. The loss forced Mr. de Vaudreuil to return to Brest.

Two months passed before the losses of this armament could be repaired. Mr. de Grasse, who would have been absolute master of the isles, could have profited from this armament to attack defenseless Jamaica. A lost opportunity never returns. Mr. de Vaudreuil departed again with three vessels less than he had before but he was already preceded by Admiral Rodney who, joined with Hood, commanded a navy of 37 ships of the line against Mr. de Grasse's 30, who withdrew to Martinique after the capture of St. Christopher.

There were more than 250 vessels in the harbors and ports of this island. They belonged to the merchants and were to set sail for Saint Domingue under the escort of his fleet. Mr. de Grasse set sail the morning of April 9 and landed his convoy. Rodney arrived to attack him. The battle began, but Mr. de Grasse rendered the outcome of the day indecisive by his maneuvers. However, he returned to Fort St. Pierre, Martinique and set sail again on the 11th. During the night of the 11th to the 12th, the 74-gun ship *Zélé* came alongside the *Ville de Paris* twice. The two vessels were damaged but the weaker *Zélé* suffered more which slowed her progress. The morning of the 12th, Mr. de Grasse saw the vessel being repaired closer to the enemy, who reappeared, than to his fleet. Unable to let her be captured without attempting at least to save her, he turned about on the enemy and made signal for his convoy to continue along their route. The battle began at 7 a.m.

It is here that one has to be an eyewitness and an artist to decide seriously if the battle should have taken place, if Mr. de Grasse could or should avoid it. Here, we must describe the pros and cons of this maneuver. It is here that we must be able to say truthfully "I saw his conduct good or bad, brave or cowardly of this or that vessel." But it doesn't matter. It is certain that, almost from the beginning of the action, the fine 74-gun vessel *le Glorieux* was dismasted of all her masts, the Baron d'Escars who commanded her was killed, and the enemy profited from the gap that this vessel necessarily had to leave to cut the French line. Thus separated, she fought poorly. Some vessels however worked wonders but, in the partial or unequal melee for the number, somewhat relentless a few [unintelligible] by their

victory against the French at the Second Battle of Ushant in 1781 and for his death when HMS *Royal George* accidentally sank at Portsmouth the following year. Kempenfelt was writing in his cabin when the ship went down. The cabin doors jammed due to the ship's heeling and he perished with some 900 people.

Brigadier General Anthony Wayne

Independence National Historical Park

duty. *Le Glorieux* dismasted, was taken first. The 74-gun *l'Hector*, the 64-gun *l'Ardent* were taken. The 74-gun *César* was captured and then blew up. The 64-gun *Caton* and *Jason* suffered the same fate. Confusion continued, supported by the fire of a few vessels. Mr. de Grasse, in the midst of the enemy, made signals which were ignored, which were poorly understood. Mr. de Bougainville, chief of the squadron who commanded a division aboard the 80-gun *Auguste*; Mr. de Vaudreuil, with the vessels under his command, did not do what they should, not even what they could. Finally, after eleven and a half hours of fighting in the midst of the entire enemy fleet and surrounded by three three-deck ships, abandoned by his two sailors, physically despairing of being saved, Mr. de Grasse surrendered to the 100-gun *Victory* commanded by Admiral Hood at 6:30 p.m.

Rodney then had an advantage of 14 vessels over a beaten and dispersed enemy. He was exhausted, surprised and enervated by his victory and did not pursue the unfortunate remains of the French Navy. A few vessels arrived at St. Domingue, a few at Curaçao, others at Martinique. Rodney could have taken most of them.

This day, we lost many excellent officers: Mr. Dupavillon(?) whose knowledge surpassed that of any officer of the Navy, the brave Mr. de la Clocheterie, Mr. de Saint Cezaire,[8] Mr. de la Vicomte,[9] Mr. de Marigny[10] and many others.

The Viscount de Morteman who commanded a frigate, having seen, in the midst of the action, a 74-gun French vessel which had lost its rudder and could hardly maneuver, threw her rope to take her in tow and thus passed under the fire of the entire British line. Mr. de Morteman was not wounded but he became ill and survived this fine action for a short time.

8 Capt. of la *Chimère*.

9 Capt. of the *Hector*.

10 Capt. of *le Vaillant*.

Rodney, the fortunate Rodney, arrived at Jamaica with his prizes and his victorious army as if in triumph. The rest of the scattered French Navy fled to several ports and then reunited at St. Domingue under the command of Mr. de Vaudreuil.

General Greene, concentrating the enemy at Charleston, sent General Wayne to Savanna in the month of April to try to capture Colonel Brown[11] who commanded shortly after Mr. Brown positioned himself. General Wayne caught up with him and defeated him at the Ogeechee River. Colonel Laurens,[12] bored by inactivity, left General Washington during the winter to go serve under General Wayne. His intrepidity, which matched his talents, led him too far on this occasion in the pursuit of the enemy where he was killed.

The news of the capture of York and of Cornwallis's army, the arrival of this general in England where he greatly enjoyed his reputation and recognition, the favor he had with the king and the court, the real wrongs which he imputed to Sir Henry Clinton necessarily brought about changes in the conduct of affairs in America. Clinton and Cornwallis himself had previously boasted to their country about the imminent defeat of the 13 states but even more particularly those in the South. This idea had received such favor in the ministry that Lord Dunmore, former governor of Virginia was sent to New York in 1780 to resume his position in this state. Success did not meet expectation. Clinton was recalled and Lieutenant-General Sir Guy Carleton, who had been commander in Canada, was named general in chief of the British Army in America. He arrived at New York on May 23, and Sir Henry Clinton and Lord Dunmore embarked for England a few days later.

The season was advancing, however, and we already enjoyed the mild temperatures of the Virginia climate for some time during the winter and especially in early spring. There were already periods of intense heat. We could have begun the campaign much earlier but we were far from any enemy. The navies were already defeated and could no longer be a great resource for us. We had no resources of our own. We had no money and we did not receive any news. Mr. de Rochambeau decided to give some of his own, to make them part of his plans and he sent the 18-gun sloop of war *Susanne* commanded by the Chevalier de Boulainvilliers[13] to France on May 29.

This sloop of war was part of the naval forces which we had remaining in the York River. Mr. de la Villebrune, an active, intelligent officer, who particularly commanded the

11 Col. Thomas Brown (1750–1825) was a southern Loyalist leader who established himself at Augusta. Following the American War of Independence, Brown was exiled first to British East Florida, and later to St. Vincent's Island in the Caribbean.

12 This note is in the manuscript: "Colonel Laurens was not killed on this occasion. He was near the Combahee River in the month of August (27) of the same year."

13 Louis-Henry de Boulainvilliers de Croÿ (1721-1797) was capitaine de vaisseau and chief of the naval squadron. He commanded the sloop of war *Susanne* and died in combat.

vessel *Romulus* and was in charge of everything in the river, was busy during the winter and spring raising most of the vessels which the British sank before the siege. Success crowned his works and, in the final analysis, he had raised the 32-gun frigate *Guadeloupe* and gave the command to the Chevalier Duquesne.

Before Mr. de Grasse's battle and after its unfortunate outcome, hardly any flour came to St. Domingue. This colony would lack this basic commodity when Mr. de Rochambeau was apprised of it. He had much corn and flour purchased in Virginia where they are better and whiter than in any of the other 13 states. He had assembled as many ships as possible and sent two convoys, the first under the simple escort of a 20-gun sloop of war commanded by Mr. de Saint Vincent and the second escorted by the 26-gun frigate *Sybille*[14] under the command of Count Kergariou-Locmaria[15]. These two convoys very fortunately arrived at St. Domingue.

These little details did not prevent Mr. de Rochambeau from taking care of what most particularly concerned his army. The capture of York made parliament and the English government renounce the plan of re-conquering united America. It was decided to maintain the troops which were at New York but that no new troops would be sent. Mr. de Grasse, having been defeated and captured, we could no longer hope for assistance from the navy. The heat became unbearable in Virginia. We already had many ill. Mr. de Rochambeau decided to leave and to rejoin General Washington who was too weak to expose himself alone before New York and had not yet left his winter quarters.

June

In the long run, Mr. de Rochambeau had already prepared various services. This precaution is necessary in a land where the settlements are sparse and where whatever existing resources are no less difficult to gather.

During the preceding campaign, we lost almost all our artillery horses, more than 600 oxen which we took in Connecticut to haul part of our baggage, the hospitals. . . . They died of exhaustion upon arriving near York but the negligence of the teamsters had also

14 *Sibylle.*

15 Théobald René de Kergariou-Locmaria (1739-7095) was promoted to Capt. on March 13, 1779 and received command of the frigate *Junon* on which he captured the British corvette HMS *Rover.* He transferred to the prestigious *Royal-Louis* in May 1781, on which he served as first officer in Guichen's squadron. He was appointed to command the 32-gun frigate *Sibylle* in June. Kergariou was given command of the frigate *Calypso* in 1786 and led a three-year expedition in the Indian Ocean. He emigrated at the beginning of the French Revolution and later took part in the British-sponsored invasion of France in 1795. He was captured by Republican forces, tried by the Revolutionaries, sentenced to death, and shot.

contributed to the losses, to delay the march which we planned and which would be over such a long distance. We passed a market where town inhabitants committed themselves to furnish horses and wagons for two dollars a day, four horses, one wagon, one teamster everything supplied by the king. They were put in one brigade under the inspection of some large owners, suppliers who were charged with overseeing their care and maintenance.

Having taken all precautions and establishing the different services, Mr. de Rochambeau, in his orders for June 24, directed all the brigades to prepare to march. We could not bring our siege artillery with us. Mr. de Rochambeau left it at West Point, York River with a detachment in order to prevent any sudden incursion of a privateer or of a partisan. He had a detachment of 400 men total selected from each regiment which he put under the command of the Chevalier de la Valette, Brigadier, Lieutenant-Colonel of the Saintonge regiment to garrison York.

For the ease and facility of the march, independently of the meager resources which the land offered, the general set the order of march by divisions in two columns. The left, composed of Lauzun's Legion, departed Charlotte Courthouse near Petersburg, and was already on the march to then find itself at the height of the first division of the right column.

On June 30, the first battalion of the Saintonge Division which was at Hampton rejoined the second Battalion at Halfway House 12 ½ miles. Mr. Desnos[16] Chevalier de Saint Louis captain commanding this division had married a fairly rich widow from the area of Halfway House a few days earlier. This is the only wedding which we had seen occur up to this time.

Departure From Williamsburg
July

On July 1, the first division composed of the Bourbonnais Regiment, a portion of the artillery park and the military officers or the administration attached to the different services left Williamsburg and camped at Drinking Spring 8 miles. The headquarters remained at Williamsburg because of the lack of convenience of this first camp and of the brevity of the march. There are only two barracks here which take their name from a nearby fountain (spring). The heat was excessive and even the night was oppressive. However, as it was a little less intense, it was decided that we would march at night. We had no enemy to fear in all of Virginia. The army staff, was more concerned with the comfort of the troops in the choice of camps than with the military aspect which we nonetheless tried to keep—near

16 Augustin-Rouxelin Denos or d'Enos or des Noes (1741-1806) was a captain in the Saintonge Regiment.

some woods for shade, water for needs. However, the duties were as usual: large guards and camp pickets.

The same day, the Saintonge Division left Halfway House and camped at York 12 ½ miles.

While being poorly received at most places in America where we had not been and where we were not known, we finished by being missed after halting only a few days. The evening before Mr. de Rochambeau's departure from Williamsburg, all the private businesses assembled to pay their compliments, to express their gratitude and to praise his conduct in the discipline of his troops, on their usefulness and to express all their regrets on his departure. These regrets were shared by all the classes of the inhabitants. The women were in tears. Never had they ever spent such an enjoyable winter. The feasts, the balls, the considerations, the attentions of society and all the little details which make the least service so precious. Nothing was forgotten on our part. Fortunes were reestablished; money circulated and we made them partly forget some of the ravages and destructions of the war in general and of the British in particular.

Living in private with Mr. de Rochambeau, my cousin, we drew on a great part of the resources which this region offered and of the company which a widow named Mrs. de Ridle[17] who had two lovable nieces, Miss Rachel and Camilla Warrington. As the song says "let's make love, let's make war." These two matters are full of appeal. We effectively sought to join one with the other and our efforts were rewarded. I particularly had the opportunity to know one of the lovely women I had seen in America, Jenny Stevenson. She lived sometimes 12 miles, sometimes 23 miles, from Williamsburg and the distance entertained me very frequently without neglecting my service however, in an activity always necessary and profitable to a man of my station. Kindness, candor, simple customs, behold in general the instinctive character of the Americans. In addition to these precious qualities, Jenny was also endowed with all the gifts of nature. We spent tender, charming moments together, always too brief. Our separation was cruel. My regrets will be eternal. Every liaison is permitted. Every attachment can be avowed when we find principles, virtues at the core of love itself. It makes us cherish them more. I would willingly linger and expound on a chapter which had nothing but appeal for me. But let's break. The trumpet sounds; the drum beats; let us surrender to duty and leave an extraneous digression. Back to the main subject— in a book it will appear strange. In a particular memorandum, I permit it to myself for my pleasure and to refresh her image.

Before leaving Williamsburg, I want to say a few words about this city. It is at 39° latitude and 37° longitude. It is only 100 and a few years since its foundation. It has become

17 Susanna Riddel.

the capital of Virginia and the seat of government. Its main street is a mile-long, wide, well-built and bounded on one end by the capital and by the university on the other. The capital is large and spacious—It is a public building destined to convene the state assembly and to house a large part of the delegates. We made it a hospital. The university is built with a fine appearance. It is composed of a large body of dormitories and two large pavilions which are not contiguous in the front. Before the war, this university was renowned. It taught Latin, the other languages and law. The governor of Virginia still had a very lovely palace at Williamsburg, built at the end of a fine street planted with catalpa which joined the main street perpendicularly. This fine building as well as one of the pavilions of the university were burned during the winter by negligence of a few American soldiers who were taken there wounded or sick after the siege of York.

The temperate climate during the winter at Williamsburg is scorching during the summer. The countryside around the city is not fertile. There are a lot of woods and marshes. The Negroes alone cultivate the land although these unfortunates have a fate a little milder than those who inhabit the sugar islands, they are nonetheless subject to the same treatment and groan equally under the weight of a harsh slavery. The fruits and vegetables from Europe grow fairly well in this part but nowhere else can we find such strong tobacco. There is also cotton and corn in abundance.

The Virginians do not have the character of the inhabitants in the North. These are passionate about their religion, cultivate their fields, live in the interior of their families, don't meddle in the affairs outside and are zealous Republicans. The others, on the other hand, accustomed from childhood to do nothing, command their Negroes, live in idleness and comfort. They raise superb horses, hunt much, have very fine teams, enjoy making bets and races. They all profess the Anglican religion and, like the British, despise the Presbyterians. Finally, this province, originally founded by the government, holds more to a monarchy as far as character and customs rather than to a Republic.

Williamsburg can never prosper much nor grow firstly because of its soil, secondly because of its distance from the sea (19 miles). Norfolk, burned by the British in 1776, will rise from its ashes. Hampton receives large vessels. The harbor is good. York, Gloucester will surely increase with time and the pleasant shores of the James and York rivers are already furnished with fine country houses. They should always be more populated than the peninsula formed by these two wide rivers which receive the largest ships—especially the York River.

The March North

On July 2, the Royal Deux Ponts Division camped at Drinking Spring, that of the Soissonnais at Williamsburg, that of the Saintonge halted at York and the Bourbonnais

Division and the headquarters camped at a mile and a half from Byrd's Tavern 8 miles, on the left of the New Kent road.

On the 3rd, the Bourbonnais Division went 7 miles and camped in front of the house of Mister Ratcliffe. The Deux Ponts division arrived at Byrd's Tavern, the Soissonnais at Drinking Spring and the Saintonge at Williamsburg.

The 4th, the Saintonge Division camped at Drinking Spring, the Soissonnais was at Byrd's Tavern, the Deux Ponts camped at Ratcliffe's house and the Bourbonnais Division made 7 ½ miles to camp at Hartfield, 2 miles beyond the New Kent Courthouse. The Pamunkey passes only 1 mile from this place.

More culture, a very different and better share than the environs of Williamsburg already distinguished this region. More distance from the sea and the cities attracts the farmers especially when the harvest responds to their care.

On the 5th, Lauzun's Legion which composed the left column joined that of the right, preceding it, however, by three marches. It camped at Little Peags Bridge,[18] a little beyond the Pamunkey Bridge.

The excessive heat forced us, so to speak, to march only at night. The soldiers also being out of breath, we only made three short marches. That of the 5th was longer. The Bourbonnais Division made 15 miles and camped 1 mile beyond New Castle. This route is hilly and not very easy and it was done almost entirely in the woods. The Deux Ponts camped at Hartfield, the Soissonnais at Ratcliffe's house and Saintonge at Byrd's Tavern.

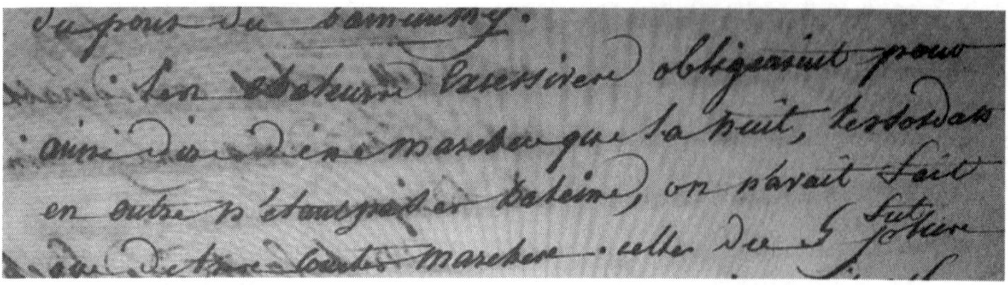
du pont du Pamunky.
Les chaleurs excessives obligeaient pour
ainsi dire à ne marcher que la nuit, les soldats
en outre [illegible] d'haleine, on n'avait fait
que trois courtes marches. celle du 5 fut plus [illegible]

The 6th, the Royal Deux Ponts Division came to New Castle, the Soissonnais at Hartfield and the Saintonge at Ratcliffe's house. This little town, capital of a small district, is lovely and consists of about 50 houses rather separated and built in a large fertile and pleasant plain. The Pamunkey passes at the bottom of the town and receives a small creek from which our camp drew water. There is excellent and abundant forage in this area. Colonel Seams, a rich individual, raises superb horses there originally from the rare Barbary and Arabian races.

18 Littlepage's Bridge.

Lauzun's Legion, Forming the Vanguard, Halted at Littlepage's Bridge.

The Soissonnais Division arrived at New Castle on the 7th, the Saintonge arrived at Hartfield, the Deux Ponts camped at New Castle and the Bourbonnais Division departed to camp near Hanovertown. This march was only 5 miles in the midst of a charming region, which experienced abundance and which proved that Cornwallis's vanguard and its parties did not stay very long. Hanover is a larger town than New Castle. It is built in a plain and the houses are brick.

Mr. the Count de Rochambeau left the army at New Castle to go to Philadelphia to meet with General Washington who was coming from Newburgh. I remained with the army and did not follow the general on this difficult route for him because he was doing it on horseback in excessive heat.

Lauzun's Legion Camped at Burk's Bridge.

On the 8th, the Bourbonnais Division made 11 miles after crossing the Pamunkey on a bridge, camped beyond Littlepage's Bridge. The Pamunkey is a river which flows from east to west. To the east it is not navigable. In many places it is fordable but not safe. It separates the county of Hanover from that of King William and after having been joined by that of West Point they formed together the York River at New Kent courthouse. This county is 2 miles from Littlepage's. I camped at this location near the plantation of a man named Mr. Gerton[19] who had the kindness to loan me some horses to go visit Secretary Nelson in King William County.

This respectable old man is as renown, recommended and regarded because of his virtues as for his personal merit because he is the head of one of the finest and oldest families in Virginia. When this colony was under British domination, he held the office of secretary which was the second of the state and the highest office to which a colonist could aspire because the governor was always English. When the revolution and the first troubles erupted, his family, even his children, embraced the cause of liberty, but he depended on his king for everything and wanted to await the outcome. He conducted himself as a prudent and wise man and also knew how to manage and to conciliate both parties. His brother's son, who was president of the state, was made Brigadier General and Governor in 1781 when Lord Cornwallis took the post of York. I spoke of his virtues, his merit, his courage

19 The name appears written as Gerto. The following paragraph indicates he held the office of Secretary of Virginia. However, no one by that name served in this post. Thomas Nelson held the office from 1743 to 1788 and his nephew, Thomas Nelson, Jr., was governor from June to November 1781.

and of his usefulness to us before and during the siege. His uncle the secretary always remained at York where he had a fine house and Lord Cornwallis who esteemed him and treated him very well, lived with him.

This house, rather high and in a fine location, received our first cannon shots when our batteries were opened. Mr. Nelson was at breakfast. The third cannon shot killed a Negro aside of him who was serving him. He then requested Lord Cornwallis for a passport to leave the place and he withdrew for the duration of the siege to Mr. Moore's where the capitulation was signed. All his goods ravaged, his house demolished by the bombs and the cannon the fall of the British, their capture are events which made him reflect on the benefits of his former sovereign. He is still very rich and lives with general admiration on one of his plantations, dividing his time between his reading, politics and society which often gathers at his house.

The same day, the 8th, the Royal Deux Ponts Division camped at Hanovertown, the Soissonnais camped at New Castle. The Saintonge Division arrived there and Lauzun's Legion camped at Bowlen Green[20].

The 9th, the Saintonge halted at the camp at New Castle. The Soissonnais camped at Hanovertown, the Royal Deux Ponts camped at Littlepage's Bridge and the Bourbonnais Division made 14 miles and camped at Burk Bridge on the left bank of the Mattaponi, 1 mile from this river. It flows like the Pamunkey from west to east. It is fordable in many places and goes to West Point. This route is not very inhabited. There are few notable points. One mile from camp, on the left of the Fredericksburg road is Mr. Kenner's Tavern.

Lauzun's Legion Camped at Dillards.

The 10th, the Saintonge Division camped at Hanover, the Soissonnais at Littlepage Bridge, the Royal Deux Ponts at Burk Bridge, the Bourbonnais made 8 miles and camped at Bowling Green. This place only has 4 or 5 houses, fairly well situated but in a mediocre region.

I stayed that day 4 miles to the rear and visited a rich inhabitant named Mr. Baylor. His father, who was a great lover of fine horses and who had raced them several times in England and at New Market, had given this name to his plantation where his son still raised some very fine ones. His brother is colonel of a regiment of light dragoons and distinguished himself several times in the Carolinas along with Colonel Washington. I halted at this house and I spent two very pleasant days with Mr. Baylor's three sisters, two

20 Bowling Green.

of his nieces, all young, kind, cheerful, and pretty, especially the one named Francine Armstead.

The 11th, the Bourbonnais Division was camped at Dillard's Run, 3 miles beyond Coos tavern. This march was 11 miles in the midst of good and cultivated land but which offers nothing remarkable.

The Royal Deux Ponts Division came to Bowling Green, Soissonnais at Burk Bridge, Saintonge at Littlepage Bridge and Lauzun's Legion marched to Falmouth.

The 12th, the Royal Deux Ponts Division camped at Dillard's Run. That of the Soissonais at Bowling Green, that of the Saintonge at Burk Bridge, and that of the Bourbonnais made 15 miles to camp at Falmouth.

It passed Fredericksburg 12 miles from Dillard's Run. This town is lovely, located at mid-coast and, even though it has only one street which is very lovely and wide, it is large enough and could pass for one of the main settlements of Virginia after Williamsburg. All the houses are well-proportioned and built of bricks. This town is a large tobacco market. It brings together many large merchants whose vessels can go up the Rappahannock to the height of the city.

The Rappahannock flows from northwest to south and empties into the Chesapeake Bay at Falmouth which is built on her left bank. It is not very wide. At this location, it is divided by an island full of rocks and large stones along its entire width. The few boats that were available to cross the river were reserved for the infantry. All the baggage, the artillery horses crossed at the ford. We cannot imagine the work that crossing this river gives us to gather the resources, prevent accidents. To account for this and to execute the appropriate order are tasks for the army staff, part of which was executed perfectly.

The road from Dillard's Run to Fredericksburg is almost level, interrupted from time to time by woods and fine houses which make the landscape very varied and pleasant. Many herds of young goats of all kinds graze in the fields. No other part of America struck me as much for the goodness of the soil as the right bank of the Rappahannock. Its left bank is not as pretty and the soil of Falmouth is not very good.

This location is, high and low, not very pleasant, generally badly built and can contain about 60 houses. Its growth will necessarily be slow because the location of Fredericksburg will always attract merchants and commerce and a large part of the population.

Lauzun's Legion camped at Garot's Tavern

On the 13th, the Bourbonnais Division halted at the Falmouth camp, that of the Royal Deux Ponts arrived there. The Soissonnais camped at Dillard's Run, the Saintonge at Bowling Green, and Lauzun's Legion at Dumfries.

The 14th, the Royal Deux Ponts halted at the camp at Falmouth. The Soissonnais Division arrived there. That of the Saintonge came to Dillard's Run and the Bourbonnais Division made 9 miles and came to camp near Colonel Garrot[t]'s Tavern. We should not be surprised, in the 13 states in general and Virginia in particular, to see taverns occupied and run by colonels, majors, captains etc.

At the beginning of a revolt, an insurrection, we always see some obscure men which nature endowed with a more hardy, exalted and vibrant talent become head of the different parties. Sometimes even the large landowners of [illegible], people commendable by themselves are chosen. This example or this principle was followed in almost all the states. In Virginia, where pride and vanity rule, the militias were filled only with mountain men, only those who reside in the interior of the country, and those not very rich who increase the value of their plantations with a very small number of Negroes. Those who are closer to the cities have all resorted to titles. Three quarters or half have never left their homes, but it doesn't matter. Without reason, without motive they precede their name with a military rank and if a sudden attack by the enemy required them to march, we would see them flee with their effects and their furniture rather than to concern themselves with the means to repulse force with force.

Lauzun's Legion Camped at Colchester.

On the 15th, the Bourbonnais Division made 13 miles and camped at Dumfries. The preceding march being only 9 miles, the Chevalier de Chastellux who commanded the first division, had a camp reconnoitered for the other three, three miles further on the same route so that in addition to camping at Garot's Tavern,[21] the Royal Deux Ponts Division marched to Pyton's Tavern[22]—13 miles. This side of the Rappahannock is not as pleasant as the right bank. It is practically a continuous forest with bad, difficult road, very steep banks.

The Soissonnais Division halted at the camp at Falmouth, that of the Saintonge arrived and Lauzun's Legion camped at [illegible][23]

21 Garrot's or Garrett's Tavern.

22 Peyton's Ordinary.

23 Possibly Alexandria.

Dumfries is built in a low land. It contains about 45 to 50 houses among which are some rather fine ones. The little Asquino[24] river passes beyond it and empties into the Patowmack.[25]

The 16th, the Saintonge Division halted at the camp at Falmouth. The Soissonnais marched to Peyton's Tavern. The Royal Deux Ponts Division camped at Dumfries, 10 miles, and that of the Bourbonnais made 9 miles to go to Colchester.

This little town which contains 30 to 40 [houses] is, like Dumfries, fairly well built. The little of Occoquant[26] river passes there and empties into the Potomac opposite Colchester. There is no bridge on this river. All the baggage and artillery crossed at a ford 6 miles above Colchester. The troops crossed on poor boats belonging to the ferry which is about a quarter mile wide.

From Colchester, the environs of Colchester are very lovely, offer a pleasant countryside which [the course] of the Potomac greatly enhances the scenery. It is notable that all the rivers we crossed retain the names the indigenous savages originally gave them: Mattapony, Paminsky, Asquino, Occoquan, Potomac.

Lauzun's Legion Camped at Georgetown.

On the 17th, the Saintonge Division camped at Peyton's Tavern – 13 miles. The Soissonnais marched to Dumfries, the Royal Deux Ponts to Colchester and the Bourbonnais Division camped beyond Alexandria after crossing [unintelligible] was 16 miles.

Guided by curiosity and the desire to know [illegible] a great man, I let the column file past and, with the Viscount de Rochambeau, strayed from the route which they were to take to go to General Washington's house. It is located in a charming location on the top of a hill called Mount Vernon, 10 miles from Colchester and 10 from Alexandria on the right bank of the Potomac which is a mile and a half wide at this location. The panorama, the glimpse over this lovely location which the course of the river offers is very long and very pleasantly bounded by the coast of Maryland which borders its left bank.

The general's house is near the river which it greatly dominates, as it is sloped. The building is a single story and 86 to 88 feet long and 20 high. It has only one ground floor and

24 Aquia Run.

25 Potomac.

26 Occoquan Creek.

one floor pierced with nine intersections [unintelligible[27]]. On each side of the main building, there is a curved, covered gallery which communicates with two outbuildings which serve as a kitchen and a commons. Together, they embrace a plot of land which forms a very fine yard. In front of each of these small buildings there is a garden enclosed by retaining walls which are spacious and very well maintained. They are preceded by a very vast approach and a drive which is not yet finished.

The side of the house which overlooks the Potomac is adorned with a colonnade or covered gallery which protects the apartments from excessive heat, gives the structure a very noble appearance at 18 feet high and 9 wide. The apartments are rather comfortable and well distributed but they are all very small.

The plantation of Mount Vernon practically produces no revenue for General Washington. The open land is generally poor, full of stones and full of sand. It is destined surely to be a place of enjoyment because there are farms and other small plantations in the neighborhood which contain 8 or 9000 acres of land between them in excellent ground, well-cultivated and well-maintained by the Negroes to make it valuable.

Visit at Mount Vernon

Since the war, General Washington had a lot of work done at Mount Vernon and, as he is a lover of privacy and devoted to domestic work by taste, he sacrificed the pleasures which they bring him to his duty to his country, to devote himself to the whirlwind of business matters. Since the beginning of the war, he spent only nine days at his home. [Seeing?] that the relatives of the same name as his wife ordinarily lived with Mrs. Washington who spends the summers and who goes to rejoin her husband every winter wherever the army is encamped.

Before marrying the general, Mrs. Washington was the widow of a rich inhabitant, a Mr. Custis.[28] She had a son who died at Alexandria sometime after the siege of York. She has nothing moral or externally physical which corresponds to the first impression which the name Washington evokes or leaves today. She enjoyed a great fortune. She could not make a better or wiser decision than to share it with a hero, with a great man, according to all accounts, and whose name will pass to his most noble heirs. William the Conqueror usurped the land where his ancestors were born, and freed from tyranny and slavery the land which one of William's successors wanted to dominate.

27 The phrase seems to be "sauve avant corpre."

28 Daniel Parke Custis (1711–1757) was an American planter and politician who was the first husband of Martha Dandridge. After his death, Dandridge married George Washington.

After examining everything which might arouse my curiosity and draw my attention at Mount Vernon, I left and took leave of Mrs. Washington to go join the first division of the army at Alexandria.

Alexandria is built on the Potomac and, after Williamsburg, is the largest city in Virginia. There are many fine houses, either in brick or in stone and there is a great commerce in tobacco and flour on the Potomac. Sixty-four-gun ships can go up this river as far as Alexandria where it is a mile wide. In 1778, when Lord Howe went up the Chesapeake Bay, a 64-gun British ship went up the Potomac and came close to Alexandria. Some soldiers, some sailors from South Carolina came along both banks of the river, pillaged a few plantations and burned others. They intended to do the same to Mount Vernon, but Mrs. Washington was warned in enough time to gather some people, to conduct some defensive maneuvers which made the enemy flee.

The countryside around Alexandria is nothing less than beautiful. It is generally dry, arid and sandy.

On the 18th, the Saintonge Division camped at Dumfries. That of the Soissonnais marched to Colchester the same day. The Royal Deux Ponts camped at Alexandria and the Bourbonnais Division made 9 miles to camp in Maryland a mile from Georgetown, on the left bank of the Potomac. We crossed this river by ferry which is a half mile. The baggage crossed above the falls where a fairly difficult ford crossed 6 miles from there.

The Potomac is the largest river in Virginia in particular and of the 13 states in general. It flows from the northwest to the southeast and empties into the Chesapeake Bay and toward the middle of this Mediterranean sea.[29] It is 21 miles wide at its mouth and separates Maryland from Virginia.

I want to cast another glance on this vast and lovely state before leaving. Its boundaries not yet well defined but it is generally understood as between the Chesapeake Bay and the banks of the Ohio. There are still a lot of savages in this area who are often at war with the newly settled colonists and who sometimes scalp. The Potomac borders it in the north and Carolina in the south. No state is better located. Nature is broadly drawn, lends itself to all kinds of cultivation, to every production which finds its market by great rivers which receive large ships and which all empty into the Chesapeake Bay which is itself 180 miles long. A spit of land or peninsula well-populated, rich and fertile but upon which I had not gone, is called the Eastern Shore[30] and still bears the name of Virginia from Cape Henry to the height of the Potomac.

29 Inland sea.

30 Translated into French.

The western part produces abundant corn, wheat and tobacco, the finest known, and a little bit of cotton. There are about 80,000 Negroes and about 20 to 30,000 whites. The weather's excessive heat renders the Virginians generally soft and, on the other hand, one must force a large number of slaves to work. Before the war, commerce was concentrated, without incentive, without vigor. It was done only with the English who took the two American products at a good price in exchange for the product of their manufacture which they sold very dearly. From there, the little emulation, the little hope of enriching oneself, commerce languished for the colonists. Their spirit did not work, became lazy, not focusing on any single well-determined object. We could not see and we did not yet have this energy which a people should have, that its interests, its productions, its fortunate and [illegible] condition naturally appeal to commerce. But the veils[31] are slowly tearing. The chains will be broken. The freedom for which we fight will be the prize of our present labors and hardships. The fortunate American, especially the Virginian, who can charge his products, his ships in the midst of his lands of his plantation, will feel the price of an advantage which he possesses more than any other state and, little by little, we will see him come to the state where his position naturally calls him.

In general, in Virginia, the large houses are scattered. Height rules more than appearance as in the north. However, the owners are fairly hospitable and receive strangers well. In the interior of the country, particularly where the roads are less traveled, the settlements are smaller and taverns very rare, travelers often enter private houses where they are well received. It is thus that the officers who were going to join their corps, whether in the North or in the South, almost always saved themselves the cost of a long and difficult voyage.

At the beginning of the revolution, Virginia took up arms and supplied a fairly large number of troops for the common cause. But since the capture of Charleston and the battle of Camden, it has not raised a single regiment. The money raised by taxes is poorly distributed, badly used and serves almost only to defray the delegates from the different counties to the General Assembly and to enrich a few individuals whose avarice more than patriotism, devotion and love of their duty called them to the various duties of the state.

To prove the neglect or the culpable indifference of their main officers, I can report what I saw around Secretary Nelson at the crossing of the Pamunkey. Twenty-one pieces of 18-pound bronze cannon which were brought from France are in the water and on the shore of this river without having tried to raise them or at least to remove them from the water for three years. We might say they have too many.

31 The word could also be translated as "sails."

The horses of Virginia are, with good reason, the most prized in North America. They are thoroughbred and have much grace and agility. There is a large number of very fine studs originally from wild Arabian breeds whose mating and breeding are carefully continued as in England. They do not descend from twins as formerly. They won race prizes and were spared from doing work. In general, they are put on an English diet and the results prove the excellence and the success of the principles of this nation as two thousand leagues away in a different climate, the same treatment (?) produces the same results.

[Illegible[32]] of the mares is very expensive and a stud brings in more money for his master then a plantation of 12 to 1500 acres of land.

Georgetown in Maryland is a small town which contains about 50 or 60 houses. Maryland tobaccos, which are the most prized of America after those of Virginia, go to market by the Potomac and there are large warehouses in this town.

On the 29th, the Saintonge Division camped at Colchester, that of the Soissonnais at Alexandria. The Deux Ponts Division crossed the Potomac and came to Georgetown and that of the Bourbonnais marched to Bladensburg where it camped after having made 8 miles.

Lauzun's Legion halted at this place since the 17th when part of it arrived from Charlotte Courthouse on July [illegible]. It had made five marches before reentering the right column. From Charlotte Courthouse to Kings land ferry 16 miles— to Richmond 8 miles. July 3 halt. The 4th 12 miles to Norrel's Tavern after crossing the Chickahominy on the 9th, it reentered the right column at Little Peags Bridge[33].

Bladensburg is pleasantly located even though it is partly built in a hollow. This place can comprise about 100 houses. The East branch of the Potomac passes through there and empties into this river a few miles from there below Georgetown. This region is very abundant in forage and we harvest much wheat.

The 20th, Lauzun's Legion camped at Patuxent Iron Works 13 miles. The Bourbonnais Division halted at Bladensburg, that of the Royal Deux Ponts arrived there and the Soissonnais Division crossed the Potomac and came to Georgetown; the Saintonge camped at Alexandria.

The 21st, Lauzun's Legion made 13 miles and camped in a field near the woods, water and its forage. The Bourbonnais and Deux Ponts Divisions halted at Bladensburg. That of the Soissonnais arrived and the Saintonge Division crossed the Potomac to camp at Georgetown.

32 The word appears to read "La louvature."

33 Littlepage's Bridge.

The 22nd, the vanguard made 12 miles and camped at Baltimore. The Bourbonnais marched to Patuxent or Snowden's Iron Works. The Deux Ponts and Soissonnais halted at Bladensburg and the Saintonge came to take the camp of the Bourbonnais Division.

The 23rd, the Bourbonnais Division made 13 miles. The Royal Deux Ponts Division camped at Patuxent Iron Works.

The Patuxent is a little river which empties into the Chesapeake Bay and which flows across a very hilly countryside. It is very deep. It is wide at its mouth and would be very capable of receiving warships.

The house of a man named Mr. Snowden is located on the right bank and an eighth of a league from this river. I made my lodging at his house. His family was originally of the Anglican religion, but his father became a Quaker and left two children. The elder is Mr. Snowden [who] is one of the most zealous proselytes of this sect and, as its strict [principles] hold the shedding of blood and slavery equally in horror, that it should always make vows and contribute essentially to the well-being of the human race, he freed all his negroes. Some remained with him in gratitude and out of attachment. George Snowden, his younger brother, lives on the opposite bank. The forges or iron works belong to him. He mocks the credulity and the good nature of his brother, does not believe in any religion for fear of making a mistake, hunts much and retains all his negroes he inherited.

On the 24th, the Bourbonnais Division camped at Baltimore. That of the Royal Deux Ponts made 13 miles. The Soissonnais came to Patuxent Iron Works and the Saintonge halted at Bladensburg.

The 25th, 26th and 27th, the three divisions of the Royal Deux Ponts, Soissonnais and Saintonge arrived at the Baltimore camp.

Mr. de Rochambeau returned from Philadelphia at this time where General Washington arrived on his part. It was extraordinary that a court which does not permit its generals to do anything without its participation and which until then, without knowing the country, the locations of the region where we were conducting war, still wanted to regulate the marches and had not yet sent, at the end of July, any dispatches for any particular plans of operation in concert with the general plan. Mr. de Rochambeau, realizing that a longer halt in Virginia would be of little benefit and that he would lose many men, had the French corps leave. The purpose of his conference was to consider and to decide what would be the best thing to do for the rest of the campaign, in the uncertainty of the resources which either might be sent to him or possibly even be demanded of him. The two generals decided that we would march toward the North River to join the American army which was too weak to undertake anything and was still in quarters. Consequently, Mr. de Rochambeau dispatched the Count de Fersen to the Chevalier de la Valette whom he left in command at York and at West Point to have his detachment embark as soon as possible and come join him at Baltimore. The time necessary to do this required the halt which we made in this city (at Baltimore) where, each day, a large number of soldiers became ill from exhaustion and the fatigues of a long march.

August

An American ship coming from Cape François[34] informed us on Friday, August 2 that Mr. the Marquis de Vaudreuil under whose escort he had arrived, was anchored off the Virginia capes with 13 ships of the line and three frigates and that he had sent some to Hampton to land his dispatches. Mr. de Rochambeau received them three days later. Mr. de Vaudreuil, after the unfortunate battle of April 12, had spent the winter in the Boston area which appeared the most suitable place to replenish his resources to refit and to repair his vessels. But, as the British followed him closely to New York, he feared that they might attack him as they were much stronger, and possibly burn him as he landed some men. He requested Mr. de Rochambeau for an officer on whose talents he could rely, some engineers and artillerists to construct some works and batteries. Mr. de Choisy was sent to Boston.

Visit with Governor Lee

The 3rd, Mr. Lee, Governor of Maryland, arrived at Baltimore. He is a man well-liked and respected as much for his manners, his knowledge, his fortune as for his public character. Under this last characteristic, he was most useful to the army in 1781 when, totally without resources, it embarked at Annapolis to go conduct the siege of York. Mr. de Rochambeau waited for him to make his general review of the summer. It was announced for the 5th which attracted a very large number of people. The troops paraded before the governor and rendered him honors. They deserved his applause as much for their comeliness, their dress, as for the order in which they passed before him and the general.

The 6th, 7th and 8th, he saw them more in detail. We conducted firing exercises. Unfortunately, a cartridge with ball was fired through the negligence of a soldier of the Soissonnais Division and seriously wounded an unfortunate woman spectator in the thigh. The maneuver, the chief surgeon of this regiment was sent to treat her free of charge and the regiment was ordered to pay her a large settlement.

The governor returned to Annapolis on the 9th, after obliging Mr. de Rochambeau to go visit him.

34 Now Cape Haitien.

It was at this very same time that Mr. de Vaudreuil arrived at Boston. In his passage, he captured six transport ships loaded with masts and other supplies necessary to repair the British Jamaica fleet.

The 10th, our general set out to march to Annapolis. Two miles from Baltimore, we cross the ferry of the West Branch of the Patapsco. It is a mile and a half wide at this location. We made 13 to go breakfast in a poor tavern at the widow Authward and, from there, we crossed a rather thin and wooded region with pine trees to the governor's at Annapolis.

The government is a fine building which belonged to the last British governor Lord Charles Eden[35] who had it built, and which the Americans configured at the beginning of the war to make it the residence of the governor of Maryland.

Mrs. Lee, whom we had seen at Baltimore, received us with the greatest ceremony. She is a woman of 35 or 36 years who is not pretty but has a very fine figure. At the same time, she has much wit, is very lovable, and made me laugh. And, a very rare thing about the retired life which women in America bring to their family, made the honors of her household very perfectly and with the greatest ease. What is even more notable for strangers to Maryland, she is Catholic, enjoys a very fine fortune and married Mr. Lee only on condition that his children would be raised and taught in the same religion as hers.

Annapolis is located on the Chesapeake Bay at the head of an extension of this bay in the land. Only very small ships can enter it. This town is the capitol of Maryland and the seat of government. As Baltimore increased by more than three quarters since the war, there is a very strong question of making it the capitol in name because it is, in fact, by its size, its population, its commerce that a more suitable location, a more spacious and deeper port would always be their preference.

There are about 200 houses at Annapolis, many very fine. The courthouse or city hall is very remarkable. It is a very large building and almost square. The hall in the middle of the interior is immense and resembles a church in its dimensions. It only receives daylight from above. On both sides of this great hall, there are some other equally fine rooms for the Chamber of Delegates and for the Senate and other large apartments for private meeting rooms.

Annapolis is one of the oldest settlements in Maryland and the [home] of the finest and richest families. It was founded during the reign of Queen Anne whose name it bears. One of the things that strikes a young man is its natural beauty, but an animated nature and even

35 Charles Eden (1673 –1722) was governor of North Carolina. His brother Sir Robert Eden,1st Baronet, of Maryland (1741–1784) served as governor of Maryland from 1769 to 1776.

further embellished by art. The beauty, the spirit, the talents should not be kept secret. It is thus that I would depict the beautiful Mrs. Lloyd, the prettiest woman I ever saw in America. Before the war, she spent a year in Paris and one in London and has perfectly known how to blend simplicity of American customs to those more studied, more refined of these great cities. She enjoys a very easy fortune at Annapolis. She speaks French. We were anxious to meet her during our brief stay and she gave me and two of my companions an elegant breakfast the eve of our departure.

Mr. de la Fayette camped near Annapolis in the month of May 1781 after the naval battle of the same month—see the month of May in the first booklet.

We departed Annapolis on the 12th and arrived at Baltimore the same day where Mr. de Rochambeau found some letters from General Washington and from Sir Guy Carlton, Commander-in-Chief at New York.

Sir Guy Carlton had received notice by way of packet boats from London to New York that the first overtures of peace had been made at Paris, that England recognized the independence of the 13 United States, that it would free the prisoners in consequence of which he was giving notice to the generals in chief and that he proposed a suspension of hostilities. Was it a lure or was it a fact? —— Mr. de Rochambeau received notice from the Chevalier de la Valette a few days earlier that the siege artillery, the detachment, and everything that still belonged to the French corps at Yorktown would leave very soon and go to Head of Elk by sea. Our general, not yet having received any dispatch from the court of France, not knowing what response Congress would make to those of Sir Guy Carlton, what would be that of Mr. Washington and whether he would be obliged to change anything to his marching plans because of that, he sent me to bring his dispatches to Congress, to Chevalier de la Luzerne, our ambassador and to Mr. Washington's headquarters at Newburgh. I left at 1 p.m. on Tuesday the 13th and hastened to the forges of Little Fall[36]. 19 There is a little stream, an abundance of forage, near this place which has about 10 or 12 houses. The forges of Little Fall are a good product and are named after the river. I cross it at a ford. From there, I proceed 13 miles[37] to Bushtown.[38] I took a fresh horse there and proceeded 12 miles to cross the Susquehanna at the ferry which is a mile and a half wide. The river empties into the Chesapeake Bay 2 miles lower. From this ferry, I

36 Little Fall was in the area near where I-95 crosses the Big Gunpowder Falls River in White Marsh, MD.

37 This note is in the manuscript: "This having been written on location and thus being able to serve as [illegible] and as information for subsequent marches, or rather for similar missions to this one, one should not be surprised if we mix a few local observations with a simple commission which we can also make into a succinct narrative."

38 Bushtown was along the Philadelphia Road in Abingdon, Maryland.

proceed to Head of Elk, 17 ½ miles after crossing at the Principio forges which are only 3 miles from the Susquehanna. They once belonged to some Englishmen. Since the war, they were confiscated for the state. Three miles further, we cross at Charleston. This place has 40 or 50 houses situated near the left bank of the Susquehanna. The area is sandy. Three miles further, we find North East, a small place in a flat land and Head of Elk is 9 miles further. I refreshed myself at this place for a moment and immediately afterward took some horses and a guide and proceeded to Wilmington during the night, 22 miles. From there to Chester, 12 ½ miles. At Chester, I found some horses to rent and left for Philadelphia. Three miles from this last town, we cross the Schuylkill on a floating bridge. It is made with large beams equally spaced and strongly joined together, on which planks are nailed. This bridge is rather long and follows the movements of the tide.

The Schuylkill empties into the Delaware opposite Mud Island. The plans of William Penn extended the city of Philadelphia all the way to this river. Although it is already very big, it will surely take much more time for his plan to become totally realized.

I arrived at Philadelphia at the Chevalier de la Luzerne at 7 a.m. on the 14th. I gave him my dispatches and those of the Congress. He dismissed me only at noon. I then left to cross the Delaware 35 miles from there at Robertson's or Corwell's Ferry[39], leaving Trenton 25 miles on my right. There are many taverns along this route, houses for three, four or five. The land is good, well-watered by small streams. Consequently, there are buildings from which we have very fine and pleasant views. The Delaware is not very wide at Robertson's Ferry. It can be crossed by a ford at all times without any risk. However, there is a ferryboat on each bank.

I found myself on the other side of the ferry in the greatest embarrassment for having horses. I wanted to complete my tedious mission promptly and I don't know how I would have managed to do so without the help of a militia colonel named Ely who [unintelligible[40]] me two guineas which I promised would serve to support me during the night and loaned me two horses. We were at Baptist town 9 miles; 5 miles further to Pitch town and 7 miles from the latter place we found Mr. Burkarit's tavern in the middle of the woods. This large tavernkeeper received me very badly because I woke him in the middle of the night. He told me he had no horses for me and after many fruitless supplications, I was forced to sleep in his substandard bar with my guide Colonel Ely. When I woke, I was very bothered for the resources to use to extricate myself from this terrible shelter. It was the morning of the 15th. I awakened my militia colonel and asked him to bring me a few miles further with his horses. The Americans are lazy and do not get moving very easily. A little

39 Coryel's Ferry.

40 The words appear to read "moy en en."

more money made me win my case and gave my guide a little incentive. We mounted on horseback and, 5 miles from there, we crossed Muscon Creek[41] on a bridge at Johnson's mill, A mile further, I found Mr. McCullough, a kind farmer, who gave me one of his plow horses with which I made 12 miles and proceeded to Hacket's town.[42]

These 12 miles of countryside are not low nor pleasant to the sight. They are full of rather dry mountains and moors scattered with shrubs which cannot grow. The neighborhood of Hackettstown is pretty. The town consists of 12 to 15 houses located halfway up a hill from which there is a view. A little brook at the bottom of the hill fertilizes and makes the fields green which a rather large number of cattle trample. From Hackettstown I made 11 miles in the midst of a high and almost continuously low forest and I arrived at Mr. Petitt's Tavern. It is built on the right of the road in a fine and rather abundant town. The Sussex Courthouse is located on the left, 6 miles from [there].

My plow horse was on edge. He gave me a lot of incentive to find another and I arrived at the home of a farmer planter called Caughe. He was [illegible]. He gave me 1000 insults. I returned them at the stroke of the whip but he did not give me any horse and I was forced to return to Mr. Petitt's Tavern where I had left mine which I pushed 8 miles further to Mr. Snider's tavern, a German, a very good man, very obliging, with whom I left Mr. McCullough's horse and he rented me two with which I arrived at Squire Cary's 6 miles away. His house, built on the left of the road, dominates a very fertile and fine valley which is very long. It contains magnificent fields. The Americans, not having any posts for horses, had thought to create some at certain distances with some rich individuals for the needs of officers dispatched for the public service. I had hoped to find some at the squire's but he had returned them to the army and I went four miles further to Beard's Tavern. I found the numerous company and a pleasant man who loaned me a horse to go 15 miles from there to Warick,[43] but I pushed on as far as Chester.—Warwick is a well-situated and pleasant place. It has only 12 to 15 houses but its location and the fertility of its surroundings will certainly increase it greatly. A rather fine brook passes there. Chester is 11 miles from Warwick and is about as large. Its neighborhood is watered by a fine brook.

The 26 miles from Beard's Tavern to Chester are cut by many mountains. There are some very extended vistas from their summits. They are generally covered with wood but they enclose, between them, some charming valleys which are very fertile, well cultivated, abundant in forage, watered by many streams and filled with superb and numerous cattle. There are very few gentlemen in this area. The houses are still separated and distant. The

41 Musconetcong Creek.

42 Hackettstown.

43 Warwick.

people are totally devoted to rural life. It provides their comfort and happiness.— A very kind resident of Chester rented me some horses with which I made 17 miles to New Windsor through a rather bad region, dry, rocky and hilly.

New Windsor is carefully built on the right bank of the North River 8 miles above West Point. It is built at the foot of a very high hill and contains about 80 houses. It is generally a very bad place whose appearance is wild and where the American army spent its winter quarters from 1780 to 1781 and from 1781 to 1782. Two miles above and on the same hill and bank as New Windsor is Newburgh where I arrived at 11 o'clock at night. I was not disappointed, as it is easy to imagine, to find a frugal meal and a bed which I owe to the kindness of Colonel Trumbull, General Washington's aide-de-camp and secretary, who could read the dispatches I brought him only the following morning. He immediately sent orders to all the general officers, even those at West Point, to come to his quarters at 10 o'clock to consider the current situation and to determine what response he should give and the wisest course of action to take. Mr. de Rochambeau and the Chevalier de la Luzerne thought that the peace which Sir Guy Carlton proposed did not seem as imminent as he led us to believe.

General Washington's opinion and the decisions of the Council of War concurred with the observations of the French and they concluded unanimously that the manner to prepare themselves or rather to make peace promptly was to maintain the most hostile and the most respectful footing before the enemy, that we should mistrust the British because they had often been deceived, that they even advised that they wanted to embark a detachment of four regiments at New York to reinforce Jamaica about which we knew, by news from Europe, that our cabinets at Versailles and Madrid had plans, that they had to remove from the enemy any thought of making any attack on Boston and on the French fleet, that a new junction of the two combined armies would produce this result, that moreover the French corps, being supplied with everything necessary for the campaign and for the march, there could be no inconvenience to continue and that, given the heat in the South, the health of the men would suffer. This opinion became that of the plurality of the members of the council.

I dined with General Washington who handed me his dispatch at 3 o'clock in the afternoon. I promised him a prompt delivery. I took my leave of him and remounted my horse. I made 70 miles and halted a few hours at Pettit's Tavern where I had already stayed. Everybody was asleep. This tavern is very small and there was no bed. But a kind American made me a little place in his. When one experiences great fatigue, everything is good. I slept three good hours and remounted my horse the following morning, the 17th. I returned by the same places. I traveled 90 miles to Philadelphia. The Chevalier de la Luzerne kept me an hour and a half to give me a few dispatches. I made another 55 miles and arrived at Head of Elk at 11:30, dying of hunger, and exhausted. I had travelled a little more than 50 leagues on my buttocks during my day. I set out early on the 18th. I made 56 miles and arrived at Baltimore before noon where I found Mr. de Rochambeau ill. The extreme and unusual speed which I made greatly surprised him but, at the same time, it induced him to give me some orders to resume the army's march. Its departure was set for the 23rd because we still had part of our troops who had been attacked by fever and were not yet in condition to march and to endure the hardships. Moreover, the *Romulus*, the *Guadeloupe* and the transports had just arrived loaded with artillery and troops. Contrary winds and the difficulty of navigating the Patapsco delayed them until the 20th when they entered the harbor.

The unfortunate detachment which landed showed us, by the pitiful condition to which they were reduced, the happiness which had accompanied our departure from Virginia. But they all had fever and they told us that three quarters of the residents had also been struck.

Arrival in Baltimore

The 21st and the 22nd, various corporations of the city of Baltimore presented addresses to Mr. de Rochambeau in which they commemorated everything he did to support the alliance in general and the states along the Chesapeake in particular. They thanked him for the powerful protection which he gave to their commerce and, at the same time, they gave him the most extensive praises for the manner in which he had his troops live among them.

Baltimore was founded at the beginning of this century by Lord Baltimore who gave it his name. Few settlements grew as quickly as that one. Its location on the Patapsco and near the bay offers a market for its commerce and for its produce. However, before the war, the continuation of the one and the encouragement of the other were illegal because of the restraints which the British imposed. And for the same reason, the colony languished and remained in stagnation from which our victories extricated it. Our fleets, victorious until now, assured the return of the merchants. Fortunes increased more than sixfold and the number of wage earners was so great that since the previous year when the army lodged in this city, we counted an increase of 100 newly built or almost completed houses.

The port of Baltimore, still leaves much to be desired, but is nonetheless much better and preferable to that of Annapolis where there is little water. This reason alone will always attract the speculator, in preference, and will make the first of these towns prosper to the detriment of the second which is much older.

The 23rd, Lauzun's Legion left the camp at Baltimore and camped at the forges of Little Fall.

The 24th, Lauzun's Legion camped at Bushtown and the Bourbonnais Division made 13 1/2 miles to camp at Little Fall. Mr. de Rochambeau left Baltimore the same day with part of his headquarters. He went to lodge at Governor Lee's sister's, Mrs. Buchanan. She was very lovable, very elegant but, at the same time, she was a sort of deranged mind whose expressions nothing could stop.

The 25th, the Lauzun Division marched to the Susquehanna ferry which it crossed; the Bourbonnais Division camped at Bushtown 14 miles. Two miles from Bushtown, we find New Town, a new settlement in the woods in an area which appears wild. The Royal Deux Ponts Division camped at Little Fall the same day.

The 26th, Lauzun's Legion halted at the Susquehanna camp, the Royal Deux Ponts Division marched to Bushtown, that of the Soissonnais camped at Little Fall and the Bourbonnais Division marched to the Susquehanna ferry which is a mile wide at this place. Despite that, they crossed entirely on the same day because of the precaution that Mr. de Béville had taken to bring all the flat boats from Baltimore for the baggage and artillery. We cannot imagine the untiring attention that a staff officer in charge of these types of embarkations must devote to diminish the frequent risks and to prevent accidents. We saw nothing remarkable in the area around the ferry except for the boatman's daughter who has a very pretty appearance, accompanied by the graces, politeness and the naïveté which we can expect of a 15 year-old, but which we cannot expect to encounter, given the rusticity which is the common state of sailors and boatmen.

Lauzun's Legion left the Susquehanna camp on the 27th and came to take one at Head of [Elk.] The Bourbonnais halted near the Susquehanna. The Royal Deux Ponts Division crossed this river the same day. The Soissonnais Division camped at Bushtown and that of the Saintonge at Little Fall Iron Works.

All the area around the Susquehanna is very wooded. There are falls or saults a few miles from the ferry going upriver and there are still savages near the source and on the banks of this river.

While we were making a long, difficult and tiring but peaceful march, General Greene's advance posts near Charleston had occasion to skirmish with the enemy from time to time. British General Leslie who did not have many provisions, attempted various sorties and excursions to obtain some rice with some success. On August 27, he made a new attempt with the same intent, but without the same success. He brought back some provisions but he had several men killed near the Combahee River.

The Americans paid for this slight advantage with the loss of Colonel Laurens, son of the president, [one] of their best and bravest officers. He is the same one who was employed, in 1781, in a negotiation with the court of France. He returned in time to find himself at the siege of York. He was named commissioner for the articles of capitulation and, not wanting to remain inactive during the winter, he requested the command of a

Lieutenant Colonel John Laurens

Independence National Historical Park

detached body in the Army of the South where he always gave new proof of his zeal, of his unflagging courage and of his ability up until the time of his death, a fatal time for his fellow citizens.

The 28th, Lauzun's Legion camped at Newport 16 miles. The Bourbonnais Division camped at Head of Elk [illegible] miles.

The Bourbonnais Division halted at the Susquehanna. The Soissonnais Division crossed this river and the Saintonge Division arrived from Little Fall to camp at Bushtown.

Head of Elk is still part of the state of Maryland. The commerce of this province is almost the same as that of Virginia, that is to say that it consists of tobacco, flour sent to the islands, and horses less prized than those of Virginia. This state is divided by the Chesapeake Bay of which the Elk River forms the head. It begins on a side to the west of the Potomac and on the east bank at Herring's Bay. In general, the soil of this state is very good. The dominant religion is Anglicanism, but Catholicism is also freely practiced. However, the number of its adherents is very small. The Negroes cultivate the plantations but they are in small numbers in the counties a little distant from the sea. The lands are also better cultivated. Maryland has always exactly supplied its quota of troops to the union. They have always distinguished themselves by their bravery, their zeal and their perfect discipline and they have supplied some officers who made themselves renown such as Morgan opposed to Tarleton, General Smallwood[44] who retreated before Lord Cornwallis at Camden in 1780.

44 Maj. Gen. William Smallwood (1732–1792) was serving as the fourth Governor of Maryland when the state adopted the United States Constitution.

The 29th, Lauzun's Legion marched to Chester. The Bourbonnais Division camped at Newport 16 miles. The Royal Deux Ponts Division camped at Head of Elk. That of the Soissonnais halted at the Susquehanna camp and the Saintonge Division crossed this river.

On the road from Head of Elk to Newport is Relley Creek[45] which is crossed on a bridge and which separates Maryland from the lower counties of the Delaware. In 1777, when General Washington marched to oppose the landing of General Howe, there was a small attack of some American militiamen at this creek on the British outposts. We can still see Christiana on this road, 6 miles from Newport. The location is very pleasant. This place still consists of only about 30 houses on a creek which carries boats and empties into the Delaware. Two miles from Christiana, we cross a creek on a bridge called Christian's bridge four miles from Newport. This last city is well situated. There is only one very wide and fairly long road even though there are only 60 or 70 houses. The great inconvenience of the lack of water which the excessive heat made us feel separated the camp one mile from the city.

The 30th, Lauzun's Legion camped at Philadelphia. The Bourbonnais Division camped at Chester 16 miles. That of the Royal Deux Ponts at Newport. The Soissonnais camped at Head of Elk and the Saintonge division halted at the Susquehanna camp.

From Newport to Chester, we pass Wilmington, capitol of the lower counties of the Delaware. It is well-built, but the air must not be healthy because of the marshes which fill the banks of the Delaware in this area.

The scarcity of water prevented us from camping at Chester. We took a position two miles further on the Philadelphia Road where the Bourbonnais division camped on the 31st after crossing the Schuylkill bridge. This division entered this town in very good order, preceded by its vanguard and followed by its artillery. Mr. Mackean, President of Congress, was at the head of the entire body over which he presided on the steps of the courthouse porch, located on Chestnut Street, to watch the troops parade. Mr. de Rochambeau placed himself at their head and saluted the president. The flags rendered him the same honor.

All the region around Philadelphia is lovely, well cultivated, open and adorned with fine houses.

The same day, Lauzun's Legion halted at Philadelphia. The Royal Deux Ponts division came to camp near Chester, that of the Soissonnais marched to Newport and that of the Saintonge came from the banks of the Susquehanna to camp at Head of Elk.

45 Ridley Creek.

September

The first of September, Lauzun's Legion left Philadelphia to go to Red Lyon's Tavern[46]. The Bourbonnais division halted there, that of the Royal Deux Ponts arrived and passed before Congress rendering the same honors as the preceding one and camped beyond the city. The Soissonnais division marched to Chester and the Saintonge division camped at Newport.

The 2nd, Lauzun's Legion camped at Trenton. The Bourbonnais division left the camp at Philadelphia and marched to the Red Lion Tavern where it camped. Mr. de Rochambeau marched with this division. That of the Royal Deux Ponts halted at Philadelphia. The Soissonnais division camped there and the Saintonge division camped at Chester.

The 3rd, the Saintonge division camped at Philadelphia. The Soissonnais division halted there and that of the Royal Deux Ponts camped at the Red Lion Tavern 14 miles. The Bourbonnais division made 16 miles and camped at Trenton and Lauzun's Legion halted there.

From the Red Lion Tavern to Trenton, we must cross the Neshaminy River. It would be considered a great river in Europe but here it can only be called a creek. It is not very wide but it is very deep and a bridge still hasn't been built. We also find Bristol on this route, a small place well-situated on the Delaware. On the opposite bank we see Burlington. It is a very industrious place.

The 4th, Lauzun's Legion came on the right and camped at King's town[47] 3 miles from Prince town.[48] We were approaching the station of the enemy and this prudent movement became necessary to cover the main army, to assure the relaxation of its march.

The same day, the Bourbonnais division halted at Trenton. That of the Royal Deux Ponts arrived there. The two other divisions arrived successively on the 5th and the 6th.

During this double halt, I went with Mr. de Rochambeau to see the camps and the positions which General Washington had taken in the month of December 1776 and the marches he made at this time and on January 3, 1777 to surprise the posts of Trenton and Princeton. For the details of the surprise, see the second booklet. August 1781. I would simply add to this detail that after having crossed the Delaware, he took the road to Allentown and, at the fork of the road to Burlington, he marched to the left and took the Quaker road and returned passing by Philips Mill (an essential post that the enemy

46 Red Lion Tavern.

47 Kingston, NJ.

48 Princeton, NJ.

neglected to guard). He found Colonel Mawhood with the 40th British regiment on the road to Maidenhead.[49]

The success of these two attempts was complete, but, regardless of the outcome, we can say, to the praise of General Washington's character and military talent, that he was, at that time, at the a, b, c of his command, that he was developing infinite knowledge and tact, that all his positions were well taken, the orders perfectly given and that if, as at Germantown, at Brandywine and on other occasions, victory did not crown him, it is because she gives her laurels only to the perfect union and general harmony of actions and of courage of the subordinates. In this, Mr. Washington was often poorly served. For independently of the cowards and deserters which he often had to restrain and rally, his generals often poorly executed his orders.

Greene himself, McDonald, got lost at Germantown. The troops fled at Brandywine. Irwin got lost at Trenton.

After passing Trenton, the order of march was shortened. The two divisions of Bourbonnais and the Royal Deux Ponts were joined in the same column. Lauzun's Legion, by itself, continued to form that of the right.

The 7th, it got in motion again, left Kingston and went to camp at New Brunswick 13 miles. The first division forming the left column camped at Princeton 12 miles.

The 8th, the Soissonnais division, forming only one with the Saintonge, camped at Princeton and that of the Bourbonnais camped at Somerset Courthouse 15 miles. A few miles from Princetown, we cross the Raritan which empties into the sea near Sandy Hook. We then marched militarily, always sticking to the hills and valleys of the region. Lauzun's Legion camped at Quibbletown 7 miles from the army. It marched without baggage and always in bivouac. This entire region is filled with Tories, people sold to the British or those who serve them, because they are their neighbors and they fear them. Despite that, we received daily intelligence of the enemy at New York and it is at this time that we learned that admirals Pigot[50] and Hood had just arrived from Jamaica with 22 ships of the line and a few frigates.

The 9th, the first division left camp at Somerset Courthouse and camped at Bullion's Tavern 14 miles. It is on this route that we find Middlebrook, a stream which flows at the bottom of a superb location which General Washington occupied in 1776. His artillery was

49 Now Lawrenceville, NJ.

50 Adm. Hugh Pigot (1769–1797) was Commander in Chief of the Leeward Islands Station during the American Revolutionary War, and later First Naval Lord. While captain of *Hermione*, his men mutinied in one of the bloodiest in the history of the Royal Navy. Pigot and nine other officers were killed. The Navy hunted down and executed a number of the mutineers and recaptured his ship from the Spanish, to whom the mutineers had turned it over.

barracked at Pluky mine.[51] The entire region is hilly, very difficult and very wooded. The height of Middlebrook is the key or dominant position.

The Soissonnais division camped at Somerset Courthouse and Lauzun's Legion left Quibbletown to go to Scotch Plains, a distance of 6 miles from most of the army.

The 10th, the Soissonnais division marched to Bullion's Tavern and that of the Bourbonnais camped at Wippany[52] 14 miles after having crossed at Morristown and Hanover. On the right, Lauzun's Legion made 8 miles and posted itself at Chatham 9 miles from the first column of the left.

The 11th, the Bourbonnais division and Lauzun's Legion did not move and the Soissonais division camped at Whippany. Part of the grenadiers and light infantry were detached and posted in front in a very fine position.

The same day, I was at Chatham with Mr. de Rochambeau where the Legion was posted. It is a small village, rather fine, in an excellent area and which furnishes us with a fairly large quantity of forage. We can see Staten Island very well from here and that's the reason that Mr. de Villemanzy chose it the preceding year to make his demonstrations of the construction of bread ovens which served so well to deceive General Clinton about our plans for this campaign.

From there, we could see the position that General Greene took at Springfield in 1780 and where part of his troops had a light engagement with the Hessians commanded by Lieutenant General Baron de Knyphausen.

Springfield is not very big. General Greene posted a regiment there and took the rest of his troops with him, consisting of 2000 men, a fine position where he camped in two lines overlooking Staten Island 7 miles away. General Knyphausen landed on the continent with 3000 men. He was advancing on Springfield to take a position but he found opposition on the part of the regiment which General Greene had placed there. On the side of Springfield, opposite the sea, there is a small brook. General Knyphausen, at the head of a column, crossed it to flank the village and cut the retreat of the American regiment. Greene discovered the movement and had his advance post retire during this maneuver. There were a few gun shots fired. The regiment then posted itself on a little hill where it again gave musket and artillery fire which made Knyphausen retreat without having accomplished his purpose, which was to surprise Springfield more than to take a footing on the continent. All this area is very hilly, very covered and suitable for a fight.

51 Pluckemin, NJ.

52 Whippany, NJ.

Captain Lippincott Affair

In the month of June of this year, an American captain named Mr.[53] at the head of a small detachment of 15 men was captured by a refugee or loyalist captain named Lippencut[54] who had the American hanged without any trial. This cruelty, in violation of the rules of war, soon came to the attention of Mr. Washington who demanded justice from the British commander who apologized very poorly. General Washington consistently demanded Lippincott and threatened retaliation. Clinton who was still at New York was very embarrassed and decided to deliver the offending captain. Oliver Delancey, Adjutant General of the British Army, a refugee himself and head of this predatory militia, threatened, at the head of this body, to no longer serve and to withdraw from New York if he surrendered Lippincott. Clinton was weak, intimidated by the threats, sought ways to minimize the affair and finally did not surrender this officer. General Washington wrote to Sir Henry Clinton that since he did not want to listen to justice, scorning the rules of war, he had in his possession the right to repress [illegible] by the offense and that more than 60 British officers prisoners would respond to him or rather would assure the redress which he demanded. Consequently, he had a prisoner selected at random and Captain Charles Asgill was the one selected. He was seized and taken to Philadelphia, locked up in prison and his trial was begun more to intimidate Clinton than for the purpose of executing him. Meanwhile, Major Gordon,[55] head of the British officers held prisoners, wrote to Mr. de Rochambeau and asked him that, having taken part in the capture and surrender of York, he requested him to stay the hand of execution as the final article of this capitulation expressly stated that no article could be infringed under pretext of reprisal. Mr. de Rochambeau responded to him that, although he was head of the French troops, he was under the orders of Mr. Washington, and had no part to play in this affair and should not meddle. Meanwhile he wrote to the Chevalier de la Luzerne, who, as our plenipotentiary minister, had the right to make observations. Those which Mr. de Rochambeau suggested he make bore effectively on article 14 of the capitulation. They had the desired effect.

53 There is a blank space for the name which is Capt. Joshua Huddy (1735–1782).

54 Capt. Richard Lippincott (1745–1826) was an American-born Loyalist who served in the British Army during the American War of Independence. He is best known for his part in the Asgill Affair in which he hanged an enemy officer, Joshua Huddy, in revenge for similar murders of Loyalists, provoking an international incident.

55 Major Andrew Gordon (died 1806) became a Maj. in the 26th Regiment of Foot in 1777. He was promoted to Lt. Col. in 1784, Col. in 1790, Maj. Gen in 1794 and a Lt. Gen in 1801 (from brevet, 1799). He was appointed Lieutenant Governor of Jersey in 1797 and died in office in 1806.

Asgill's trial was adjourned and he was kept prisoner at Philadelphia where he remained two months with the horrible expectation of being hanged. He was transferred to Chatham where he was imprisoned without parole.[56] Major Gordon accompanied him.

The captain, knowing that Mr. de Rochambeau was passing by Chatham, immediately requested him to visit him. Our general consented. Asgill thanked him very much for the part he knew he had played for his benefit. Mr. de Rochambeau, not wanting to compromise anything with the Americans, dismissed everything, spoke a little about the mercy, the nobility of feelings which Mr. Washington always assumed, saluted Asgill and remounted his horse to return to his camp at Whippany. Asgill is interesting. He could be 24 or 25 years old. He is sorrowful, militarily innocent and despite that to have these horrible [torn] of being slaughtered at his age and with his great fortune [torn]

September 1782

The 12th, Lauzun's Legion, still marching on the right, came from Chatham to camp at Forks[57] 10 miles from the army. The first division left Whippany and camped at Pompton Meetinghouse 14 miles. The Soissonnais Division halted at the Whippany camp.

The neighborhood of Pompton, which was only woods 40 years ago, is now well cleared and offers a very fine field.

The 13th, the Bourbonnais Division camped at Suffrang[58] 16 miles, fine land, fine roads. The Soissonnais Division marched to Pompton and Lauzun's Legion approached the North River and took a post near Parames[59] which is only a few miles.

The 14th, the Bourbonnais Division made 15 miles to go camp near Haverstraw Bay and the North River, 2 miles from the fort at Stony Point. Lauzun's Legion remained at Paramus and the Soissonnais Division camped at Suffren.

The 15th, the first division halted at Haverstraw and the Soissonnais division came to camp; Lauzun's Legion left Paramus and came to post itself at KiaKiat,[60] thus forming the rearguard of the army after having cleared its right flank after several marches.

56 It is difficult to determine if the word is "sur" (on) or "sans" (without).

57 Two Bridges, NJ.

58 Suffren, NJ.

59 Paramus, NJ.

60 Kakiat, New Hempstead, NY.

The 16th, the two divisions halted together at the Haverstraw camp. The artillery descended to King's Ferry[61] where boats were prepared and it crossed the North or Hudson River. Lauzun's Legion remained at New Hempstead.

General Washington, not being strong enough to go on campaign alone and moreover not having any operation which he could undertake without us, only left his headquarters at Newburgh and the quarters at New Windsor and West Point on August 30. He came down as far as Peekskill in front of which he took a very fine position, his right extending from the fort of Verplanck's Point or Fort Lafayette. He detached his light infantry 3 miles ahead on the road from Tariton[62] to King's Ferry. Our junction was to be effected at the camp at Peekskill. Mr. de Rochambeau crossed the North River on the 16th to go reconnoiter the position he would occupy near the Americans. General Washington had already determined it. He came with us and even Mr. de Rochambeau on the ground. All the banks of the North River are very hilly, steep, difficult and wooded and are so much better for a defensive position. Ours was chosen a little to the left of the American camp on five different small hills, but the key and the most dominant of the others was the one on the left which had a view of the Crumpound Road[63] and which the Saintonge Division later occupied.

After this tour, we returned to the American camp which Mr. Washington had kept on parade to welcome the French general. All the troops were camped on the same line and nothing was more pleasant than the glimpse of the front of the stanchions of each regiment. They were arranged in colonnades, arcades or greenery to remain in the shade. The soldiers got the idea and the plans of an immense hall of greenery which Mr. de Villefranche,[64] a French officer in the American service, oversaw and had constructed at West Point for a feast which the American army gave on the occasion of the birth of Mr. the Dauphin.

After a forced and difficult labor, the artillery found itself all on the left bank of the river. The same evening, Mr. de Rochambeau left General Washington, recrossed the river and returned to his camp.

The 17th, we again reembarked on the North River with the first division which all crossed on the same day with its baggage without accident. Our troops passed in review

61 North of Stony Point.

62 Tarrytown, NY.

63 Crompond Road. Crompond is now Yorktown Heights, NY.

64 Jean-Louis Ambroise de Genton chevalier de Villefranche (1747-1784), or his younger brother Louis Joseph de Genton de Villefranche (1754-1794).

before the American camp and made a total of 7 miles of march to camp and occupy the position reconnoitered the day before.

The 18th, the Soissonnais division crossed the river and camped at Peekskill. Lauzun's Legion left New Hempstead and made such an effort to cross that it also arrived at the camp near Peekskill the same evening.

We were, until then, adequately supplied with all the necessary provisions and staples but our junction with the American army did not delay our hunger.

Review of the Troops

While our armies were not very large, we should not, however, be surprised by this statement which would not occur in a very populated area, cultivated and entirely cleared. The latter is very good but only small groups can survive there. The means of transportation in the interior of the land are very difficult to muster, the roads difficult, the quantities very meager, consequently the transports are necessarily slow and costly. These reasons felt by Mr. de Rochambeau persuaded him to propose to Mr. Washington to let him go toward Yorktown Heights to take a position there. He had it reconnoitered on the 19th.

Independently of this allegation which would soon have become imperative, our discipline might have suffered from the close proximity of the American camp. This militia better dressed, or (simply) dressed (because it never was prior to this time) is still very poorly paid and often malnourished. It required the mind of General Washington to rally and to maintain a body so discordant and multi-form committed to their duty. When provisions lacked or were going to lack without hope of replenishment in a regiment, in a brigade, 3, 4, or 500 men were permitted to go to the countryside to search for the means of subsistence as best they could for which a misunderstanding or concessionary administration had not foreseen. This example could have found some imitators among our soldiers who, despite living under a more abundant administration, it was therefore prudent, on this occasion, to merge the rules of economy and discipline.

The 20th, the French corps, on parade in front of its camp, passed in review before General Washington. It acquired, on this occasion, a new proof of what daily oversight of the chiefs over their subalterns and the frequency of a little attention can do. For after a march of 250 leagues in mid-summer, our soldiers appeared with as fine a dress as could be expected of a peacetime garrison. The American leaders were ecstatic and made their compliments to the colonels. Meticulousness certainly accounted for much, but, on the other hand, it is always difficult to think that such results are obtained only at the expense of relaxation, of unfortunate laziness which tired from a long march, the ravages of time, of guard duty etc. they devote to bleaching their uniforms and accoutrements, most of the time that nature requires for relaxation after an excess of work. War and pity have never agreed. The first harvests under the reports which come from thousands of men; the second which should derive from self love should also guarantee it.

The 21st, General Washington passed his army in review in the same manner on parade in front of his camp. Up to the time of the first junction of the French and the Americans, the latter, for the better appearance of the troops, had not thought that the men ranked by height would produce a better effect in a corps. They were arranged by ranks of seniority. We saw a man who was barely 5 feet tall aside of one who was almost 6, a black with a white, a soldier armed with a saber, another with a musket and other similar disparities. Tactics were not known even though they had won some battles. The campaign of 1781 was generally regarded as a model campaign. We also saw an extraordinary difference in the actual state of the army compared to that which we had left the preceding year. The regiments well-dressed, well-armed, well-maintained in every way, would not have been odd in a European army and to this exterior polish, they joined adequate instruction. The total of those present came to about 7000 men who paraded before the general, after which Mr. the Baron de Steuben,[65] a German officer and Major General in the service of the United States who was named Inspector General, had them drill. He first had them form a closed column and then deployed in two lines. Two regiments lost their place in this deployment. An erroneous command caused this disorder which was soon repaired. He reformed the columns, changed front to the right on the march and deployed again. Much silence, attention was observed during these two maneuvers. They had adequate precision and we could not ask for more from a body composed of three quarters of recruits and commanded by brave officers full of goodwill but who do not know what they command much better than those who execute it.

According to the example of the incentives which Mr. de Monteynard[66] had instituted among our troops during his Secretariat in the War Department, General Washington also founded some in his army as a stimulus to duty and a support for emulation. Only the span of time is different. The first chevron is given after three years, the second after six and a

65 Friedrich Wilhelm Ludolf Gerhard Augustin Baron von Steuben (1730–1794) served as Inspector General and a Major General of the Continental Army. He taught the soldiers the essentials of military drills, tactics, and discipline. He wrote *Regulations for the Order and Discipline of the Troops of the United States*, the book that served as the standard United States drill manual until the War of 1812. He also served as Gen. George Washington's Chief of Staff in the final years of the war.

66 Louis François, marquis de Monteynard, (1713–1791) was a French soldier and statesman. He served as Secretary of State for War 1771–1774. He died in Paris during the French Revolution.

Major General
Frederick William
Augustus, Baron Von Steuben

Independence National Historical Park

heart worn on the left side for all those whose conduct and loyalty would have been tried or who might have accomplished a particularly fine action.

The 22nd, Mr. de Rochambeau received some dispatches from Mr. de Vaudreuil at Boston. He requested a reinforcement of men and an officer who might have some standing among the Americans in order to put himself in a new state of defense to receive the enemy who, according to the reports he had received, were preparing to attack him. Mr. de Fleury, Major of the Saintonge Regiment who had previously served in America, was the officer on whom Mr. de Rochambeau cast his eye and he sent me to bring him the order to prepare to leave for Boston where he would take orders from Mr. de Vaudreuil.

We could no longer have any vague presumption on the manner, more or less advantageous, about how this campaign would end. Some warnings, scattered intelligence and confirming reconciliation, simply gave us some indications about what was being planned in Europe. And we were still unaware if our movements or our more or less relaxation on the continent would be counted in the balance, some troops to put in action for planned operations in one or another world.

Frigates *Aigle* and *Gloire*

The 44-gun frigate *Aigle*,[67] commanded by the Count de la Touche Levassor, Captain of Vessel, and the 36-gun frigate *Gloire*[68] commanded by the Chevalier de Vallongue departed Rochefort at the beginning of August to sail together along the coast of the

67 Meaning "eagle."

68 Meaning "glory."

United States to bring us 2,500,000#[69] and to land some passengers of distinction whom they had aboard and the ministerial dispatches which the Count de Ségur,[70] son of the Marquis, then Minister of the Department of War, was charged. These two frigates had orders not to chase any ships encountered, rather to avoid them in order to not go astray in anything for the purpose of their mission which was mainly to arrive at their destination. Some small events which later became consequential occurred on this occasion.

Mr. de la Touche had a mistress whom he loved passionately and who loved him dearly. She saw him depart from places several times, witness of their mutual happiness. She saw him return wounded, victorious and promoted. As admiral, she said that "glory is a rival which should always alarm me." She wanted to follow her other fox wherever destiny would lead him. The strict order of the French Navy which forbids the embarkation of women removed one means from her, so she thought of chartering a ship which she would board and from which she could go aboard the *Aigle* when she wanted. Mr. de la Touche consented. The three vessels set sail, but it soon became apparent that the ship carrying love had no wings. It dragged much and, to obviate this obstacle, Mr. de la Touche took her in tow which made him lose at least 3 or 4 hours of travel per day. Along the way, the lookouts announced that they discovered a large ship. Night was approaching. It was not avoided. It proved to be the *Hector*, a 74-gun ship which we had lost in the battle of April 12[71] and which was part of a fleet returning to England from the West Indies. The *Aigle* left her tow and, together with the *Gloire*, attacked the enemy who fought poorly because they had an insufficient number of men. Mr. de la Touche would have taken her were it not for the vessels which were coming at full sail to the *Hector's* assistance.

Mr. de la Touche retook his tow. The Chevalier de Vallongue[72] hailed him near the land and told him that if he did not leave it, he would sail alone. Some distance from there, someone cried, "ship ahead." It was a little sloop of war detached from the British fleet on a cruise from New York to the Chesapeake.

69 Livres Tournois. A livre is equal to a franc.

70 Louis-Philippe, Comte de Ségur (1753–1830), son of the Marquis de Ségur, was the minister of war, and the Marquis de Lafayette's uncle. He was recently appointed colonel-en-second of the Soissonnais Regiment. He was sent as minister plenipotentiary to Saint Petersburg in1784 and was sent on a mission to Berlin in 1791. He became a member of the council of state, grand master of the ceremonies, and senator in 1813. He supported the Revolution of 1830 but died shortly afterwards in Paris.

71 Battle of the Saintes.

72 Captain Louis Marie Casimir, Chevalier de Vallongue (d. 1815), was a navy officer with the rank of capitaine de vaisseau (1783). He emigrated during the French Revolution, returned to France and became mayor of Nîmes in 1815. He died in office that same year.

Mr. de la Touche committed the unbelievable error of amusing himself chasing this sloop of war which crowded her sails to the point that she knew what fleet she was. He was at the mouth of the Delaware and lost 4 hours of unrecoverable time searching for her which he should have used to go in search of pilots to enter the river. He was spotted by the enemy fleet. He himself took chase. He made signals from a distance to some pilots who did not arrive and, without any other guide than a map, he entered a channel of the river which he thought was good. La *Gloire* preceded him. She passed a bar where the *Aigle* remained because it drew more water.

The enemy arrived and the *Centurion*, a 50-gun vessel, aboard which Prince William Henry, 3rd, son of the King of England, served in the capacity of a marine guard. He put himself amid ship and cannonaded the French frigate, grounded and on its side. In this sad position, Mr. de la Touche put all his boats to sea and unloaded the money he had aboard, along with the Baron de Vioménil, the Duc de Lauzun, the Duc de Laval, the Comte de Ségur, the Prince de Broglie, the Viscount de Vaudreuil, the Count de Boson Talleyrand, the Chevalier Alexandre de la Meth, the Count Frederic de Chabannes, the Viscount de Metfort, the Count de Liliehorn, a Swede who was a passenger. The enemy had these boats followed by their own. The pursuit was lively to the point that we were obliged to throw a few chests of silver with a few observation buoys to lighten the French skiffs. Mr. de la Touche meanwhile disencumbered himself of whatever hindered him the most, cut his masts, scuttled the frigate and surrendered. His vessel did not have time to sink. The enemy raised it and brought it to New York along with the ship which had the unfortunate mistress of the French captain aboard.

The 22nd, the Count de Ségur arrived at Peekskill and gave his dispatches to Mr. de Rochambeau along with the details of the disaster suffered by the *Aigle*.

Very fortunately for the desired quickness in executing the orders from the court, which Mr. de Rochambeau's foresight put him in the state of submission, it is unbelievable that he received no notice, until this time, of any plans or of the destination of the body under his command. There was then a large armada at Cadiz where Mr. d'Estaing, who commanded it, was in person and from whence he would leave to go to Jamaica. Rochambeau's army was supposed to complement it. That's why the navy was then halted at Boston where Mr. de Vaudreuil's fleet was to transport him.

The 23rd, our general received several Knights of St. Louis. General Washington himself presented the cross to them.

Camp at Croton

In the reconnaissance that Mr. de Rochambeau made of the position he expected to take near Yorktown Heights, he did not find any water nearby. A marsh was discovered to the rear of the right, and as neither the enemies nor the lack of time could oppose this operation, a detachment was sent to dig a canal which was brought around to the camp. It also restored the livelihood of a resident mill owner as enemy detachments had previously damaged the dikes and water conduits. The canal finished, the army marched to Yorktown Heights on the 24th. It camped there on a hill overlooking the entire region, facing the Croton Bridge. The center was occupied only by the road which led to this river and the left occupied a small, very high hill which made the other bastion. By our separation of 9 miles from the American army, we found ourselves in a better position to have our provisions supplied from Danbury, Newtown, etc. and our discipline would no longer be relaxed by bad example.

Lauzun's Legion was camped 2 miles ahead on a very high plateau overlooking the Croton and Pines Bridge where it placed a post of infantry and cavalry. Newbridge is 9 miles from there, near the mouth of the Croton. The American light infantry had a post there which communicated with that of Pines Bridge by the left bank of the Croton outside our position. Our cavalry posts still communicated by their left with Sheldon's American dragoons. They had posts all the way to the Sound, an arm of the sea which separates Long Island from the continent such that from this point to the North River for a distance of 44 miles, nothing could pass which our respective patrols could not discover and recognize.

The Croton is a fordable river in many places but it is extremely enclosed and offers crossings only at common fords and at the points of Golden Bridge in front of our left, Pines Bridge in the center and Newbridge in front on the right. All these routes were visited and reconnoitered by the general himself the first two days of our arrival at Yorktown Heights.

September, October 1782

The 26th, General Washington crossed Newbridge with his light infantry and had them forage on the Dobbs Ferry side, a few miles from our former camp of Philipsburg. Mr. de Rochambeau, with a light escort, crossed to the other side of Newbridge where we discovered only the sad remains of the devastation and pillage of the refugees. The American forage was not harassed and returned to camp at Peekskill on the 27th.

It is physically impossible to attempt anything at New York without a navy superior in numbers and master of the sea. The American and French armies were at a rather short distance away which nonetheless left them without worry on the part of the enemy. The British, realizing the goodness of their position, must have lived with great security. Our junction however assured Mr. de Vaudreuil's tranquility in Boston and gave them enough uneasiness to disarm their ships and to recall the detachments sent to destroy or burn his fleet. It was a retroactive effect of our presence which had the benefit of protecting the region from any incursion. In the errands and reconnaissance which we made every day on the other side of the Croton, at Sing Sing,[73] North Castle,[74] etc. it was horrible to see the pitiful state to which the plundering of the refugees had reduced this part of the country, once rich and abundant. These unfortunates are dangerous enough to encounter when they think they are the stronger. They pillage, steal and often give no quarters. On a patrol which Sheldon's dragoons made, they took eight and it is the only small military event which occurred prior to October 18 when some letters from Mr. de Vaudreuil arrived from Boston which reported that the preparations for embarking would soon be made. Our preparations to go join him had already been made for some time but this admiral was accused of slowness, inactivity. His fleet was anchored in the port of Boston 8 miles from the city where he was lodged and, even though he was in charge, he never gave any oversight to his subordinates.

After halting a month at the camp at Yorktown Heights, we began to move. On the morning of the 22nd, the second division relieved all the posts of the first which took the Salem Road where it was camped after having crossed Croton at Golden Bridge and from there to Haits Tavern.[75]

Salem is 13 miles from Yorktown Heights in a region which, although filled with hills is, however, less steep as we go away from the banks of the North River. There are two Salems: upper Salem where we camped and lower Salem, 5 miles from that one, on the Bedford Road to the east.

The second division commanded by the Baron de Vioménil, recently arrived from France, departed Yorktown Heights on the 22nd to camp at Salem.

Rochambeau's Arrest

Upon the departure of Mr. de Rochambeau from Yorktown Heights, I should not forget a unique anecdote. Always preferring his duty to his ease, at every camp we took, he always ordered the staff officers to select the house closest to the camp for his headquarters. At Yorktown Heights, he was lodged at an individual, a type of half ruined miller, who had a few possessions near the camp which, like almost all those in America, were enclosed by fences or long wooden rails crossed in zigzag one upon the other. The properties of our host had also been cleared as much as possible near the camp. We even

73 Now Ossining, NY.

74 Mount Kisco, NY.

75 Hunt's Tavern.

repaired his mill and recovered part of his house and we also left him two very large ovens which we had built for the troops.

I was lodged in an attic with two of my comrades. We were very surprised to be awakened in the middle of the night by a sheriff or a judge who came to ask us to sleep. We put him on the floor aside of us and we would have treated him less well had we known that, at dawn the following day, he would, with our host, arrest our general and make him prisoner.

Effectively after a light and frugal breakfast at the moment that Mr. de Rochambeau was to put his foot in the stirrup, our host escorted by his sheriff, came to tell him that having made the tour of his possessions, he had remarked that they had suffered some damage due to the neighboring troops, that he wanted to be paid, that he recognized the important services that his Excellency the General had rendered to his country, that he prized his virtues and everything he had seen from him during his stay at Yorktown Heights but that all of that could not prevent him from making him his prisoner to assure himself of redressing the grievances which he alleged and the replacement of his losses which he estimated at 15,000#. After this brief preamble, he put his hand on his neck and the sheriff grabbed him by the other side. Our first reaction was to beat both the host and the sheriff with the flat of the sword but Mr. de Rochambeau, with the calm appearance that nothing ever disturbs, stopped us. He began to laugh and responded to his captors that he believed he was the first example of a general arrested by two men in the midst of his army. He explained the irregularity but he especially stressed the danger of their conduct if they had to deal with a less popular and less thoughtful man than he. He told them that despite the unusual manner in which they brought their complaint, he wanted to examine the reasons and he ordered me to go tell Mr. de Villlemanzy, Commissioner of War, to come to the locations with the commissioners they would appoint themselves to mutually estimate the damages and to pay for them.

After the report was made to him, he had them hand over 50 louis, half of which could be regarded as a bonus. He then spoke to them about the circumstance, but they appealed to their qualification of free men, independent of everything that is not law and on the Constitution of their country— . . . . which did not excuse the exaggeration they made of the loss and the compensation that they demanded. This scene ended in this manner and we left to rejoin the column which marched toward Salem. For the rest, I devoted myself to the account of this fact only to give an idea of the manner in which we have to deal with the civil part of our allies almost daily and of the character of liberty which accompanies their actions. As for the army, I should render them a new homage. We have always found in it all the sentiments of the sacrifices that France, in general, our friendship, our hardships and our mutual labors seem to demand of it — I resume the march of the army.

The first division left Salem on the 23rd and camped at Danbury 13 miles.

Part of this town which still contains about 150 houses along a mile stretch was burned by the British who embarked at New York on April 24, 1777 and landed on the continent on the 25th 4 miles east of Norwalk and 20 from Danbury under the orders of Major General Tryon[76]. They marched as far as Riding[77] without being discovered and they then went to Danbury without being harassed except by some small parties which were repulsed. Militia General Wooster[78] who commanded them was killed. The British then captured the warehouses, well-supplied with all sorts of provisions, which the Americans had at this location. They also burned the village. It is believed that, after this damned arson, they wanted to go to Peekskill to also destroy the other American warehouses before returning to New York by the North River but General McDougal went along this route with some militiamen. They had received intelligence and consequently took the road to Ridgefield to re-embark. General Arnold (the traitor) posted himself in this village with a few militiamen but the British repulsed him and spent the night of the 28th there, after which they rejoined their vessel despite being harassed by the Americans who had received some reinforcements of men and cannons.

The fine location of Danbury assures the future prosperity of this place. A lovely little creek crosses it. There is much pasture around but the roads, like all those in Connecticut, are not very easy.

The 24th, the second division left the camp at Salem and came to that of Danbury and the first went 8 miles to go to Newtown where it occupied the same location as the preceding year. The grenadiers and light infantry were placed in front on a height from which they commanded the whole region and covered the headquarters.

The 25th, the first division halted at the camp at Newtown and the Soissonnais Division camped there. Mr. de Rochambeau reconnoitered the neighborhood. We found it pleasant and well-inhabited. The area has many roads. Agriculture is well understood and even though all the fields are generally full of loose rocks, the harvests are no less good.

76 William Tryon (1729–1788) was a British general officer and a colonial official who served as the eighth governor of North Carolina from 1765 to 1771 and then the 39th governor of New York from 1771 to 1780. He returned to his home in London, England in September 1780 and directed the affairs of his 70th Regiment of Foot still in the colonies. He was promoted to lieutenant-general in 1782 and was made colonel of the 29th Regiment of Foot, which was stationed in Canada, in 1784.

77 Redding.

78 Brig. Gen. David Wooster (1711–1777) was an American general who served in the French and Indian War and in the American Revolutionary War. He died of wounds sustained during the Battle of Ridgefield, Connecticut.

The 26th, the first division made 17 miles and camped at Breakneck[79] and the second halted at Newtown. On June 28 of the preceding year, I had already passed through Windsor to rejoin the army after my wound. I will not add any further detail on this location than those I gave already.

The 27th, the second division left Newtown and camped at Windsor. The first left in a terrible rainstorm the same day to go camp at Baren's Tavern[80] after crossing the Mad River at Waterbury, a picturesque and charming place, on a wooden bridge somewhat like that of Carlton's bridge on the Stradtford River.[81]

The 28th, the second division left the camp at Windsor and came to camp at Barnes's Tavern from which the first division left to take its camp at Farmington, passing by Southington, a lovely place which gives its name to the region.

The 29th, the first division left camp at Farmington and camped at East Harfort[82] after passing West Hartford, Hartford and the Connecticut River which it crossed in scows and boats. The neighborhood of Hartford, capitol of the state of Connecticut, generally offers a glimpse of ease and simplicity and happiness. We don't see landowners who encompass a whole county, as in Virginia, where Negro people languish in much difficulty, but we encounter planters everywhere, rich farm owners and never a poor!! Good and solid horses, very large oxen, fine cows, very fat and numerous hogs near all the dwellings and in the woods. They vary very pleasantly the glimpse of the rich valleys and the routes of Connecticut. And if I were to live in one of the 13 states, the temperature and the healthy climate of this one together with the local advantages which always seemed to me to be discovered every time I traveled it, would make me decide without doubt for Connecticut or certain parts of Massachusetts where I saw the same benefits.

The same day the Soissonnais division camped at Farmington.

The 30th, the first division halted at the East Hartford camp and the second crossed the Connecticut River and camped on its left.

I profited from the halt at East Hartford to travel in the neighborhood of Hartford. I left this city and went to Wethersfield which is 4 miles away. Wethersfield is a lovely town built near the right bank of the Connecticut River. It is in the middle of a vast and very fertile field. The belfry of the church is very high and draws the attention of the curious of the area. In addition, the town, which contains 2000 inhabitants, does not offer anything

79 The camp was on a hillside off Artillery Road, about 200 feet from the intersection with Breakneck Hill Road in Middlebury, CT.

80 Barnes's Tavern.

81 Stratford River.

82 East Hartford.

special but its environs are renowned in Connecticut for the goodness of its rutabagas and onions which are exported to the West Indies as well as for the horses which are raised for the same purpose.

A dispatch which Mr. de Rochambeau received from Boston from Mr. de Vaudreuil made him decide to remain in camp at East Hartford longer than he had expected. He spent the 31st and set up his headquarters there.

Along all the routes that we have taken, I spoke little about the troops in general because, in a friendly country where we only have to fear a few Tories, there could be very few military actions to note. I should not forget, however, to write a few lines in praise of all the brave regiments which comprise our little army. It has already been more than four months that it camped and decamped almost daily.

The extreme heat of Virginia, sometimes hunger, fatigue of the load and of the route, often repeated in very active military service, the frequent rain and storms, the almost constant bivouac, in a word, everything which (except for the risk of musket shots which were not found during this campaign) can be called the hardships of war never brought any complaints. If there were ever any murmurs, they concerned only individual leaders who often surpassed in severity and even harshness the orders of the general whom they adored and whom they would follow anywhere. In the marches of the previous campaign, we managed, with much difficulty, to train and bring to our military order all the Americans whom we were obliged to employ. In this, a more active supervision, or which I think is more correct to say, a better knowledge of their customs and of their manners and of their most common shortcomings put us in a position to counter them so that we never heard speak of marauding, pillaging, nor any other act of this type committed by any teamster, valet, or sutler for the provost would have executed quick and good justice. The manner employed in redressing the above-mentioned offenses was less frightening and less cruel and surely just as effective as any employed by our generals in Germany. There, it was hanging, here 25 or 50 good blows with a stick on the buttocks of the offender, according to the nature of the infraction, and on the site where he was found guilty had the double advantage of repressing all disorders and to preserve the men.

November

On November 2, we received confirmation of the news of full powers being given to Mr. Fitzherbert[83] to act as Plenipotentiary Minister of the Court of London to that of

83 Alleyne FitzHerbert,1st Baron St Helens (1753–1839), was sent to Paris in August 1782 by Lord Shelburne. He served as plenipotentiary to negotiate a peace with the crowns of France

France and to treat for peace. This circumstance threw a new veil on the purpose and the object of our march northward. It did not appear very probable to us that we should stay any longer on the continent, because seeing much agreement between our march and the possible operations of our navy at Boston, the following correspondence between the admiral and our general gave us new indications and the different speculations began to bear on the more probable bases. When we saw the artillery receive orders to hold themselves ready to march the following day, the 3rd, in a single division and to precede the army on the march, it was then clear that it would only stop at Boston and that it received the order only for the greater ease and speed of its embarkation.

The 3rd, the artillery division began to march toward Bolton 13 miles. The following day, the 4th, it left to go to Windham 17 miles. The first division of troops camped 2 miles beyond Bolton at the bottom of a very long hill. All this area is very wooded and hilly. The houses are not yet very close nor the outlets easy.

The 5th, the artillery camped at Plainfield. The first division at Windham and the second left East Hartford to go beyond Bolton.

The three divisions camped successively at Plainfield, Waterman's Tavern and Providence where the artillery arrived on the 7th and the second division on the 9th.

I had not seen New London. I left the army on the 5th with the Count de Rochambeau to go there. We first made 6 miles on the road to Windham which we left on the left and then 10 more to get to Lebanon. This town or rather county is very inhabited. The Lebanon Road is lined with houses where everything around them announces wealth. In general, a large population in a county announces its goodness. This word about the population reminds me that I often heard it said in Connecticut that it increased by more than 150,000 souls in 10 years.

Lebanon is located on a green of moderate size. There are 12 or 15 houses at this place which had served as the quarters for Lauzun's hussars during the winter of 1780 to 1781. Governor Trumbull resides here. He is an old man whose life was always blameless and the respect given him always kept him in his place, that he never owed it to great talent. Under British domination, the states of Rhode Island and Connecticut retained the right to appoint their own governor. Mr. Trumbull took office 10 years earlier. At the time of the Declaration of Independence, he did not waver between the happiness of living free among his fellow citizens and with their support and the always difficult role he had to play to

---

and Spain and with the States General of the United Provinces. The preliminaries of peace with the first two powers were signed on January 20, 1783. He was Minister Plenipotentiary to Russia from 1783 to 1788, appointed Chief Secretary for Ireland and a member of the Privy Council (Great Britain Ireland) in 1787, serving in the former position until 1789. He was Minister Plenipotentiary to Spain from 1790 to 1794. He retired from diplomatic life in 1803.

maintain himself in favor and to obtain a few favors from the despotism and the tyranny of Parliament and the court of England. He espoused the cause of liberty with ardor, a cause so laudable, so fine and so natural to embrace and to defend and as a reward for his patriotism, the Connecticutians, his fellow citizens, reelected him governor of this state.

Generally, all the planters of Connecticut know their laws fairly well, especially their Bible, the gazette or newspaper of their state, but that is the limit of their knowledge of luxury. The arts of Europe never struck their minds and the politics of this part of the world even less. They weave their own wool, make their own clothing at their plantations, live off the produce of their labors and with the cattle that they raise, they truly give the image of a patriarchal life, of the mild manners of earlier times, of this purity, of this innocence which we rarely find on our continent. Finally, they are happy because they have hardly any knowledge of and even less the practice of any vice.

It is not surprising, then, that they often gave themselves over to asking us questions which would have seemed very unusual with other customs and in another country. One of the most lovable Frenchmen that I have ever seen, of a most constant gaiety, of a most pleasant wit turned toward the people, and of the most original and most mild humor is without doubt the Duc de Lauzun. He was admirable for his responses among all these good planters whom he entertained much for he spoke English very well. When the hussars of his legion were quartered at Lebanon, he was often with Governor Trumbull. Dining with him one day, an American asked him touching him on the shoulder "what does your father do?" The duke responded "my dear, my father is a loafer who does nothing and who lives on the fortune which his parents left him, but I have an uncle who is a marshal[84]. "Ah!" Responded the other, "that is a good job, that one. It assures the life of everyone who practices it." The Duc de Lauzun left him in his error and never corrected him about the double meaning of the word Marshal in France or Marshal of France.

Governor Trumbull was ill and we did not see him in our passing. We went from Lebanon to Nordwhich[85] which is only 9 miles. The entire region is broken with fine valleys and creeks. Two miles from Norwich we find some rather large forges called Baker's Ironworks. We cross a bridge over a little river which makes them run.

Norwich is very large. We could give three different names to each group of houses which make up this place. There are many very fine ones. It is the home and the place of residence of Mr. James Huntington, former president of Congress and of Brigadier

84 This note is in the manuscript: Marshal Biroy.

85 Norwich.

General Huntington,[86] his cousin. Right from the beginning of the troubles, the former was known and respected for his attachment to the American cause. He was charged with some very important commissions and then elected member of Congress for the state of Connecticut. It is after having been seated among this body that he was elected president.

We have generally enough remarked that Congress always had the politic of never appointing an ardent man as its leader, a project engineer or systematician, one of the people who has a large enough fortune that he is able, under any circumstance, to be independent of the events, finally one of those people for whom ambition could suggest thoughts of promotion for them or their family!! Mr. Huntington is full of love for his country, but in promoting him to the first place of the state, it was rather to reward his virtues. They only wanted to make his talent shine and for him to conduct himself according to his or the administration's political views. He received us perfectly well. He even had the kindness to mount a horse and to guide us a rather long distance along the route to New London where we wanted to go sleep. We passed a part of Norwich called Chelsea or Norwich Landing. The Thames River, which flows to the sea at New London, passes through and receives at this place a brook which passes below Windham. A little above, it receives the one which operates Mr. Baker's forges.

Chelsea is situated in a very advantageous location for commerce. Vessels of the port of 200 tons can go up the Thames river as far as here but can go no further. The place exports much salt, cattle, boards, draught horses destined for the West Indies. The air must be very pure and very healthy. The area is very scenic and very pleasant and the population of this township is about 7 or 8000 inhabitants.

Chelsea is 12 miles from New London. We travel them in very open country, but probably of a lesser value than the rest of Connecticut. The road follows the banks of the Thames for some distance which are often seen on the left and which appears, like the North River, among the rocks and the hills. There are some very impressive views, but it would take a very experienced paintbrush to render them well.

New London and Fort Griswold

There's a little neighborhood 6 miles from New London still inhabited by natives who have always maintained themselves and have preserved their customs and traditions, for the most part, amid the draft and the war made on their race. They are easily recognized by

86 Brig. Gen. Jedediah Huntington (1743–1818) served in the Hudson Highlands and New Jersey in 1779 and 1780. He remained in the Highlands during the Yorktown campaign. After the war, he served in numerous civilian posts.

their olive bronze color and their very dark hair. Their village is called Mahowgey and consists of about 40 families. They very much enjoy rum and hard liquor and they easily and often become inebriated. There are many places along this entire route which would be very advantageous to occupy if a body of enemy would land on the right bank of the Thames with the intention of penetrating the country by marching on Norwich.

New London is located at the base of a rather long and mild hill on the right bank and at the mouth of the Thames River at the entrance to the Sound or arm of the sea which separates Long Island from the continent. This town contains 4 or 500 houses built of wood as most of the houses in North America. It was always very commercial and it is from this port that the largest shipments of salt and cattle to the West Indies are made. Its inhabitants also did business with the coast of Guinea and we have seen more than 300 ships sail from this port before the war. Since the break with the mother country, they armed several privateers but most of them were unfortunate because of the nearness of New York and Long Island occupied by the British. We can see this island perfectly from New London as well as Gardner's Bay where the British fleet commanded by Admiral Arbuthnot spent the winter of 1780 to 1781 observing our movements in Newport Harbor.

The port of New London merges a very safe anchorage with several other advantages such as that of being vast, having great depth and containing enough water to enter at any time.

Its entrance is almost North and South and is defended by two forts. The one on the west bank is called Fort Trumbull. Its position is well situated but little more attention could have been brought to its construction and it would have been capable of greater perfection. It has seven sides more or less long with embrasures fairly well spaced and open to fire successfully on any vessel before it enters the channel. When it is there and when it is in the harbor, this last fire would be especially advantageous if, despite the fire from the forts, a vessel would be imprudent enough to anchor and cannonade the town a mile away from Fort Trumbull.

Upon arriving at New London, we were introduced to the American commander called Colonel McLenellan whose kindness is impossible to over appreciate. His oversight and his multiple offerings left us nothing to desire in relation to the objects we wanted to obtain and to bring back any details. It was he who had us visit the fort I just spoke of on the morning of the 6th and who, despite a type of rain, wanted to accompany us to the lighthouse placed along the shore of the sound, 3 miles from the city, for navigation and from which we could see Sandy Beach, the landing site west of the lighthouse. The rain was too strong. We could not see Long Island. We saw Fisher's Island, however, 9 miles away. We returned to New London by the heights, following the road along the crest. A mile and a half from town, we saw a fort which the Americans called Fort Nonsense since they recognized its uselessness. It does not overlook any interesting place. It could easily be flanked and left without danger by an enemy who might march to New London. Not even a guard is sent here today. But it is too bad, for it should either be destroyed or maintained by the principle that what is not useful for defense can very much become so to take a position after a landing.

We had breakfast at New London after which we crossed the port or ferry which is a mile wide and we got off on the eastern bank at Groton hill which is high and rather steep. Groton contains 12 or 15 houses at the base of the hill. It is at the highest point of its summit that the second fort was built to guard the entrance to the port of New London. It is a parallelogram whose angles facing northwest and southwest form two bastions in front of which a battery was raised which dominates the pass. The north side is defended by a half moon and the south side is flanked by a sally port in the form of a redan with an embrasure on each side from which the cannons dominate the countryside. The development of this work is large enough to require at least 350 men for its defense. Its approach is defended by a very strong and very thick abatis and it is in the best possible shape in every way today. It bears the name of Fort Griswool[87] and it is a mile from Fort Trumbull.

To the south and two musket shot range from Fort Griswold there is a rather steep point whose position seems to me would have been better and more advantageous to seize for the defense of the pass. Its fire would have been less annoying than that of Fort Griswold which is higher. It would have crossed much better with that of Fort Trumbull which is at least 160 toises closer and whose elevation would still be sufficient to not be exposed to the fire of the zone of any vessel. The location of Fort Griswold was preferred only because of its height.

In the month of September 1781, when the traitor Arnold returned from Virginia (where he had left his troops after their junction with those of Lord Cornwallis), he proposed to General Clinton an expedition or surprise attack on New London for which he took command of 3000 men. The garrison of the forts was then very weak, the guard poorly mounted and the local militia not assembled or prepared in the least. Arnold personally landed with 1500 men at Sandy Beach, of which I spoke, without hardly being discovered and he put Major Montgomery in command of 1500 who landed on the east side, or of Groton, at a point opposite the lighthouse.

Arnold marched toward New London without difficulty, always keeping the heights. He entered Fort Nonsense where he found not even a guard for the few old cannons which he spiked. From there, he advanced toward the town and sent some men to capture Fort

87 Griswold.

Trumbull, which is not closed on the land side by its throat. The garrison, seeing itself too weak to defend itself, abandoned it, boarded and went to reinforce that of Fort Griswold.

Arnold entered Fort Trumbull, spiked the cannons, broke the trunnions and marched to the town which he found undefended. He entered as a conqueror. He had himself given a good breakfast after which Arnold, born to obscure parents at New Haven, 8 leagues from New London, the Connecticutian Arnold set fire to one of the main cities of the state which promoted him to the rank of major general of his country. Finally, he had the unfortunate inhabitants pillaged.

While this scene of horror and barbary was happening at New London, Major Montgomery[88] advanced on Fort Griswold. He emerged in columns from the gap of a small wood which is far out of cannon range and southeast of the fort. He deployed [his men] a short time later and advanced in good order. On the side where he marched, there was then a small redoubt in front of the fort where 20 or 30 men were positioned and killed many of his troops. It was finally evacuated as he approached. When he arrived near the fort, he divided his men into platoons of 30 or 40 men to surround it on all sides and to attack simultaneously. This disposition, although very bad if the work were well-garrisoned, succeeded for him here before 150 militiamen who accomplished marvelous deeds of valor and who defended themselves very vigorously. But, unable to guard the parapet everywhere, they were taken. Those who were unable to escape were killed by the sword. Colonel Ledyard who commanded them handed his sword to a British officer who took it only to plunge it into the breast of this brave man and deprived him of a life which he had always adorned with civil and military virtues. Major Montgomery himself was killed during the attack. The British also left many of their own at the place. The Americans lost 84 men.

Everything which I have just written occurred in one morning. The alarm spread quickly. The militias of Norwich and the other surrounding towns were already en route. Arnold was informed of their approach and withdrew. The militiamen however arrived in enough time to harass him greatly on his retreat. The traitor succeeded in embarking after adding to his other exploits the pillage, the massacre, the arson of a city, almost his homeland, and the loss of almost 500 men which this expedition cost him.

Colonel McLenellan commanded at New London only since this happened. Governor Trumbull appointed him to this post with the injunction to make all the expenses and the repairs to Fort Griswold. This officer acquitted himself well and it is he who also added the abatis to the defense of the fort which is there today and which probably would have cost

88 Major William Montgomery (d. 1781) commanded the 40th Regiment of Foot in the assault on Fort Griswold. He was fatally stabbed with a spear in hand-to-hand combat near the northeast part of the fort when the British scaled the fort's walls.

the British many men if it were there at the time of their attack. The garrison was not increased.

There is not a single cannon nor an embrasure in condition at Fort Trumbull. The first lesson however was good enough for the state of Connecticut to turn its attention to the defense of this essential post. It is true that today New London does not offer the same appeal as at the time of Arnold's expedition. This city still flourished; its warehouses, its shops were well furnished and, at the present time, we can only see the foundations of many of them and the ashes produced by their burning.

We left Colonel McLenellan exiting Fort Griswold. We expressed our farewell and our thanks and we took the road to Westerly which is 16 miles from New London. We judged the area that we traveled rather poorly because the rain always followed us, but, as much as the weather allowed, we realized that this region is poor and very unproductive. There are only boulders and large rocks and woods beaten by the ocean winds and which grow very poorly. Here and there, there are some rather large sounds. We pass by Stonington, a place of 8 or 10 houses fairly well located on a brook called the Mistick River[89] which goes from there to the ocean. It is 8 miles from Stonington to Westerly. We encounter some houses rather frequently and many rocks and stones.

Westerly consists of about 15 houses. It is located on the Packettuck River[90] which we cross on a bridge. This little river empties into the ocean and separates the state of Connecticut from that of Rhode Island. There are many Quakers in this region which is not very rich but which is however very comfortable. We dried ourselves a bit at Westerly. We ate lightly and departed to go 10 miles from there to the tavern of Captain Champlain where we planned to sleep. There, we saw a land better cultivated and less stony than on the other side of Westerly.

Return to Newport

Our intent was to go to Newport. We left Captain Champlain's Tavern for this purpose the morning of the 7th. We had gone only a few miles when we encountered a loyal American, who, seeing that we were French, wanted to bring us to his house on the seashore for breakfast. I can only recall with gratitude all the kindness which he bestowed on us. His wife, his daughters, his entire household hurried to serve us. Their simple but pleasant manners as well as their hospitality, devoid of any interest, charmed us so much that they surprised us. After a pause of an hour, we took our leave of this kind family, whose

89 Mystic River.

90 Pawcatuck River.

name I cannot remember, and we took the Narragansett Ferry Road which is 10 miles away. Three miles from the ferry we find Tower Hill where there are seven or eight houses located on a hill surrounded by fine fields. The Narragansett ferry, which is 3 miles wide, is formed by a sound which separates Conanicut island from the continent. We cross it as well as the island and we reembark to arrive at Newport.

Conanicut island is the first land where I walked after three months at sea and Newport is the first American city where I lived. I had left many friends and acquaintances there in 1781 and I saw them again with great pleasure. It was the cradle of the new customs which we adopted, forgetting or casting aside our own. It was there that we learned a new language. It was there that our good conduct won us the affection of an entire population which our presence saved from the pillage of their enemies. Finally, it was there that we spent an entire winter!! I can cite many names here if I surrender to the pleasure of naming the individuals who saw me again with very touching expressions of delight. I had the happiness of being useful to many and to render them rather important services; but, at 21 years of age, it is permitted to occupy oneself in preference with those which have a hold on our heart. I do not write here without a tender remembrance the names of Miss Peggy Champlain, Betsy Stevens and Polly Laughton, a young Quaker whose simplicity of manners, like that of the clothing of her sect, imparted new charms.

We found in this city the Prince de Broglie, the Count de Ségur, the Count, and Frederick de Chabannes[91] and the Count von Fersen who had come from Providence. We collected, along with the Counts de Deux Ponts and de Vauban who also came, a rather large sum of money to give a general ball to all the ladies on the 12th. We sought, in this manner, to repay them for all their goodness. Some of us also thus prepared some new regrets. But as we saw, from time to time, some enemy sloops of war along the coast and that, in an exposed city, it would not have been prudent to stay very long, we all departed on the 14th to go to the camp at Providence.

Since the departure of the army, Newport and the island of Rhode Island was constantly and still is today without defense. The enemy could often put this island under requisition or to recapture it. This fear and that of pillage alienated many inhabitants. Others went to seek their fortune. And this city, which once was one of the most flourishing of the 13 states, is now little inhabited.

91 Jean Frederic de Chabannes marquis de la Palice (or La Palisse) (1762-1836) was aide de camp to the Baron de Vioménil. He went to Naples in 1790, returned to France and accomplished some missions for the comte d'Artois in London and Paris in 1791. He served in the Army of the Princes and was charged with a variety of missions in 1793 and 1794. He was taken prisoner upon his return from the island of Yeu. He managed to escape and return to London. He returned to France in 1802, served as Louis XVIII's aide-de-camp in 1813 and 1814. He fell into disgrace in 1815 and went into exile, first in London, then Brussels.

General Washington had ordered us to destroy all the works which we had constructed, seeing that they would not be garrisoned, but the order was never executed and we found them all in very good condition.

Newport harbor which is probably one of the finest and safest and best of the world, sooner or later, will make this city return to its former state because its location and its port which can be entered under almost any weather condition and at any time will make it an excellent relief or a large storehouse.

The first camp which the army occupied at Providence was to the east of the city coming from Waterman's Tavern but the cold becoming very biting, Mr. de Rochambeau had the camp broken the morning of the 13th and took another near the woods 2 miles on the other side of Providence on the road to Boston. Snow soon covered the earth. We built some barracks where we lit big fires and we awaited Mr. de Vaudreuil, aboard whose fleet the army was to board, was ready to receive it.

The artillery began its march to Boston on the 18th and had orders to arrive in this city in four days to proceed forthwith to the embarkation of its carriages, wagons, caissons and ammunition.

Mr. de Rochambeau, at the request of many residents of Newport, left Providence on the 22nd to go there. I accompanied him. He received some addresses, good wishes and gratitude of the residents that evening and we departed on the 23rd to return to camp after having said farewell, probably for good, to the good and appreciative inhabitants of this city and the island.

Nothing remarkable happened at Providence. The troops endured the bitter cold with courage. Their discipline reassured the inhabitants and, in the city, they treated us not as allies but as they would their own relatives. They observed the preparations for our imminent departure from their city and from the continent with sadness. But the moment finally arrived and the departure was set for December 1.

December

We then knew that an attack upon Jamaica was being considered with the united and combined forces of France and Spain, that the landing troops would arrive from different points and that our army would take part. All the speculation and probabilities considered by those who were not in on the secret were converging on this point of view. Mr. d'Estaing was appointed commander in chief of the expedition. He would have Mr. de Bouillé as second-in-command who was recently promoted to lieutenant-general and who was much younger than Mr. de Rochambeau. It thus became impossible for our general to follow the destiny of his army. Consequently, he gave instructions and his orders to the Baron de Vioménil, his second, and looked forward only to his return to France. Mr. de Vaudreuil, having advised that he was ready to set sail and that the troops could march to get aboard, the order of march was set to that of the 4 divisions, one day apart.

December 1 was a day of general sadness and mourning both for the city and for the army. The residents had only received signs of kindness and goodwill from us. We had saved their country and their properties. Our preceding campaign assured their independence and promised them a prosperous peace. We made their commerce flourish anew. Our consumption spread money everywhere. Many people previously saddled with debts prospered since our sojourn among them. These are the general reasons for the affection they bore for us; but personal friendships cemented it even more. All the delegates of the state assembly led by Lieutenant Governor Bowen[92] came to present their addresses and their good wishes to Mr. de Rochambeau. We shared their sentiments and the really profound sadness which they exhibited in taking leave of him and of us; but these types of visits and the farewells which they expressed to us were those of all the bodies of the army. Having been away from our country for three years, we all lived together under the kind but firm direction of our leader. We experienced the same misfortunes, endured the same hardships. When a confluence of many reasons would not have bound us closely together, the custom of seeing each other frequently would have become an imperceptible link, at first sight, but it is no less real or less felt at separation. Mr. de Rochambeau made a visit to the camp, gave his well-deserved praises to all the corps, exhorted them to follow the orders of his successor just as they did his own, and received, in return, from the soldiers a reward always flattering (although he well deserved it from them for all the attention he made to assure their well-being as much as circumstances permitted) the least equivocal proofs of their esteem, of their confidence, of their regrets, and of their love for him.

Part of the army staff, that of the infantry, was retained; the other was destined to return to France. I would have followed the army to its destination in my capacity of sub-assistant quartermaster general if I had not received the promise of a sub-lieutenancy in the King's bodyguards. If I received it, it would render my going to the isles very useless for my promotion. Therefore, I did not waver to in my decision to accompany Mr. de Rochambeau to Philadelphia where he was to take a frigate to return to France.

Some pieces of artillery had already been loaded a few miles from Providence in the Patuxet River (which is an extension inland of Newport Harbor) aboard the *Fantasque*, an

92 Jabez Bowen, Sr.(1739-1815) was Deputy Governor of Rhode Island from May 1778 to May 1780 and from May 1781 to May 1786. He was a delegate to the Annapolis Convention in 1786 and the Constitutional Convention in 1790. He served as a Superior Court judge in, 1776 and became Chief Justice in 1781. He served as Chancellor of Brown University from 1785 until his death.

old ship of 64 guns, armed en flute and commanded by the Chevalier de Vaudoré. Mr. de Vaudreuil had sent him for this purpose and to take two companies of the Soissonnais Regiment who were to make the crossing on board this vessel. He was then to go to Newport to join the army of Mr. de Vaudreuil when it would cross.

Snow fell very heavily on December 1. The first division of troops under the command of the Baron de Viomenil to whom Mr. de Rochambeau transferred the command this day, left from Providence to go to Boston. I will always have the very vivid memory of the moment of our departure and of our separation. The sorrow and the regrets of taking different paths was evident after having followed the same ones for so long. The regret of leaving, in a word, was well expressed on all the faces. The morning at headquarters, we embraced our friends who were going where duty called them and Mr. de Rochambeau, his son, the Count de Vauban and I mounted our horses to go to Philadelphia.

The Chevalier de Chastellux and his aides-de-camp, Mr. de Béville and several staff officers of the army, Mr. de Choisy etc. took the same route on different days with the same intent.

I will only have a few details from hearsay and from individual letters to write about the army. I leave it on the road to Boston. I believe it is already embarked and ready to sail. I am only a traveler from tavern to tavern. Despite that, I will write the account of our travels even though detailed in many ways. But when we tell the truth, and the truth to remember it for oneself, when we have no intention of publishing our compilations, when we also have the intention of concealing them from the knowledge of any individual, we can allow ourselves all the details and occupy ourselves only with the circumstances, of their aridity and often their lack of interest.

We stopped at Angel's Tavern 9 miles from Providence and we then made 16 miles to go sleep at Dorance's Tavern. When we come from Europe, where in general, except in England and Holland, the hotels are dirty and bad, we cannot help admire that in the woods and in an absolutely new country, that there could be any so neat and well-served as that of Mr. Dorance. The Chevalier de Chastellux, in a voyage which he made two years ago and which he even had printed, spoke of his crossing at Voluntown at Mr. Dorance's and he paid tribute to the Misses Dorance who are very tall, very well-built and very pretty. They are conversationalists and speak a sort of Babel sufficient to interest strangers, the French, because, as for the Americans, they never speak a word to them. A girl whom they do not seek to please with the intent to marry is not a prize. In America, the rights of all men are recognized as being equal. Every profession which makes an honest living is good. None excludes civilian or military employment and every bar keeper believes and effectively is as equal as any other man, even though the upper class families seek to support and maintain themselves among them.

Voluntown is the name of the district where there are only five or six houses near Mr. Dorance's.

On the 2nd, we made 9 miles to go to Well's Tavern beyond Cantorbery[93] and, after traveling 15 miles, we arrived at the tavern of Mr. Hills, 6 miles from Wyndham which we passed without stopping.

The 3rd, we had breakfast 11 miles from our last lodging at Bolton. From there, we went to Hartford which is 14 miles away. The days are short, the cold is biting, and the snow which covered the earth prevented us from making long days.

I employed my evening very pleasantly and to give, one last time, an idea of the customs and the innocence which still prevailed in this pleasant country where the corruption of vices has not yet been experienced, I will speak about what occurs of interest to three quarters of the young people of both genders.

The days of prayer and Sundays are no longer religiously observed anywhere except among Presbyterians. They spend most of their day reading the Bible. They go to church several times. They don't play any games out of fear of violating a holy day; nor do they play music at home; nor do they ride a horse. This exaggerated attention to rules is also observed among the Anglicans. I was once witness to a very touching scene at Hartford which I saw repeated. After work and the evening tea, almost all the young girls and young boys go to church on certain days of the week where they sing very melodious songs, psalms and hymns in perfect harmony and unison of all the voices and raise their young hearts to the creator.

All the girls get on one side and the boys on the other but they break into groups more or less according to the tone of their voices, each one taking the part of the song assigned by the minister who presides over this meeting and who always gives the tone by a few notes at the beginning of each song. The tone is repeated by each part which will participate. The most profound silence is always observed the moment after the song begins and in all those which I have heard, I have never noticed any dissonance in harmony, strained voices, false notes in any of the parts and I don't exaggerate excessively my enjoyment and the pleasure which I experienced in saying that I have never had as much at any of the operas of Gluck,[94] Piccini,[95] or Grétry.[96] Here I do not speak of theatrical effects, striking and unexpected scenes of ballets. I concentrate on the part of the song. It is also permitted to create pleasant

93 Canterbury, CT.

94 Christoph Willibald Gluck (1714 –1787) was the composer of Italian and French opera, including *Orfeo ed Euridice*, *Alceste*, *Iphigénie en Tauride*, *Echo et Narcisse*.

96 André Ernest Modeste Grétry (1741-1813) was a composer from the Prince-Bishopric of Liège (present-day Belgium). He is most famous for his opéras comiques.

illusions in whatever position in which we find ourselves, and we can imagine the type of prestige which should arise, the ideas we can have when fortune serves you enough to make you enjoy a performance so new that it is touching.

No other emotion than the one which arouses the desire to do well is depicted on any of these young faces. On many of them, we see so much grace, appeal, freshness, innocence, tranquility of soul and of candor. The interior of all their families is the picture of unity and peace. Active ambition, so worrisome elsewhere, does not devour them here. The thirst for honors, dark concerns disappears. Consequently, happiness resides. Yes, happiness almost everywhere else, ideal and fleeting joy, surely resided in the four so-called New England states before the war. The independence for which they fought will never be, for them, adequate compensation to the origins of all the vices of the old world which the inhabitants implanted and which time and a different population and exterior politic would grow, develop and propagate.

It is our laws, it is the government under which we live, which has, without thinking about it, the most direct influence on the customs of our life and on our character. We see a certain nation, active, industrious occupying the channels which are open to all types of speculation. We notice that another is slow, lazy, cold when one finds them all encumbered or busy. That's precisely the case of the Americans living under the tyrannical and innumerable restrictions imposed upon them by the mother country. The children reflect the milk which they have sucked. We do not see them here noisy, impolite, forgotten as they always are at home, almost everywhere where they are the masters, alone and gathered together or else when they leave school or any exercise whatever where their attention was forcibly captured and held by fear.

One hundred and fifty young girls from 9 to 16 or 18 years of age and as many boys of the same age leave church into the street without hurrying or throwing themselves on each other, without hardly talking to each other. Each one goes home peacefully and only brings wise, virtuous and inspiring thoughts. To finish this article, I would almost say that I saw virtue reside on a corner of the earth. If this idea were not in my principles, beaten by this other: that what we often take for virtue is only a lack of passion, that we are never naturally virtuous but only by effort, by inclination or by weakness of organs and that, in the end, there is merit to being truly virtuous, that in the midst of all sorts of illicit temptations and of true or false attractions which the world offers us. That is my little digression which is not suitable for a military journal, but so what. I let myself be led without perceiving it. It is written; it will remain. I resume our route.

The 4th, we had breakfast at Farmington 10 miles. Two routes leave this place and both go to the banks of the North River. The lower one is the most traveled but, as it is closer to the ocean, and as there are many Tories and evil-minded people, we took that of Lichfield[96] and we left Farmington to go there. Eight miles from the latter place is a new settlement called West Briton.[97] Six or seven barracks comprise it and the appearance of the neighborhood is wild and full of woods which cover the crest of the hills and rocks. The valleys, however, appeared to me to be a very good soil for farming which already becomes apparent in some places. This district only needs laborers.

Six miles from West Briton is Harrington[98] comprising 15 or 18 houses rather distant from one another and located on a hill. The land is still very wooded, difficult, very hilly and cut by many streams. Litchfield, which gives its name to the county, is 8 miles from there and is located on an elevation with a very pleasant view. We count 70 or 80 houses located along a very wide road. There is a rather lovely church in the middle. According to the last census and totals, the population of this village and its environs amounted to 2000 souls.

We departed again on the 5th and we stopped at Washington, a place established a few years ago, at the tavern of Mr. Coggswell. All this region is very little inhabited and the land is full of rocks, hills, ravines and woods.

Washington is still dependent on the state of Connecticut but 4 miles further, we cross the Stratford River on a bridge which forms the boundary with that of New York. Its bed is full of rocks and, 100 toises from the bridge, we notice one which forms a rather high cascade or waterfall.

One mile from the Stratford River we cross another small river. It flows peacefully in a rather long valley. Mr. Moorehouse's tavern, where we slept, is 9 miles. Mr. Moorehouse's tavern is a rather poor lodging! And despite being accustomed to sleeping on the ground for a long time, on a bear skin or on straw in a barn, I cannot prevent myself from making the remark.

The 6th, we left Mr. Moorehouse's tavern early in an extraordinarily biting and piercing cold and entered into the Highlands, part of New York state, whose name means high or mountainous land. This told us pretty much what we would travel. It is also full of rocks and valleys and the houses are not very frequent. After traveling 14 miles, we arrived at Mr. Strom's tavern where we found very attentive hosts, a good fire which we certainly needed, and a good breakfast. We resumed our march, after having taken all these types of refreshments, to go to the shore of the North River at Fishkill Landing, passing Fishkill which is 4 miles from there. This town, which is the largest of the Highlands, contains about 80 houses. Since General Washington made West Point an important post, Fishkill

96 Litchfield, CT.

97 New Britain, CT.

98 Harwinton is more than 16 miles from New Britain.

was always one of the main storehouses of the American army and the winter quarters of a rather large number of troops. It is covered by two good redoubts or forts called the North and the South. The land is unusually difficult and wooded, full of defiles and gorges. It would require an enemy of very superior numbers and very sure fire to dare to attack this post.

Because it is surrounded by wooded mountains which [unintelligible] bad and rocks, this land cannot be very pleasant. Its inhabitants are not very numerous. Before the war, they lived very comfortably and they raised many cattle for export and salt which proves that there are good fields in the valleys. Since New York was occupied by the British, their only outlet which was the North River is closed, which together with a neighboring friendly army but an army which until now was poorly paid, malnourished and living on forage gathered by necessity or by lack of discipline reduced them to misery. There are about ten houses at Fishkill Landing.

The American army always has a certain number of big and small boats at this place for its use. We profited by it, on the morning of the 7th, to cross the North River. We landed on the shore of Newburgh and we arrived at General Washington's where we spent the day to rest along with our baggage. Moreover, it was probably the last we would spend with this great man.

Mistress Washington, who spends every winter with the general wherever he made his quarters since the beginning of the war, had arrived at this one eight days ago. She is not young nor very pretty and does not seem to respond to the grandeur of her husband in everything but she was very rich and this reason which always prevails and which conceals so many other defects made the general decide to marry her. In addition, it is very meritorious on her part to deprive herself of all the comforts and pleasures which she could experience in Virginia at Mount Vernon in a climate that is always mild and serene, even in this season, to come live among the ice and snow, of the noise and the rigors (we can say it) of a camp and of an area of nature which the American army then occupied. Our day was not happy. We thought only of the following day which would be that of farewell, maybe forever, and of the people we held dear and in high esteem. We have to render this justice to General Washington's aura. He bears the imprint of the manners and the character of a leader. It often occurred to us to think, in hearing him speak or seeing him only pass, to consider that one officer or another had often approached or lived with this general. It was a different tone, more relaxed mannerisms, a different and better deportment and the most perfect kindness.

The 8th, the snow fell in large flakes. Despite this bad weather we left Newburgh and General Washington had the kindness to mount his horse to accompany us to the other side of his camp.

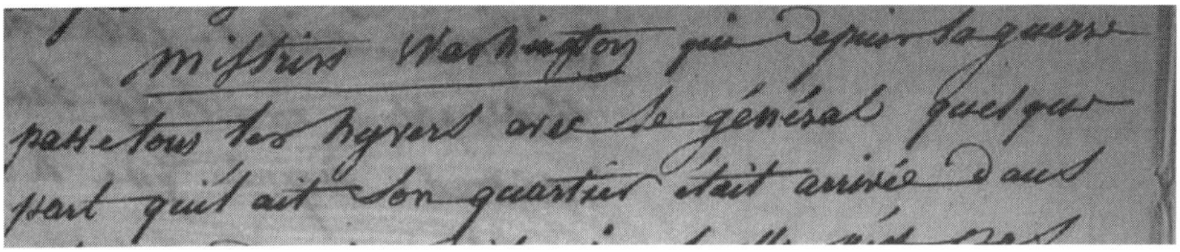
Mistriss Washington qui depuis la guerre
passe tous les hyvers avec le général quelque
part qu'il ait son quartier était arrivée dans

Part of his troops were still under their tents; the other had entered their barracks which we visited. The soldiers constructed them entirely. It was they who, at the beginning of winter, cut the trees, sawed the planks, made the loads etc. and in all their construction, not a pound of iron was used. They are arranged in three parallel lines forming two roads three toises wide. Each barrack was 7 feet high and housed 32 men in two rooms. At each end of the barrack there is a chimney and the distance from one to the other, from 2 in 2, is 4 feet because two barracks or four rooms contain a company. The officers barracked behind.

The conditions of war and the lack of place or of good posts for shelter and safety, the extreme difficulty of the land which removes access to the enemy and the rigors of winter in this region which creates an obstacle for any operation on both sides, also the proximity of West Point had been, for several years, sufficient reasons for General Washington to establish his quarters in this part of the Highlands, but the manner in which the troops were barracked is only practicable in America and only in certain regions. The barracks which had served one winter are destroyed and new ones constructed the following winter (similarly to nomadic people who camp, break camp and change location when they have exhausted it to go in search of a more abundant one), are set up in wooded areas in order to avoid horses, wagons etc. to transport wood for heating to the camp. The land is also little inhabited. The small number of owners who live there do not have enough influence to protect what they own, so the quantity of wood needed for the construction of the barracks and for heating (for a soldier never spares anything) is inconceivable. This part of essential territorial riches is neither appreciated nor understood in a land where it abounds where even in certain counties we pay to remove it. I have often seen it happen that the finest tree is cut for the least use, just as that which is only good to burn.

All the barracks of the lines of New Hampshire, Massachusetts, Connecticut and New York were on one and the same line. That of the lines of the Jerseys, some Pennsylvania troops and the Maryland recruits were on another. New Windsor was 2 ½ miles from the barracks.

As I already said, the weather was very cold and very bad. This condition coupled with our repeated requests could never prevent Mr. Washington from accompanying us along with a few other American generals more than 6 miles from the barracks. We finally had to leave. We can add nothing to what the general told us in kindness, affection even tenderness. His virtues equally command respect, esteem and admiration, but to all these feelings we will add those of regret! His were depicted on his face and he embraced us all in a mournful silence, even though this custom is unknown between men in America as in England! This scene was touching for everyone and we can understand their reasons, on the part of the Americans especially when we think of the state in which we found their affairs and that in which we put them. . . . Mr. Washington and Mr. de Rochambeau embraced each other once more!!! And we soon lost sight of each other. We had dinner at Chester, 18 miles from the barracks and we slept at Warwick which is 9 miles away.

We left Warwick on the 9th. Four miles from this small place, there are two or three small streams which separate the state of New York from that of the Jerseys. All this land is very wooded. The little that there is of value is from a good report from what the residents tell us. We had breakfast at Beard's tavern and from there we slept at Sussex Courthouse which is 14 miles. This place located on a hill contains eight or ten houses. The courthouse is a terrible structure.

The 10th, we left Sussex. Three miles to the right we find the road to Easton, 3 miles further Mr. Pettit's tavern where I had already slept during the summer. It is 10 miles from Hacket's town,[99] poor land, hilly, few inhabitants, very wooded.

From Hackettstown to Johnson's mill is 12 miles. The land which they cross is very arid. Six miles from Johnson's mill, we find Mr. Burkirt's Tavern on the left where we slept. I was better received with my general than I was the first time I stayed there.

The morning of the 11th, we left Burkirt's tavern. We made 6 miles and crossed at Pitch town which is in a pleasant location. Four miles further is Baptist town where Hart's tavern, where we had breakfast, is 4 miles away. There is a small brook near there which we cross on a bridge.

Five miles from Hart's tavern, we crossed the Delaware at Robert's Sons Ferry[100] and we slept at Benet's tavern which is 7 miles away.

The 12th, we made 27 miles and arrived at Philadelphia in time for dinner at the Chevalier de la Luzerne and in enough time to find ourselves at a ball which he gave that evening for some of the ladies of this great and fine city. All the land which we had just traveled is furnished and adorned with many houses, was well-inhabited, well-cultivated and offered interesting and very varied views.

In the various errands and sojourns more or less extended which I had already made to Philadelphia, I had never yet enjoyed the spectacle of any particular great feast or dress ball. The progress which luxury has made in three years in this capitol of Pennsylvania and, for

99 Hackettstown.

100 Robertson's Ferry.

the moment, of the federal union of the United States is astonishing. The women arrived and were dressed with an elegance and with a refinement which we did not have in our large provincial cities in France. There is not a single vessel from our ports which is not loaded with an infinity of fashion objects, of all sorts and types. The French hairstyle, the practice of curling, of braiding hair, powders and pomades which they used to find so ridiculous and bothersome has prevailed and a woman today would not appear in a gathering of several people if she were not coiffed by a French hairdresser or if she did not have her dress made in the latest French style. Despite that, their grooming with new and fresh pieces of cloth is nothing remarkable because, in general, they do not know how to adjust or place the works of our fashion products or of a Parisian tailor. Their corsets, in general, are very poor and need work. Patience, they'll come around! . . . Daintiness, almost unknown to this new people until now, makes progress each day. The men who generally lived among them respond a little in the gatherings. The French appeared everywhere and often presented to the women a language to which their ears were not accustomed but which was very agreeable and pleased them! Our customs and our manners are not as severe as theirs. Gallantry is a moral power which has always been embraced by the female gender and which would not be repulsed as odious and dangerous in America.

The Chevalier de la Luzerne lives in a noble and grand manner in Philadelphia. For the Dauphin's birthday, he gave a splendid and very brilliant feast for which he had built a very large hall of a very noble interior architecture which he continued to use to give balls during the winter. From 150 to 200 women were present at this ball and there were a very large number of very beautiful and very lovely ones among them. Among the first?, a Mrs. Bingham seemed to win the prize. Only English contra dances were danced! However, almost everywhere where the French army halted for some time, only French contra dances or French cotillions were danced. Since the war and the arrival of the French army, there are many balls given by subscription at Philadelphia. Thus, this city, once inhabited by Quakers whose austere morality is far removed from every pleasure and every kind of popular entertainment, is now the most merry city in America. Many of the entertainment teachers, most of them French, have introduced themselves and established themselves there! For the moment, those of the French language and dance enroll the most students. I had the curiosity to go visit some of the schools. In one of them, one day, I saw the comic operetta *Annette* and *Lubin*[101] performed by some young girls 8 to 15 years old who did not do too badly.

The French army is the cause of a great circulation of money in the United States. If the war continues or even if peace is signed, and that professors, all types of teachers,

101 Written by Jean-François Marmontel (1723–1799) in 1761.

artists, artisans of merit come to establish themselves a large part of this money would remain momentarily in France. The actual avarice with which they seize everything which comes from us is the guarantee and will become ever more so if the French are always proper in their conduct and scrupulous as honorable in their business and in their markets.

The Frigate *Danaé* Runs Aground

The frigate *Danaé* commanded by Mr. the Count de Capellis, ship captain, arrived in the Delaware from France on December 13 with a very strong wind and very heavy snow. She took a river pilot aboard who, despite Mr. de Capellis and the bad weather, wanted to bring her immediately to Philadelphia! Either out of ignorance of the soundings or because of the bad weather which did not permit him to judge his position well, the said pilot ran the *Danaé* aground near the place or the sand bar which had already been fatal to the frigate *l'Aigle* on September 22. The bottom being muddy, the *Danaé* did not strain and Mr. de Capellis got everything under way to extract her from this misstep. Colonel Gouvion[102] (a Frenchman in the service of the American engineers) was a passenger on board. He brought the news to the Chevalier de la Luzerne and asked for the necessary assistance for Mr. de Capellis. It was sent but, in the meantime, he was obliged to cut his masts and, despite lightening the frigate of everything that was possible, she was not refloated until all her artillery was thrown overboard. She then went up the Delaware and arrived at Philadelphia on the 24th.—

La Danaé had 1,800,000# in specie aboard which he had put ashore near Dover, Maryland[103] when she entered the river, along with the government dispatches which were immediately put under escort of a detachment of the hussars from Lauzun's Legion. As soon as Mr. de Rochambeau had opened them, he sent Captain Baron de Fock[104] (a Swede)

102 Jean-Baptiste Gouvion (1747-1792) was a Lt. at the engineering school of Mézières when he left the service of France to join the Continental Army. He returned to France and was given the rank of Lt. Col. in the French Army in 1783. The following year, he was recognized as a Knight of Saint Louis and was promoted to mestre de camp in 1787. He was active in the French Revolution from the start and was appointed major general of the Parisian National Guard in August 1789. Two years later, he was promoted to maréchal de camp in the regular army and appointed inspector general of the 17th military division. He was elected to the Legislative Assembly as a deputy for Paris in September 1791 and he joined the military committee the following month. He resigned his position in the government in April 1792 to serve in the army. He was killed by a shot from a cannon near Maubeuge. His name appears on the Arc de Triomphe.

103 Delaware.

104 Johan Henrik Fock; John Fock, 2nd Baron de Robeck (1753-1817), the Duc de Lauzun's aide-de-camp in America. After the war, he moved to England and was naturalized as a British

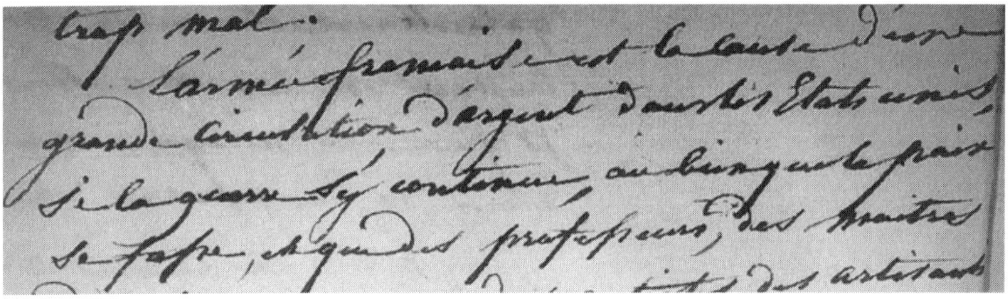
trop mal.

l'armée française et la cause d'une

grande circulation d'argent dans les Etats unis

si la guerre s'y continue, au lieu que la paix

se fasse, et que des professeurs, des maitres

des artisans

following Lauzun's Legion to Mr. the Count de Vaudreuil at Boston and to bring him the dispatches and letters for the navy.

Lauzun's Legion, which, in leaving the camp at Yorktown Heights, went to establish itself at Burlington on the left bank of the Delaware, to wait until its quarters at Willmington [DE] were ready to receive them, passed by Philadelphia on their way on the 21st and the 22nd.

The 24th, during the day, [unintelligible[105]] admiral de Vaudreuil with 12 ships and three frigates set sail from Nantasket harbor, bringing with him the troops under the command of the Baron de Viioménil. He left the crew of the lost ship le *Magnifique* at Portsmouth (in New Hampshire) to board the *America*, a 74-gun American ship given to France as soon as it would be finished and seaworthy.

The frigate *l'Iris* had to separate from Vaudreuil's fleet to go to France to bring dispatches there. —- Lauzun's Legion and a detachment under the command of the Chevalier de la Valette, future colonel of the Saintonge Regiment, were to remain in the United States for the time being.

Captain Baron de Fock arrived from his mission to Boston the night of December 28! Mr. the Count de Rochambeau at this time had very honorably fulfilled his own for which the king had sent him and his army to the United States. According to the orders of the court (peaceful as it was today for the fate of this army and on the excellent turn of political affairs of this country), he only had to think of leaving it to return to France. He could have embarked immediately on the frigate *Gloire* which had arrived from France last September and which was still in the Delaware, but this frigate also sails poorly. The number of British cruisers at the mouth of the Delaware Bay was such that the 44-gun American frigate *South Carolina* had just been taken by the enemy cruisers and that having received news of the

subject under the name "John Henry Fock, called Baron de Robeck," by an Act of the British Parliament in 1789.

105 The text seems to read J W le m qiers which would translate to J W quartermaster.

imminent departure of the French general, they seemed to double their surveillance to intercept him and to capture him.

Campaign of 1783

Introduction

After a three week stay, General Rochambeau and his retinue departed Philadelphia on January 2 . Having sold their horses, the Duc de Lauzun graciously supplied mounts for the departing party. While the officers of the various branches of service boarded ships in Baltimore to return to France, Rochambeau's party proceeded instead to Annapolis.

Lauberdière recorded his thoughts and emotions about his imminent departure and the people he met. He described the city of Annapolis and the government of Maryland. The governor wished to give a banquet in their honor, but the French decided to take advantage of the favorable weather to depart. However, the winds changed before they could set sail. Prudently, they remained on board until fairer circumstances. The banquet went on as planned but without the French.

When the winds shifted again, they set sail. Fickle as ever, the winds died out while underway; forcing them to anchor at the mouth of the Potomac. When they finally proceeded out of the Chesapeake Bay, a British fleet engaged them. Their foes nipped at their heels, firing upon them. After a twenty-nine-hour chase, they slipped away from their pursuers.

Storms and other dangers at sea beset the travelers. Off the coast of Spain, they hugged the land to the Isle of Groix. Some Nantais sailors recognized the shores of the Loire. The ship sailed up the river to anchor opposite St. Nazaire after a crossing of thirty-one days.

Before going to Paris and Versailles, to give an account of their mission to the king (and to pay him homage for his glory and his victories), Rochambeau went to Nantes. Lauberdière accompanied him as far as Angers, veering off to visit his parents for just over a week.

The King awarded the Count de Rochambeau a promotion, a government position and a pension. Lauberdière also benefitted. He rose from Captain to the Sub-Assistant Quartermaster General in the Royal Normandy Regiment.

A series of important milestones followed. The Continental Army disbanded on June 13. In July, most of the troops who departed Boston and headed home via the West Indies, returned to France in July. The British evacuated New York City on November 25.

The Diary

Rochambeau's Departure
January 1783

These considerations made him [Rochambeau] decide to go to Annapolis on the Chesapeake Bay where the fine frigate *l'Emeraude* was located. She was a much better sailor, commanded by Mr. de Quémy,[1] ship captain. Mr. de Rochambeau set his departure from Philadelphia for January 2, 1783. Since our arrival in this city we had sold our horses. Mr. the Duc de Lauzun gave us some horses from his hussars to go to Annapolis. After having spent three weeks at Philadelphia, far from the noise of war, during the holidays and in pleasure, the time of departure having rung, we took leave of our good, hospitable, even charming, hosts, and of Mr. the Chevalier de la Luzerne, Ambassador of France who has showered us with attention.

We set out on the road again and had breakfast at Chester where Mr. de Lauzun and several officers of his corps came to join us. From there we went to Wilmington, Mr. de Lauzun's headquarters, where Mr. Collot,[2] Assistant Quartermaster General of the Army had prepared fine stables. Horses and men will be very well in this winter

1 Lt. Louis-Alexandre Macquerel, Chevalier de Quémy served as Capt. of the French frigate *l'Emeraude*.

2 Georges-Henri-Victor Collot (1750–1805) served as an aide-de-camp and *maréchal des logis* (quartermaster) under General Rochambeau. He served as governor of Guadeloupe, 1792–1794. He is best known for his expedition down the Ohio and Mississippi rivers in the spring and summer of 1796. He is the author of *Voyage dans L'Amérique Septentrionale, ou Description des Pays Arrosés par le Mississipi, l'Ohio, le Missouri et Autres Riviéres Affluentes . . . Avec un Atlas de 36 Cartes, Plans, Vues et Figures* (Paris: A. Bertrand, 1826), which was simultaneously published in English.

quarters. The officers of Lauzun's Legion came with the duke at their head to make a final corps visit to the general. They gave him an honor guard which he thanked and sent back. He received respectful and sincere farewell wishes, signs of affection and best wishes. We remounted our horses to go to sleep at Christian[3] 36 miles, after having passed Newport, a lovely little town where the army had camped twice and which is 4 miles from Christiana.

January 3, we made 13 miles in a very bitter and very hard cold and had breakfast at Head of Elk. We left to go sleep at the Susquehanna ferry on the right bank of this river. We were rewarded for the smallness and the narrowness of our accommodations by the pleasant babble of a very lovely person, daughter of our host. She helped us pass a very pleasant evening. Our customs became simple and all American! She had made our beds herself and we slept very well.

A gentleman, a landowner at the mouth of the Susquehanna, wanting to increase his revenues without much work, founded a town at that place. He named it Havre de Grace. He made a very fine map of his land which I saw. He measured it and divided it himself laid out the various roads. He had already sold very dearly more than 300 little lots of land to build and already there are about 30 houses constructed. For the time being, the proximity of Baltimore, which becomes richer and more commercial every day, might present Havre de Grace with some obstacles to prosperity. But, to the point, there will probably be much emigration of people from Europe for the United States having become free, independent and happy and so the views of the founding proprietor [illegible] will find themselves neither frustrated nor out of place.

On January 4th, in a very thick and heavy snow, we left the Susquehanna ferry and went to have breakfast at Bushtown. From there, we set out on our march to Baltimore where we arrived at night, after a march of 39 to 40 miles during our day. Baltimore is not yet paved and we experienced trouble and difficulty to extricate ourselves from the mud of this city to reach Mr. the Chevalier de la Valette's lodging with whom we supped.

The Baltimore city council convened recently and resolved to pave the city and the work had begun. By virtue of this resolution or municipal decision, each resident owner must pay, for this purpose, two dollars per foot that the house occupies facing the street. This tax, however, will not suffice because, in addition to the roads being very fine and wide, the stones are intermittently rare and the labor very expensive. On the other hand, the great extent of business and the population which already brings in

3 Christiana, DE.

what Baltimore would receive each year by its location after the peace, will surely amply furnish her administration with the means to make the city lovely and healthy.

After his arrival, Mr. de Rochambeau, together with Mr. de la Villebrune, captain commanding the 50-gun *Romulus*, and Mr. Duquesne, captain commanding the frigate *Guadeloupe*, then in Baltimore harbor, together with Mr. the Chevalier de la Valette, made all the final arrangements to board the officers of the various branches of the service who continued in their functions and to return to France. Since the departure of the army, we made our wishes for the expansion and future prosperity of Baltimore which already comprises 15 to 18,000 souls. We departed the morning of January 5th to go to Annapolis.

The bad weather frustrated us very much to cross the ferry from the west branch of the Patapsco. We were forced to return and to try to cross 9 miles higher, near Mr. Gammonds's house. We ventured out in a boat in very poor condition and which was on the verge of sinking in the middle of the ferry. We succeeded in attaining the opposite shore only by force of labor. Everybody applied himself. Our life, our salvation depended on it— however we landed without any damage. We made 12 miles across level but wild ground, little inhabited, very wooded and sandy. We stopped at the widow Auckward who hospitably gave us a very fine dinner. Warmed near a big fire, lit and maintained by her attention, we then resumed our route and after twelve (14) miles of march, we finally arrived at Annapolis on January 5.

Thus ends the course of our march by land and our voyage from Boston, Providence and Newport in Rhode Island fortunately without any accident! Of all the many trips I made at different times over three years in the United States, this one, begun with a very deep freeze and a very rude winter, seemed to me the longest. I experienced a type of interior pain and sorrow to see our army dissolve, so to speak, and the separation of many brave soldiers and fellow warriors with whom we have experienced the same hardships and the same dangers.

I am only 22 years old and sometimes find myself susceptible to being more or less sensitive to the impulses of the heart which visits, farewells, the expression of regret etc. etc. can produce. All those who made us witness in general and in particular to Mr. de Rochambeau, both by the army and by the entire population, wherever we passed, touched me because of the respect and friendship which I bear him. The Americans are still a new people whose basis of customs is especially simplicity and frankness. Their manners are neither refined nor affected. Equality, unity within gatherings of the same party reign among them and amply reward them for what art procures for enjoyment in Europe. If some of their customs are different from ours, the habit of living among them and with them made me adopt them. Finally, on my account and as a simple individual, I lived perfectly happy and content! It is true that in my position as aide-de-camp to the general in chief and his close relative, I should find my fate preferable to that of most of the individuals who comprise the army. If my service was sometimes difficult, it was usually pleasant and mild. It was always ordered with as much kindness as justice and my comrades and I can say it depended only on reason.

Return to Annapolis

I return to Annapolis: The assembly of the state of Maryland which was in session had not adjourned at our arrival. As soon as it was known, the president of the Senate and several delegates came to pay their respects to Mr. the Count de Rochambeau. In the state of Maryland, the governor is elected for three years. Mr. Lee,[4] whom I had previously met at Baltimore, had not been reelected and Mr. Paca[5] had been elected governor three months earlier. He is a very suitable man for this position and also has a remarkable ability and talents for business. He has the advantage of being very tall, of possessing a very fine figure, and of having good form and the appearance of a European diplomat. He invited us to a very fine dinner where toasts were drunk to the king of France, to his brave army, to his generals and admirals, to the nascent glory and prosperity of the United States, to their perpetual union, to peace etc. etc.

Annapolis is one of the most populated cities of North America, probably because of a type of comfortable or rich landowners, the former aristocracy of the country. In the summer, they live on their properties; in the winter, they come to Annapolis to spend their income, which, despite being much smaller than Baltimore in population, has become the seat of government of the state of Maryland. We renewed acquaintance there with Mr. Carroll,[6] an excellent man, who treated us so well and received us so

4 Thomas Sim Lee (1745–1819), governor of Maryland from November 12, 1779 - November 22, 1782 and April 5, 1792 - November 14, 1794. Although not a signatory to the Declaration of Independence, the Articles of Confederation or the US Constitution, he was an important participant in the process of their creation. He also served as a delegate of Maryland in the Congress of the Confederation in 1783 and was a member of the House of Delegates in 1787.

5 William Paca (1740–1799), a signatory to the Declaration of Independence from MD, a delegate to the First Continental Congress and the Second Continental Congress from MD and Governor of MD from 1782 to 1785. He was also a judge of the United States District Court for the District of Maryland from1790 until his death.

6 Charles Carroll (1737-1832) served in the Continental Congress, on the Board of War, through much of the War of Independence, and simultaneously participated in the framing of a constitution for Maryland. He returned to MD in 1778 to participate in the formation of the state government. He was elected to the MD Senate in 1781 and to the first Federal Congress in

perfectly in 1782. Mr. Carroll is a very rich planter and an enlightened philanthropist. He is a Catholic. He has already made several attempts to plant vines. They were successful and he had us drink a white wine from his harvest which was not bad. He showered us with foresight and kindness in everything as did Mr. Lloyd whose sister-in-law earned, among her fellow citizens, the title of the prettiest woman of the 13 states. She was born in England and spent more than a year in Paris. It is said that in the first, she brought back to America the taste of fashion. She is very lovable and speaks French fairly well.

The frigate *l'Emeraude*, of 42 18-pound cannons, commanded by Mr. the Chevalier de Quémy, ship captain, was anchored below Annapolis, 3 miles from this city at the mouth of the South River in the Chesapeake Bay. Mr. de Rochambeau, on the reputation of his march and of his qualities, was destined to make his way from Philadelphia to return to France. The 7th, he boarded this frigate and he decided that, if the winds were favorable, we would embark the following day along with Mr. the Chevalier de Chastellux, Major General of the Army; Mr. de Béville, Brigadier and Quartermaster General; Mr. de Choisy, Brigadier of the King's Armies, Commander of St. Louis; the Viscount de Rochambeau; the 1st and 2nd regiments of the Bourbonnais and some other persons including Mr. Dr. Coste Surgeon General of the Army; Mr. the Baron de Montesquieu[7]; the Viscount de Vaudreuil; Mr. de Béville's eldest and youngest sons, a few others.

Mr. the Duc de Lauzun received orders to take his winter quarters at Wilmington with his legion, infantry and hussars and the Chevalier de la Valette had received orders to encamp at Baltimore with a detachment of infantry and the rest of the administrative services of the army which did not go from Boston to the West Indies with Mr. de Vaudreuil.

The city of Annapolis and Governor Paca had decided to give us a feast on the 8th and we promised to attend, but the same day, 8, the winds were favorable and we had decided to board the *Arethuse*. I said goodbye to the pretty and charming Mrs. Lloyd with whom I was supposed to spend this evening. But alas! We had to get in a boat and

---

1788. He returned to the State Senate in 1790 and served for another 10 years. He retired from that post in 1800. He was the last surviving member of those who signed the Declaration.

7 Charles-Louis de Secondat, Baron de La Brède et de Montesquieu (1749-1824),was aide-de-camp to the Marquis de Chastellux. He became Mestre de camp en second of the Bourbonnais Regiment in 1782 and of the Royal Grenadier Regiment of Orléanais in 1788. He resigned in August 1791 and emigrated to England in October. He took part in the Quiberon expedition, was appointed Mestre de camp (Camp Marshal) in 1793 and Lieutenant General in 1814. He returned to France during the Restoration but returned to England when he was not made a Peer of France. He became a Chevalier de Saint Louis in 1786.

go aboard despite the very severe cold. No sooner had the general in chief and other passengers noted above arrived, than the wind changed and became absolutely contrary. The cold was very bitter. However, as all the individuals and all the baggage were aboard, prudence dictated that we remain without complaint and await favorable wind.

January 9 and 10 were spent in this situation. All our rigging, our sails furled, were taken by a deep freeze but on the 11th, the winds turned to the north. Captain Quémy had his crew prepare to set sail. We weighed anchor and set sail. We made little way that day because we were forced to anchor as the wind died almost suddenly.

Departure

The morning of the 12th, we weighed anchor and set sail again with a rather fine wind. It died again that evening and we anchored near Lookout Point at the mouth of the Potomac. As the winds were poor, we spent the 13 at anchor in this anchorage.

January 14th, a very favorable breeze picked up. We raised the anchor early and set sail to continue going down the Chesapeake Bay. The chills had ceased and we enjoyed the mild temperature of Virginia weather. We arrived at the latitude of Cape Henry early and we did not see any vessel beyond! At this location, Captain Quémy thought he could send back the coastal pilot whom he had taken aboard to navigate the bay. We continued our route under a very favorable wind and everything seemed auspicious for our crossing.

However, night came. The moon was very clear and we were out of the capes less than two hours when we discovered several vessels which we thought were neither strong nor dangerous. They were headed straight for us and, despite the night, on their approach, they were considered ships of war! (It was a British division on a cruise consisting of the 64-gun *Lion*, the 50-gun *Centurion*, two 36-gun frigates and a sloop of war). We found ourselves very close to the lead which was the 64-gun ship. She fired a few cannon shots at us, hoisted all her sails to turn athwart us. It was 6 o'clock in the evening. We took chase, hoisting all our sails also, but our position became critical because we no longer had a pilot to risk re-entering the bay. We found ourselves between the land and the enemy chase vessels. The wind fortunately changed a little, giving Captain Quémy hope of being able to follow the coast which is north-south and to go obliquely to the southeast to escape. Meanwhile, the enemy fleet followed us, but especially one of the frigates and the 64-gun ship, a fine sailor, and which still kept the lead of his own. About 9 o'clock at night, he had gained enough to think that he could put himself across our bow and fire a broadside. It wounded a provision ox which was aboard, tore a few sails, but did no other damage. This crossing the bow by the enemy was probably the cause of our salvation. Our captain did not return fire but was busy raising sails. Thus, we gained some distance at 10 p.m. At 11 o'clock, we believed that the enemy was certainly gaining on us. Captain Quémy had his boat thrown overboard, replacement masts for his brig, many different objects and came to tell Mr. de Rochambeau to even prepare to throw his papers overboard in case we were in danger of being caught. In the confusion of the night, the sailors threw many useful objects. The enemy, within cannon range and within our waters, constantly fired their chase guns at us and we responded with two retreat guns. Our anxiety was great and became more so when the wind howled and the ocean became rough. We had the greatest fear of breaking something. We were reduced to risk everything for everything.

Meanwhile, day came. We lost sight of the enemy 50-gun ship, the two frigates and the sloop of war and we were only chased by the 64-gun ship which we thought sailed at least as well as we! Too well, without a doubt, for its chase being well-supported, continued ceaselessly all the day of the 15th when, about 4 p.m., we thought sure we would be approached and taken! Captain Quémy then had his bow anchors, his fore and aft Faillard[8] guns, spars, spare topmasts etc. etc. jettisoned. Everything went! We found ourselves overcome with joy when we gained some distance. The wind became fresh. The enemy was greeted by two brief wind storms which struck him and not us, forcing him to furl some sails. The sky became cloudy and, at nightfall, we hoped that we might lose him from sight, despite the bright moon. Our expectation was not in vain for, the wind being fresh, about 11 p.m., the enemy finally gave up the chase after 29 hours, almost constantly within cannon range, and we lost him from sight. We then headed southeast and southeast ¼ east. We continued on this wind stream until the morning of the 16th when we found ourselves at 33° latitude.

Thus free of the enemy, we were not yet out of all other dangers and other difficulties as the wind became very strong. It became a storm and forced us to spend the night of January 16th to the 17th at the Cape on very rough seas. The furor of the waves continued to increase throughout the day of the 17th. We spent it without sails, fearing to be dismasted. We had no replacements. We were either very uneasy or very sick as were several young crewmen. Finally, around evening, the wind abated but the

8 Jean Charles, chevalier Folard (1669–1752), authored *Nouvelles Decouvertes Sur La Guerre: Dans Une Dissertation Sur Polybe. Ouvrage Utile & Necessaire Tous Les Generaux, Commandant & Officiers D'armées.* 2. éd., rev. par l'auteur. ed., F. Foppens, 1724 and *Histoire De Polybe, Nouvellement Traduite Du Grec Par Vincent Thuillier. Avec Un Commentaire Ou Un Corps De Science Militaire, Enrichi De Notes Critiques Et Historiques, Ou Toutes Les Grandes Parties De La Guerre, Soit Pour L'offensive, Soit Pour La De´fensive, Sont Explique´es,* Par M. De Folard. Nouv. édition revue, corrigeé & augmentée d'un supplement. ed., Chez Zacharie Chatelain Et Fils, 1759.

ocean, extremely rough, gave us little rest by its bellowing, the creaking of the vessel, its canons etc. during the night. We finally saw the sun and good weather again on the 18th, but, as the ocean was still very rough and agitated, it was only on the 19th that we were able to completely repair whatever damage was done by the commotion of the chase, by the 64-gun ship and by the windstorm.

The 20th, the wind being favorable, we navigated to pass north of the Bermudas heading east ¼ northeast. We arrived without accident nor any mishap whatsoever until the 28 of the month by the shortcomings of [unintelligible] on the map by 38° 20' latitude and 41° 40' longitude of the tides of Iron Island. We headed two quarters further north to pass it and we resumed eastward on the 29th. It is mere luck that makes us recognize these directions exactly for [unintelligible] no navigator is concerned about its approach too close and what one might take more care for the breakers on some rocks could very well have occurred for a totally different reason.

The 30th, the wind shifted to the south southwest. We were then very close to the Isle of Flora,[9] the westernmost one of the Azores. We headed east southeast to avoid any accident. The captain navigated to the northeast ¼ north until the following morning.

At 8 a.m. on the 31st, we discovered a ship in front of us. We continued our route and soon joined her. It was a brig flying the Austrian Imperial flag coming from St. Domingue and going to Ostend. The wind howled; the sea was rough. We hailed the ship. We could not hear ourselves. We continued our route under very few sails.

In order to avoid British cruisers as much as possible, leaving the Chesapeake Bay, Mr. de Rochambeau's intention was to land at Cadiz and to cross Spain by Madrid. Mr. the Chevalier de Escémy, without saying anything and, on the contrary, not being preoccupied with getting to this port where he feared to encounter Mr. the Vice Admiral Count d'Estaing who was preparing and gathering considerable naval forces there to go to the West Indies. It was being said that he was going to conquer Jamaica, so he only navigated to recognize the capes Laroque and St. Vincent, saying that he would then hug the coast and arrive at Cadiz.

February

February 2, the wind shifted and became very violent. We then headed to the closest one. Captain Quémy advised the general to make his route to Coruña where the winds were then taking us and where we would be only 130 leagues from our

9 Flores Island.

destination. Mr. de Rochambeau agreed. We sailed to the northeast ¼ north all night and all day February 3.

From the 3rd to the 4th, we made 80 leagues and we found from our point that we were near land.

At noon on February 5th, all our pilots had arrived at their post. We continued to skirt the land to reconnoiter Cape Finisterre. We did not see it that day and we sailed on one side and then the other all night to keep ourselves in position toward the landings.

The morning of the 6th, we headed to shore. The winds changed. The captain then decided openly to enter the Gulf of Gascony. We were then never sure of any point. In the Gulf, the sea is no longer as black and we find the soundings very far off the coast.

February 7, 8 and 9, the winds were variable. We only sailed during the day.

Return to France

The 10th, as the weather was very cloudy, we thought we were close to land according to our soundings. We brought ourselves to the Isle of Groix from where we could either enter Quibéron Bay, to the east or the mouth of the Loire for Nantes. Fortune prevented every reconnaissance. The wind became very violent, but there was a clearing which allowed several good Nantais sailors aboard the frigate *l'Éméraude*, which had been launched and armed at Nantes, to recognize the shores of the Loire and announce that we were at the mouth of this river. We headed to go up river and we anchored in the river opposite St. Nazaire without risk nor danger about 11 a.m. and without a pilot. We had barely dropped anchor when a coastal pilot came aboard and gave us the first news of the signing of the peace. Mr. Bufry, Ship Ensign aboard the frigate *Iris* which came from Boston and had been in the river for 15 days, soon confirmed this news. Mr. the Count Admiral Marquis de Vaudreuil (fleet commander) had sent it there upon its departure.

Thus ends our navigation and our crossing from Annapolis in Maryland to France aboard the king's frigate *Émeraude* in 31 days from January 11 to February 10 inclusive, 1783.

As soon as the frigate had anchored, Mr. de Rochambeau had nothing else in mind than to find the means to get to Nantes. He sent me in a fragile boat from the town which had come alongside at St. Nazaire to prepare horses for him for that purpose. The Viscount de Rochambeau and Mr. de Choisy, bored as they were being aboard, also wanted to be among the first to disembark and they joined me. A cockswain and twelve rowers comprised our crew. The wind was too strong, the river, or rather the sea, was too rough. We raised a small sail and were obliged to run some large waves. We ran one too far out. A wave entered our boat and was on the verge of sinking us! We emptied the water all together as best we could.

The wind was absolutely against us to land and was getting stronger. We found ourselves in danger of sinking in our fragile skiff, when, after an hour and a half of useless struggle, we found ourselves overjoyed to be able to board a Dutch vessel anchored near the mouth of the river. The captain threw us a hawser which we finally reached after several attempts and we arrived alongside him. He received us with hospitality and signs of joy which he expressed for having saved us from imminent danger. It would have been cruel to die at the port or in the port! Strong liquors were offered to us to warm ourselves. We dried our clothing, completely soaked with water. We then supped with the Dutch crew and finally, about 11 p.m., the wind became completely calm and the tide was rising. We retook our boat and, after having thanked our humane and good Dutch captain again, we headed out and arrived at the large town or small city of St. Nazaire.

The Viscount de Rochambeau and Mr. General Choisy then went to bed in the best hotel in the area. I went to find the mayor or leader of this place and other prominent people to help me find the horses that I needed. I went here and there during the night to obtain them and succeeded in finding about 30 the morning of the 11th. At this time, one of the *Émeraude's* boats arrived at St. Nazaire. The general advised me that he decided to embark for Nantes without a crew and that Captain de Quémy had offered to bring him to Paimboeuf in one of his remaining boats. He decided to take this route to go to Nantes. Messrs. de Béville and de Choisy, &c. profited by the horses I had gathered at St. Nazaire. I re-embarked with the Viscount de Rochambeau to return aboard the *Émeraude* where, upon our arrival, Mr. Lieutenant-General Count de Rochambeau accompanied by Mr. the Chevalier de Chastellux and some aides-de-camp disembarked to go to Paimboeuf. Upon the departure of the general in chief, the frigate *Émeraude* fired 13 guns in a salute of honor. About 2 to 3 o'clock in the afternoon of February 11, 1783, we arrived at Paimboeuf safe and sound and thus ended our navigation and our return from the United States of North America to France, from where we left on April 15 and May 2, 1780.

On the morning of February 12, we mounted horses and went to Nantes where, on the 14th, Mr. the Count the Rochambeau departed to go to Paris and Versailles to give an account of his mission to the king and to pay him homage for his glory and his victories.

In 1492, Christopher Columbus discovered America!! 300 [years] later, on January 21, 1783, a vast country had become established in the north of this continent, acquired its independence from British power and monarchy through the military conquest of

France and concluded a solemn peace treaty!!! Freedom reigns! Who can yet tell or foresee what will be the consequences of this immense and glorious event?

On February 14, I accompanied Mr. the Count de Rochambeau as far as Angers from whence I went to Bauges and to the countryside near Cotterville where I spent 8 or 10 days with my parents. From there, I went to Paris.

After the war in America, the king promised Mr. the Count de Rochambeau the first great government position vacant which would bring him 60,000# per year and, while awaiting it, a government pension of 30,000#.—- The king also appointed Mr. de Rochambeau, who already had the great cross of St. Louis, Knight Commander, or popularly blue ribbon.

Since April 15, 1780, I had the brevet of captain and in 1781 captain of cavalry in the Royal Normandy Regiment commanded by the Prince de Croi.[10] The general staff of the American army was preserved in part and reestablished on a regular and stable footing of peace. I was retained in this corps under the title of Sub-Assistant Quartermaster General.

The Duc de Lauzun who, at our departure from Philadelphia in January 1783, had remained at Wilmington with his legion, embarked on the frigate *l'Active* upon receiving the news of the peace and returned to France in July 1783 as did the Chevalier de la Valette and all who remained with him from our army at Baltimore. —- Most of our troops, who had left from Boston aboard Mr. de Vaudreuil's fleet and had gone to the West Indies, also returned to France in the month of July.

End of Journal

10 Anne-Emmanuel-Ferdinand-François de Croÿ, 8th Duke of Croÿ and 4th Prince de Solre, (1743-1803) a French soldier who attained the rank of Maréchal de camp. He had previously served as a member of the Assembly of Notables in 1788 and 1789 and as a member of the National Constituent Assembly of 1789 representing the Bailiwick of Le Quesnoy, Hainaut. He emigrated from France during the French Revolution and received the sovereignty of Dülmen in Westphalia after the Congress of Ratisbon (1797).

Index

About the Editor

Norman Desmarais is professor emeritus at Providence College, Providence, Rhode Island, and an active reenactor. He is a member of Le Régiment Bourbonnais, the 2nd Rhode Island Regiment and the Brigade of the American Revolution.

Mr. Desmarais is the author of *Guide to the American Revolutionary War* series (six volumes about the war on land and seven volumes about the war at sea and overseas), as well as *America's First Ally: France in the American Revolutionary War*, and is the editor-in-chief of *The Brigade Dispatch*, the journal of the Brigade of the American Revolution.

He translated the *Gazette Françoise*, the French newspaper published in Newport, Rhode Island by the French fleet that carried the Count of Rochambeau and 5,800 French troops to America in July 1780. It is the first known service newspaper published by an expeditionary force.

Mr. Desmarais is also fluent in French and Italian, and has a reading knowledge of German and Spanish as well as classical Latin and Greek. He served as Vice President of Le Foyer Club and the Richelieu (which became the Aram Pothier Club), social organizations for the preservation and promotion of the French language and culture. He serves on the Board of Directors of the Boivin Center, University of Massachusetts, Dartmouth.

He was a pioneer in the CD-ROM industry. He set up and managed the first CD-ROM network in Rhode Island and served as Senior Editor of *CD-ROM World*, contributing editor of *Optical Information Systems*, and was the founding editor and editor-in-chief of *Electronic Resources Review*. He is listed in *International Directory of Distinguished Leadership*, the *Dictionary of International Biography*, *Who's Who of Information Technology*, *2000 Outstanding Intellectuals of the 20th Century*, and *Marquis Who's Who*.

Norm was inducted into the American French Genealogical Society French-Canadian Hall of Fame in 2015, and received the Albert Nelson Marquis Lifetime Achievement Award in 2019 and 2020.

Other Titles of Interest from Savas Beatie

Jerome A. Greene
The Guns of Independence: The Siege of Yorktown, 1781 (2005)

Theodore P. Savas and J. David Dameron
A Guide to the Battles of the American Revolution (2006)
Winner, 2006, Gold Star Award for History, Military Writers Society of America

John C. Luzader
Saratoga: A Military History of the Decisive Campaign of the American Revolution (2008)
Finalist, 2014, Army Historical Foundation Distinguished Book Award

Michael C. Harris
Brandywine: A Military History of the Battle that Lost Philadelphia but Saved America, September 11, 1777 (2017)
Finalist, 2014, Army Historical Foundation Distinguished Book Award
Winner, 2015, American Revolution Round Table of Richmond Book Award

Germantown: A Military History of the Battle for Philadelphia, October 4, 1777 (2020)

Justin Glenn
The Washingtons: A Family History (2014 - 2018)
(9 vols., plus the 2-vol. Index)

An excerpt from Michael Harris' *Germantown: A Military History of the Battle for Philadelphia, October 4, 1777.*

Chapter 1

The Philadelphia Campaign

June – September 1777

"Our people behaved well but Heaven frowned upon us in a degree. We were obliged to retire after a very considerable slaughter of the enemy."[1]

— Henry Knox, Chief of Artillery, Continental Army, September 1777

George Washington spent the six months after his victories at Trenton and Princeton in late December 1776 and early January 1777 around Morristown, New Jersey, building a new army nearly from scratch. His one-year enlistments—which comprised most of his army in 1776—had expired. During the long and arduous process, Washington harassed British outposts scattered across northern New Jersey in a series of raids and skirmishes. Fortunately for him, British Gen. William Howe was more concerned with strategic planning and writing letters to London than with what he considered the minor doings of the Continental Army.[2]

1 Noah Brooks, *Henry Knox: A Soldier of the Revolution* (New York, 1900), 104.

2 For more information on the opening months of the campaign, as well as the Battle of Brandywine, refer to my first book on the Philadelphia Campaign, *Brandywine: A Military History of the Battle that Lost Philadelphia but Saved America, September 11, 1777* (El Dorado Hills, CA, 2014).

Between January and June 1777, these small-scale raids and skirmishes were the only military operations that took place in northern New Jersey. The American Revolution had devolved into something more closely resembling a guerilla war than the more traditional European-style of combat. Washington described this form of war in a letter that February. "There have been and almost daily are, some small Skirmishes," he explained, "but without much loss on either side." Happily for Washington and the American cause, this form of warfare continued for the next four months, giving the general the precious time and space he needed to rebuild his weakened army. The stress built up during the extended off-tempo, low-intensity war simmered through the spring of 1777 until it boiled over into the savageness exhibited later in the campaign—especially at Paoli. The rains of April ended in early May and Washington, his army still in flux, shifted his command from the winter encampment at Morristown to a position at Middlebrook, New Jersey.[3]

General Howe mostly ignored Washington's change of base and made little effort to open the 1777 campaign season. He intended to capture Philadelphia as rapidly as possible and return to New York to join forces with Gen. John Burgoyne and the northern army, yet he showed no sign of urgency to actually do so. Nicholas Cresswell, an Englishman soon to return to England, noted in his journal, "I am as ignorant of the Motions or designs of our Army as if I had been in Virginia." The British soldiers, added Cresswell, "seem very healthy and long to be in action."[4]

June 1777

William Howe finally lurched into action in June by ordering an expedition to Middlebush, New Jersey. The British commander decided his best bet was to attempt the overland route to Philadelphia in the hope of luring Washington down from his mountain stronghold. Defeating Washington in New Jersey and then marching to Philadelphia offered Howe the best chance to take the colonial capital and leave in time to aid Burgoyne in New York. Howe's delay in opening the campaign triggered some dissatisfaction within the British officer corps. Timing was crucial to the British plan, and the army could have moved weeks earlier when

3 John D. Fitzpatrick, ed., *The Writings of George Washington from the Original Manuscript Sources, 1745-1799*, 39 vols. (Washington, D.C., 1933), vol. 7, 196.

4 Nicholas Cresswell, *The Journal of Nicholas Cresswell, 1774-1777* (New York, 1928), 229.

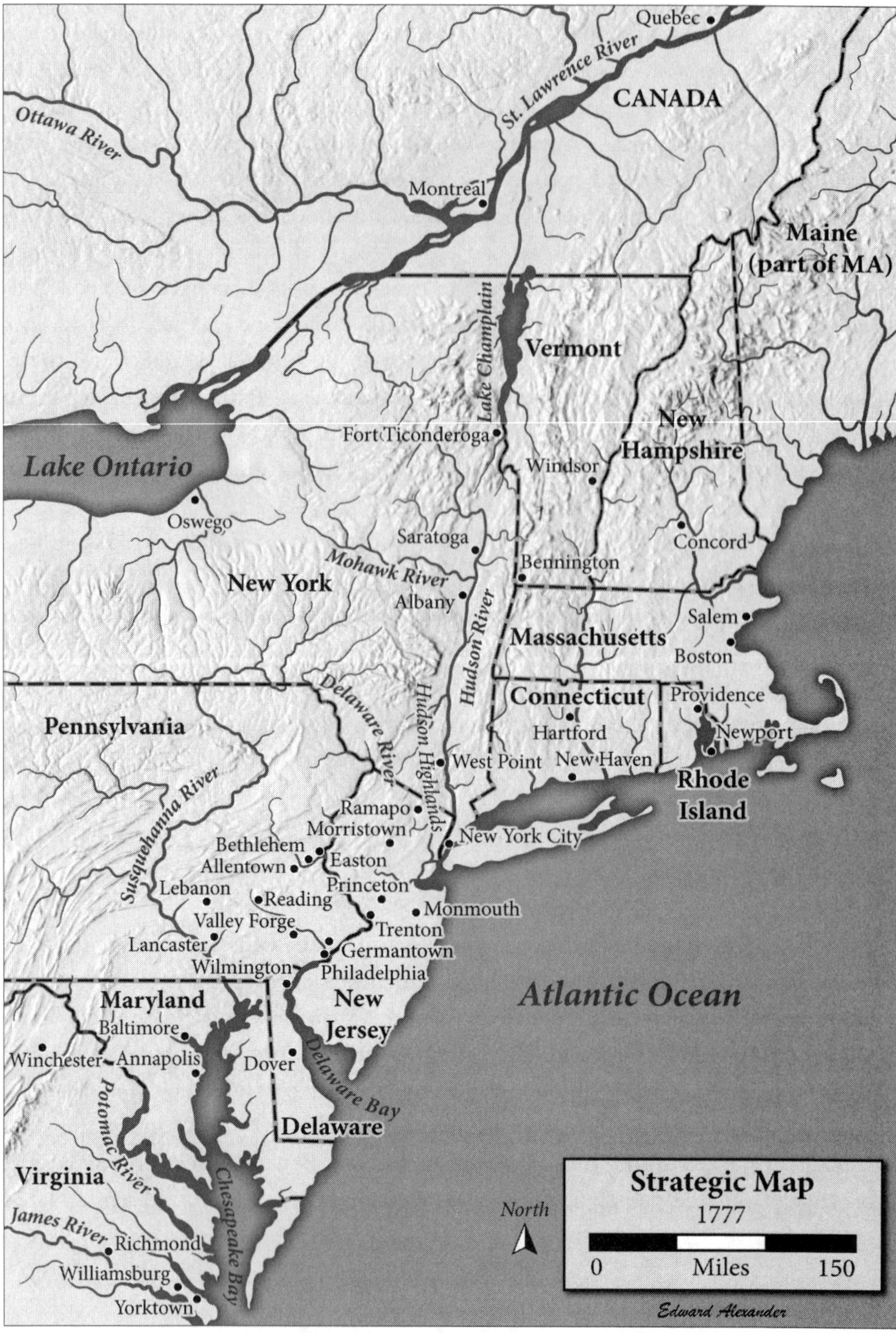
Quebec
St. Lawrence River
CANADA
Ottawa River
Montreal
Maine
(part of MA)
Lake Champlain
Vermont
New
Hampshire
Fort Ticonderoga
Lake Ontario
Windsor
Oswego
Saratoga
Concord
Mohawk River
Bennington
New York
Albany
Hudson River
Salem
Massachusetts
Boston
Delaware River
Hudson Highlands
Connecticut
Providence
Pennsylvania
Hartford
Newport
West Point
New Haven
Susquehanna River
Rhode
Island
Ramapo
Morristown
New York City
Bethlehem
Allentown
Easton
Lebanon
Reading
Princeton
Monmouth
Valley Forge
Trenton
Lancaster
Germantown
Wilmington
Philadelphia
Maryland
New
Jersey
Atlantic Ocean
Baltimore
Winchester
Annapolis
Dover
Delaware Bay
Potomac River
Delaware
Virginia
Chesapeake Bay
Strategic Map
1777
North
James River
Richmond
0
Miles
150
Williamsburg
Yorktown
Edward Alexander

the winter rains stopped and the warmer weather dried the roads. However, Howe did not move into northern New Jersey until June 13.[5]

To the disbelief of officers on both sides, the British army stopped after a march of about ten miles and established camp the day after reaching its destination. Not only did the army stop its advance, but Howe ordered fortifications erected; he apparently no longer intended to move any farther toward Philadelphia through New Jersey. "Nobody in the world could be more careful than he is," wrote Howe's Hessian aide, Capt. Levin Friedrich Ernst von Muenchhausen, in defense of his chief's actions. "This is absolutely necessary in this cursed hilly country." By remaining stationary, Howe intended to draw Washington down from the high ground and offer him battle in the relatively flat country east of the mountain range. To Howe's dismay, Washington refused to take the bait.[6]

The failure to lure the Americans into a fight flummoxed Howe, whose army of professional soldiers was being stymied by Washington's ragtag collection of militia, frontiersmen, and Continental Regulars. No one believed Washington's force was formidable, including Washington himself. His was not the army of veterans that would become hardened and molded in the grueling campaign still ahead of them, followed by the reckoning that would take place at Valley Forge the following winter. Four days ticked past as Howe waited in frustration for Washington to move. Other than light skirmishing and the launching of small raiding parties to plunder the countryside, Howe accomplished nothing. By remaining idle during perfectly good weather, Howe had effectively removed his army from the war effort.

Howe gave up the game and returned to New Brunswick on June 19 as elements of the Continental Army followed, skirmishing fitfully with his rear guard. Howe's actions dumbfounded British Maj. Charles Stuart. "These retrograde movements appear just as incomprehensible to us as they can possibly to you," he wrote his father in England. Howe's half-hearted attempt in New Jersey was as baffling then as it is today. Even though he was on a tight schedule, he moved thousands of troops ten miles, went into camp and constructed earthworks, waited

5 For a complete discussion of the campaign, its strategy, and the relationship between Howe and Burgoyne, see John F. Luzader, *Saratoga: A Military History of the Decisive Campaign of the American Revolution* (Savas Beatie, 2008).

6 Friedrich von Muenchhausen, *At General Howe's Side: 1776-1778: The Diary of General William Howe's aide de camp, Captain Friedrich von Muenchhausen*, trans. Ernst Kipping, ed. Samuel Steele Smith (Monmouth Beach, NJ, 1974), 16.

four days, and returned to his starting point a week later. Most historians attribute Howe's actions to a failed effort to pull Washington from the mountains for an open-field fight. However, Washington had never so obliged his enemy, and in fact rarely fought a battle under his enemy's terms. The more logical explanation is that Howe never intended to assault Philadelphia by marching through New Jersey. He would reach his objective by using the British fleet to transport his army.[7]

On June 22, Howe retired farther to Amboy, New Jersey, to load his army and its baggage for the voyage to the Delaware River. The Americans pressed Howe's rear guard, harassing the tail of his column. Washington remained cautiously optimistic about the state of affairs. "I cannot say that the move I am about to make towards Amboy accords altogether with my opinion," wrote the army commander, "not that I am under any other apprehension than that of being obliged to loose Ground again, which would indeed be no small misfortune as the Spirits of our Troops, and the Country, is greatly reviv'd (and I presume) the Enemys not a little depress'd, by their late retrograde motions."[8]

Washington's willingness to come down off the high ground and pursue Howe's retreating army, however, provided the British general with the opportunity he had been seeking. The Continental Army was on more engageable terrain, and Howe had his chance to attack. He did just that on June 25 by turning and assaulting Maj. Gen. Lord Stirling's isolated and heavily outnumbered American division of some 2,500 men. Stirling waged a well-crafted fighting withdrawal and took up a strong defensive position in the area of Ash Swamp and Scotch Plains. The British pushed hard and forced Stirling's command back once more toward Westfield. Suffering under an intense sun, Howe called off the pursuit and the day's fighting ended. The defensive action cost Stirling perhaps as many as 100 killed and wounded, in addition to 70 men and three cannons captured, while British losses totaled just five killed and 30 wounded. "The Battle of Short Hills," as it became known, bought precious time for Washington to move the balance of his army into the hill country to deny Howe the opportunity of the larger pitched battle he so craved. The affair also demonstrated that Washington's vaunted spy network had been surprised and thus had failed him. The British army, camped a mere eight miles away, had stolen a march on Washington and defeated a portion of the Continental Army. Howe had been unable to bring Washington to battle, but his

7 Mrs. E. Stuart Wortley, ed. *A Prime Minister and His Son: From the Correspondence of the Third Earl of Bute and Lt. General The Honourable Sir Charles Stuart, K.B.* (London, 1925), 110-113.

8 Fitzpatrick, *Writings*, vol. 8, 295-296.